Research in the Social Scientific Study of Religion

Volume 23

Edited by

Ralph L. Piedmont
Loyola University Maryland

and

Andrew Village
York St. John University, UK

BRILL

LEIDEN · BOSTON
2012

Published with the kind support of Loyola University Maryland, USA.

Library of Congress Cataloging-in-Publication Data
LC control number 89650738

This publication has been typeset in the multilingual "Brill" typeface. With over 5,100 characters covering Latin, IPA, Greek, and Cyrillic, this typeface is especially suitable for use in the humanities. For more information, please see www.brill.nl/brill-typeface.

ISSN 1046-8064
ISBN 978 90 04 22953 2 (hardback)
ISBN 978 90 04 20954 9 (e-book)

This book is printed on acid-free paper.

Printed by Printforce, the Netherlands

Research in the Social Scientific Study of Religion

Series Editors

RALPH L. PIEDMONT
ANDREW VILLAGE

VOLUME 23

Research in the Social Scientific Study
of Religion

CONTENTS

PREFACE

As a type of publication, *Research in the Social Scientific Study of Religion* lies somewhere between a one-off edited book and a journal. As such it offers a regular forum for papers in the field that may come from a wide range of disciplines connected by the umbrella of the series' title. Edited books often have a particular subject focus, and the editors of *RSSSR* have tried to incorporate this aspect into the series over the last few years by inviting guest editors to put together contributions from different authors on a particular topic of interest. These topics are often linked to emerging fields or to those where there is considerable debate as to how a subject should be conceptualized and studied. The format of a book series allows different sorts of contributions, ranging from short, data-driven reports to longer essays that may be entirely theory-driven.

The current volume reflects well the nature of the series, with general articles covering diverse topics and a special section dealing with the fascinating, but often contentious, subject of theism and psychology. To study religion within the broad discourse of the social sciences is to employ the methods of empirical enquiry, as well as to interact with some of the key constructs used to help our understanding of human beings. It also requires a recognition that the very nature of religion obliges claims about human beings and the nature of existence that are not easily enveloped within methods open to social scientists. The development of methods of study goes hand in hand with the development of ideas: Some questions can only be meaningfully asked when we have the means to answer them. The general papers in this volume reflect both empirical and theoretical attempts to understand the ways in which human behavior is both influenced by and influences religious or spiritual expression:

Mark Cartledge is based in the UK, but he reports on a study of a Pentecostal denomination in the USA. He uses quantitative data from over 50 churches to investigate the way in which the context of socialization of Pentecostal congregants shapes their experiences of Godly love and Pentecostal expression. The study is an example of how theoretical constructs (in this case socialization, Godly love, and Pentecostal religion) are operationalized into quantitative measures that can then allow underlying relationships to emerge. One interesting finding from this study is the key role played by married women in promoting and sustaining the *born again* experience and, by implication, the importance of marriage for the maintenance of Pentecostal spiritual life in these communities.

Judith Muskett's paper emerges from her work on social capital among the Friends Associations of English cathedrals. In this theoretical exploration, she reviews sociological studies of the capacity of *passive* members of voluntary associations to generate social capital. The literature is divided on the extent to which simple membership of an organization can meaningfully contribute to social capital unless it is accompanied by active participation. Although most of the work to date derives from secular organizations, it has clear implications for religious groups. Muskett uses Grace Davie's notion of *vicarious religion* to show how passive membership of religious organizations may be important in generating social capital. This work offers some clear avenues for future empirical study that might test these interesting ideas.

RSSSR has a long-standing interest in fostering work that helps us to understand the meaning and implications of the terms religiousness and spirituality. The development of instruments such as the *Assessment of Spirituality and Religious Sentiments* (ASPIRES) has opened up a range of possibilities for investigating the different ways in which religion and spirituality might impact individuals. Teresa Wilkins, Ralph Piedmont, and Gina Magyar-Russell investigate the contributions of these two factors to well-being among a sample of over 500 people from the United States. One important aspect of this study was the way that personality differences could be controlled for in order to identify more clearly effects that relate directly to religious or spiritual constructs. Although religion had some independent effects on measures of resilience and pro-social behavior, these were much smaller than the more significant effects of spirituality. This is further evidence to support the idea that religiosity and spirituality are related but separate phenomenon.

The special section edited by Kari O'Grady and Richard York deals with the subject of theism and psychology. This is where the social scientific study of religion confronts in a very direct way the ambiguities and tensions of working at the interface of different human discourses. Religions resist the attempts of sociologists and psychologists to subsume them under the study of human sciences. Social scientists often feel they have to study religion as a purely human phenomenon to retain their credibility and position within the wider scientific discourse. Those of us who work at this interface can be subject to criticism from theologians for not being sufficiently theological and from social scientists for not being sufficiently scientific. This is not an easy tension to resolve, so a collection of papers that seeks to move beyond sterile debate is most welcome. The editors have brought together in one place papers from those who believe a theistic psychology is possible and those who do not. The creation of an arena where different views are set alongside each other results in a fruitful dialogue.

A "fruitful dialogue" by no means implies agreement, or even "agreeing to disagree." Some of the contributions in this section are putting forward arguments that cannot be meaningfully reconciled. This makes the concluding section all the more important, and the editors have done a deft job of recognizing the difficult but necessary avoidance of the *groupthink* that can arise when people with particular worldviews retreat into the safe haven offered by the company of those with whom they always agree. Wrestling with the notions of theism and psychology is very much an exercise in leaving the security of our safe havens, and the editors of *RSSSR* are grateful to all those who contributed to this section and especially our invited editors.

As this series moves towards its quarter-century, the editors believe that there remains a place for this sort of publication within the field. We invite readers and researchers to continue to use this forum to develop new ideas, report original research, and debate important issues related to the social scientific study of religion.

ACKNOWLEDGEMENTS

The editorial staff and I are grateful for the contributions and cooperation of a large number of people without whom publication of *RSSSR* would not be possible. Most obvious among them are the authors and coauthors of the published articles. There were a number of researchers, scholars, and clinicians who have served as anonymous reviewers of the manuscripts that were received for current publication. These individuals are noted at the end of this volume. They not only have functioned as professional referees evaluating the appropriateness of the respective manuscripts for publication, but they also have given the authors significant suggestions to improve the quality and scope of their future research in this area. Their efforts helped to insure a high quality among those reports that are published.

I would also like to acknowledge the efforts of Dr. Kari A. O'Grady and Dr. Richard H. York for their wonderful work in managing the Special Section on Theism and Non-Theism in Psychological Science. The series of papers presented here makes a significant and substantial contribution to the literature. The variety of topics is very relevant for both researchers and clinicians. The articles presented here are informative and should provide highly stimulating reading.

Teresa Wilkins has served as the editorial assistant for this volume. Her experience, talent, and painstaking work contributed immeasurably to the high standards of production. Throughout this process, she was always patient and quick to smile. Although the work load got very heavy at times, her commitment and diligence were always in evidence, and she maintained a very high level of professionalism. Thank You, Teri!

My own academic institution has provided many critical necessities for the production of this volume. Loyola University Maryland, especially its graduate Department of Pastoral Counseling, has provided office space, funds for the editorial assistant, telephone services, computer technology, postage, access to its admirable support infrastructure, and related services. I am very grateful for both the Department's and Graduate Administration's support for this worthy endeavor.

I am grateful, too, to the production staff of Brill Academic Press who have efficiently published this attractive and useful volume. Brill's marketing department (www.brill.nl or e-mail brill@turpin-distribution.com for

R.O.W. and cs@brillusa.com for North America) is eager to fill orders for either single volumes or on-going subscriptions to *RSSSR*.

Please recommend *RSSSR* to your professional and academic colleagues. Also support its addition or continuation in your academic, religious, research, and public libraries for its rich contents are relevant to everyone, both lay and professional, who is interested in keeping up with the rapidly expanding frontiers of scientific knowledge about spirituality and religion.

Ralph L. Piedmont, Ph.D., Co-Editor

MANUSCRIPT INVITATION

For future volumes we welcome the submission of manuscripts reporting on research which contributes to the behavioral and social science understanding of religion, whether done by members of those disciplines or other professions. *RSSSR* is an annual interdisciplinary and international volume that publishes original reports of research, theoretical studies, and other innovative social scientific analyses of religion. (However, we do not include studies that are purely historical or theological.) Manuscripts should be original contributions (not reprints) based upon any of the quantitative or qualitative methods of research or the theoretical, conceptual, or meta-analytical analysis of research on religion in general or on any specific world religion. They should not be under consideration for publication by any other journal or publication outlet and should comply with the professional ethical standards of psychology, sociology, and other social science professions.

Manuscripts may be submitted at any time during the year, although those received within the calendar year have the best chance of inclusion in the next volume. Manuscripts must conform to the style guidelines of the *Publication Manual of the American Psychological Association,* 6th edition. Papers not in APA style will be returned to the author un-reviewed. (Authors who lack access to the *Publication Manual* may contact Dr. Piedmont for sample materials to help in the final preparation of their papers.) Send three copies, double spaced on standard paper to:

Ralph L. Piedmont, Ph.D., Editor
Research in the Social Scientific Study of Religion
Department of Pastoral Counseling
Loyola University Maryland
8890 McGaw Road, Suite 380
Columbia, MD 21045 USA

Questions about suitability can be directed to Dr. Piedmont electronically (rpiedmont@loyola.edu). Manuscripts that are judged by the editors as relevant to the coverage of *RSSSR* are reviewed anonymously for quality and then either accepted (usually along with constructive suggestions for revision) or rejected. Manuscripts relevant to our subject that are not

accepted for publication also receive the benefit of critiques and suggestions that can aid their improvement for submission elsewhere. Authors
will be required to complete a copyright transfer form giving Brill the
rights to publish the work.

RSSSR is also interested in developing "special topic sections" for inclusion in future editions. Special topic sections would include a series of
papers (5–7) on a specific theme. These sections would be "guest edited"
by a single individual who would be responsible for the solicitation of the
manuscripts and their review. If you have a suggestion for a special topic
section or would be interested in editing such a section, please do not
hesitate to contact Dr. Piedmont for details.

FAMILY SOCIALIZATION, GODLY LOVE, AND PENTECOSTAL SPIRITUALITY: A STUDY AMONG THE CHURCH OF GOD (CLEVELAND, TN)

*Mark J. Cartledge**

ABSTRACT

This study explores data from a congregational survey of the Church of God (Cleveland, TN) Pentecostal denomination (N = 1,522). It considers the relationship between family socialization and the concept of Godly Love, understood as a perceived relationship of love with God and neighbor, in relation to Pentecostal spirituality. This research discovered that the home is an important context for conversion and that married women in particular are socializing agents of Godly Love and Pentecostal spirituality. They are supported in this key role by other family members. They are also key agents within congregational expressions of Pentecostal spirituality. These are important findings and lend further support to the understanding that women are empowered by Pentecostal spirituality even if they are in tension with aspects of Pentecostal patriarchy. These findings have implications for the role of marriage, gender relations, and religious experience in American society.

Keywords: socialization, family, altruism, Pentecostalism, spirituality

This paper emerges from the Flame of Love Project funded by the John Templeton Foundation, in association with the University of Akron. The author is working with Kimberly Ervin Alexander and James Bowers to consider the influence of religious socialization on Godly Love and its impact on vocation in church and society. This paper uses quantitative survey data (N = 1,522) to explore the nature of family socialization as it relates to the notion of Godly Love and its influence on key features in Pentecostal spirituality. Family socialization refers to the influence that close family members, as well as the home as a context, have in the transfer of beliefs, values, attitudes, and behavior on its members. Godly Love is defined as the dynamic between individuals' experience of God's love for them and their love for God in return that leads to the acquisition of love energy as an expression of this dynamic. This dynamic can also

* *Author Note*: Mark J. Cartledge, School of Philosophy, Theology, and Religion, University of Birmingham, UK.

Correspondence concerning this article should be sent to Mark J. Cartledge, Director, Centre for Pentecostal and Charismatic Studies, School of Philosophy, Theology, and Religion, University of Birmingham, ERI Building, Pritchatts Road, Edgbaston, Birmingham, B16 2TT, UK. Email: m.j.cartledge@bham.ac.uk be described in Sorokin's (1954/2002) terms of *intensity* (how it affects various aspects of the person's life) and *extensity* (how widely this love is shared beyond oneself). Pentecostal spirituality is discussed in terms of church activity, Spirit baptism, charismatic experience in general as well as healing, prophecy, and evangelism in particular.

The Church of God (Cleveland, TN) began as part of the Holiness movement in Tennessee in 1886, as nine people agreed to commit themselves to imitate the primitive church and allow each other freedom of conscience in the interpretation of the New Testament (Conn, 1996). The group was led by Spurling and known as the Christian Union. It planted new churches and conducted revival meetings in the Holiness tradition. Subsequently, this group was joined by A.J. Tomlinson in 1902, and he became the leading pastor of the movement, relocating its center of operation to Cleveland, TN. In 1906, they adopted the name the *Church of God* (Cleveland, TN; hereafter: CoG). As news spread of the Azusa Street revival, Tomlinson was eager to experience the Pentecostal blessing for himself. In 1908, he invited G.B. Cashwell to preach at CoG services, and Tomlinson experienced Spirit Baptism and spoke with other tongues. From that time the CoG adopted what became known as Wesleyan Pentecostal spirituality. The denomination believed in justification by faith experienced in conversion, a Wesleyan crisis experience of entire sanctification, and a third experience of Spirit Baptism as power for witness, as evidenced by glossolalia, and a gateway into the domain of the *charismata*. Thus they adopted a three stage *ordo salutis*. With the practice of healing and the premillennial expectation of the imminent return of Christ, the denomination expressed the full gospel as a five-fold one. Jesus Christ is savior, sanctifier, baptizer in the Spirit, healer, and soon to be coming king. This fivefold model is still popular today and functions as a central theological identity marker for Wesleyan Pentecostals (Thomas, 2010). Currently, the CoG denomination has 7000 congregations in the USA and 6.8 million members in 181 countries around the world. The majority of the US congregations are located in the southeast of the country, with the largest churches especially in Charlotte, NC.

The aim of this paper is threefold: (a) to explore the influence of family socialization factors among the CoG in the USA concerning conversion experience, gender, and Pentecostal experience; (b) to test whether the factors of gender and family socialization predict the degree to which members of this denomination engage with aspects of Pentecostal spirituality; and (c) to reflect on the implications of this study for the relationship between family and religion more generally. In order to achieve this aim, socialization theory will be outlined, Godly Love will be described and defined, Pentecostal spirituality will be outlined before the survey is described, and the results presented and discussed.

SOCIALIZATION THEORY

Socialization refers to the process whereby individuals are integrated into a particular social group, becoming members and adopting certain roles and behavior. In so doing, they become actors in the various scenarios of life in the context of particular cultures. It is a process that usually begins within a family context (often referred to as primary socialization) and continues throughout the life of individuals as they proceed through formal education and on into the world of paid employment (often referred to as secondary socialization). There are a number of theoretical perspectives that seek to provide an overarching framework for this process, for example role theory, associated with the structural-functionalist tradition, symbolic interactionism, and psychoanalytic theory (Fulcher & Scott, 2003). Sociologists of religion are usually concerned with the ways in which beliefs, values, attitudes, and behavior are transmitted either generationally or as individuals join new religious groups, thus moving from the outside to the inside (Hunt, 2003). The process enables a particular religious subculture to survive and be maintained as the person adapts to the new culture and fits into its ethos (Berger, 1969). It is through a set of ongoing relationships within the group that shared attitudes and accepted roles are maintained and indeed owned by the incomer (Furniss, 1995). It is in this process of integration that beliefs owned by the group also become beliefs owned by the individual such that they become internalized. As Berger stated, "He [sic] draws them (meanings) into himself and makes them *his* meanings. He becomes not only one who possesses these meanings, but one who represents and expresses them" (Berger, 1969, p. 15). In order for the person to remain part of a religious group, these beliefs must continue to be both represented and expressed in his or her life by means of specific religious practices and experiences. This is especially pertinent to the study of experiential forms of religion, such as Pentecostalism.

There are a number of key factors associated with socialization theory that influence the ways in which individuals are raised within religious groups or are brought into religious groups from outside and retained. The first is a group of peers often called a *reference group* (Furniss, 1995).

It can be quite small or really quite large, for example a church congregation, and it encourages and supports the acquisition and maintenance of new beliefs, values, and practices. The reference group mediates the existing beliefs and values of the religious culture that it represents. It is this mediation that allows individuals coming from outside to be more easily integrated into the existing social structures and internalize the religious values of the group. And it is the integration of individuals which functions as a mechanism of retention. The greater the integration of the individual within the group then the greater is the likelihood of retention. A reference group maintains shared meaning among its members and enables that shared meaning to be "taken-for-granted" (McGuire, 2002, p. 37). It has been called the chorus group that routinely affirms one's place in the general scheme of things (Berger & Luckmann, 1967). In today's pluralistic network, culture reference groups are chosen for a variety of reasons and even religiously affiliated individuals can find themselves engaging with a number of different kinds of competing references groups (Furniss, 1995).

Second, all social groups have individuals who stand out and who represent in a public manner the beliefs and values of the group; they are *significant others*. These people provide role models for the rest of the group and indeed for wider society. They also, along with the reference group, contribute to the plausibility of the religious identity they represent (Aldridge, 2000). Therefore plausibility is an important dimension of socialization (Berger, 1969). A significant other epitomizes the beliefs and values of the religious tradition and contributes to the maintenance of the religious reality (Furniss, 1995). This means that there is always an important relationship between the significant other and the reference group (Berger & Luckmann, 1967). They are guardians of the religious tradition and hand it on to the next generation (van der Ven, 1996). Significant others may be officially sanctioned as authorized church leaders, or they may in fact be gifted lay leaders, who nevertheless command the respect and allegiance of others. Their influence can be considerable, and they usually police the boundaries of the group ideologically and socially, including the management of group expectations and social discipline where necessary (Richards, 1970). Therefore the relationship between the reference group and the significant other is important. Conflict between them can lead to fractures in the plausibility structure and loss of group membership or worse.

Third, religious groups express their beliefs and values in cultural artefacts, such as literature of one kind or another, media in a broader sense including radio, television, and the internet, and buildings or places of worship. Pentecostal Christians from the earliest days produced statements of faith, magazines, and tracts, all of which mediated their beliefs and values to others and importantly to themselves. Over the course of the 20th century, they embraced new electronic media, such as radio and television, and it is now relatively easy to find out about certain groups via cyberspace. There is a huge market in popular books, music CDs, and DVDs of worship and Christian teaching, all of which assist in the wider socialization of individuals and groups into Pentecostalism more generally. They have tended to construct functional worship spaces rather than grand cathedrals, suggesting that God is immediate and active rather than transcendent and remote. It is the combination of all of these factors which contribute to the construction of a worldview embodying and supporting particular beliefs and values, enabling individuals to acquire the appropriate language to use and engage in meaningful social discourse (White, 1977). The power and ubiquity of these media are culturally sanctioned and religiously endorsed by different kinds of groups (Danziger, 1971).

It is important, fourthly, to consider the role that personal agency plays in the process of socialization; otherwise, it could be construed as an entirely deterministic process. Clearly the very different ways that religious groups emerge, develop, transmute, and disintegrate suggest that personal agency factors play a significant role in these processes. Individuals enter and position themselves in relationship to a religious culture with differing degrees of commitment. Some individuals become so committed to the values of the group that the self becomes a tough task master with high expectations of success and conformity (White, 1977). Highly socialized individuals can be anxious about the limits of what might be considered acceptable behaviour, while less socialized persons ignore convention and can be considered unreasonable or selfish (Danziger, 1971). Indeed, self-identity is never purely an individual affair because it is developed in constant interaction with others, be they the reference group, the significant other, or via media, broader society, and culture (Berger, 1969; Berger & Luckman, 1967). Nevertheless, in the ebb and flow of human relations in all their complexity, there is always the dimension of personal human agency (McGuire, 2002).

In terms of socialization and religiosity, the existing literature suggests that the family continues to be essential for the socialization of religious beliefs and values. Marriage and childbearing have been found to boost religious participation (Sherkat & Ellison, 1999). Higher religiosity is also associated with greater satisfaction in marriage (Willits & Crider, 1988).

The frequency of a spouse's church attendance is linked to the attendance of the other, especially in young adulthood (Willits & Crider, 1989). Indeed, when both spouses attend church there is a lesser likelihood of divorce compared to when only one spouse attends church (Call & Heaton, 1997). Where the parents' beliefs and practices are learned in the home, then continuity of religious practice is expected between parents and children. Parental warmth and acceptance facilitate imitation and model learning and can predict the following by children of their parents' religion (Bao, Whitbeck, Hoyt, & Conger, 1999). Thus, family harmony and overall family religious interaction can promote the transmission of religious values (Kieren & Munro, 1987), especially when parents discuss religious issues (Hayes & Pittelkow, 1993). Other family members can function as reinforcers, substitutes, and contrasts to parental socialization roles (Park & Eck-lund, 2007). Mothers tend to be the most influential in the socialization of religious beliefs and values in children (Martin, White & Perlman, 2003; Hitlin & Piliavin, 2004), while fathers are more likely to influence specific behavior such as church attendance (Hayes & Pittelkow, 1993).

Given this theoretical and empirical background, socialization in this research project tests specific factors for the support given to enable the respondent to experience a relationship of love with God. It also tests the perceived impact of a direct encounter with God. In this context, it is important to appreciate the way in which this relationship of love, defined as Godly Love, is understood.

GODLY LOVE

Godly Love has been defined as the dynamic interaction between divine love and human love that enlivens benevolence which allows for "remarkable self-forgetfulness in the agent" (Post in Lee & Poloma, 2009, p. i). It is an expression of the love of God and the love of neighbor as oneself. Further, it is a love energy produced through two-way interaction of loving and being loved by God. Poloma and Hood defined Godly Love as the "dynamic interaction between human responses to the operation of perceived divine love and the impact this experience has on personal lives, relationships with others, and emergent communities" (2008, p. 4). The main theory of love energy is drawn from the work of Sorokin (1954/2002; Lee, Poloma & Post, 2008, pp. 9–11). For Sorokin, love energy was constantly being produced through the process of human interaction and was embedded within culture, including religious cultural values. Sorokin acknowledged the possible hypothesis that the inflow of love can originate in a transcendental reality, although it was recognized that this reality is beyond empirical measurement. Nevertheless, inferences may be drawn from the perception, experience, and behavior of individuals and groups engaged in benevolence.

Sorokin developed five dimensions of love, which are understood as criteria by which the presence of love can be assessed. The first dimension is intensity, by which is meant the degree to which acts of loves are expressed and the cost to the person acting in such a way. Therefore a low intensity of love would mean, for example, distributing a few small coins to a beggar or giving up one's seat on a bus. High intensity love would be costly in terms of time, energy, and resources and which is freely given. The second dimension of love is called extensity and refers to the range of persons to whom love is given, ranging from self, family and friends, ethnic group, nationality through to those that have never been met but only heard about. The third dimension is duration, which refers to benevolence expressed over time. This may vary enormously due to circumstances. The fourth dimension is purity and refers to the degree to which "egoistic motivation" (Lee, Poloma & Post, 2008, p. 10) is present or lacking. To love for personal advantage or profit would be a sign that the purity level is low. Pure love would be regarded as that which is disinterested in any return. The fifth and final dimension is adequacy and refers to the consequences that an act of love can generated. An inadequate kind of love results in undesirable consequences, for example the pampering of a child. For adequate love, intention and consequences should be aligned.

Lee and Poloma (2009), as well as Poloma and Green (2010), attempted to correlate this sociological theory with a Pentecostal theological account. They used the work of Macchia (2006) who adopted the metaphor of "baptism in the Spirit" as focus for theological construction. This pneumatological emphasis understands the experience of baptism in the Spirit as liberating and reordering, such that human lives are better placed to know something of the love and reign of God. It is not just a one-off experience related to glossolalia but part of an ongoing spirituality process (Cartledge, 2006; Macchia, 2006, p. 117). In turn, the love generated in an ongoing manner can be made real to others in solidarity with victims and in opposition to unjust structures and attitudes (Macchia, 2006). Of course, Macchia agreed that Pentecostals have fallen short of this ideal; nevertheless, at a theological level, he wished to see it as a normative outcome for a theology of Spirit baptism and for which there are exemplars

(Lee & Poloma, 2009). This means for Lee and Poloma that they take perceived experiences of the divine seriously, but this does not mean that any
or all attribution of an experience to a divine cause can be accepted sim-
pliciter. However, neither of them wish to reduce Pentecostal "behaviors
and feelings to purely secular causes" (Lee & Poloma, 2009, p. 101).

PENTECOSTAL SPIRITUALITY

Pentecostal spirituality can be described as one that specifically and
explicitly emphasises the experience of the Holy Spirit in corporate and
dramatic ways. Although Christ is always at the center of the rhetoric,
hence he is the Spirit baptizer, it is the person and presence of the Holy
Spirit that is searched for via corporate worship and private devotional
practices. Conversion through the convicting work of the Holy Spirit is
regarded as the beginning of the spirituality process, which in the Wesleyan tradition is followed by a purifying experience whereby the Holy
Spirit is considered to have cleansed the heart of the believer in preparation for the power of Pentecost. Without purity there cannot be power.
Even in non-Wesleyan forms of Pentecostalism there is still an emphasis
on holiness of life and conduct, as evidenced in codes of various kinds
which function to maintain identity and mark out a lifestyle boundary.
The dramatic experience of Spirit baptism is experienced subsequent to
conversion and it is regarded as an overwhelming experience of the presence of the divine life, as on the day of Pentecost (Acts 2.1–4). Indeed
early Pentecostals used to refer to it as one's *personal Pentecost*. And just
as on the day of Pentecost, many experience an accompaniment of glossolalia (unidentifiable speech) as a sign of its occurrence, followed by its
practice as a form of prayer and praise in private and corporate worship.
The empowerment of Spirit baptism is for witness, and Pentecostal spirituality is expressed in evangelism, whether through personal conversation, evangelistic events and services, or through major campaigns and
revival type meetings. The call to commit all to Christ will surely be one of
the key features of these events. The drama of Spirit baptism is matched
by healing practices, the use of prophetic speech as individuals feel led
by the Holy Spirit to speak out a message for a congregation or to an
individual. Often the prophetic and the healing are intertwined as pastors
and members share words of knowledge regarding a condition or ailment
in the congregation, which it is believed encourages members and visi-
tors to respond in faith. All of these features contribute to a process of

search-encounter-transformation, whereby the person encounters and is transformed by participation in this kind of spirituality (Cartledge, 2006). At the heart of this process is Godly Love, whereby individuals experience God's love for them and express it to God and neighbor in return and out of a very real sense of gratitude.

In order to conceptualize the relationships involved in this understanding of Godly Love in the context of Pentecostal spirituality, a model was developed by colleagues in the Flame of Love project (Lee & Poloma, 2009).

In this model, it is posited that love energy produced in the context of a relationship with God and a set of relationships with others leads to benevolent attitudes and action towards other beneficiaries. Godly Love is not the same as altruism, but it includes it with its focus on benevolent action and draws attention to the process of interactions surrounding it (Lee & Poloma, 2009, see Figure 1). In Pentecostalism in particular there are many testimonies of church leaders, as well as ordinary members, who have had profound experiences of what they perceive to be God's love such that they are transformed into people able to love others with considerably more energy than before. The ways in which benevolence is expressed are indeed varied, but all agents of benevolence are influenced by others sharing similar norms and values. This is where the role of socialization takes its place in so far as attitudes and behavior are supported by different factors such as significant others and the reference group. Indeed, for strongly communal religious groups there may be a case for modifying the *exemplar* category into simply *Pentecostal agent* because the primary role of agency cannot so easily be distinguished between the *exemplar* and the

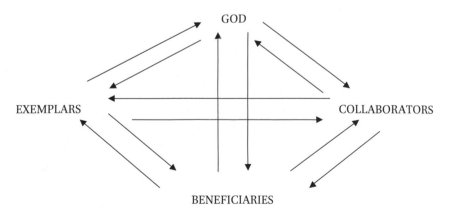

Figure 1. *The Diamond Model.*

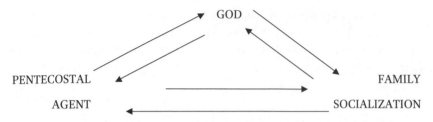

Figure 2. *The Family Socialization Model.*

group. In this study, the focus is on the role that family socialization plays in the context of broader socialization processes (see Figure 2).

This study is primarily concerned with the perception of a relationship with God, family socialization, and the Pentecostal person embodying spirituality and agency.

RESEARCH QUESTIONS

In order to guide the analysis, a number of research questions can now be stated. First, does the context of a born again experience influence how congregants are socialized in relation to their experience of Godly Love? Second, in particular, does the context of the born again experience influence how congregants are socialized by specific family significant others? Third, are men and women socialized differently in their relationship of love with God? Fourth, is there an association between family socialization and Pentecostal experience and spirituality? Fifth and finally, what family socialization factors are understood to predict specific features of Pentecostal experience and spirituality?

METHOD

Procedure

The survey aimed to sample 100 congregations from the denominational list of member churches in the USA. It used a computerized process to randomly selected 800 congregations to be approached. Church leaders were approached and their congregations invited to participate. From this number, 127 congregations agreed to participate in the survey. The data was collected through a questionnaire completed by congregation members during a worship service on a typical Sunday morning. From the congregations agreeing to participate in the research, 52 returned completed questionnaires, which amounts to a congregational response rate of 41%. This provided 1,522 usable questionnaires, which were subsequently scanned and converted to a Statistical Package for the Social Sciences (SPSS version 11.00) computer program data file.

Participants

In this sample, 61.0% were women and 39.0% were men. There was a good age spread: 5.1% aged between 11–19, 12.0% aged between 20–29, 15.7% aged between 30–39, 19.4% aged between 40–49, 23.6% aged between 50–59, 15.7% aged between 60–69, 6.8% aged between 70–79, and 1.7% aged over 80. Of these congregants 13.1% were single, 9.1% divorced, 1.7% separated, 6.1% widowed, and 70.0% married. In terms of ethnicity, they were 78.9% White, 12.2% African American, 6.5% Hispanic or Latino, 1.1% Multi-racial, 0.8% Native American, 0.4% Asian, and 0.1 Eastern Indian. Educationally, 3.4% had grade school experience, 11.0% had some high school experience, 27.4% were high school graduates, 36.8% had some college trade school experience, 14.2% were college graduates, 5.4% had attended graduate school and 1.8% experienced postgraduate education. The largest occupational categories were: Church work (10%), Heathcare support (9.7%), Management (9.0%), Office and Administrative support (8.8%), Sales and related (8.4%), and Education, training and library (7.1%).

The respondents stated that 78% were members of the church in which they completed the questionnaire, with 18.5% identifying as a regular attender without being a member. Thus this data represented core members of the CoG denomination. Their membership status was relatively young, with 39.3% having been members for 0–4 years, 18.1% for 5–9 years, 14.3% for 10–14 years, and 8.7% for 15–19 years. Thus the majority (80.4%) had been members for less than 20 years, suggesting a relatively high level of congregational mobility. The denominations attended at the age of 15 years old included: the Church of God, Cleveland, TN (25.5%), Baptist (19.2%), Pentecostal other than the Church of God (11.7%), Roman Catholic (8.2%) and Methodist (5.5%), with 13.7% not attending any church as a teenager. The participation in church worship was high, with 93.3% attending a Sunday morning worship service three or more times per month and 62.5% attending at least three mid-week church activities per month.

Measures

The socialization measures built on earlier work by Cartledge (2012) and aimed to develop them. The question asked: "How much have the following helped you to *experience* a relationship of love with God?" The response options were in a Likert format and offered a range from 1 = *very little* to 5 = *very much*. The items were developed into four scales: (a) Reference Group (camp meetings, church holidays, close friends, men's group, women's group, small group) with a Cronbach's alpha score of .71; (b) Significant Other (evangelists, father, mentors, mother, other family members, pastors, prayer partners, worship leaders, and youth pastors) with a Cronbach's alpha score of .76; (c) Personal Agency (individual decision, deliberate choice, step of faith, personal bible study) with a Cronbach's alpha score of .73; and (d) Christian Media (Christian teaching on DVDs, church music, Christian music on CDs, Christian media, sermon recordings, Christian literature) with a Cronbach's alpha score of .80. For the purpose of this study, family members were in focus: mother, father, spouse and other family member and represented both significant others and members of the family reference group. In addition, the answer option for the perceived influence of a "direct encounter with God" was also included.

Following an item developed by Poloma (1989), the survey asked: "Do you consider yourself a born again Christian?" The follow up question asked: "If you are a born again Christian, which of the following best describes the circumstances of that experience?" The answer options included: (1) I was raised in a Christian home; (2) A response to an altar call; (3) After a personal and unusual spiritual experience, (4) As a result of a deep personal crisis, (5) Through the testimony of friend or family member, (6) In response to an invitation during a Christian television program, (7) As part of a discipleship or small group ministry, and (8) I cannot identify the particular cause or event of my accepting Jesus.

Pentecostal experience and spirituality was measured through a number of items, again initially developed by Poloma (1989). Five scales of measurement were used from her previous research.

Church Activity was measured by the question: "Indicate how many times in a typical month you participate in the following church activities." The response used a Likert scale 0–4, where 0 = *none*, 1 = *once*, 2 = *twice*, 3 = *three times* and 4 = *4 times or more*. The scale (comprising the items: Sunday morning worship, Sunday school, Midweek service/activity, Small group, Other activities) delivered a Cronbach's alpha score of .70.

Charismatic Experience was measured by the question: "How often have you been involved in the following practices during a worship service within the past year?" The response used a Likert scale 1–4, where 1 = *never/almost never*, 2 = *once in a while*, 3 = *fairly often* and 4 = *very often*. The scale (comprising the items: speaking out a message in tongues, giving interpretation to a tongues message, speaking a prophetic word, singing in the Spirit, giving a testimony [salvation, healing, etc.], physical manifestations [laughter, jerking, shaking, etc.], being slain in the Spirit, dancing in the Spirit, prayer for deliverance, prayer for healing, prayer for baptism in the Spirit) delivered a Cronbach's alpha score of .87.

Healing was measured by the question: "Divine healing has played an important part in Pentecostalism and is practiced in many churches. Please answer the following questions having to do with healing, health and wellbeing." The response used a Likert scale 1–4, where 1 = *never/almost never*, 2 = *once in a while*, 3 = *fairly often* and 4 = *very often*. The scale (comprising the items: I pray with others for healing, I have been prayed with for healing, I have heard accounts of what I regard as "miraculous healing," I have personally experienced a divine healing in my own life, I have witnessed miraculous healing in the lives of family members and/or friends) delivered a Cronbach's alpha score of .81.

Prophecy was measured by the question: "To what extent can you say that you have had the following spiritual experiences?" The response used a Likert scale 1–6, where 1 = *never/almost never*, 2 = *once in a while*, 3 = *some days*, 4 = *most days*, 5 = *everyday* and 6 = *many times a day*. The scale (comprising the items: giving a prophecy privately to another person, receiving a personal revelation from another, receiving a revelation directly from God during times of prayer, an experience with God in which you lost awareness of time and things around you, hearing a divine call to perform some specific act, I have seen future events in dreams or visions before they happen) delivered a Cronbach's alpha score of .89.

Evangelism was measured by the question: "How many times have you performed the following activities *within the past six months*?" The response used a Likert scale 0–5, where 0 = *none*, 1 = *once*, 2 = *twice*, 3 = *three times*, 4 = *four times* and 5 = *five or more times*. The scale (comprising the items: invited a non-member to a church event, invited children of a non-member to attend worship on a Sunday school at your church, helped a visitor or new member get acquainted with others in the church, talked with friends and neighbors about your church, offered the services of your pastor or church to someone in need) delivered a Cronbach's alpha score of .82.

Finally, the central feature of classical Pentecostalism, Spirit Baptism, was measured by the question: "Given your personal experience, indicate how strongly you agree with the following statements." The response used a Likert scale 1–5, with 1 = *very little* to 5 = *very strong*. The scale (comprising the items: Spirit Baptism is an experience of the love of God, Spirit Baptism is subsequent to an experience of inner cleansing, Spirit Baptism is experienced subsequent to conversion, Spirit Baptism results in a new love for God, Spirit Baptism is an experience of the power of God, Spirit Baptism results in a new love for neighbor, Spirit Baptism results in a new zeal for reaching the lost, Spirit Baptism is an experience of inner cleansing) delivered a Cronbach's alpha score of .91.

RESULTS

Table 1 shows the results of one-way analysis of variance conducted to explore the impact of different kinds of conversion experience categories (independent variable) on the socialization factors (dependent variables). This test was repeated for nine socialization dependent variables. There was a statistically significant difference for seven out of the nine dependent variables.

Post hoc pairwise comparisons using Bonferroni correction revealed that the context of conversion experience elicited differences in the degree of socialization via significant other, especially the family members of mother, father, and other family member. For significant other, there were significant differences in means scores between Christian home as the context for conversion and (a) response to an altar call $(+/-3.36, p < .000)$, (b) personal and unusual spiritual experience $(+/-4.00, p < .000)$, (c) a result of a deep and personal crisis $(+/-3.92, p < .005)$, (d) testimony of a friend or family member $(+/-4.64, p < .001)$ and (e) cannot identify the particular cause or event $(+/-5.07, p < .001)$. For mother, there were significant differences in means scores between Christian home as the context for conversion and (a) response to an altar call $(+/-0.961, p < .000)$, (b) personal and unusual spiritual experience $(+/-1.272, p < .000)$, (c) result of a deep and personal crisis $(+/-1.799, p < .000)$, (d) testimony of a family or friend $(+/-1.658, p < .000)$ and (e) cannot identify the particular cause or event $(+/-1.065, p < .000)$. In addition for mother, there was a significant difference in mean scores between as a result of a deep and personal crisis and response to an altar call $(+/-0.838, p < .000)$ and between testimony of friend or family member and response to an

Table 1. One-way ANOVA: Conversion Experience by Socialization Factors and Family Members

	Christn Home		Altar Call		Experience		Crisis		Testimony		Christn TV		Small Gp		Not id		F
	M	SD	M	SD	M	SD	M	SD	M	SD	M	SD	M	SD	M	SD	
Ref Gp	18.3	5.9	17.5	5.8	16.9	6.4	17.0	5.0	17.3	5.6	15.5	7.1	19.0	5.3	16.2	6.6	1.58
Sig Other	30.9	7.6	27.6	7.0	27.0	7.5	27.0	7.1	26.3	7.8	26.7	9.9	31.9	8.0	25.9	7.8	7.64***
Cn Media	19.2	5.6	18.9	5.3	18.9	6.0	19.4	5.6	18.3	6.0	19.4	7.4	23.1	5.7	17.2	6.0	2.75*
Pers Agen	15.7	3.6	15.8	3.5	16.6	3.1	16.3	3.2	15.8	3.5	17.5	3.1	17.9	2.7	14.8	4.3	2.29*
Dir Enc	4.3	1.1	4.2	1.2	4.5	1.0	4.2	1.2	4.2	1.3	4.5	1.3	4.3	1.4	3.5	1.6	4.80***
Mother	4.2	1.2	3.2	1.6	2.9	1.6	2.4	1.5	2.5	1.6	2.9	1.5	3.4	1.6	3.1	1.6	27.80***
Father	3.1	1.7	2.1	1.5	1.9	1.4	1.9	1.4	1.7	1.2	2.1	1.5	2.0	1.6	1.8	1.3	18.74***
Spouse	3.4	1.7	3.4	1.6	3.4	1.6	3.0	1.7	3.0	1.7	3.4	1.4	3.2	1.8	2.9	1.7	1.66
Oth Fam	3.5	1.4	2.9	1.4	2.8	1.5	2.5	1.4	3.0	1.6	3.2	1.4	3.5	1.7	3.1	1.4	6.76***

Note: Circumstances of the born again experience: Christn Home = raised in a Christian home; Altar Call = response to an altar call; Experience = personal and unusual experience; Crisis = result of a deep personal crisis; Testimony = through the testimony of friend or family member; Christn TV = in response to an invitation during a Christian television program; Small Gp = as part of a discipleship or small group ministry; and Not id = cannot identify the particular cause or event. Socialization factors: Ref Gp = Reference Group; Sig Other = Significant Other; Cn Media = Christian Media; Pers Agency = Personal Agency; Dir Enc = direct encounter with God; Oth Fam = Other Family Member.

* $p < .05$ ** $p < .01$ *** $p < .0001$

altar call (+/– 0.696, p < .007). For father, there were significant differences in means scores between Christian home as the context for conversion and (a) response to an altar call (+/– 1.046, p < .000), (b) personal and unusual spiritual experience (+/– 1.228, p < .000), (c) as a result of deep and personal crisis (+/– 1.190, p < .000), (d) testimony of a family or friend (+/– 1.403, p < .000) and (e) can't identify the particular cause or event (+/– 1.330, p < .000). For other family members, there were significant differences in means scores between Christian home as the context for conversion and (a) response to an altar call (+/– 0.536, p < .000), (b) personal and unusual spiritual experience (+/– 0.655, p < .000) and (c) result of a deep personal crisis (+/– 0.963, p < .000).

Other post hoc pairwise comparisons revealed that the context of conversion experience elicited differences in the degree of socialization via Christian media, between discipleship or small group ministry and cannot identify a particular cause or event (+/– 5.94, p < .007) and sense of personal agency, between personal and unusual spiritual experience and cannot identify a particular cause or event (+/– 1.81, p < .049). There were also differences in the context of conversion and the degree of perception of direct encounter with God. These differences are for cannot identify a particular cause and event and (a) response to an altar call (+/– 0.74, p < .000), (b) personal and unusual spiritual experience (+/– 1.01, p < .000), (c) deep personal crisis (+/– 0.69, p < .016) and (d) testimony of a friend or family member (+/– 0.66, p < .025).

No post hoc pairwise comparisons were made for reference group and spouse because the analysis of variance indicated there were no statistically significance differences between these contexts for conversion.

Table 2 shows the results of an independent t test. There were statistically significant differences between women and men in relation to two family socialization factors. Men were especially indebted to the role of their spouse in their relationship of love with God. Women were appreciative of other family members in their relationship of love with God.

Table 3 shows the statistically significant correlations between the family socialization factors and Pentecostal spirituality experiences. All of the correlations were statistically significant, except for mother and church activity and mother and prophecy. This suggests that mothers do not provide the strongest family socialization for Pentecostal spirituality overall, although their influence on the key experience of Spirit baptism is noteworthy. Fathers tend to support the socialization of church activity the most, while the spouse tends to support charismatic experience and evangelism most strongly. The most important family socialization factor

Table 2. *Comparison of Mean scores for Men and Women for Family Significant Others*

	N	Men Mean	SD	N	Women Mean	SD	t	95% CI
Mother	375	3.32	1.6	592	3.46	1.6	−1.32	[−0.35, 0.07]
Father	360	2.35	1.6	531	2.36	1.6	−0.08	[−0.23, 0.21]
Spouse	369	3.59	1.6	544	3.06	1.7	4.82***	[0.31, 0.74]
Oth Fam	383	2.81	1.4	593	3.30	1.5	−5.04***	[−0.67, −0.30]

Note: CI = confidence interval; Oth Fam = Other Family Member
*** $p < .0001$

Table 3. *Pearson Product-Moment Correlations between Family Significant Others and Pentecostal Spirituality*

	Mother	Father	Spouse	Oth Fam
Church Activity	.063	.158**	.140**	.076*
Charismatic Experience	.136**	.114**	.187**	.166*
Healing	.150**	.123**	.117**	.208**
Prophecy	.035	.114**	.094**	.101**
Evangelism	.073*	.109**	.170**	.205**
Baptism in the Spirit	.175**	.096**	.156**	.206**

Note: Oth Fam = Other Family Member.
* $p < .05$ ** $p < .01$

was the "other family member," which supports healing, evangelism, and Spirit baptism most strongly.

Table 4 shows the results of a standard multiple regression analysis and presents four models where there is statistical significance, even though the models are very weak. Church activity (variance of 0.5%) can be predicted by the family socialization factors of father and spouse as well as gender (code: *1* = men; *2* = women; the positive score refers to women). The strongest correlation is for father. Charismatic Experience (variance of 0.7%) is predicted by the family socialization factor of spouse and gender (women). The strongest correlation is for spouse. Healing (variance of 0.6%) is predicted by the family socialization factors of other family member and spouse as well as gender (women). The strongest correlation is for other family member. Evangelism (variance of 0.6%) is predicted by the family socialization factors of spouse and other family member. The strongest correlation is for other family member. The spouse is the most consistent predictor of Pentecostal spirituality, especially when associated with gender (women), but the other family member strongly supports the role of the spouse in healing and evangelism.

Table 4. *Standard Regression Analysis: Predictors of Pentecostal Spirituality*
(*B = standardized Beta scores*)

	Ch Activity		Charis Exp		Healing		Evangelism	
	B	95% CI	B	95% CI	B	95% CI	B	95% CI
Constant	7.413***	[5.68, 9.15]	14.145***	[12.10, 16.18]	10.199***	[9.16, 11.24]	12.48***	[10.48, 14.48]
Gender	.132***	[0.60, 2.18]	.117***	[0.63, 2.50]	.124***	[0.42, 1.36]	.026	[-0.56, 1.26]
Mother	-.009	[-0.31, 0.25]	.076	[-0.02, 0.64]	.068	[-0.02, 0.32]	-.033	[-0.46, 0.19]
Father	.140***	[0.17, 0.71]	.010	[-0.28, 0.36]	.018	[-0.12, 0.20]	.022	[-0.22, 0.40]
Spouse	.135***	[0.18, 0.65]	.184***	[0.44, 1.00]	.105**	[0.08, 0.36]	.141***	[0.30, 0.85]
Oth Fam	-.017	[-0.37, 0.24]	.079	[-0.04, 0.69]	.133***	[0.14, 0.49]	.184***	[0.49, 1.18]
Adj R^2	.05		.07		.06		.06	
F	7.78***		11.97***		13.07***		11.85***	

Note: CI = confidence interval; Ch Activity = Church Activity; Charis Exp = Charismatic Experience; Oth Fam = Other Family Members
* $p < .05$ ** $p < .01$ *** $p < .0001$

DISCUSSION

The evidence suggests that the category of significant other is important for socialization in general, and this is especially the case when the context of conversion experiences is being raised in a Christian home. But this feature needs to be held in tension with a perception of direct encounter with God. The Christian home consistently scores more highly than other categories such as responding to an altar call, personal and unusual spiritual experiences, the result of a deep and personal crisis, through the testimony of a friend or family member, and not being able to identify the cause or event of conversion. This is a significant finding given the role that Pentecostal spiritual practices play within the movement. As part of this movement, there is a great emphasis placed upon responding to God's call by means of the altar call (Albrecht, 1999). Often Pentecostal narratives are composed of unusual spiritual experiences, and many conversion narratives contain a crisis event (Rambo, 1993). Pentecostals emphasize the role of testimony as a means of witnessing to their faith and of reinforcing the faith of those within the movement (Cartledge, 2010). But the empirical evidence suggests that conversion is rooted in family socialization in the Christian home. Therefore, this feature needs to be held in tension with the sense of direct encounter with the divine, which does emphasize the altar call, unusual spiritual experiences, personal crisis, and testimony. Personal and unusual spiritual experience is noted in relation to personal agency in particular, which again supports the theory of Rambo (1993) that the conversion process is active rather than passive. This dynamic is captured in the conceptual model between the perception of God and active quest for God, socialization factors, and religious experience. This basic tension between the Christian home in relation to a significant other and spiritual experiences in relation the perceived direct encounter with God is also supported in a minor way by the role of the discipleship or small group in relation to Christian media.

Given the broad dynamic discussed above, can we identify the particular family socialization members who might be regarded as significant others as far as the conversion experience is concerned? The evidence indicates that family members are important in general and that mothers stand out in particular, although supported by fathers and other family members. A born again experience in the context of being raised in a Christian home does indeed provide an important context in which to socialize its members into a relationship of love with God, even if other influences can also be appreciated. The pairwise comparisons show that the Christian home is by far the most important context for family social-ization. This is an important finding because it is so often assumed that such conversion type experiences are associated with evangelistic cam-paigns and church-related events. The role of the mother, however, does extend beyond the family context and it does include some influence in the appropriation of the altar call as a context in which to experience the born again experience. Therefore, the Christian home is significant for establishing the first step on the way to a Wesleyan-Pentecostal *ordo salutis*, although it may be supplemented by the church ritual of the altar call and in this way echo the tension noted above between the Christian home and spiritual experience. This means that the mother is the key player when it comes to socializing "born again" experiences and that her influence extends beyond the domain of the home to include Pentecostal altar call rituals in order to ensure the Pentecostal identity of the family.

Men and women are clearly socialized differently, but, interestingly, not in relation to the role of mothers and fathers. Rather, men are assisted in their relationship with God by their spouses, and women are assisted by other family members. This, of course, begs the question as to why the relationship is not reciprocal. Men draw on the resources of their wives, but wives draw on the resources of other family members, suggesting an interesting family dynamic is at work. Men seem to be satisfied with their spouse's support, but women need support outside of their marriage. An important role for married women in the maintenance of spirituality gen-erally is suggested by this research and supports previous research which places women at the heart of the Pentecostal family dynamic, especially in sustaining the Pentecostal gender paradox of simultaneous submis-sion and empowerment (Martin, 2001). This paradox associated with the study of Pentecostals in Latin America suggests that, despite accepting an outward patriarchal social convention symbolized by men in official church leadership roles, women are empowered by Pentecostal spiritual-ity which in turn brings greater social mobility and family stability (Cox, 1996). The paradox is that they do not use this power to challenge patriar-chal structure in the home and in the congregation; rather, they comple-ment it with their own spiritual power normally associated with the key features of Pentecostalism such as Spirit baptism, healing, and prophecy. "The implicit deal seems to be that a substantive shift towards greater gender equality will be tolerated so long as women are not seen to be publicly exercising formal authority over men" (Martin, 2001, p. 54). Any permanent resolution of the tension associated with the paradox would ultimately mean disempowerment for them (via disaffiliation), thus the paradox continues (Brusco, 1995, 2010; Cartledge, 2003; Martin, 2001). This research shows how the paradox is maintained from the women's perspective in the COG: The spirituality is itself empowering, and women are supported by other family members who together enhance its impact.

This research suggests that when the family is extended or functions in close proximity to other family members, then socialization is also extended beyond the nuclear structure thus modifying this modernizing impulse (Martin, 2001). This influence is likely to extend to the spiritual practices of healing, evangelism, and Spirit baptism. Of course, the category of "other family member" does not specify which persons are in view, and it could be speculated as to whether it largely denotes sibling or aunt/uncle or cousin. One suspects that the key role is that of sibling and further research is required to identify this more precisely. For the sake of this discussion, the role of the extended family is noted as an important one for family socialization purposes. If, as one suspects, extended families are also members of the same congregation, it means that this category also functions as a bridge between family socialization and congregational socialization.

It is clear that women are significant factors in the engagement with church activities, charismatic experience, healing and evangelism, but not in the role as mother rather as spouse. Here the Pentecost gender paradox comes to the fore again as spouses may not be the most obvious influence in terms of up-front ministry in the denomination. Nevertheless, they do appear to influence congregational life and witness. The category of spouse should be interpreted as female for three out of the four models since the gender score refers to women. This suggests that married women also exercise significant congregational influence. This dynamic is important because it suggests that marriage, especially for women, lies at the heart of family socialization for Pentecostal spirituality. Other family members are important for more outward-facing features such as evangelism, and fathers are important for more inward facing features such as Church activities. But is it the wife, as spouse to her husband, and as supported by other family members who is central to the maintenance of Pentecostal spirituality. The literature on the role of women in Pentecostalism, as noted above, underscores this finding and challenges earlier stereotypical characterizations of fundamentalist patriarchy (e.g. Rose, 1999). Married women fulfill a significant role beyond the family unit and indeed function as the social glue connecting both family and congregation, especially when supported by other family members. There are significant implications for the study of the relationship between the family and religion, especially conservative Protestantism, in the USA.

This study confirms the importance role of the family, and in particular the Christian home, for the socialization of children and young people into religious experience. This experience may be supported by outside socialization factors (e.g. the media and small groups), but they have a generally weaker influence than the home and the power of the spirituality itself. The roles of both mother and father are significant, although it is especially the case for mothers. It is important to note the role of the "other family member," who functions as a *reinforcer* for the wife, while she in turn functions as the reinforcer for the husband (Park & Ecklund, 2007). The husband might support church activities in general, thus giving an impression of leadership (Hayes & Pittelkow, 1993), but it is the wife who mediates the spiritual capital (Martin, White & Perlman, 2003). This is not a fully reciprocal relationship and requires a wider family network to be sustained. Where there is marriage breakdown, therefore, it is more likely that the husband disaffiliates altogether because of a lesser commitment to the actual spirituality as opposed to the attendance at church activities, compared to the wife who is more like to switch affiliation but not spirituality (Lawton & Bures, 2001). Thus it can be seen that religiosity and family life are sufficiently supportive to lead to satisfaction within the marriage and greater involvement in organized religion (Willits & Crider, 1988).

The family as an institution can be confirmed as a positive contributor to religiosity in the USA, but there are numerous expressions of family life and a variety of Christian churches. Miller, Miller-McLemore, Couture, Lyon, and Franklin (2000), in a study of family and religion in American society, identified three kinds of marital and family love: (a) mutuality or equal regard ("giving your spouse and children the same respect, affection, and help as you expect from them"); (b) self-sacrifice ("putting the needs and goals of your spouse and children ahead of your own"); and (c) self-fulfillment ("fulfilling your personal needs and life goals") (Miller et al., 2000, p. 18). This research suggests that among CoG Pentecostals there is not full mutuality, at least with regard to the socialization of Pentecostal spirituality, which could be classified as the values guiding the family. There is some sharing of values both in the home and the congregation; nevertheless, it could be suggested that women are more likely to understand familial love as self-sacrifice rather than equal regard because of the investment in others (notably spouse and congregation), although there is also some self-fulfilment in the process as well. Here they exhibit Sorokin's (1954/2002) notion of intensity if not extensity. The power to love in this way comes from a high degree of participation in the key practices of Pentecostal spirituality. In this way women, demonstrate in their religious practices the notion of the family as "first church" and as "little church" and with other family members display continuity between the gathered ecclesia and the church at home (Miller et al., 2000, p. 308).

This study clearly confirms the accepted and well documented general picture that women are more religious than men (Sherkat, 1998; Woodhead, 2001), but it nuances the picture by suggesting that this kind of Pentecostal religiosity is fundamentally about personal and congregational spiritual practices rather than official roles. Indeed, it might be suggested that it is through religious traditions emphasising experience that such spiritual power is gained and that these experiences are "feminized" to some extent because of their important relational contexts (Woodhead, 2001, p. 78) and the "feminine and fluid intimacy of the Spirit or through a feminized Jesus appealing from the heart to the heart" (Martin, 2002, p. 104). It does need to be noted from Ammerman's (1987) study of a conservative Protestant community that women's deference to men in the home does not mean that they are without influence in the decision making and that this influence is, to some extent, accepted by men and often leads to a process of negotiation (Bartkowski, 1997; McNamara, 1985). The Pentecostal gender paradox gives an answer to the question as to why this is the case when allied to the previous point about religious socialization and marital benefits. There appears to be something of a trade-off between access to spiritual power and stable family life, despite patriarchy, which appear to be accepted as worthwhile and beneficial. Following Brusco, victimization and marginalization as explanations of Pentecostal women's experience can be rejected as simplistic (2010), even if self-sacrificial love might not ultimately lead to complete equal regard. This access to power, despite patriarchy, is mirrored in both home and church because of the overlap between the two institutions, which in turn reinforce and legitimate the other. What is fascinating is that a model of gender relations developed out of studies in Latin American has proven to have application to American Pentecostalism (even if Brusco might be surprised by this finding, 2010). Martin's comment that Latin American Pentecostal women "have been 'empowered' by a 'regressive,' 'fundamentalist' Christian movement whose theological rawness and lack of intellectual sophistication causes

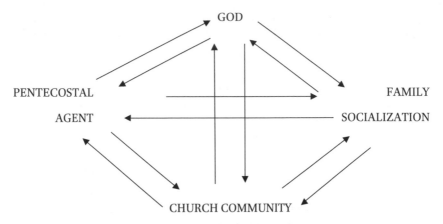

Figure 3. *The Revised Family Socialization Model.*

problems and embarrassment to enlightened western observers" (2001, p. 57), could also be said for its North American cousin.

There are also implications for the emerging conceptualization of Pentecostalism and religious experience. The earlier model (Figure 2) that conceptualized the perceived interaction between the individual, family socialization, and God can now be developed even further. The relationship between the individual and religious experience should not be conceived as a simple quest for an encounter with the divine irrespective of either the family or the wider community of the church. Rather, it should include all of these dimensions (Figure 3).

Clearly there is a dynamic between individuals and their perception of a direct encounter with God but this is always set within the context of the church community and largely influenced by dynamics within the nuclear family and wider family structure. Pentecostal spiritual practices are indeed mediated via significant others and at the same time engaged with via a high degree of personal agency. Models of religious experience that conceive of this and similar forms of spirituality as either passive, focusing on the influence of the group, or active, focusing on the individual and individualizing features, cannot be supported by this research. Religious experience is both undergone (here socialized by external communal factors) and pursued (exercised by individuals with personal agency; cf. Franks Davis, 1999). Indeed, it requires this double feature for its ongoing meaningfulness. Therefore, Pentecostalism is a highly socialized and communal form of religion even in its western expression and cannot be fully understood without this realization (Cartledge, 2006). As a form of global religion, it resonates deeply with various primal and communal expressions of religiosity from around the world (Cox, 1996).

Conclusion

This study has shown that the Pentecostal home is an important context for born again experiences and influences the socialization of congregants in their perceived relationship of love with God. Married women, especially, assist their spouses in their experience of a relationship of love with God, while they themselves are supported by other family members. Indeed the role of other family members is important for the engagement with Pentecostal spirituality. Married women provide the strongest support for the ongoing maintenance of Pentecostal experience and spirituality. This is a significant finding that places marriage at the heart of Pentecostal socialization. By implication, marriage breakdown is likely to be an important factor in the weakening of such socialization for Pentecostals, impacting the role of women most severely. This research has implications for appreciating the role of the family in the socialization of Pentecostal spirituality but also among conservative Protestants more generally. It lends even further support to the proposed Pentecostal gender paradox, whereby women are empowered despite patriarchy. Further research is now required to understand its applicability more widely, not just for Pentecostal studies but also for the study of Christianity more broadly, and to explore more precisely the role that other family members play in the socialization process.

References

Albrecht, D.E. (1999). *Rites in the Spirit: A ritual approach to Pentecostal/Charismatic spirituality*. Sheffield, England: Sheffield Academic Press.
Aldridge, A. (2000). *Religion in the contemporary world: A sociological introduction*. Cambridge, England: Polity.
Ammerman, N.T. (1987). *Bible believers: Fundamentalists in the modern world*. New Brunswick, NJ: Rutgers University Press.
Bao, W-N., Whitbeck, L.B., Hoyt, D.R. & Conger, R.D. (1999). Perceived parental acceptance as a moderator of religious transmission among adolescent boys and girls. *Journal of Marriage and Family, 61,* 362–374. Retrieved from http://www.jstor.org/stable/353754
Bartkowski, J.P. (1997). Debating patriarchy: Discursive disputes over spousal authority among Evangelical family commentators. *Journal for the Scientific Study of Religion, 36,* 393–410. Retrieved from http://www.jstor.org/stable/1387857
Berger, P. (1969). *The social reality of religion*. London, England: Faber and Faber.

Berger, P. & Luckmann, T. (1967). *The social construction of reality: A treatise in the sociology of knowledge*. London, England: Penguin.

Brusco, E.E. (1995). *The reformation of machismo: Evangelical conversion and gender in Colombia*. Austin, TX: University of Austin Press.

Brusco, E.E. (2010). Gender and power. In A. Anderson, M. Bergunder, A. Droogers & C. Van der Laan (Eds.), *Studying global Pentecostalism: Theories and methods* (pp. 74–92). Berkeley, CA: University of California Press.

Call, V.R.A. & Heaton, T.B. (1997). Religious influence on marital stability. *Journal for the Scientific Study of Religion, 36*, 382–392. Retrieved from http://www.jstor.org/stable/1387856

Cartledge, M.J. (2003). *Practical theology: Charismatic and empirical perspectives*. Carlisle, England: Paternoster.

Cartledge, M.J. (2006). *Encountering the Spirit: The Charismatic tradition*. London, England: Darton, Longman & Todd.

Cartledge, M.J. (2010). *Testimony in the Spirit: Rescripting ordinary Pentecostal theology*. Farnham, England: Ashgate.

Cartledge, M.J. (2012). Socialization, empirical studies and Godly love: A case study in survey research. In M. Lee & A. Yong (Eds.), *Godly love: Theological, interdisciplinary, and methodological essays* (pp. 183–199). Dekalb, IL: Northern Illinois University Press.

Conn, C.W. (1996). *Like a mighty army: A history of the Church of God, definitive edition 1886–1995*. Cleveland, TN: Pathway Press.

Cox, H. (1996). *Fire from heaven: The rise of Pentecostal spirituality and the reshaping of religion in the twenty-first century*. London, England: Cassell.

Danziger, K. (1971). *Socialization*. Harmondsworth, England: Penguin.

Franks Davis, C. (1999). *The evidential force of religious experience* (2nd ed.). Oxford, England: Oxford University Press.

Fulcher, J. & Scott, J. (2003). *Sociology*. Oxford, England: Oxford University Press.

Furniss, G. (1995). *Sociology for pastoral care: An introduction for students and pastors*. London, England: SPCK.

Hayes, B.C. & Pittelkow, Y. (1993). Religious belief, transmission and the family: An Australian study. *Journal of Marriage and Family, 55*, 755–766. Retrieved from http://www.jstor.org/stable/353355

Hitlin, S. & Piliavin, J.A. (2004). Values: Reviving a dormant concept. *Annual Review of Sociology, 30*, 359–393. doi:10.1146/annurev.soc.30.012703.110640

Hunt, S.J. (2003). *Alternative religions: A sociological introduction*. Aldershot, England: Ashgate.

Kieren, D.K. & Munro, B. (1987). Following the leaders: Parents' influence on adolescent religious activity. *Journal for the Scientific Study of Religion, 26*, 249–255. Retrieved from http://www.jstor.org/stable/1385797

Lawton, L.E. & Bures, R. (2001). Parental divorce and the "switching" of religious identity. *Journal for the Scientific Study of Religion, 40*, 99–111. Retrieved from http://www.jstor.org/stable/1388184

Lee, M.T., Poloma, M.M. & Post, S.G. (2008). *Researching Godly love in the Pentecostal tradition: A white paper for the Flame of Love Project*. Akron, OH: University of Akron.

Lee, M.T., & Poloma, M.M. (2009). *Social filters of Godly love: A sociological study of the great commandment in the Pentecostal context*. Lewiston, NY: Edwin Mellen Press.

Macchia, F.D. (2006). *Baptized in the Spirit: A global Pentecostal theology*. Grand Rapids, MI: Zondervan.

Martin, B. (2001). The Pentecostal gender paradox: A cautionary tale for the sociology of religion. In R.K. Fenn (Ed.), *The Blackwell companion to the sociology of religion* (pp. 52–66). Oxford, England: Blackwell.

Martin, D. (2002). *Pentecostalism: The world their parish*. Oxford, England: Blackwell.

Martin, T.F., White, J.M. & Perlman, D. (2003). Religious socialization: A test of the chan-
neling hypothesis of parental influence on adolescent faith maturity. *Journal of Adolescent Research, 18*, 169–187. doi:10.1177/0743558402250349

McGuire, M.B. (2002). *Religion: The social context.* Belmont, CA: Wadsworth Thomson.

McNamara, P.H. (1985). Conservative Christian families and their moral world: Some
reflections for sociologists. *Sociological Analysis, 46,* 93–99. Retrieved from http://www
.jstor.org/stable/3711053

Miller, D.S., Miller-McLemore, B.J., Couture, P.D., Lyon, K.B. & Franklin, R.M. (2000). *From
culture wars to common ground: Religion and the American family debate* (2nd ed). Louisville, KY: Westminster John Knox Press.

Park, J.Z. & Ecklund, E.H. (2007). Negotiating continuity: Family and religious socialization for second-generation Asian Americans. *The Sociological Quarterly, 48,* 93–118.
doi:10.1111/j.1533–8525.2007.00072.x

Poloma, M.M. (1989). *The Assemblies of God at the crossroads: Charisma and institutional
dilemmas.* Knoxville, TN: The University of Tennessee Press.

Poloma, M.M. & Hood, R.W. (2008). *Blood and fire: Godly love in a Pentecostal emerging
church.* New York, NY: New York University Press.

Poloma, M.M. & Green, J.C. (2010). *The Assemblies of God: Godly love and the revitalization
of American Pentecostalism.* New York, NY: New York University Press.

Rambo, L. (1993). *Understanding religious conversion.* London, England: Yale University
Press.

Richards, A.I. (1970). Socialization and contemporary British anthropology. In P. Mayer
(Ed.), *Socialization: The approach from social anthropology* (pp. 1–32). London, England:
Tavistock.

Rose, S.D. (1999). Christian fundamentalism: Patriarchy, sexuality, and human rights. In
C.W. Howland (Ed.), *Religious fundamentalism and the human rights of women* (pp.
9–20). Basingstoke, England: Macmillan Press.

Sherkat, D.E. (1998). Counterculture or continuity? Competing influences on baby boom-
ers' religious orientations and participation. *Social Forces, 76,* 1087–1115. Retrieved from
http://www.jstor.org/stable/3005704

Sherkat, D.E. & Ellison, C.G. (1999). Recent developments and current controversies in
the sociology of religion. *Annual Review of Sociology, 25,* 363–394. Retrieved from http://
www.jstor.org/stable/223509

Sorokin, P. (2002). *The ways and power of love: Types, factors, and techniques of moral transformation.* Radnar, PA: Templeton Foundation Press. (Original work published 1954)

Thomas, J.C. (2010). *Towards a Pentecostal ecclesiology: The church and the fivefold Gospel.*
Cleveland, TN: Center for Pentecostal Theology Press.

van der Ven, J.A. (1996). *Ecclesiology in context.* Grand Rapids, MI: Eerdmans.

White, G. (1977). *Socialisation.* London, England: Longman.

Willits, F.K. & Crider, D.M. (1988). Religion and well-being: Men and women in middle
years. *Review of Religious Research, 20,* 281–294. Retrieved from http://www.jstor.org/
stable/3511225

Willits, F.K. & Crider, D.M. (1989). Church attendance and traditional religious beliefs in
adolescence and young adulthood: A panel study. *Review of Religious Research, 31,* 68–81.
Retrieved from http://www.jstor.org/stable/3511025

Woodhead, L. (2001), Feminism and the sociology of religion: From gender-blindness to
gender difference. In R.K. Fenn (Ed.), *The Blackwell companion to the sociology of religion*
(pp. 67–84). Oxford, England: Blackwell.

FROM *VICARIOUS RELIGION* TO VICARIOUS SOCIAL CAPITAL? INFORMATION AND PASSIVE PARTICIPATION IN VOLUNTARY ASSOCIATIONS

*Judith A. Muskett**

ABSTRACT

This article proposes a theory of passive involvement in voluntary associations admitting passive and active members. The theory draws on key principles of Davie's (2008) concept of *vicarious religion*, which accounts for contrasting behaviors of the active (in that case, those who believe in God and belong to a church) and the passive (who may believe yet do not belong). It is suggested that, through *understanding* and *approving of* active members' participation, passive members share in and possibly also experience the benefits of stocks of social capital generated/embedded within the association. Despite a tendency on the part of theorists to trivialize association newsletters, the Vicarious Social Capital Model ascribes a pivotal role to information in the social process: By compensating for an absence of activity, information is predicted to be the mechanism through which passive members are empowered to contribute to an extent greater than researchers have hitherto recognized.

Keywords: information, passive participation, social capital, vicariousness, voluntary associations

Although early social capital research focused on formal voluntary associations because this was convenient from a methodological point of view (Newton, 1999; Putnam & Goss, 2002), much scholarly attention continues to be given to the study of voluntary associations, as generators or, at the very least, repositories of social capital. The interest in voluntary associations stems in large part directly from Putnam's early work (1993, 1995a). Indeed, the level of associational membership has now become "a standard litmus test for the health of a society's social capital" (Stolle & Hooghe, 2005, p. 152; see also Holmes & Slater, 2007; Maloney, van Deth, & Rossteutscher, 2008).

* *Author Note*: Judith A. Muskett, Theology and Religious Studies, York St John University. I thank Andrew Village for helpful comments on drafts of the manuscript.

Correspondence concerning this article should be addressed to Judith A. Muskett, Theology and Religious Studies, York St John University, Lord Mayor's Walk, York YO31 7EX, United Kingdom. Email: j.muskett@yorksj.ac.uk

Nevertheless, the significance of voluntary associations for social capital has been contested (Li, Pickles, & Savage, 2005). Researchers risk presenting an incomplete or even distorted account of social capital (Li et al., 2005) because studies tend to count the number of memberships in specific voluntary associations as an index of the stocks of social capital in a community, region, or country at a given time (Hall, 1999; Paxton, 1999; Putnam, 1995a). For instance, indicators which focus exclusively on formal acts of participation may overlook women, who traditionally prefer more informal connectedness and participation (Stolle & Hooghe, 2005), and also disadvantaged social groups, who can be deterred from entry to civic associations that require formal application for membership, the payment of fees, and knowledge about how to behave within the organization (Li et al., 2005). Yet, it is hard to underestimate the importance of voluntary associations when, for example, empirical research leads to claims that "associational affiliations are more central to respondents' lives than their neighbours, work, or politics" and come a very close second to family and friends (Maloney et al., 2008, p. 284).

The focus of this article is the capacity of formal voluntary associations to generate social capital, or perhaps merely embed it, through passive membership. The main aim is to use ideas from religious affiliation to construct a model that will advance theory in relation to passive involvement where the passive and the active co-exist within the membership. First, existing literature on the hallmarks of voluntary associations and on the role of passive participants is reviewed. Next, it is argued that key principles of Davie's (2008) *vicarious religion* construct have wider applicability. There are two main contentions. The first is that through *understanding* and *approving of* active members' participation, the passive may share in and possibly also experience the benefits of stocks of social capital; the second is that information is the mechanism through which this is achieved. There has been a tendency for theorists to downplay and/or trivialize the role of information in the social process within voluntary associations (see, for example, Putnam, 1995a; Wuthnow, 2002). In reality, communication may compensate for an absence of activity, but precisely how it functions as an integrative mechanism has been unclear (Knoke, 1981).

The study of religion arguably benefits from engagement with ideas generated from non-religious or quasi-religion organizations, so the mechanism discussed in the article can deepen understanding of Davie's concept. Furthermore, the mechanism may also elaborate the concept in a fruitful manner: See Muskett, 2011 for how the theory might be applied to the role of Anglican cathedrals.

VOLUNTARY ASSOCIATIONS

The Hallmarks of Voluntary Associations

It is common for authors to discuss associations without defining the characteristics by which such entities are recognized (Cameron, 2004). Fundamentally, a distinction is made between four types of groups (Newton, 1999): involuntary groups (e.g., a compulsory professional organization for doctors), voluntary groups (e.g., a parish church choir), informal groups (e.g., Bible-reading or Lent groups) and formal associations (e.g., the Christian charity Mothers' Union).

Specific criteria by which a formal, voluntary association can be identified encompass such aspects as nomenclature, constitution, articulated purposes, criteria for access to membership, rules, conduct of business, democratic decision-making processes, resources provided by members, and the supportive role of any paid staff (Billis, 1983; Cameron, 2004). However, governance arrangements and decision-making per se may not hold a particular interest for members, who tend to seek from voluntary associations "expressive" social and personal benefits, like friendship, reciprocal support, and exchange of news (Harris, 1998, p. 608). The kernel of a voluntary association, according to Cameron (2004), is membership by fulfilling criteria and democratic decision-making, and, according to Hall (2002), is involvement of members in at least some face-to-face interaction and engagement of members in a common endeavor.

Not every entity that uses the label *association* should be regarded as a safe indicator of social capital (Offe & Fuchs, 2002; Wuthnow, 2002). For example, the ubiquitous neighborhood watch association fails the test: In Putnam's (1995b) view, this represents "only a partial, artificial replacement for the vanished social capital of traditional neighborhoods—a kind of sociological Astroturf suitable only where you can't grow the real thing" (p. 681, note 8). Similarly, special-interest groups (such as the American Association of Retired Persons) "do little to promote social capital because membership may consist of little more than sending in a check once a year and receiving a seldom-read publication in return" (Wuthnow, 2002, p. 91).

Intensity of Involvement in Associational Life

A key characteristic that marks out one type of voluntary association from another is the intensity of involvement of individual members: The essential distinction is whether the membership is active or not. As noted above, in Hall's (1999) analysis, active supporters engage in some face-to-face interaction with fellow members. The corollary is that passive members do not. But associations are complex and do not necessarily fit neatly into a binary classification. Putnam has been criticized for overstating the amount of socialization taking place in organizations (Wollebaek & Stromsnes, 2008) and also for failing to take account of secondary associations where many or even most members are passive, which is said to be common, for example, in Scandinavia and the Netherlands, although not in the United States (Wollebaek & Selle, 2002a). To represent the full range of expression of voluntary associations, the detailed taxonomy of Offe and Fuchs (2002) encompasses the spawning of secondary-type groups in tertiary associations (termed "nested associability," pp. 193–197). Examples of the latter would be national fundraising charities with active local branches.

Passive Involvement, Check-Book Participation, *and the Consequences for Social Capital*

Wollebaek and Selle (2002a) have called for studies to give greater attention to passive membership, which has been poorly researched. Passive involvement should not necessarily be regarded as a negative contribution to an association. If the passive are shown to contribute more than previously recognized, it may be possible to assuage anxieties about the future vitality of democracy.

Passive support is important for at least four fundamental reasons. First, it is a source of numerical strength and legitimacy for associations (Wollebaek & Selle, 2003). A growth in membership may enable a campaigning association to be more effective in lobbying a government for changes in policy. Second, passive support is important in straightforward economic terms: the greater the number of members (however intensely they relate to the association), the greater the capacity to raise funds, not least through regular fees/donations. Third, viewing passive memberships dynamically may reveal a valuable latent energy, which could be harnessed (Wollebaek & Selle, 2003): Different events in the life-course (children leaving home, retirement, partner loss) and changes in motivation or in the availability of resources may all present opportunities for passive support to be transformed into active membership. Fourth, passive members appear to have sticking power. The most active members of voluntary associations are among the least persistent, and the most persistent members are among the least active; organizations requiring more of their members will have trouble keeping their members (Cress, McPherson, & Rotolo, 1997). Given the demands of modern life, it may be easier to commit to a membership that does not require too much in return.

In the de Tocqueville (1956) model of social capital (deriving from the principle that there is a causal relationship between the effect of associationalism and the capacity for civic participation; see, for example, Rudolph, 2004; Whiteley, 1999), it is the social connection within voluntary associations that creates social capital. The logic is that social capital will not be formed in an association lacking social connection: "What really matters from the point of view of social capital and civic engagement is not merely nominal membership but active and involved membership" (Putnam, 2000, p. 58). Elaborating this model, Putnam (1995b) argued that as classic secondary associations have declined in recent years and tertiary associations (such as the American Association of Retired Persons and Greenpeace) have flourished, so there has been a reduction in social connectedness and thus also in stocks of social capital.

But, while Putnam (1995b), Hall (2002), and Offe and Fuchs (2002) have argued that not every type of association has the capacity to generate social capital, others (Maloney, 1999; Whiteley, 1999; Wollebaek & Selle, 2002b, 2004) have expressed a different opinion. Along the lines of Putnam's (1995a) notion of tertiary association (where writing a check for fees and occasionally reading a newsletter are the hallmarks of membership, and those who belong are unlikely ever to meet), a new form of engagement was identified. First, McCarthy and Zald (1973) referred to paper organizations with newsletter members. Subsequently, the label *credit card participation* (Richardson, 1995) was applied to the new form of engagement, where individuals express support through monetary gifts but play no further role in the activities of the organization to which they "belong." Later, the notion of *check-book participation* came into its own (Hilton, McKay, Crowson, & Mouhot, 2010; Jordan & Maloney, 1997; Maloney, 1999; Whiteley, 2011). According to Richardson, this mode of engagement can be regarded as a kind of

> surrogate activism in which individuals support a particular cause—often single issue—but leave the formulation and delivery of the campaign to organizational professionals or to the few genuine activists within the

> organization. Having paid one's contribution, one can rest in the knowledge
> that the organization will campaign on one's behalf...Like other forms of
> activity in a post-industrial society, it is easy to "contract out" the tasks one
> does not want to, or need to, perform oneself. (Richardson, 1995, p. 135)

Yet, there is a paradox here, because while such protest and participation can be regarded as coordinated collective action, most participants are actually acting alone (Stolle & Hooghe, 2005). Nevertheless, the rise of a range of check-book associations carries with it the implication that passive members will become more important (Stolle & Hooghe, 2005).

The growth of check-book participation is widespread not only in the United States but also in the United Kingdom (Maloney, 1999). Surprisingly, the label has stuck in the U.K. despite the prevalence of bankers' orders in favor of voluntary associations (with the consequence that participation need not even extend to conscious delivery of the annual subscription by check). Newton (1999) identified two major types of "low-commitment" check-book associations. In the first, citizens join merely for the benefits and service they receive in return (p. 12). The extent of the membership and income renders such associations powerful interest groups. The Automobile Association would be a prime example: This has a very large but almost totally inactive membership comprising individuals who pay an annual fee for various services connected with motoring. In Newton's second type, individuals are motivated to join organizations not for the services they provide but for largely symbolic reasons. In subscribing, a member makes a symbolic gesture, desiring to be allied with the cause. Such a gesture could be made by joining the Friends of a heritage site, for example. However, Newton concluded that both these types of organizational membership have no obvious implications for civic engagement and the formation of norms of social capital (1999); moreover, he argued that they have little internal effect on members so far as the creation of social capital is concerned.

Having initially questioned whether check-writing can be regarded as meaningful participation (Jordan & Maloney, 1997), Maloney (1999) subsequently conducted a postal survey of supporters of Amnesty International British Section (AIBS) and Friends of the Earth (FoE) in order to examine attitudes and behavior patterns. Responses demonstrating that supporters seek the group goal, rather than active political participation, led Maloney to endorse Richardson's appraisal and then to consider the salience of participation by proxy. By choosing to fund professionals to influence policy, supporters of AIBS and FoE were contracting out of the function, resulting in what Maloney termed "vicarious participation" (1999, p. 114).

He concluded that there was little or no strong evidence to suggest that check-book participation is detrimental in the way that Putnam implied or envisaged. In a deliberate echo of the claim by John Stuart Mill that "any participation, even in the smallest public function, is useful," Maloney argued that the check-writers' contribution may be small but is better than no participation at all (p. 117).

Voluntary associations relying on passive support are said to bear a resemblance to the notion of an imagined community (Anderson, 1991), where a large-scale membership shares emotional ties (the nation being the most obvious example; Maloney, 1999; Wollebaek & Selle, 2002a). Turning to social-psychological literature on social identity, Whiteley (1999) made a similar point about imaginary communities, claiming that empirical data show that individuals do not have to interact directly with other members of the preferred group in order to identify with it. For their part, Wollebaek and Selle (2002b) argued that passive affiliations may foster a sense of affinity to a cause that individuals know is not only important to themselves but also to others: "If the association is successful, the membership, regardless of activity level, conveys a sense of the value of cooperation for common purposes . . . and of a shared belonging to something important" (p. 57). Slater's (2005) three-fold typology of voluntary associations supporting cultural and heritage organizations identified that "Integrated Membership Schemes" (at one end of the spectrum) will foster a sense of community/belonging through programmes and communication (p. 37).

In a study of social capital in Norway, Selle (1999) asserted that Putnam's understanding of norms and social integration was old-fashioned, because it did not pay sufficient attention to aspects of the communication structure of societies in the information age. Selle proceeded to argue that it is feasible that identities and trust can be built when the primary method of communication is not face-to-face contact, leading him to the proposition that new types of organization where face-to-face contact is not the rule may after all be important as producers of social capital. Subsequent analyses of data from a Norwegian survey by Wolleback and Selle (2002a, 2002b, 2004) did not support Putnam's emphasis on face-to-face contact:

> While those affiliated with associations consistently displayed higher levels of social capital (measured as social trust, civic engagement, and breadth of social networks) than outsiders did, the difference between those spending little or no time participating and highly active participants was very small or altogether absent. (2004, p. 239)

Wollebaek and Selle suggested that a central issue is how passive supporters are affected by what is termed their participation by proxy. They distinguished between four understandings of the relationship between these individuals and their association: the association as social system, imagined community, information system, and network of political influence (p. 248). Three key insights emerging from that distinction were: Some passive members, recruited through already existing social networks, can keep in touch with the association through pre-existing networks of contact with active members; the shared belonging to something important in the imagined community is a virtue conducive to social capital; and, even though passive members do not interact personally, they are in touch with what is happening in the association through the dissemination of information.

Wollebaek and Selle (2004) therefore challenged the emphasis of social capital theory on face-to-face contact. While acknowledging the importance of this mode of connectedness, they noted that associations actually provide little opportunity for it, in contrast to, for example, families, friends, and workplaces; they pondered whether the sense of belonging and commitment to a cause which arise from associational membership (even when passive) are more significant in the formation of social capital. Wollebaek and Selle (2004) did not demonstrate precisely how these virtues generate social capital: They simply suggested that a sense of belonging and commitment to a cause are conducive to social trust and civic engagement. In fact, they raised the question of whether associations should be viewed "as institutionally-embedded stores of trust, norms, and networks of civic engagement, rather than as generators, catalysts, or vehicles," thus bringing to the forefront the scope of involvement (multiple, overlapping memberships) over intensity (degree of face-to-face contact) (p. 252). Together with Stromsnes, Wollebaek (2008) subsequently argued that the main contribution of voluntary organizations lies not in socializing active members but in institutionalizing social capital.

VICARIOUSNESS

As described above, Maloney (1999) and Wollebaek and Selle (2004) have suggested that participation by proxy may be a consequence of passive associational membership. Within the sociology of religion, Davie's (2008) theory of vicarious participation accounts for contrasting behaviors of the active and the passive: In that case, the active are those who believe in

God and belong to a church, and the passive are those who may believe yet do not belong. The premise of the present article is that aspects of Davie's theory have wider applicability and that her ideas can benefit from engaging with theory drawn from non-religious organizations. The debate surrounding intensity of involvement in voluntary associations can be illuminated by her construct which, with a more nuanced approach, may account for how passive participants contribute to social capital in voluntary associations. It is not unusual to advance theory by comparing voluntary associations and religious congregations. Just as Harris (1998) and Cameron (2004) shed light on the organizational structure of congregations by identifying that they resemble voluntary associations in certain respects, so it is argued here that the discourse on social capital can be informed by applying principles of congregational normative behavior to voluntary associations; this in turn sheds light on the behavior of religious organizations.

From Believing Without Belonging *to* Vicarious Religion

The decline in the popularity of Christian churches in Britain over the 20th century was credited with stimulating research into the attitudes and beliefs of those who are outside organized religion but not opposed to it (Bruce & Voas, 2010). To understand this constituency (reckoned to be approximately half of the population), Davie sought to develop tools and concepts, of which the phrase "believing without belonging" was the first attempt, subsequently refined by the notion of "vicarious religion" (2010, p. 261). Believing without belonging was Davie's way of depicting the way large parts of the population in Europe continue to be attached to their historic churches, even though they may not they attend these institutions regularly. It is one of the most accepted theories within the sociology of religion (Day, 2011), but Davie reckons the notion should now be retired, and she is not alone in reaching that view (Voas & Crockett, 2005). Her successor concept, vicarious religion (claimed to be more penetrating and accurate; Davie, 2007, 2008), is one way of probing implicit and explicit connections between this body of people and the historic churches (Davie, 2010). The intention of the term vicarious religion is to convey "the notion of religion performed by an active minority but on behalf of a much larger number, who (implicitly at least) not only understand, but, quite clearly, approve of what the minority is doing" (Davie, 2007, p. 22, original emphasis removed). Davie (2010) illustrated the more explicit acceptance of vicarious religion by reference to parts of Europe

(Nordic countries and Germany) where a form of church tax is still in force: With only a relatively small number of tax-payers choosing to contract out of this system, she concluded that most tangibly support their churches.

By considering the standpoints of both the passive majority and the active minority, the sceptical Bruce and Voas have criticized Davie's vicarious religion concept on a number of grounds. For example, they claimed she misunderstands the etymology of her own term. Appearing to assume that vicariousness can operate only in one direction, they used Davie's concession in a footnote (2007, p. 33, note 2) that vicars serve on behalf of a superior to suggest that vicarious religion cannot apply to the active minority "doing religion on behalf of others," who are not similarly in a position of superiority (Bruce & Voas, 2010, p. 254). They concluded that Davie's construct amounts to a descriptive theory about the meaning of peripheral religious involvement. Preferring Voas' own concept of *fuzzy Christians*, the pair contended that it is inappropriate to use the adjective religious (even when qualified by vicarious) for individuals with no church connection and who do not see themselves as religious but approve (for example) of the active minority "doing religion on behalf of others" (pp. 257–258). But it is not immediately clear why describing these individuals as Christian, albeit qualified by the adjective fuzzy, should be acceptable, when Davie's use of the adjective religious is judged not to be. In criticizing Davie in this manner, the detractors missed the very point of her concept. It is not the inactive majority whom Davie is describing as religious. The essential aspect of the construct lies in the "on behalf of" element (Davie, 2010, p. 265). Her focus is on the activity of the minority, which she claims is implicitly (at least) understood and appreciated by the majority.

A theological definition of vicariousness will firmly overthrow Bruce and Voas' etymological objection to Davie's concept. According to Saxbee (2009), vicariousness is the essence of Jesus' life and death: "Jesus lived and died vicariously, and faith in Jesus can be likewise vicarious insofar as it is about the same overflowing of God's grace and goodwill in solidarity with those around us" (pp. 90–91). He observed that vicarious faith "continues to flourish in ways that tend to confound those who espouse without question theories of secularization" (p. 86). Saxbee argued that individuals go to church for the sake not only of the God who is present but also for the people who are not. This chimes with one of the more famous sayings often attributed to William Temple, Archbishop of Canterbury 1942–44: "The church is the only society on earth that exists for the benefit of non-members." Saxbee continued:

> That we are in church to worship God is presumably beyond question, but we pay little regard to this vicarious role whereby we represent a community to God and God to a community in ways which may be implicit rather than explicit, but are nevertheless significant. (p. 86)

He concluded, first, that "as a function of solidarity with those who may not yet have accepted Jesus' invitation into His life, [vicarious faith] goes to the heart of our purpose as the People of God and the Body of Christ"; and, second, that vicarious faith can be "the calling card whereby God's invitation into the life of Christ is conveyed and communicated" (pp. 91–92).

Vicarious Action and Intentionality

In responding to the criticism of Bruce and Voas, Davie (2010) explained the next phase of her thinking. Highlighting a more philosophical question about the vicarious religion concept, prompted by insights of German scholars, she pondered: "Does the notion of acting vicariously imply intentionality? Is it necessary, in other words, for the actor to be conscious of what s/he is doing?" (p. 266). Theologians would point to the fact that the believing community should indeed be conscious of what it does and thereby acts intentionally. The theme of intentionality could also be explored in relation to the reverse side of the equation. Is it necessary for the passive majority to be conscious of what is being done for it? Is it necessary for the *on behalf of* element to be understood by the passive and welcomed by them, implicitly or explicitly? Such questions could likewise be posed about vicarious action in social capital theory.

Benefits Accruing to the Passive from Vicarious Action

The idea of the passive benefiting from vicarious action resonates with the public good aspect of Coleman's (1990) theory of social capital. He provided the example of a school Parent Teacher Association, which constitutes social capital not only for the participants (organizers) but also for the school and non-participants (the students and other parents). Burt's (2000) discussion of social capital being "borrowed" by managers in firms (pp. 400–405) may also suggest that the notion of vicarious social capital has salience.

In the case of campaigning tertiary associations like Friends of the Earth and Amnesty International, the participatory process is also relatively straightforward. The argument would proceed as follows. A small number of professionals acts explicitly on behalf of the many supporters who fund the association. The passive are conscious of this action and welcome it and are enabled thereby to participate in the political process by proxy or vicariously. That participation, although minimalistic, is conducive to the formation of social capital, because it builds generalized trust and civic engagement.

But what about the case of an association which blurs the categories: where active and passive members are found in combination within, say, a tertiary association having a nested secondary-type group? An example would be the Friends' association of an historic cathedral: A nationwide membership subscribes to raise money for the fabric and in return receives news of the cathedral, while a nested subset of active Friends in the vicinity are additionally advocates and volunteers for the cause. Another example, this time with two nested levels, would be Mothers' Union, which admits *central members*, who support the charity simply by payment of an annual subscription, and in return receive magazines including news and a prayer diary; *diocesan members*, who not only subscribe but also get involved in local social outreach; and *branch members*, who meet like-minded people on a more regular basis and share in prayer and fellowship within a group linked to a local church (Mothers' Union, 2011). It could be speculated that there is an *on behalf of* element in such hybrid scenarios and that behaviors conducive to the formation of social capital are performed by an active constituency on behalf of a broader passive membership. Naturally, this performance may or may not acquire intentionality.

Voluntary Associations, Information, and Social Capital

The essential principles of Davie's concept are that the passive, implicitly at least, not only *understand* but also *approve of* what the active do on their behalf. If these are imported to the social capital field and applied to life in a tertiary association with a nested secondary-type group (hybrid membership), there is at once need of a *mechanism* (Knoke, 1981; Simon, 1979) whereby the passive can understand what the active do. The contention here is that associational information fulfils that role.

Constructing the Model

Preliminary support for the proposition that the supply of information in the form of associational newsletters plays a vital role in sustaining the sense of belonging has been provided by the findings of Wollebaek and Selle (2004). Echoes are found in the writing of de Tocqueville (1956), who pointed to the importance of information, gleaned through newspapers, in the formation of voluntary associations. The bi-directional relationships between belonging, participating, and information might be depicted as in Figure 1 (below). First, information about the association leads to individual decisions to join, and members' belonging generates associational information (that is, without a corpus of members there will be no planning and no reason to communicate). Second, through belonging, members participate in organizational activities, and, in turn, participation reinforces the sense of belonging to the organization. Third, information about activities (in the form of notices/invitations) encourages participation, and, in order to sustain the sense of belonging, information flows about the activities in which members have been involved. The contention implies that the characterizations of tertiary associations by Putnam (1995a) and Wuthnow (2002) trivialize newsletters and downplay their value in the social process.

The potential of information in relation to voluntary associations and/or social capital has been highlighted in both theoretical and empirical research (Burt, 2000; Coleman, 1990; Knoke, 1981; Widén-Wulff et al., 2008). Association memberships entail access to sources of knowledge and information (Wollebaek & Selle, 2002), which is important in providing a basis for action (Coleman, 1990). A prerequisite for a group's unity as a network is the mutual exchange of information (Widén-Wulff et al., 2008).

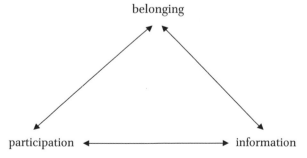

Figure 1. *Schematic representation of the role of information in a simplex voluntary association.*

The basic model (Figure 1) is expanded below (Figure 2) to depict the creation of social capital and the effects of this resource. Here, the participation leads directly to increased levels of social capital, which has effects such as volunteering and greater levels of generalized trust (that is, trust in the organization and also trust in organizations more generally); these in turn sustain a sense of belonging. However, it should be acknowledged that to identify which way causation flows is not straightforward (Newton, 1999). Putnam's (1995b) findings demonstrated that "people who join are people who trust" (p. 666), whereas Brehm and Rahm's (1997) research suggested that the effect of civic engagement on interpersonal trust was much stronger than the effect of interpersonal trust on civic engagement. For such reasons, all linkages are bi-directional in the expanded model.

In an article that predated the major theorizing on social capital, Knoke (1981) claimed that the absence of normative communication (encompassing, implicitly, both verbal and non-verbal forms) would lead to a worsening of members' commitment and an increasing indifference to the group (p. 144). He tested empirically the proposition that "the more extensive the amount of communication within a voluntary association, the greater the level of members' commitment and the lower their detachment from the organization" and proposed two alternative models. The first, *consistency*, following Smith and Brown (1964), asserted that to elicit high levels of member involvement, the communication and decision-making processes must complement each other; whereas the second, *compensation*, asserted

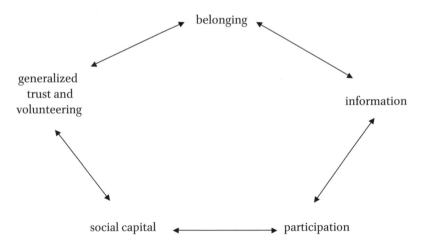

Figure 2. *Schematic representation of the role of information in the building of social capital in a simplex voluntary association.*

that extensive communication may offset or compensate for the weakness of direct participation. Knoke's data demonstrated that to a certain extent communication can offset an absence of personal involvement in the policy process, especially in the case of those members whose support might be at most risk without such contacts. The problem with Knoke's research is that it focused on the internal political structure of voluntary associations: The author acknowledged that the effects might be suspect on the grounds that some voluntary association members do not desire extensive involvement in the internal politics of the organization. Nevertheless, there were two key findings. First, "group norms of loyalty and dedication to the group are reinforced by the flow of information about the prevailing orientations, evaluations, and behaviours of the organization's participants." Second, the socializing function of information appears to be of especial importance where members lack first-hand involvement (p. 155). Knoke concluded that his analyses left little doubt about the primary function of communication in producing supportive memberships but conceded that further work was needed on precisely how information functions as an integrative mechanism. To flesh out Knoke's (1981) compensation model requires a novel dimension. This is where Davie's principles (2007) can be applied. The putative mechanism whereby the passive can understand what active fellow members do is illustrated in the final model below (Figure 3). Here, generalized *participation* has been replaced by two parallel loops: The first depicts the norms of the nested secondary-type group, and the second characterizes the norms of the passive members.

On the one hand, the link between information and activity remains bi-directional: The dissemination of information (notification of forthcoming events) spawns action, and action is subsequently captured in a rather more collaborative form of information (first-hand accounts and photographs of events), which in turn reinforces experience. Again, this process resonates with de Tocqueville's insights about the role of newspapers in the initial formation of associations: "there is . . . a necessary connection between public associations and newspapers: newspapers make associations, and associations make newspapers" (1956, p. 203). On the other hand, the relationship between information and passivity is uni-directional in the final model. The transmission of information by the gate-keeper officials is hierarchical rather than collaborative. Written communication compensates for and/or offsets the lack of direct personal involvement by the passive. By means of information, the passive supporters learn about and understand associational affairs and, in particular, about the normative behavior of the active members. The advantage of the new model over

Davie's construct is that it accounts for how the passive participants understand the *on behalf of* element. Whether the passive also approve of the action is a moot point but one susceptible to testing empirically. This reasoning ascribes greater significance to the role of information than in, say, Wollebaek and Selle's (2004) and Slater's (2005) characterization of associations, where its dissemination merely sustains the sense of belonging (Figure 1).

Taking a further step, beyond the patterns of vicarious participation, to adapt Davie's concept to social capital theory more broadly would raise the question of whether the effects of vicarious social capital can be experienced equally by the passive. If a secondary-type group generates social capital by its activity in a fundamentally tertiary association (for example, active local fundraisers who belong a national Friends' charity in support of an historic place of worship), can the passive membership feel the benefit of the vicarious social capital? That is, according to Hall's (1999) definition, can the passive see an effect upon their level of general trust in others and their commitment to voluntary work? In the Vicarious Social Capital Model (VSCM; Figure 3), the dashed arrow between (vicarious) social capital and its effects hints at this process. Again, a hypothesis along these lines could be tested empirically. It is likely that the second arrow is bi-directional in so far as increased trust and volunteering, experienced even by the passive supporter of the original association, form ever greater social capital.

It would be myopic to disregard Wollebaek and Selle's (2004) alternative proposition that voluntary associations merely embed stores of trust, norms, and networks of civic engagement, rather than as act as generators, catalysts, or vehicles of such virtues. Even if that proposition were supported, social capital created outside the association but embedded within it could accrue vicariously to passive participants through the putative VSCM described. In addition, it is feasible that extra social capital accruing to passive participants through their own voluntary action elsewhere and spawned by the initial embedded social capital could also become embedded in the association, and that, in turn, this assists in the formation of even further stocks for the whole community.

The Vicarious Social Capital Circle: Virtuous or Vicious?

According to Brehm and Rahm (1997), there is the potential for a virtuous circle in a social capital model. On the one hand, increase any of the elements in the model, and the positive reciprocal relationships would pre-

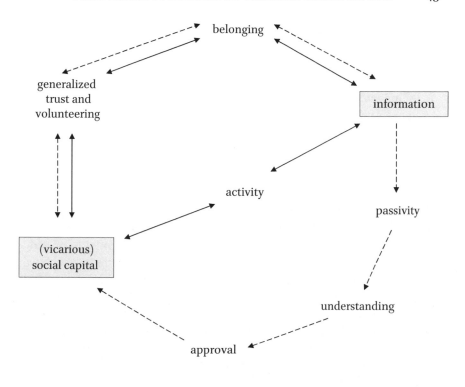

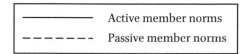

Figure 3. *The Vicarious Social Capital Model (VSCM): the pivotal role of information in generating/embedding social capital within a voluntary association having hybrid membership.*

dict a positive symmetrical effect on the reverse side: More activity yields yet more social capital; increased social capital results in greater levels of trust and volunteering, and so on. It follows that if a voluntary association increases the frequency of its written communication to members, there may be a positive consequence: More extensive information may compensate for and/or offset to an even greater degree the absence of direct participation. Yet there may come a point at which an over-supply of information has a deleterious outcome.

On the other hand, a decline in any element in the model would result in lower levels of the virtue on the reverse side. Less activity yields a reduction in social capital; lower levels of social capital result in less trust and volunteering, and so on. Hence, there is potential for a vicious circle. As Brehm and Rahm observed, the cycle can erode over and over as a consequence of the reciprocal relationship between the virtues. Accordingly, such a model can account for a decline in social capital over time.

Directions for Future Research

After the detailed account of how the model was constructed, attention now shifts to its possible applications. At one level, the message is a simple one: It is that the conceptual framework has the potential to provide reassurance to voluntary associations that their passive members have a worthwhile role to play, by contributing not only to financial capital through paying their dues but also to institutional stocks of social capital. In addition, the focus on associational information within the construct may prompt those who govern organizations to reflect on the nature of the information which they share with members through newsletters, magazines, and annual reports. A recognition that information may play a role in the social process, beyond that of simply building a sense of belonging, could also inform policy discussions about the frequency with which such information is disseminated.

However, all this is speculation at present. The VSCM is now ready for conceptual critiques and empirical testing. In designing an instrument, it will be important to pay heed to repeated warnings from Davie (2007, 2010) that vicariousness is not necessarily easily measured. In particular, she has argued that the phenomenon is relatively invisible to those using quantitative methods, because it cannot be counted. However, the claim here is that the identification of information as a mechanism within the VSCM may facilitate quantitative research around vicariousness: It offers an independent variable that may allow researchers to test causal links. Indeed, a similar point has been made (Muskett, 2011) in connection with a refined model of vicarious religion, where Anglican cathedrals have been highlighted as a potential element in the mechanism that acquaints the passive with the religious practices of their active counterparts.

So, with empirical research, the VSCM may prove to be a useful tool for analyzing the social process in voluntary associations admitting both active and passive members. The rewards of empirical studies could be reaped not only by secular voluntary associations but also by religious organizations. This would be especially fitting given that the new social capital model has been shaped by use of a theory of religion. But in what specific circumstances could the model be tested, and what practical benefits might be felt there? Three examples of how the VSCM might be applied in real-life situations follow: All have a religious context, but that is not to imply that the model has practical implications only in that domain. Two were mentioned earlier as examples of tertiary associations with nested secondary-type groups: Friends' associations of Anglican cathedrals and Mothers' Union.

The prior example relates to how information might operate within and outside a congregation to foster capital among non-participants. Take the role of parish magazines, which have been said by the Archbishop of Canterbury (Beckford, 2009) to be the most widely read Christian publications in the country. They have a combined readership of more than 1.3 million, which is greater than that attracted by a British national daily newspaper such as *The Guardian* or *The Independent* and approaching the readership of *The Daily Express* or *The Times* (National Readership Survey, 2011). Parish magazines are read by many people who never set foot inside a church (Beckford, 2009) and have a capacity to serve as "cordage" in network communities that develop from parochial association, linking individuals who may not live in the locality yet share a parochial interest or sense of belonging, especially through on-line publication (Snell, 2010, p. 47).

The VSCM predicts that (a) information is crucial in order for the active to build the vicarious social capital from which the passive ultimately benefit, and (b) information about activity is crucial for the passive to experience such capital. Thus, in this scenario, the prediction is that parish magazines are one mechanism by which active members of a parish church congregation build social capital. In the first instance, information therein about church events mobilizes the active to participate. Second, the model predicts that interested individuals outside the congregation understand and approve of the vicarious activity. The monthly parish magazines compensate for the lack of first-hand involvement by these passive individuals. They share vicariously the congregational stocks of social capital and experience the effects, in terms of generalized trust and volunteering. A critical test of the model would be to examine the extent to which the passive subscribers actually read the parish magazines, rather than discarding them: If higher levels of social capital (as indicated by social trust and volunteering) were correlated with reading the magazines, and lower levels of social capital with receiving but not reading the information, then this would suggest the model is correct. Data from such a study could influence decisions about precisely how to share church information (weekly pew sheets and/or parish magazines), with whom (gathered congregation and/or passive parishioners), and at what cost to the recipient (free or not).

Likewise, in a Friends' charity that supports an historic parish church or cathedral, active local Friends and geographically distant Friends able/willing to travel are mobilized by newsletters conveying information about future social events, volunteering opportunities, and trips. The model predicts that passive members of the charity understand and approve of the vicarious activity. Through accounts and photographs of events, outings, and volunteering, the regular associational newsletters and annual reports compensate for the lack of first-hand involvement by the passive, who share vicariously the charity's stocks of social capital and experience the effects thereof. A critical test of the VSCM would be to examine the extent to which the passive Friends actually read the newsletters and reports: If higher levels of social capital (as gauged by social trust and volunteering) were discovered in the readers, and lower levels of social capital in the non-readers, then, again, this would suggest support for the model.

An organization with not two but three levels of nested associability could hold particular interest in relation to the VSCM. Thus, a third voluntary association in which to test the model would be Mothers' Union. First, the model predicts that branch members, and to a lesser degree the diocesan members (who meet less often), build social capital through their own regular participation in meetings, prayer, and volunteering. The sharing of information about branch/diocesan activities encourages such engagement. Second, the model predicts that the central members understand and approve of the vicarious activity by their branch and diocesan counterparts. The regular M.U. news magazines compensate for the lack of first-hand involvement on the part of the central members. These individuals share vicariously the associational stocks of social capital and also experience the effects, in terms of generalized social trust and volunteering. A critical test of the model would be to examine the extent to which passive central members read the magazines: If higher levels of social capital were correlated with reading M.U. magazines, and lower levels of social capital with not reading them, then this too would suggest the model has salience. In this and the other two scenarios, longitudinal data could reveal whether adjustments to the volume and/or frequency of information are also likely to have an effect. For example, more extensive information may compensate for and/or offset to a greater degree an absence of direct participation; conversely, disseminating less information may have a deleterious effect.

Thus far, the model and suggested applications have focused on the one-directional dissemination of information by voluntary associations to their audience through conventional, printed means. Conveying associational information by alternative, two-directional means, such as email or social media, holds open the possibility of recipients' reacting and responding to the communication relatively easily through the same channels (Hogan & Quan-Haase, 2010). But does keeping in touch with the off-line world of an association through social media imply a blurring of the distinction between active and passive members? This would appear to be unlikely. The effects of the Internet on social contact have been shown to be supplementary: Participants in the off-line sphere use it to augment and extend their participation, and on-line participants get more involved in person with organizations (Wellman, Haase, Witte, & Hampton, 2001). Rather than blur the categories, social media may affirm or reinforce them: The Internet provides another tool for getting the active involved (Stern & Adams, 2010). To test the VSCM in the context of a voluntary association that uses Facebook and/or Twitter as a platform to convey its information would make a fascinating study.

CONCLUSION

In summary, the goal of this article was to use a concept about religious affiliation in order to advance theory in connection with passive involvement in voluntary associations, specifically in those organizations that boast both passive and active members. The goal has been achieved by the construction of the Vicarious Social Capital Model (VSCM), which in one respect runs counter to certain scholars' assumptions about the role of associational information. Testing precisely how information functions as an integrative mechanism by means of the new model will complement the original study by Knoke (1981). Three scenarios have illustrated how the model could be applied in real-life situations, and it has been suggested that voluntary associations which use social media to convey their information are likely to be equally profitable contexts in which to test the model.

REFERENCES

Anderson, B. (1991). *Imagined communities: Reflections on the origins and spread of nationalism*. London, England: Verso.

Beckford, M. (2009, 13 January). Archbishop of Canterbury, Dr Rowan Williams, celebrates 150 years of parish magazines. *The Telegraph*. Retrieved from http://www.telegraph.co.uk/news/religion/4228972/Archbishop-of-Canterbury-Dr-Rowan-Williams-celebrates-150-years-of-parish-magazines.html

Billis, D. (1983). *Organizing public and voluntary agencies*. London, England: Routledge.

Brehm, J., & Rahn, W. (1997). Individual-level evidence for the causes and consequences of social capital. *American Journal of Political Science, 41*(3), 999. doi:10.2307/2111684

Bruce, S., & Voas, D. (2010). Vicarious religion: An examination and critique. *Journal of Contemporary Religion, 25*(2), 243–259. doi:10.1080/13537901003750936

Burt, R.S. (2000). The network structure of social capital. *Research in Organizational Behavior, 22*(345–423). doi:10.1016/S0191–3085(00)22009–1

Cameron, H. (2004). Are congregations associations? In M. Guest, K. Tusting & L. Woodhead (Eds.), *Congregational studies in the UK : Christianity in a post-Christian context* (pp. 139–151). Aldershot, Hants, England: Ashgate.

Coleman, J.S. (1990). *Foundations of social theory*. Cambridge, MA: Harvard University Press.

Cress, D.M., McPherson, J.M., & Rotolo, T. (1997). Competition and commitment in voluntary memberships: The paradox of persistence and participation. *Sociological Perspectives, 40*(1), 61–79. Retrieved from http://ucpressjournals.com/journal.asp?j=sop

Davie, G. (2007). Vicarious religion: A methodological challenge. In N.T. Ammerman (Ed.), *Everyday religion: Observing modern religious lives* (pp. 21–35). New York, NY: Oxford University Press.

Davie, G. (2008). From believing without belonging to vicarious religion. Understanding the patterns of religion in modern Europe. In D. Pollack & D.V.A. Olson (Eds.), *The role of religion in modern societies* (pp. 165–176). New York, NY: Routledge.

Davie, G. (2010). Vicarious religion: A response. *Journal of Contemporary Religion, 25*(2), 261–266. doi:10.1080/13537901003750944

Day, A. (2011). *Believing in belonging: Belief and social identity in the modern world*. Oxford, England: Oxford University Press.

de Tocqueville, A. (1956). *Democracy in America. Specially edited and abridged for the modern reader by Richard D. Heffner*. New York, NY: New American Library.

Hall, P.A. (1999). Social capital in Britain. *British Journal of Political Science, 29*(3), 417–461. doi:10.1017/S0007123499000204

Hall, P.A. (2002). Great Britain: The role of government and the distribution of social capital. In R.D. Putnam (Ed.), *Democracies in flux: The evolution of social capital in contemporary society* (pp. 21–58). New York, NY: Oxford University Press.

Harris, M. (1998). A special case of voluntary associations? Towards a theory of congregational organization. *The British Journal of Sociology, 49*(4), 602–618. doi:10.2307/591291

Hilton, M., McKay, J., Crowson, N., & Mouhot, J.-F. (2010). *Civic participation and social responsibility. Briefing paper presented to the Strategy Unit of the Cabinet Office, 15 June*. Birmingham, United Kingdom: University of Birmingham Retrieved from http://www.birmingham.ac.uk/news/thebirminghambrief/items/civicsocietydecline.aspx

Hogan, B., & Quan-Haase, A. (2010). Persistence and change in social media. *Bulletin of Science Technology & Society, 30*, 309–315. doi:10.1177/0270467610380012

Holmes, K., & Slater, A. (2007). Social capital and voluntary membership associations: Heritage supporter groups in the United Kingdom. In M. Collins, K. Holmes & A. Slater (Eds.), *Sport, leisure, culture and social capital: Discourse and practice.* (pp. 101–117). Eastbourne, England: Leisure Studies Association.

Jordan, G., & Maloney, W.A. (1997). *The protest business: Mobilizing campaign groups*. Manchester, England: Manchester University Press.

Knoke, D. (1981). Commitment and detachment in voluntary associations. *American Sociological Review, 46*(2), 141–158. doi:10.2307/2094975

Li, Y., Pickles, A., & Savage, M. (2005). Social capital and social trust in Britain. *European Sociological Review, 21*(2), 109–123. doi:10.1093/esr/jci007

Maloney, W.A. (1999). Contracting out the participation function: Social capital and chequebook participation. In J. van Deth, M. Maraffi, K. Newton & P. Whiteley (Eds.), *Social capital and European democracy*. London, England: Routledge.

Maloney, W.A., van Deth, J.W., & Rossteutscher, S. (2008). Civic orientations: Does associational type matter? *Political Studies, 56*, 261–287. doi:10.1111/j.1467–9248.2007.00689.x

McCarthy, J.D., & Zald, M.N. (1973). *The trend of social movements in America: Professionalization and resource mobilization*. Morristown, NJ.: General Learning Press.

Mothers' Union. (2011). Get involved. Join Mothers' Union. Retrieved from http://www.themothersunion.org/joinmothersunion.aspx

Muskett, J.A. (2011). *Reflections on the shop-windows of the Church of England. A role for Anglican cathedrals in a model of vicarious religion*. Unpublished manuscript, Theology and Religious Studies, York St John University, York, England.

National Readership Survey. (2011). Latest top-line readership (July 2010 to June 2011) Retrieved from http://www.nrs.co.uk/toplinereadership.html

Newton, K. (1999). Social capital and democracy in modern Europe. In J.W. van Deth, M. Maraffi, K. Newton & P.F. Whiteley (Eds.), *Social capital and European democracy* (pp. 3–24). London, England: Routledge.

Offe, C., & Fuchs, S. (2002). A decline of social capital? The German case. In R.D. Putnam (Ed.), *Democracies in flux: The evolution of social capital in contemporary society* (pp. 189–243). Oxford, England: Oxford University Press.

Paxton, P. (1999). Is social capital declining in the United States? A multiple indicator assessment. *American Journal of Sociology, 105*(1), 88–127. doi:10.1086/210268

Putnam, R.D. (1993). *Making democracy work: Civic traditions in modern Italy*. Princeton, NJ: Princeton University Press.

Putnam, R.D. (1995a). Bowling alone: America's declining social capital. *Journal of Democracy, 6*(1), 65–78. doi:10.1353/jod.1995.0002

Putnam, R.D. (1995b). Tuning in, tuning out: The strange disappearance of social capital in America. *PS: Political Science and Politics, 28*(4), 664–683. doi:10.2307/420517

Putnam, R.D. (2000). *Bowling alone: The collapse and revival of American community*. New York, NY: Simon & Schuster.

Putnam, R.D., & Goss, K.A. (2002). Introduction. In R.D. Putnam (Ed.), *Democracies in flux: The evolution of social capital in contemporary society* (pp. 3–19). New York, NY: Oxford University Press.

Richardson, J.J. (1995). The market for political activism: Interest groups as a challenge to political parties. *West European Politics, 18*(1), 116–139. doi:10.1080/01402389508425060

Rudolph, S.H. (2004). Is civil society the answer? In S. Prakash & P. Selle (Eds.), *Investigating social capital. Comparative perspectives on civil society, participation, and governance* (pp. 64–87). London, England: Sage.

Saxbee, J. (2009). *No faith in religion. Some variations on a theme*. Ropley, Hants, United Kingdom: O Books.

Selle, P. (1999). The transformation of the voluntary sector in Norway. A decline in social capital? In J.W. van Deth, M. Maraffi, K. Newton & P.F. Whiteley (Eds.), *Social capital and European democracy* (pp. 144–166). London, England: Routledge.

Simon, H.A. (1979). The meaning of causal ordering. In R.K. Merton, J.S. Coleman & P.H. Rossi (Eds.), *Qualitative and quantitative research: Papers in honor of Paul F. Lazarsfeld* (pp. 65–81). New York, NY: Free Press.

Slater, A. (2005). Developing a typology of membership schemes in the UK. *International Review on Public and Non Profit Marketing 2*(1), 23–39. doi:10.1007/BF02893248

Smith, C.G., & Brown, M.E. (1964). Communication structure and control structure in a voluntary association. *Sociometry, 27*, 449–468. doi:10.2307/2785658

Snell, K.D.M. (2010). Parish Pond to Lake Nyasa: Parish magazines and senses of community. *Family & Community History, 13*(1), 45–69. doi:10.1179/146311810X12710831260815

Stern, M.J., & Adams, A.E. (2010). Do rural residents really use the Internet to build social capital? An empirical investigation. *American Behavioral Scientist, 53*(9), 1389–1422. doi:10.1177/0002764210361692

Stolle, D., & Hooghe, M. (2005). Inaccurate, exceptional, one-sided, or irrelevant? The debate about the alleged decline of social capital and civic engagement in Western societies. *British Journal of Political Science, 35*(01), 149–167. doi:10.1017/S0007123405000074

Voas, D., & Crockett, A. (2005). Religion in Britain: Neither believing nor belonging. *Sociology, 39*, 11–27. doi:10.1177/0038038505048998

Wellman, B., Haase, A.Q., Witte, J., & Hampton, K. (2001). Does the Internet increase, decrease, or supplement social capital? *American Behavioral Scientist, 45*(3), 436–455. doi:10.1177/00027640121957286

Whiteley, P.F. (1999). The origins of social capital. In J.W. van Deth, M. Maraffi, K. Newton & P.F. Whiteley (Eds.), *Social capital and European democracy* (pp. 25–44). London, England: Routledge.

Whiteley, P.F. (2011). Is the party over? The decline of party activism and membership across the democratic world. *Party Politics, 17*(1), 21–44. doi:10.1177/1354068810365505

Widén-Wulff, G., Ek, S., Ginman, M., Perttilä, R., Södergård, P., & Tötterman, A.-K. (2008). Information behaviour meets social capital: A conceptual model. *Journal of Information Science, 34*(3), 346–355. doi:10.1177/0165551507084679

Wollebaek, D., & Selle, P. (2002a). Passive support: No support at all? *Nonprofit Management and Leadership, 13*(2), 187–203. doi:10.1002/nml.13206

Wollebaek, D., & Selle, P. (2002b). Does participation in voluntary associations contribute to social capital? The impact of intensity, scope, and type. *Nonprofit and Voluntary Sector Quarterly, 31*(1), 32–61. doi:10.1177/0899764002311002

Wollebaek, D., & Selle, P. (2003). The importance of passive membership for social capital formation. In M. Hooghe & D. Stolle (Eds.), *Generating social capital. Civil society and institutions in comparative perspective*. New York, NY: Palgrave Macmillan.

Wollebaek, D., & Selle, P. (2004). Passive membership in voluntary organizations: Implications for civil society, integration, and democracy. In S. Prakash & P. Selle (Eds.), *Investigating social capital. Comparative perspectives on civil society, participation, and governance* (pp. 235–256). London, England: Sage.

Wollebaek, D., & Stromsnes, K. (2008). Voluntary associations, trust and civic engagement: A multilevel approach. *Nonprofit and Voluntary Sector Quarterly, 37*(2), 249–263. doi:10.1177/0899764007304754

Wuthnow, R. (2002). The United States: Bridging the privileged and the marginalized? In R.D. Putnam (Ed.), *Democracies in flux. The evolution of social capital in contemporary society* (pp. 59–102). Oxford, England: Oxford University Press.

SPIRITUALITY OR RELIGIOUSNESS: WHICH SERVES AS THE BETTER PREDICTOR OF ELEMENTS OF MENTAL HEALTH?

Teresa A. Wilkins, Ralph L. Piedmont, and Gina M. Magyar-Russell*

ABSTRACT

Social scientists contend that significant advancements in religion and spirituality research may be achieved via incremental validity studies using the Five Factor Model of personality. This study examined spirituality and religiousness as predictors of elements of mental health, which was operationalized as a combination of purpose in life, resilience, satisfaction with life, and pro-social behavior, while controlling for personality. Based upon the findings from existing research, it was hypothesized that spirituality would predict purpose in life and satisfaction with life better than religiousness, and religiousness would predict resilience and pro-social behavior better than spirituality. Using Piedmont's ASPIRES instrument, and controlling for personality, a study was performed utilizing a series of hierarchical regression analyses. Results supported the incremental validity of the ASPIRES instrument (ΔR^2 scores ranged from .06 to .02). Contrary to the hypotheses, spirituality was a better predictor than religiousness for resilience and for pro-social behavior.

Keywords: ASPIRES, Five Factor Model, spiritual transcendence, religiousness, personality, purpose in life, resilience, satisfaction with life, pro-social behavior

With the advent of positive psychology, emphasis has shifted from ascertaining deficits to examining people's strengths. The Search Institute (see Benson et al., 2006) has developed comprehensive lists of 40 developmental assets that appear to provide protective factors for children and adolescents. Examples include having a sense of personal power, awareness of a purpose in life, resistance skills, and providing service to others. The Substance Abuse and Mental Health Services Administration (SAMHSA) has recommended concentrating on wellness and has begun a campaign to improve life expectancy for people with mental illness (see Center for Mental Health Services, 2010; SAMHSA, 2010). They have determined that the eight domains of wellness encompass emotional, environmental,

* Author Note: Teresa A. Wilkins, Department of Pastoral Counseling, Loyola University Maryland; Ralph L. Piedmont, Department of Pastoral Counseling, Loyola University Maryland; Gina M. Magyar-Russell, Department of Pastoral Counseling, Loyola University Maryland.

Correspondence regarding this article should be addressed to Ralph L. Piedmont, Department of Pastoral Counseling, Loyola University Maryland, 8890 McGaw Road, Suite 380, Columbia, MD 21045. Email: rpiedmont@loyola.edu financial, intellectual, social, physical, occupational, and spiritual aspects of people's lives. Peterson and Seligman (2004) provided a comprehensive classification of character strengths and included spirituality and religiousness as strengths of transcendence. They noted that these elements "inform the kinds of attributions that people make, the meanings they construct, and the ways they conduct relationships" (p. 600). For this study, a strengths-based model was utilized, and mental health was operationalized as a combination of purpose in life, satisfaction with life, resilience, and pro-social behavior, based on the burgeoning research showing associations between these variables and psychological wellness.

If spirituality and religiousness impact mental health, which domain appears to bring forth the greatest results? Does spirituality exert more power in certain areas, while religiousness has its distinct fields of influence? Current research indicates spirituality appears to impact purpose in life and satisfaction with life, while religiousness has stronger associations with resilience and pro-social behavior. Also, if the constructs are elements of individual differences, what do they contribute over and above personality factors? Based on Piedmont's advice to advance the field via incremental validity research using the Five Factor Model (1999b), existing theory (in this case, Frankl's [1959] notion of the will to meaning), and empirical studies, we hypothesized that spirituality would predict purpose in life and satisfaction with life better than religiousness, and religiousness would predict resilience and pro-social behavior better than spirituality.

UNDERSTANDING SPIRITUALITY AND RELIGIOUSNESS AS PSYCHOLOGICAL CONSTRUCTS

Spirituality and religiousness provide insights into the human condition and consequently are fundamental concepts for studying the psychology of religion. While many early psychologists equated these elements with pathology, there were some notable exceptions. For example, Jung (1938/1966) spoke of the religious nature of the human psyche, emphasized that devotion could be healthy, and included the Deity in his archetypes. He viewed religion as the "fruit and the culmination of the completeness of life" (p. 50). Allport (1950) identified the *religious sentiment* as the fundamental underpinning of the personality, which impacted additional elements of mental health, and he identified attributes distinguishing mature from immature religion. While examining the relationship between religious practice and prejudice (Allport & Ross, 1967), he developed the concepts of intrinsic and extrinsic religious orientation and created a trait scale, the Religious Orientation Scale (ROS), to measure internalized versus utilitarian styles. Frankl (1959, 1964) explained logotherapy as an approach which honored people's yearning for making meaning and emphasized the adaptive qualities of finding a purpose in life.

Despite growing acceptance, finding a clear definition of those concepts continues to prove problematic. Zinnbauer, Pargament, and Scott (1999) examined the various meanings of the terms and distinguished between traditional (e.g., spirituality is not seen as distinct from religiosity) and modern approaches (e.g., polarization of the constructs, with spirituality seen as positive and religiousness seen as negative). Pargament, Magyar-Russell, and Murray-Swank (2005) posited that religion may be a unique process, with *the sacred* as its springboard. Saroglou (2002, 2010; Saroglou & Muñoz-García, 2008) suggested personality predicts religiousness, which is seen as a cultural adaptation associated with openness and conscientiousness, while spirituality, also an outcome, is associated with openness and agreeableness. Wink (2010) distinguished between *R-type* and *S-type* spirituality. He declared R-type to have the source of authority springing from external factors and S-type to have a more intrinsic orientation.

Piedmont's Model of the Numinous

Our study worked within Piedmont's model (1999a) of the numinous; that is, the ability to touch cosmological transcendence. Spirituality and religiousness are important components: They are viewed as separate, albeit highly correlated constructs, which are inputs rather than outcomes. Spirituality is considered a sixth factor of personality, specifically "an individual's efforts to construe a broad sense of personal meaning within an eschatological context" (Piedmont, 2001, p. 5). Spirituality serves as a *motive*: an innate, genotypic quality that drives, directs, and selects behavior. Religiosity, however, is a *sentiment*: an emotional tendency that can vary across time periods and cultures (Piedmont, Kennedy, M. Sherman, N. Sherman & Williams, 2008). Consequently, spirituality works as an internal, affective force, while religiousness is a propensity that may be subject to societal and educational influences.

Saucier and Skrzypińska (2006) made a compelling case for considering the two variables to be overlapping yet distinct constructs. They differentiated between the subjective aspects of spirituality and the fundamental importance of tradition in religiousness. Utilizing a sample ($N = 375$) of predominantly female Christians, they correlated the variables with multiple indicators, including personality factors, attitudes, behaviors, and facets of language usage. They noted the dimensions were "substantially intertwined...but should not be lumped together" (p. 1286).

Piedmont created an instrument to measure the distinct constructs of spirituality and religiousness. Working within the framework of the Five Factor Model (FFM, see Costa & McCrae, 1985; McCrae & Costa, 1987), he gathered an interfaith focus group of theological experts who identified commonalities of many religious traditions. Their contributions were factor analyzed along with the elements of the FFM: *Neuroticism (N), Extraversion (E), Openness (O), Agreeableness (A), and Conscientiousness (C)*. The instrument appeared to capture a universal, motivational quality independent of the Big 5: The Spiritual Transcendence Scale (STS) emerged, containing the facets of *Connectedness, Universality*, and *Prayer Fulfillment*. Later refinement to his work saw the addition of the *Religious Sentiments* (RS) portion, which contains the domains of *Religious Involvement* (RI) and *Religious Crisis* (RC). Together, STS and RS compose the *Assessment of Spirituality and Religious Sentiments* (ASPIRES) instrument. ASPIRES measures the intrinsic, genotypic quality of spirituality as well as the social and behavioral aspects of religiousness. Self-report as well as observer ratings forms are available, and both have long as well as short versions. Strong evidence for convergent, discriminant, construct, and incremental validity has accrued in the research literature (see Piedmont, 2010).

Utilizing structural equation modeling (SEM), Piedmont, Ciarrocchi, Dy-Liacco, and Williams, (2009) examined the results of two studies (one sampling 467 college students from the United States and the other sampling 654 adult Filipinos; both had a majority of women subjects) addressing the relatedness of spirituality and religiousness. In the first study, they presented six possible models (p. 168): Model 1 examining the constructs as independent causes of growth, Model 2 examining the constructs as correlated causes of growth, Model 3 examining the constructs as one numinous dimension, Model 4 examining growth as the cause of the constructs, Model 5 examining religiousness as the cause of spirituality and growth, and Model 6 examining spirituality as the cause of religiousness and growth. Self-actualization and purpose in life were used to define growth. The second study utilized the first four models. Via the use of the ASPIRES instrument, specifically the spiritual transcendence and religious involvement scales, and by incorporating the use of the observer ratings as well as the self-report forms, the authors found the constructs to be non-redundant. In addition, spirituality and religiousness demonstrated incremental validity over personality factors and over each other.

The elimination of the emphasis on Christianity exhibited by some of the other available measurements in the field of the psychology of religion makes the ASPIRES instrument particularly appealing. It can be used in cross-cultural research, and results have been promising. It has been translated into Spanish, Chinese, Tagalog, Korean, Hungarian, and Czech. Studies in China (Chen, 2011), India (Piedmont & Leach, 2002) and in the Philippines (Piedmont, 2007) provided evidence for the universality of spirituality. In addition, Rican and Janosova (2010) found Piedmont's model to generalize to an atheistic culture. Working with the author, they developed the *Prague Spirituality Questionnaire* (PSQ), and using a sample of 323 secularized Czech college students, they replicated Piedmont's findings of spirituality as a separate personality factor. In a study using SEM, Dy-Liacco, Piedmont, Murray-Swank, Rodgerson, and Sherman (2009) found Western measures of the constructs of spirituality and religiosity to generalize to a non-Western sample of 654 mostly female Filipinos ranging in age from 16 to 75 years old (M = 30). Included in their measures were the self-report and observer ratings forms of the ASPIRES scale; they utilized the STS and RI portions of the instrument. They examined the fit of four structural equation models through the use of the chi-square test and found spirituality to be a predictor of purpose in life (among other variables). They also found evidence for the cross-cultural incremental validity of spirituality and religiousness, when controlling for personality variables.

Burris and colleagues utilized a sample of predominately Caucasian, female, Christian college students in two separate studies (Burris, Sauer, & Carlson, 2011; Burris, Smith, & Carlson, 2009) employing the STS and Worthington et al.'s Religious Commitment Inventory (2003). They found additional support for considering spirituality and religiousness to be overlapping but distinct concepts. They discovered (Burris et al., 2009, p. 287) a strong correlation between the variables for total scores ($r = .54$, $p = .01$, $N = 353$) and for two of the subscales ($r = .64$, $p = .01$ for prayer fulfillment; $r = .45$, $p = .01$ for universality). In addition, the authors found that participants who were more religious were less likely to participate in risky sexual behaviors, and, after controlling for alcohol use, impulsivity, and religiousness, they noted a moderating effect for gender. Women with higher spirituality reported a higher incidence of risky sexual behaviors. The authors posited that the aspect of connectedness was the driving force for the difference in the females' attitudes and actions.

In the second study, they examined the associations between underage alcohol use, alcohol-related problems, spirituality, and religiousness. While they did not find a significant correlation for alcohol-related problems at the p = .05 level or below (Burris, et al., 2011), they discovered a contradictory relationship for underage alcohol use. Using hierarchical regression analysis, they controlled for demographic variables, impulsivity, attitudes about alcohol, and the overlap between spirituality and religiousness. They found that when entered together on the third step (p. 236), spirituality and religiousness explained an additional amount of the variance over and above the other elements (ΔR^2 = .07, p = .000, N = 344). In addition, religiousness appeared to act as a protective factor (β = −.32, p = .000), while spirituality appeared to be a risk factor (β = .17, p = .005) for underage drinking. The authors emphasized that, based on their findings as well as additional support in the research literature, the variables should not be considered interchangeable but distinct.

Additional Support for the Impact of Spirituality and Religiousness on Elements of Mental Health

While this study utilized the ASPIRES instrument, current research has examined the impact of spirituality and religiousness on purpose in life, satisfaction with life, resilience, and pro-social behavior via multiple methods. Working from the perspective of Frankl's (1964) logotherapy and Tornstam's (1989) gero-transcendence theories, Jewell (2010) inspected the effect of personality, religiosity, and additional variables on purpose in life (PIL) in a sample of over 400 elderly British Methodists. Using quantitative questionnaires (n = 420) and qualitative interviews (n = 17), he found that gender, age, extraversion, and neuroticism were key predictors of PIL. PIL decreased with age and was lower in women, introverts, and those higher in neuroticism. Jewell noted a positive correlation between PIL and spiritual transcendence and PIL and intrinsic religion. After controlling for personality, age, and gender he found (p. 153) that predictive power was added by both spiritual transcendence (ΔR^2 = .05, p < .001) and intrinsic religion (ΔR^2 = .24, p < .01).

Waldron-Perrine et al. (2011) examined the relationships between spirituality, religiousness, satisfaction with life, distress, and functional ability in a sample of people struggling with traumatic brain injuries. Participants were primarily male, African-American, and Christian. Self-report (n = 88) and observer ratings (n = 88) were utilized. Spirituality was assessed via Ellison's (1983) Spiritual Well Being Scale (SWBS). The researchers included both the Existential Well-Being and Religious Well-Being subscales. Religiousness was measured via frequency of religious practice.

They performed hierarchical multiple regression analyses to determine that spirituality (i.e., the Religious Well-Being subscale, which measures connectedness with a higher power) predicted satisfaction with life (ΔR^2 = .26, p < .001), after controlling for injury-related elements and social support (p. 111). Existential well-being and religiousness were not significant.

Jonker and Greeff (2009) used a mixed methods design to explore the impact of religiousness and spirituality on resilience. They compiled semi-structured interviews of family members (N = 34) dealing with relatives who were diagnosed with Axis I disorders and who were receiving treatment at a local mental health clinic. Subjects were residents of Western Cape Province, South Africa. Ages ranged from 28 to 75 (M = 48) years old. The majority were female (94%) and spoke Afrikaans (n = 32). Participants were Colored (n = 30) or White (n = 4); there were no Black African subjects. All were categorized as having low income. Manifest coding was utilized to obtain three resilience factors from the interviews: home-based, external, and patient-focused. Religion and spirituality were named as contributors to the home-based resilience but not to the other factors. Religious and spiritual resources included "Bible study," "church activities," "prayer," "faith," and "a relationship with God" (p. 867). The importance of religion and spirituality was noted by 67.6% of the participants.

Saroglou, Pichon, Trompette, Verschuren, and Dernelle (2005) studied the association between religiousness and spirituality and pro-social behavior and proclivities via peer ratings. Religiousness was assessed with a short Likert-style scale asking for information about "(a) the importance of God in personal life; (b) the importance of religion in personal life; and (c) the frequency of prayer" (p. 327). Spirituality was measured by one item asking participants to rate its importance in their lives. Pro-social behavior was assessed via an altruism scale (Rushton, Chrisjohn, & Fekken, 1981). In a sample of 105 Belgian high school students and their peers (n = 103 for siblings; n = 105 for friends), the authors discovered small to moderate partial correlations (after controlling for gender) between altruism and religiousness and altruism and spirituality as reported by the participants as well as their peers. In an additional study, using the same measure for religiousness and spirituality, an additional scale for emotional religion, and a different one for altruism (Krueger, Hicks, & McGue, 2001), they surveyed 109 adult Belgians and their peers (n = 88 friends, n = 77 colleagues). While the self-reports reflected results similar to those in the previous study, colleagues' reports only showed small associations for religiousness and altruism, and friends' reports did not reflect any associations for any of the variables with altruism.

Unfortunately, the lack of clear definitions for many of the variables across studies noted above underscores the need for consistent operational definitions. On a more positive note, the successful utilization of those variables across cultures (also see Bahrami, 2011; Greeff & Du Toit, 2009; Webber, 2011; and Yick, 2008) demonstrates that the concepts are not limited to Western perspectives. Overall, studies have provided a foundation for the continued examination of spirituality as a predictor of purpose in life and of satisfaction with life and of religiousness as a predictor of resilience and of pro-social behavior, after controlling for personality factors. In addition, there is sufficient empirical support in the research literature to justify the consideration of the variables as overlapping yet distinct indicators of elements of mental health.

METHODS

Participants

Five hundred fifty-eight subjects (67% female) from a convenience sample completed surveys. They ranged in age from 15 to 90 (M = 40.90). For those providing demographic information, religious affiliations included Catholic (48.48%), Other Christian (14.83%), Episcopal (6.65%), Methodist (6.46%), Baptist (5.89%), Other Faith Tradition (5.51%), Atheist/Agnostic (3.80%), Lutheran (1.71%), Buddhist (1.52%), Presbyterian (1.52%), Jewish (1.52%), Mormon (.76%), Unitarian (.76%), and Muslim (.57%). The majority were Caucasian (66.67%), with African-American (15.89%), Asian (7.17%), Other (4.67%), Hispanic (3.12%), Indian (1.56%), and Middle Eastern (.93%) subjects also represented.

Measures

Demographic questionnaire. In addition to completing information about age, religious affiliation, and ethnic background, participants provided data concerning marital, employment, and vocational status as well as educational and income level.

ASPIRES (Self-Report Short Form). Developed by Piedmont (1999a; 2010), this instrument contained the *Spiritual Transcendence* scale (STS) and the *Religious Sentiments* scale (RS). The STS contained nine items; respondents completed a Likert-type scale ranging from *Strongly Agree* to *Strongly Disagree.* Two items were reverse coded, and then T-scores were calculated. Items addressed the facets of Prayer Fulfillment, Universality, and Connectedness. The manual (Piedmont, 2010) noted alpha reliabilities of .95 for Prayer Fulfillment, .82 for Universality, and .68 for Connectedness, and .89 for Total Score. For this study, Cronbach's alpha was .91 for Prayer Fulfillment, .58 for Universality, .64 for Connectedness, and .71 for Total Score.

The RS contained four items which examined the level of religiosity. Participants responded to questions about their frequency of reading sacred texts and other literature, praying, and attending religious services. Answers ranged from *Never* to *Several Times a Week* or *Quite Often*. No reverse coding was necessary. T-scores were calculated. The manual noted alpha reliability of .89 (Piedmont, 2010). For this study, Cronbach's alpha was .84.

The manual also listed evidence of convergent, discriminant, construct, and incremental validity for the ASPIRES instrument. For example, the STS demonstrated very little overlap with the domains of the Five Factor Model (Piedmont, 1999a), and the scale has been shown to generalize to an atheistic culture (Rican & Janosova, 2010).

Bipolar Adjective Rating Scale (BARS). Created by McCrea and Costa (1985), this scale examined the domains of the Five Factor Model of personality: Neuroticism, Extraversion, Openness, Agreeableness, and Conscientiousness. It contained 80 items; respondents chose from 1 (*Very Much Like Me*) to 7 (*Very Much Like Me*) on a Likert-type scale across a choice of two adjectives which were antonyms of each other. After reverse coding of several items, sums of scores for each domain were transformed into T-scores. For this study, Cronbach's alpha was .81 for Neuroticism, .81 for Extraversion, .74 for Openness, .81 for Agreeableness, .87 for Conscientiousness, and .82 for the full scale. Dy-Liacco et al. (2009) found internal consistency alpha coefficients of .70 (N), .74 (E), .58 (O), .83 (A), and .90 (C). McCrae and Costa (1987) found "convergent and discriminant cross-observer and cross-instrument validation for all five factors" (p. 86). Piedmont and Aycock (2007) found an association with staggered emergence of personality descriptors and with specific historical eras.

Purpose in Life Scale. Developed by Crumbaugh (1968), this scale examined evidence of an "existential vacuum" (Domino, 1972, ¶2), and drew upon Frankl's (1959) concept of the search for meaning in one's life. It contained 20 items, and respondents chose from 1 to 7 on a Likert-type scale across a choice of two situations which were opposite in nature. After reverse coding of several items, responses were added together for a total score. High scores signified a high purpose in life. Possible answers ranged from 20 to 140. For this study, scores ranged from 47 to 140, and Cronbach's alpha was .89. Split-half alpha reliabilities in the low .90s have been demonstrated (Braun, 1972; Domino, 1972). Research has shown convergent validity with the Srole Anomie Scale, the MMPI Depression scale, and the California Psychological Inventory Achievement via Conformance scale (Braun, 1972; Domino, 1972).

Satisfaction with Life Scale. Developed by Diener, Emmons, Larsen, and Griffin (1985), this scale consisted of five items on a Likert scale. Anchors were *strongly agree* and *strongly disagree.* Examples of items included "The conditions of my life are excellent" and "So far I have gotten the important things I want in life." Pavot and Diener (1993) provided examples of convergent validity with multiple measures of life satisfaction as well as several examples of discriminant validity. They reported test-retest reliabilities ranging from .50 to .84 and coefficient alphas ranging from .79 to .89. Waldron-Perrine reported a coefficient alpha of .81. For this study, Cronbach's alpha was .83.

Sense of Coherence Scale. Created by Antonovsky (1987), this scale examined resiliency; that is, an internal buoyancy enabling one to make sense of and to deal with life events. The short form contained 13 items, and alpha reliabilities in 16 studies have ranged from .74 to .91 (Antonovsky, 1993); the author also noted criterion validity in four domains: global orientation, stressors, general health, and behaviors. Studies conducted in 20 countries provided evidence of construct and cross-cultural validity. Respondents chose from 1 to 7 on a Likert-type scale across a choice of opposites. After reverse coding some items, responses were summed for a total score. High scores indicated a strong sense of coherence. Usually, possible answers would range from 13 to 91. Unfortunately, a typographical error in the questionnaires compromised two of the items: Only choices *1* and *2* were available; the other choices were inadvertently omitted. Cronbach's alpha for this sample was .81 with all items retained; when the compromised items were removed, Cronbach's alpha remained at .81 indicating that the reliability of the scores was not affected by those particular items.

Pro-social Behavior Scale. Developed by Rushton et al. (1981), this 20-item scale measured altruism. Individuals rated the frequency of their pro-social behaviors on a 5-point Likert-type scale. Anchors were *never* and *very often.* Convergent validity has been established via psychological tests such as the Social Interest Scale as well as altruistic behaviors such as reading to the blind. Alpha reliabilities provided by the authors of the scale have ranged from .78 to .86. For this study, Cronbach's alpha was .90.

Procedures

The data were collected as a requirement for a pastoral counseling doctoral class. Students created packets containing several scales and varied the placement of those scales to control for order effects. Each student obtained 20 participants who were mainly friends and family members residing in the Baltimore/Washington area and who constituted a sample of convenience. Subjects completed the requested information, replaced the scales into the packets, sealed them, and returned them to the experimenters. The information was added to a database which contained material accrued over a period of 3 years.

RESULTS

Histograms were scrutinized to assess normality of distributions, and the data were examined for possible outliers and for multicollinearity. Histograms demonstrated no distributions were significantly deviant from normalcy. All of the scores on all of the variables were transformed into z-scores and were examined for univariate outliers. No case exceeded a z-score of $|4.5|$ which was assumed to represent the absence of problematic univariate outliers. Multivariate outliers were determined utilizing procedures outlined by Tabachnick and Fidel (2007). Mahalanobis distances were derived, and five multivariate outliers met the chi square value for significance and were deleted. Means and standard deviations were calculated on all variables (see Table 1) and were within acceptable levels.

Zero order correlations were run on all variables to search for substantial relationships between spirituality, religiousness, personality factors, purpose in life, satisfaction with life, resilience, and prosocial behavior (see Table 2). Among the predictors and the outcomes, there appeared to be a number of significant correlations, except with Religious Involvement which seemed to be independent of all but one of the outcomes (pro-social behavior). Further examination of the matrix did not reveal any evidence of multicollinearity. Therefore, the data appeared to be appropriate for parametric analysis.

Hierarchical regression analyses were performed to examine the incremental validity of the ASPIRES scales. With Purpose in Life as the dependent variable, the five personality scales were entered on the first step via forced entry; Prayer Fulfillment, Connectedness, Universality, and Religious Involvement were requested on the second step via the forward entry method (see Table 3). Results supported the incremental validity

Table 1. *Means and Standard Deviations*

	M	SD	N	α
Connectedness	51.29	9.30	510	.64
Universality	56.00	7.63	510	.58
Prayer Fulfillment	56.82	7.22	510	.91
Total Score	55.91	6.96	510	.71
Religious Involvement	54.02	9.83	510	.84
Neuroticism	47.44	9.05	524	.81
Extraversion	49.48	9.74	524	.81
Openness	52.26	9.67	524	.74
Agreeableness	52.65	9.18	524	.81
Conscientiousness	49.40	11.11	524	.87
Total Score				.82
*Purpose in Life	105.76	15.08	169	.89
*Satisfaction with Life	14.01	5.44	547	.83
*Sense of Coherence	58.64	10.87	168	.81
*Pro-Social Behavior	55.14	12.43	546	.90

* All scores except Purpose in Life, Satisfaction with Life, Sense of Coherence, and Pro-Social Behavior are reported as *T*-scores ($M = 50$, $SD = 10$).

of the scale for measuring spirituality. While conscientiousness, extraversion, and neuroticism explained the majority of the variance, spirituality added predictive power and explained an additional 6% of the variance, over and above the personality variables: $\Delta R^2 = .06$, $p < .001$; partial $F(1, 136) = 21.10$, $p < .001$. However, the only scale contributing was Prayer Fulfillment: $\beta = .27$, $t(136) = 4.59$, $p < .001$.

With Satisfaction with Life as the dependent variable, the five personality scales were entered on the first step via forced entry; Prayer Fulfillment, Connectedness, Universality, and Religious Involvement were requested on the second step via the forward entry method. Results supported the incremental validity of the scale for measuring spirituality (See Table 4). While neuroticism, extraversion, and conscientiousness explained the majority of the variance, spirituality added predictive power and explained an additional 2% of the variance, over and above the personality variables: $\Delta R^2 = .02$, $p < .05$; partial $F(1, 478) = 9.37$, $p < .01$. Again, the only scale contributing was Prayer Fulfillment: $\beta = -.13$, $t(478) = -3.06$, $p < .01$.

With Sense of Coherence as the dependent variable, the five personality scales were entered on the first step via forced entry; Prayer Fulfillment, Connectedness, Universality, and Religious Involvement were requested on the second step via the forward entry method (see Table 5). The partial

Table 2. *Correlations of Personality, Spirituality, and Religiousness Variables with Purpose in Life, Satisfaction with Life, Sense of Coherence, and Pro-Social Behavior*

	N	E	O	A	C	UN	CN	PF	RI	PIL	SWL	SOC	PSB
Neuroticism(N)	–												
Extraversion(E)	-.26**	–											
Openness(O)	-.08	.29**	–										
Agreeableness(A)	-.39**	.47**	.10*	–									
Conscientiousness(C)	-.45**	.28**	.09*	.40**	–								
Universality(UN)	-.12*	.18**	.19**	.29**	.13**	–							
Connectedness(CN)	-.03	.15**	.10*	.06	.11*	.16**	–						
Prayer Fulfillment (PF)	-.11*	.18**	.08	.22**	.14**	.43**	.06	–					
Religious Involvement (RI)	-.04	-.01	-.10*	.12**	.03	.24**	-.14**	.54**	–				
Purpose in Life (PIL)	-.48**	.47**	.10	.39**	.55**	.22**	.05	.43**	.15	–			
Satisfaction with Life (SWL)	.37**	-.24**	-.07	-.15**	-.31**	-.13**	-.09*	-.18**	-.08	-.56**	–		
Sense of Coherence (SOC)	-.55**	.35**	-.02	.30**	.42**	.16	.19*	.30**	-.02	.69**	-.49**	–	
Pro-Social Behavior (PSB)	-.18**	.28**	.17**	.21**	.16**	.21**	.15**	.16**	.10*	.33**	-.18**	.18*	–

Ns ranged from 140 to 542 ** *p* < .01 (two-tailed) * *p* < .05 (two-tailed)

Table 3. *Hierarchical Regression Predicting Purpose in Life*

Predictor Variables	B	SE B	β	t	ΔR^2
Step 1 (forced entry)					.55***
Conscientiousness	.46	.08	.37***	5.45***	
Extraversion	.48	.10	.30***	4.55***	
Neuroticism	−.49	.11	−.29***	−4.63***	
Agreeableness	.12	.11	.08	1.11	
Openness	.04	.09	.03	.47	
Step 2 (forward entry)					.06***
Prayer Fulfillment	.32	.11	.27***	4.59***	

Note: Total R^2 = .61, partial $F(1, 136)$ = 21.10, *** $p < .001$

Table 4. *Hierarchical Regression Predicting Satisfaction with Life*

Predictor Variables	B	SE B	β	t	ΔR^2
Step 1 (forced entry)					.19***
Neuroticism	.17	.03	.28**	5.83***	
Conscientiousness	−.09	.02	−.19***	−3.80***	
Extraversion	−.09	.03	−.15**	−3.13**	
Agreeableness	.05	.03	.09	1.75	
Openness	−.01	.03	−.02	−.44	
Step 2 (forward entry)					.02**
Prayer Fulfillment	−.10	.03	−.13**	3.06**	

Note: Total R^2 = .39, partial $F(1, 478)$ = 9.37, $p < .01$ *** $p < .001$ ** $p < .01$

F test supported the incremental validity of the instrument for measuring both spirituality (again, the only scale contributing was Prayer Fulfillment) and religiousness. While neuroticism, extraversion, and conscientiousness explained the majority of the variance, the numinous variables explained an additional 7% of the variance, over and above personality: Prayer Fulfillment ΔR^2 = .03, $p < .01$; Religious Involvement ΔR^2 = .04, $p < .01$; partial $F(2, 134)$ = 9.67, $p < .001$. For Prayer Fulfillment, β = .36, $t(134)$ = 4.36, $p < .001$. For Religious Involvement, β = −.25, $t(134)$ = -3.18, $p < .01$. The negative correlation for Religious Involvement was unexpected.

    An additional test was run to determine which one of the independent variables was the better predictor. With Sense of Coherence as the dependent variable, the five personality scales were entered on the first step via forced entry. Spiritual Transcendence (total score) and Religious Involvement were requested on the second step (forward entry method). Both were statistically significant. A t-test was run to determine if there was a significant difference between the beta weights. Contrary to the hypothesis,

Table 5. *Hierarchical Regression Predicting Sense of Coherence*

Predictor Variables	B	SE B	β	t	ΔR²
Step 1 (forced entry)					.45***
Neuroticism	−.55	.09	−.45***	−6.39***	
Extraversion	.25	.08	.22**	2.99**	
Conscientiousness	.18	.07	.19*	2.56*	
Agreeableness	.08	.09	.06	.85	
Openness	−.04	.07	−.04	−.58	
Step 2 (forward entry)					.03**
Prayer Fulfillment	.23	.08	.20**	2.91**	
Step 3					.04**
Religious Involvement	−.25	.08	−.25**	−3.18**	

Note: Total R^2 = .52, partial $F(2, 134)$ = 9.67 $p < .001$
*** $p < .001$ ** $p < .01$ * $p < .05$

Table 6. *Hierarchical Regression Predicting Pro-Social Behavior*

Predictor Variables	B	SE B	β	t	ΔR²
Step 1 (forced entry)					.12***
Extraversion	.26	.07	.20***	3.92***	
Openness	.11	.06	.08	1.78	
Agreeableness	.11	.07	.08	1.49	
Neuroticism	−.10	.07	−.07	−1.41	
Conscientiousness	.07	.06	.07	1.27	
Step 2 (forward entry)					.02**
Universality	.24	.08	.14**	3.14**	
Step 3					.01*
Connectedness	.12	.06	.09*	2.05*	

Note: Total R^2 = .40, partial $F(2, 477)$ = 7.07, $p < .01$ *** $p < .001$ ** $p < .01$ * $p < .05$

spirituality was a significantly better predictor: $t(140)$ = 2.18, $p < .05$ than religiousness for Sense of Coherence.

With Pro-social Behavior as the dependent variable, the five personality scales were entered on the first step via forced entry; Prayer Fulfillment, Connectedness, Universality, and Religious Involvement were requested on the second step via the forward entry method. While extraversion explained the majority of the variance, spirituality explained an additional 3% of the variance, over and above personality (See Table 6). For the Universality subscale, β = .14, $t(478)$ = 3.14, $p < .01$; for the Connectedness subscale, β = .09, $t(477)$ = 2.05, $p < .05$. Only spirituality was statistically significant, contrary to the hypothesis.

Discussion

Spirituality did predict purpose in life and satisfaction with life better than religiousness. However, religiousness did not demonstrate a substantial improvement over spirituality when predicting resilience nor when predicting pro-social behavior. In fact, with resilience as the dependent variable, both religiousness (i.e., religious involvement) and spirituality accounted for additional variance after controlling for personality variables, albeit small percentages. Conscientiousness, extraversion, and neuroticism were the personality factors that consistently explained the majority of the variance.

While religiousness did evidence some impact on resilience, spirituality was more influential. Of the two, spirituality appeared to be a better predictor for each of the dependent variables. The Prayer Fulfillment subscale, which measured a sense of peace, wholeness, and growth attained via prayer and/or meditation, evidenced the most predictive power. Recent studies showing the impact of prayer and/or meditation (especially mindfulnesss) on improving mental health underscore this finding (e.g., see Robins, Keng, Ekblad, & Brantley, 2012; Rosmarin, Auerbach, Bigda-Peyton, Björgvinsson, & Levendusky, 2011).

Limitations of our study could have influenced the results, however. The reliability score for the Universality subscale of the ASPIRES instrument was rather low (.58), and convenience rather than random sampling was used. Because the data were cross-sectional rather than longitudinal, no causal links can be determined. The sample consisted of predominantly Caucasian, female, and Catholic participants, which could have influenced the unexpected negative correlation for Religious Involvement and Sense of Coherence: In previous research, Alferi, Culver, Carver, Arena, and Antoni (1999) found distress increased as religious involvement increased for Catholic women, and Tagay, Erim, Brähler, and Senf (2006) found no significant correlation between religiosity and SOC in a German sample of primarily Catholic women. In addition, including observer ratings would have decreased the possibility of correlated method error due to the utilization of multiple self-report measures.

We hope that this study has advanced the field of the psychology of religion by replication of some of the aspects of the aforementioned studies which examined the impact of spirituality and religiousness on purpose in life, satisfaction with life, resilience, and pro-social behavior. In addition, by establishing clear definitions of the concepts of spirituality and religiousness, separating them as distinct (although overlapping) concepts, and examining the extent of their impact upon the dependent variables, some of the confusion surrounding the terms may be ameliorated. Finally, this study has provided additional incremental validity for the ASPIRES instrument as a measure of spirituality which explains variance over and above personality variables. Counselors may consider assessing levels of spirituality and religiousness in clients and need to have confidence that they are using instruments which have been demonstrated to be reliable and valid for particular populations.

Recently, Sperry (2010) noted that spiritual issues may arise within counseling sessions and listed three situations that psychotherapists need to be attuned to: using spirituality for coping, addressing religious crises, and spiritual growth. He asserted that clients may turn to psychotherapists to assist in their quest. Consequently, clinicians need to be informed about the impact of spirituality and religiousness on many areas of psychological functioning, such as risky sexual behavior (Burris, et al., 2006), depression (Koenig, 2010; Wink, Dillon, & Larsen, 2005); anxiety (Koenig, 2010); alcohol and substance abuse (Burris, et al., 2011; Koenig, 2010; Piedmont 2004); quality of life (Sawatzky, Gadermann, & Pesut, 2009), burnout (Golden, Piedmont, Ciarrocchi, & Rodgerson, 2004), and adaptive reconstruction of one's sense of self (Sinnott, 2009). This study has provided additional information about the influence of spirituality on purpose in life, satisfaction with life, resilience, and pro-social behavior and its apparent advantage in prediction, over religiousness, of all of those variables. Our assumption has been based on secondary correlations, however, so more direct links will need to be established via future research.

CONCLUSION

The field needs to take a closer look at spirituality and religiousness and become more discerning in its use of these terms. Keeping the two terms separate, rather than folding them together into one overarching concept, is a necessary first step. Based on our data and our review of the literature, they carry with them different implications that researchers and clinicians need to examine in depth.

Spirituality and religiousness are intertwined but unique elements, which are mediated by diverse psychological systems. Our study has provided additional evidence for their discriminant validity and for the identification of spirituality as a motive and religiousness as a sentiment. Spirituality encompasses an innate aspect of being human, while religiousness is driven by contextual influences.

While both variables influence behavior, spirituality, especially, appears to be a robust predictor of elements of mental health, after controlling for personality factors. Clinicians can enter the counseling room equipped with the knowledge that those constructs are not redundant with other predictors of behavioral health; spirituality and religiousness provide insights into the inner life of their clients and can provide a foundation for interventions that foster purpose in life, satisfaction with life, resilience, and pro-social behavior.

References

Alferi, S.M., Culver, J.L., Carver, C.S., Arena, P.L., & Antoni, M.H. (1999). Religiosity, religious coping, and distress: A prospective study of Catholic and Evangelical Hispanic women in treatment for early-stage breast cancer. *Journal of Health Psychology, 4*(3), 343–356. doi:10.1177/135910539900400304

Allport, G.W. (1950). *The individual and his religion.* New York, NY: Macmillan.

Allport, G.W. & Ross, J.M. (1967). Personal religious orientation and prejudice. *Journal of Personality and Social Psychology, 5,* 432–443. http://www.apa.org/pubs/journals/psp/

Antonovsky, A. (1987). *Unravelling the mystery of healthy.* San Francisco, CA: Jossey-Bass.

Antonovsky, A. (1993). The structure and properties of the sense of coherence scale. *Social Science Medicine, 36,* 725–733. doi:10.1016/0277-9536(93)90033-Z

Bahrami, M. (2011). Meanings and aspects of quality of life for cancer patients: A descriptive exploratory qualitative study. *Contemporary Nurse: A Journal for the Australian Nursing Profession, 39,*(1), 75–84. http://www.contemporarynurse.com/

Benson, P.L., Scales, P.C., Hamilton, S.F., Sesma, Jr., A., Hong, K.L., & Roehlkepartain, E.C. (2006). Positive youth development so far: Core hypotheses and their implications for policy and practice. *Search Institute Insights & Evidence, (3)*1, 1–13. http://www.search-institute.org

Braun, J.R. (1972). Review of the Purpose in Life Test. In O.K. Buros (Ed.), *The seventh mental measurements yearbook.* Retrieved from the Buros Institute's *Test Reviews Online* website: http://www.unl.edu/buros

Burris, J.L., Sauer, S.E., & Carlson, C.R. (2011). A test of religious commitment and spiritual transcendence as independent predictors of underage alcohol use and alcohol-related problems. *Psychology of Religion and Spirituality, 3,* 231–240. doi:10.1037/a0022204

Burris, J.L., Smith, G.T., & Carlson, C.R. (2009). Relations among religiousness, spirituality, and sexual practices. *Journal of Sex Research, 46*(4), 282–289. doi:10.1080/00224490802684582

Center for Mental Health Services. (2010). *The 10 X 10 campaign: A national action plan to improve life expectancy by 10 years in 10 years for people with mental illnesses. A report of the 2007 National Wellness Summit.* HHS Publication No. (SMA) 10–4476. Rockville, MD: Center for Mental Health Services, Substance Abuse and Mental Health Services Administration.

Chen, T.P. (2011). *Cross-cultural psychometric evaluation of the ASPIRES in mainland China* (Unpublished doctoral dissertation). Baltimore, MD: Loyola University Maryland.

Costa, P.T., Jr., & McCrae, R.R. (1985). *The NEO Personality Inventory manual.* Odessa, FL: Psychological Assessment Resources.

Crumbaugh, J. (1968). Purpose-in-life test. *Journal of Individual Psychology, 24,* 74–81. http://www.utexas.edu/utpress/journals/jip.html

Diener, E., Emmons, R.A., Larsen, R.J., & Griffin, S. (1985). The satisfaction with life scale. *Journal of Personality Assessment, 49*, 71–75 http://www.tandf.co.uk/journals/authors/hjpaauth.asp

Domino, G. (1972). Review of the Purpose in Life Test. In O.K. Buros (Ed.), *The seventh mental measurements yearbook.* Retrieved from the Buros Institute's *Test Reviews Online* website: http://www.unl.edu/buros

Dy-Liacco, G.S, Piedmont, R.L, Murray-Swank, N.A, Rodgerson, T.E, & Sherman, M.F. (2009). Spirituality and religiosity as cross-cultural aspects of human experience. *Psychology of Religion and Spirituality, 1*, 35–52. doi:10.1037/a0014937

Ellison, C.G. (1983). Spiritual well-being: Conceptualization and measurement. *Journal of Psychology and Theology, 11*, 330–340. http://journals.biola.edu/jpt

Frankl, V. (1959). *Man's search for meaning.* Boston, MA: Beacon.

Frankl, V. (1964). The will to meaning. *Christian Century, 81*(17), 515–517. http://www.christiancentury.org

Golden, J., Piedmont, R.L., Ciarrocchi, J.W., Rodgerson, T. (2004). Spirituality and burnout: An incremental validity study. *Journal of Psychology and Theology, 32*, 115–125. http://journals.biola.edu/jpt

Greeff, A.P. & Du Toit, C. (2009). Resilience in remarried families. *American Journal of Family Therapy, 37*(2), 114–126. doi:10.1080/01926180802151919

Jewell, A. (2010). The importance of purpose in life in an older British Methodist sample: Pastoral implications. *Journal of Religion, Spirituality & Aging, 22*(3), 138–161. doi:10.1080/15528030903321170

Jonker, L. & Greeff, A.P. (2009). Resilience factors in families living with people with mental illnesses. *Journal of Community Psychology, 37*, 859–873. doi:10.1002/jcop.20337

Jung, C.G. (1966). *Psychology and religion.* New Haven, CT: Yale University Press. (Original work published 1938)

Koenig, H. (2010). Spirituality and mental health. *International Journal of Applied Psychoanalytic Studies, 7*(2), 116–122. http://www.wiley.com/WileyCDA/WileyTitle/productCd-APS.html

Krueger, R. F., Hicks, B.M. & McGue, M. (2001). Altruism and antisocial behavior: Independent tendencies, unique personality correlates, distinct etiologies. *Psychological Science, 12*, 397–402. http://www.psychologicalscience.org/index.php/publications/journals/psychological_science

McCrae, R. & Costa, P.T., Jr. (1985). Updating Norman's "adequacy taxonomy": Intelligence and personality dimensions in natural language and in questionnaires. *Journal of Personality and Social Psychology, 49*, 710–721. doi:10.1037/0022-3514.49.3.710

McCrae, R.R. & Costa, P.T., Jr. (1987). Validation of the five-factor model of personality across instruments and across observers. *Journal of Personality and Social Psychology, 52*, 81–90. http://www.apa.org/pubs/journals/psp/

Pargament, K.I., Magyar-Russell, G.M., & Murray-Swank, N.A. (2005). The sacred and the search for significance: Religion as a unique process. *Journal of Social Issues, 61*(4), 665–687. doi:10.1111/j.1540-4560.2005.00426.x

Pavot, W., & Diener, E. (1993). Review of the satisfaction with life scale. *Psychological Assessment. 5*, 164–172. doi:10.1037/1040-3590.5.2.164

Peterson, C. & Seligman, M.E.P. (2004). *Character strengths and virtues: A handbook and classification.* Washington, D.C.: American Psychological Association and New York, NY: Oxford University Press.

Piedmont, R.L. (1999a). Does spirituality represent the sixth factor of personality? Spiritual transcendence and the Five-Factor Model. *Journal of Personality, 67*, 983–1013. http://onlinelibrary.wiley.com/journal/10.1111/(ISSN)1467-6494

Piedmont, R.L. (1999b). Strategies for using the Five-Factor Model of personality in religious research. *Journal of Psychology and Theology 27*(4), 338–350. http://journals.biola.edu/jpt

Piedmont, R.L. (2001). Spiritual transcendence and the scientific study of spirituality. *Journal of Rehabilitation, 67*, 4–14. http://www.questia.com

Piedmont, R. (2004). Spiritual Transcendence as a Predictor of Psychosocial Outcome From an Outpatient Substance Abuse Program. *Psychology of Addictive Behaviors, 18*(3), 213–222. doi:10.1037/0893-164X.18.3.213

Piedmont, R.L. (2007). Cross-cultural generalizability of the Spiritual Transcendence Scale to the Philippines: Spirituality as a human universal. *Mental Health, Religion & Culture, 10*(2), 89–107. doi:10.1080/13694670500275494

Piedmont, R.L. (2010). *Assessment of Spirituality and Religious Sentiments, technical manual* (2nd Ed). Timonium, MD: Author.

Piedmont, R.L. & Aycock, W. (2007). An historical analysis of the lexical emergence of the Big Five personality adjective descriptors. *Personality and Individual Differences, 42*, 1059–1068. doi:10.1016/j.paid.2006.09.015

Piedmont, R.L., Ciarrocchi, J.W., Dy-Liacco, G.S., & Williams, J.E.G. (2009). The empirical and conceptual value of the Spiritual Transcendence and Religious Involvement scales for personality research. *Psychology of Religion and Spirituality, 1*, 162–179. doi:10.1037/a0015883

Piedmont, R.L., Kennedy, M.C., Sherman, M.F., Sherman, N.C., & Williams, J.E.G. (2008). A psychometric evaluation of the Assessment of Spirituality and Religious Sentiments (ASPIRES) scale: Short form. *Research in the Social Scientific Study of Religion* (19), 163–181. http://www.brill.nl/rssr

Piedmont, R.L. & Leach, M. (2002). Cross-cultural generalizability of the Spiritual Transcendence Scale in India: Spirituality as a universal aspect of human experience. *American Behavioral Scientist, 45*(12), 1888–1901. doi:10.1177/0002764202045012011

Rican, P. & Janosova, P. (2010). Spirituality as a basic aspect of personality: A cross-cultural verification of Piedmont's model. *International Journal for the Psychology of Religion, 20*, 2–13. doi:10.1080/10508610903418053

Robins, C.J., Keng, S., Ekblad, A.G., & Brantley, J. (2012). Effects of mindfulness-based stress reduction on emotional experience and expression: A randomized controlled trial. *Journal of Clinical Psychology, 68*(1), 117–131. doi:10.1002/jclp.20857

Rosmarin, D.H., Auerbach, R.P., Bigda-Peyton, J.S., Björgvinsson, T.T., & Levendusky, P.G. (2011). Integrating spirituality into cognitive behavioral therapy in an acute psychiatric setting: A pilot study. *Journal of Cognitive Psychotherapy, 25*(4), 287–303. doi:10.1891/0889-8391.25.4.287

Rushton, J.P., Chrisjohn, R.D., & Fekken, G.C. (1981). The altruistic personality and the self-report altruism scale. *Personality and Individual Differences, 2*, 293–302. http://www.journals.elsevier.com/personality-and-individual-differences/

Saucier, G. & Skrzypińska, K. (2006). Spiritual but not religious? Evidence for two independent dispositions. *Journal of Personality, 74*, 1257–1292. doi:10.1111/j.1467-6494.2006.00409.x

Saroglou, V. (2002). Religion and the five factors of personality: A meta-analytic review. *Personality and Individual Differences, 32*(1), 15–25. doi:10.1016/S0191-8869(00)00233-6

Saroglou, V. (2010). Religiousness as a cultural adaptation of basic traits: A Five-Factor Model perspective. *Personality & Social Psychology Review, 14*(1), 108–125. doi:10.1177/1088868309352322

Saroglou, V. & Muñoz-García, A. (2008). Individual differences in religion and spirituality: An issue of personality traits and/or values. *Journal for the Scientific Study of Religion, 47*(1), 83–101. http://www.brill.nl/rssr

Saroglou, V., Pichon, I., Trompette, L., Verschuren, M., & Dernelle, R. (2005). Prosocial behavior and religion: New evidence based on projective measures and peer ratings. *Journal for the Scientific Study of Religion, 44*, 323–348. doi:10.1111/j.1468-5906.2005.00289.x

Sawatzky, R., Gadermann, A., & Pesut, B. (2009). An investigation of the relationships between spirituality, health status, and quality of life in adolescents. *Applied Research in Quality of Life, 4*(1), 5–22. doi:10.1007/s11482-009-9065-y

Sinnott, J. (2009). Complex thought and construction of the self in the face of aging and death. *Journal of Adult Development, 16*(3), 155–165. doi:10.1007/s10804-009-9057-z

Sperry, L. (2010). Psychotherapy sensitive to spiritual issues: A postmaterialist psychology perspective and developmental approach. *Psychology of Religion and Spirituality, 2*(1), 46–56. doi:10.1037/a0018549

Substance Abuse and Mental Health Services Administration (2010). *10 × 10 wellness campaign: Information for general health care providers.* HHS Publication No. (SMA) 10-4566. Rockville, MD: U.S. Department of Health and Human Services.

Tabachnick, B.G. & Fidell, L.S. (2007). *Using multivariate statistics* (5th ed). Boston, MA: Pearson.

Tagay, S., Erim, Y., Brähler, E. & Senf. W. (2006). Religiosity and sense of coherence: Protective factors of mental health and well-being? *Zeitschrift für Medizinische Psychologie, 15*(4), 165–171. http://www.zmedpsychol.de/

Tornstam, L. (1989). Gero-transcendence: A reformulation of the disengagement theory. *Aging, 1,* 55–63. http://www.ncbi.nlm.nih.gov/pubmed/2488301

Waldron-Perrine, B., Rapport, L.J., Hanks, R.A., Lumley, M., Meachen, S., & Hubbarth, P. (2011). Religion and spirituality in rehabilitation outcomes among individuals with traumatic brain injury. *Rehabilitation Psychology, 56*(2), 107–116. doi:10.1037/a0023552

Webber, R. (2011). Volunteering among Australian adolescents: Findings from a national study. *Youth Studies Australia, 30,* 9–16. http://www.acys.info/journal

Wink, P., Dillon, M., & Larsen, B. (2005). Religion as moderator of the depression-health connection: Findings from a longitudinal study. *Research on Aging, 27*(2), 197–220. doi:10.1177/0164027504270483

Wink, P. (2010). Trouble with spirituality. *Research in the Social Scientific Study of Religion, 21,* 49–69. http://www.brill.nl/rssr

Worthington, Jr., E.L., Wade, N.G., Hight, T.L., Ripley, J.S., McCullough, M.E., Berry, J.W., & ... O'Connor, L. (2003). The Religious Commitment Inventory—10: Development, refinement, and validation of a brief scale for research and counseling. *Journal of Counseling Psychology, 50,* 84–96. doi:10.1037/0022-0167.50.1.84

Yick, A. (2008). A metasynthesis of qualitative findings on the role of spirituality and religiosity among culturally diverse domestic violence survivors. *Qualitative Health Research, 18,* 1289–1306. doi:10.1177/1049732308321772

Zinnbauer, B.J., Pargament, K.I., & Scott, A.B. (1999). The emerging meanings of religiousness and spirituality. *Journal of Personality, 67,* 889–919. http://www.wiley.com/bw/journal.asp?ref=0022-3506&site=1

SPECIAL SECTION

ON THEISM AND NON-THEISM IN PSYCHOLOGICAL SCIENCE

THEISM AND NON-THEISM IN PSYCHOLOGICAL SCIENCE: BEYOND THE CONFLICT

Kari A. O'Grady and Richard H. York

The topic of theism has garnered a great deal of attention throughout the recorded history of scientific, theological, and philosophical thought (e.g. Bergin, 1980; Ellis, 1980; Freud, 1939; James, 1956; Sartre,1956; Whitehead, 1933). In modern times, theism waned somewhat in its acceptance, with most scholars and researchers avoiding the discussion altogether (Burtt, 2003; Ferngren, 2002). More recently, however, theism has surfaced as a provocative issue for debate—with debate being the operative word! The controversial nature of this topic could be attributed to the fact that it hits at such fundamental levels for scholars and researchers on both sides of the issue. Those who argue that theistic assumptions should be considered in psychological science and practice feel passionately about giving voice and validation to what they consider to be one of the most prized and protected area of human experience: spiritual values and beliefs. On the other hand, many who assert that theistic assumptions should not be included in psychological science are valiantly striving to guard science from religious dogma, operationalization chaos, and loss of respect from the scientific community at large. With so much at stake, it is no wonder that the issue of theism in psychological science has been both adamantly avoided and vehemently battled.

In recognition of the divisive tendency of this discussion, editor of a recent issue on theism, Teo (2009), who described himself as non-religious and skeptical of theistic beliefs, petitioned both "sides" to remain open-minded to the other's views. He reminded the opponents of theism that even if they disagree with the theistic viewpoint, they need not dismiss their arguments on the premise of subjectivity or social construction because psychology has always dealt with issues of human subjectivity. He then cautioned theists to humbly learn from the critics of their perspective even if they do not agree with their basic premise. Ultimately he invited both sides to engage in respectful dialogue "even if, or because, they have very strong convictions" (p. 62). Although we agree with Teo's plea for civility, we suspect that his request was largely ignored by his audience.

Research in the Social Scientific Study of Religion, Volume 23
© Koninklijke Brill NV, Leiden, 2012

When we were invited to co-edit this special issue, we were asked to edit a special issue on "theism *versus* non-theism in psychological science." It is not surprising that the invitation was proposed as a debate, as proponents on either side of the argument continue to throw punches at one another—each returning to their corner of the ring just long enough to come out swinging in response to the last scholar's jab. We propose a truce in which those who align with theistic assumptions and those who lean towards non-theistic approaches to psychology retreat to the neutral corner of the ring to engage in respectful and open dialogue. We invite scholars, researchers, and practitioners to resist the temptation to frame the discussion as an *either, or* conversation.

We opted to address this special issue as theism *and* non-theism in psychological science, with the intention of encouraging scholars, researchers, and practitioners to reach for a level of creativity and inventiveness wherein bifurcation is avoided, and difference are viewed as essential to the refinement of the science and the responsible treatment of those in our care. In an effort to enrich the discussion and encourage cross-disciplinary conversations, authors from diverse affiliation and academic backgrounds were invited to contribute. Some authors have offered various views about what they deem necessary elements of a viable theistic psychology. Other authors have also expressed their views about the impossibility of such an endeavor. The line-up of authors and their approach to the topic are as follows:

Vogel, Gerdin, and McMinn point out that traditional science and a theistic view of science are both context-dependent, tradition-based ways of knowing. They suggest that the inclusion of theism in psychological science is relevant as it represents the views of many psychologists and psychologists in training. Further, they state that APA ethics codes call for respect for various worldviews including theistic worldviews.

Nelson and Thomason draw upon Patristic literature as foundational texts for the development of theistic psychology. Based upon these writings, they assert that a strong theistic psychology must include explicit statements of the assumptions that underlie theistic models and a holistic and relational view of humans that includes relationship with God. They also suggest that a strong theistic psychology would foster psychotherapy interventions that focus on correcting distorted relationships.

Hibberd points out the flaws in three paradigms of theism: (a) classical theism, (b) Plantinga's modal argument for God, and (c) Griffin's process theism. She postulates that attempts by theists to fashion a coherent concept of deity are unsuccessful and that theism continues to be an unreasonable approach to psychology.

O'Grady asserts that alignment between worldview and practice is essential for responsible and effective therapeutic assessment and intervention. An example of a theistic community intervention conducted following the 2010 earthquake in Haiti is presented to illustrate theism in psychological practice.

Larmer cautions the field to avoid demarcations of "scientific" and "unscientific," stating that attempts to delineate sufficient conditions for science have failed in the past. Instead, he proposes that views of science be evaluated based upon their own merits. He asserts that the role of true science is to follow the evidence where it leads and to remain open to the unexpected.

York proposes a resolution to the theistic/non-theistic controversy. He suggests a number of research projects to study the concepts of the Indwelling Spirit and the Self-Critic from a theistic research perspective.

Mirman approaches the topic of theism from the view that theism or not theism is not a relevant issue in the debate, but rather the issue is the structure of one's psyche. The latter affects people's relationships with themselves and their relationships with the world, as well as their ability to transcend their own egos. He states that the preoccupation with external spiritual entities has diverted the field from the more constructive task of fostering personal, spiritual transformation through focusing on internal psychic realities.

Reber, Slife, and Downs describe two research studies. The first study presented provides some evidence that experiences of God is an important predictor of theists' attachment to God, even when controlling for parental attachment. The second study demonstrates how theistic ideas can lead to a new program of psychological research, as well as illustrating that theistic students often become less theistic following their doctoral training.

Slife, Reber, and Lefevor suggest that many of the fundamental differences between secular and theistic conceptions of psychological science justify the need for a theistic view of psychology to complement secular views of psychology. They explicate some of the assumptions that undergird conventional methodology and practice and compare these assumptions to the theistic assumption of a currently and practically relevant God.

Bishop discusses revelation as one possible way of considering human nature. He focuses on the implications of special revelation for human inquiry and the consideration of theism in psychological science.

Johnson and Watson postulate that a psychological science that seeks to be comprehensive of all human beings ought to permit various worldview considerations. They also call for researchers to be explicit about their worldviews. Along with these arguments, Johnson and Watson present a research agenda illustrating the explication of worldviews in research.

Invitation to the Reader

We hope that the articles in this issue enlighten and/or disturb you enough to prompt re-evaluation and increased sophistication in the way you view theism in psychological science. As you read through these articles, we invite you to reflect on your personal worldview. We also encourage you to contemplate the potential influences of "groupthink" in the study of theism and non-theism in psychological science. Finally, we invite you to conceptualize innovative strategies for fostering future dialogues on the topic. These areas of consideration will be discussed in the concluding article of this issue.

References

Bergin, A.E. (1980). Psychotherapy and religious values. *Journal of Consulting and Clinical Psychology. 48*, 95–105. doi:10.1037/0022-006X.48.1.95

Burtt, E.A. (2003). *The metaphysical foundations of modern science.* New York, NY: Dover.

Ellis, A. (1980). *Case against religion: A psychotherapist's view and the case against religiosity.* Austin, TX: American Atheist Press.

Ferngren, G.B. (2002). *Science and religion: A historical introduction.* Boston, MA: John Hopkins Press.

Freud, S. (1939) *Moses and monotheism.* London, England: Hogarth Press and the Institute of Psycho-Analysis.

James, W. (1956). *Reflex action and theism.* In *The will to believe and other essays in popular philosophy.* Mineola, NY: Dover Publications, Inc.

Sartre, J-P. (1956). *Being and nothingness: An essay on phenomenological ontology.* Translated by Hazel E. Barnes. New York, NY: Philosophical Library.

Teo, T. (2009). Editorial. *Journal of Theoretical and Philosophical Psychology, 29*(2), 61–62. http://www.apa.org/pubs/journals/teo/index.aspx

Whitehead, A.N. (1933). *Adventures of ideas.* New York, NY: Macmillan.

THEISM AND PSYCHOLOGICAL SCIENCE:
A CALL FOR RAPPROCHEMENT

*Michael J. Vogel, Tyler A. Gerdin, and Mark R. McMinn**

ABSTRACT

The authors offer two arguments for the inclusion of theism in natural science. First, an argument against excluding theism is offered. Though early roots of science promoted a view that it is a way to accumulate knowledge that is untainted by presuppositions and traditions, postmodern critiques call this into question. Scientists have sometimes rejected religion as a context-dependent, tradition-based way of knowing, yet science itself is also context-dependent and tradition-based. Second, an argument for including theism in psychological is offered. Theistic beliefs are relevant insofar as they are part of human experience for many, they represent a form of human diversity, and they have been associated with some positive health outcomes.

Keywords: psychological science, theism, philosophy of science, ethics

> To the psychologist the religious propensities of [individuals] must be at least as interesting as any other of the facts pertaining to [their] mental constitution. It would seem, therefore, as a psychologist, the natural thing for me would be to invite you to a descriptive survey of those religious propensities.
>
> —William James (1902/1961, p. 4)

James, the founding figure of American psychological science, was committed to the study of religion (Fancher, 2000). For him, the scientific exploration of theism was as interesting as it was necessary for understanding the human experience. There was no desire to separate science and religion. However, this position began to shift during the 20th century as particular philosophical assumptions took root in psychological science (Miller & Thoresen, 2003). It now seems common to notice shelves full of

---

* *Author Note*: Michael J. Vogel, Department of Psychology, George Fox University; Tyler A. Gerdin, Department of Psychology, George Fox University; Mark R. McMinn, Department of Psychology, George Fox University.

The authors wish to thank Roy Gathercoal, Kathleen Gathercoal, and Bradford Holl for their willingness to read through and offer helpful feedback on drafts of this article.

Correspondence concerning this article should be addressed to Michael J. Vogel, Department of Psychology, George Fox University, 414 N. Meridian Street, #V104, Newberg, OR 97132. Email: mvogel08@georgefox.edu

bestselling books attempting to discredit theistic religion and demanding its exclusion from science (e.g., Dawkins, 1996, 2006; Dennett, 1996, 2006; Stenger, 2007). The once strong relationship between theism and psychological science is at present on the brink of collapse, and much is at stake.

In what follows, we suggest that the usual grounds for excluding theism are insufficient and begin by acknowledging some of the philosophical assumptions at the core of this debate.

The Argument against Excluding Theism

The earliest justifications for science were predicated on belief in a divine being (Stark, 2003). It seemed that a divine being had created an ordered, intelligible world for humanity to freely explore, and the methods that would become central to science made this exploration possible. That a theistic worldview created the initial rationale for the scientific endeavor renders the present charge to defend the possibility of theism in science quite an intriguing paradox.

Although common objections to the inclusion of theism in psychological science are complex, they often pertain to incompatible ways of knowing. Owing to the fact that science seems accountable to highly rigorous, context-independent standards for knowledge, it has been given prerogative over the extra-scientific conclusions of theistic traditions. Context-independent refers to knowing that is reliable and not limited to particular reference points or audiences. We prefer this term to *objective* knowing. Context-dependent, on the other hand, refers to knowing that is reliable but limited to particular reference points or audiences. We prefer this term to *subjective* knowing. Extra-scientific refers to claims that are not known through scientific methods; they are situated outside of the province of science.

It seems that many psychological scientists reject the extra-scientific claims of theists because they are based on context-dependent and tradition-based ways of knowing. We contend that this view pervades many arguments for excluding theism from psychological science, and it has important historical and philosophical contexts that warrant some consideration. In the sections to follow, we provide a selected history for the philosophy of modern science, some postmodern appraisals of modern science, and the conclusion that there are insufficient grounds for excluding theism from psychological science based on the common objections to its inclusion.

Early Roots of Science

Though many individuals contributed to the origins of contemporary science, we focus here on two: René Descartes and Isaac Newton. Descartes left a most indelible mark on the annals of scientific and philosophical inquiry with his leap from radical skepticism to absolute certainty (see Toumlin, 1992). His ideas ushered in an era of scientific and philosophical progress that forever changed the pursuit for knowledge (cf. Buckley, 1987). Newton's extraordinary ideas about physics and the nature of reality revolutionized the scientific endeavor. The mysteries of the whole universe, it seemed, were now subject to the certainties of mathematics (Newbigin, 1995).

For the field of psychological science, the Cartesian legacy informs a number of significant philosophical assumptions regarding the standards of claims to knowing, whereas the Newtonian legacy influences several philosophical assumptions primarily about the nature of reality. These have helped to form the usual grounds for excluding theism from psychological science; they define what science is and what it is not. Although a comprehensive review of their impact (or that of other influential figures) is beyond the scope of this article, we briefly discuss the early roots of four such assumptions.

The Cartesian legacy. Descartes (e.g., 1637/2007) influenced psychological science in at least two fundamental ways. The first is evident in the broad scientific ambition to discover context-independent knowledge (cf. Newbigin, 1995). This is an extension of the Cartesian summons to reject the context-dependent ways of knowing embedded within all traditions (Cottingham, 1988; Matson, 2000). Since at least the 17th century, context-independent knowledge has been separated from and preferred over context-dependent ways of knowing (Newbigin, 1995; Van Belle, 2005). And, because modern science appears to be so well sanitized of context-dependent knowledge, many seem to render it more true or legitimate than other ways of knowing (Newbigin, 1995). Therefore, it is considered authoritative and is privileged over the extra-scientific conclusions of many traditions (this position is typically called *scientism*). Science has become venerated as a result of the Cartesian program, whereas theism has been categorically dismissed for its context-dependent, tradition-based ways of knowing.

A second fundamental way that Descartes influenced psychological science is apparent in its justifications for what counts as knowledge (Murphy, 1997). These justifications stem from his presumption that structures of knowledge should be built in a gradual, floor-by-floor manner on established foundations (Cottingham, 1988; Matson, 2000). The Cartesian program also tends to distrust any claims that do not follow a linear, bottom-up approach to knowing; alternative approaches are considered less valid (Murphy, 1997). Psychological scientists generally embrace this theory of knowledge (called *epistemological foundationalism*). In doing so, they justify their research activities as extensions or clarifications of those things already known though the methods of science, and they assume that their scientific conclusions will justify future research activities. However, many theistic traditions tend to make claims that are not knowable in this way, which inclines some psychological scientists to discredit them completely. Descartes' epistemological foundationalism has forever shaped scientific knowing and served as an impetus for excluding the extra-scientific approaches to knowing used by many theistic traditions.

And all was light. Newton (e.g., 1687/1999), with his remarkable accomplishments in physics, also shaped the field of psychological science in at least two important ways (Newbigin, 1995). First, he provided a mathematical account of complex phenomena in the natural world using more basic units of matter (Feingold, 2004; Murphy, 1997). His calculations of mass and force explained "everything from the movement of the stars to the fall of an apple" and seemed to reveal a model of reality independent of faith commitments (Newbigin, 1995, p. 29). In other words, the Newtonian program not only categorized the world into more basic elements (a position on reality called *atomism*), it also made sense of more complex phenomena using only those basic elements (*reductionism*: Murphy, 1997; Van Belle, 2005). It did so without a theistic explanation of reality; the universe seemed to make sense independent of a divine being (Newbigin, 1995). The impact of this shift cannot be underestimated for psychological science. It has resulted in the rejection of theistic truth claims that are not reductionist; explanations of reality now must be purged of a divine being (Van Belle, 2005).

The apparent success of Newton's atomist-reductionist model has resulted in a second, though related, influence over psychological science. It follows from his presumption that all phenomena can and should be explained by reference to physical matter, motion, and natural laws (Van Belle, 2005). The Newtonian program ascribes to a model of reality that can be manipulated to produce any desired effect, like a grand machine, and which science seems to promise the means to control (Murphy, 1997; Van Belle, 2005). This position on reality is called *mechanical materialism*. For the field of psychological science, this serves as a primary working premise in the pursuit of knowledge (Murphy, 1997), making claims about causation in the material world privileged over alternative explanations of reality. Since theists tend to hold extra-scientific explanations of reality, which are unknowable through the methods of science, they are rejected under the Newtonian program. Many psychological scientists refuse to accept any theistic claims about reality that are not knowable through the methods of science.

Appraisals of Modern Science

It seems the Cartesian program has succeeded in convincing many psychological scientists that they can know in context-independent, tradition-free ways. However, many postmodern philosophers (e.g., Foucault, 1972; Kuhn, 1996; Lakatos, 1981) have argued that science is itself a context-dependent paradigm—a tradition. For instance, Polanyi (1974) suggested that becoming a scientist involves apprenticeship to a tradition of knowledge to acquire the necessary skills and worldviews to carry out future scientific endeavors (see also Newbigin, 1995). This is, in no small way, a significant objective of graduate training as a psychological scientist. Students learn to *indwell* the scientific tradition and rely on particular methodologies and landmark studies to continue the acquisition of knowledge (Polanyi, 1974). It seems that psychological science is a tradition and has context-dependent ways of knowing. This is not necessarily a bad thing, but it does deserve some consideration insofar as it serves as a major premise for the exclusion of theistic traditions from psychological science.

Not only is science a tradition, it is many traditions. The *demarcation problem* in the philosophy of science (e.g., Feyerabend, 2010; Lakatos, 1981) has highlighted that there do not seem to be very clear distinctions between ways of knowing that are scientific, pseudo-scientific, and non-scientific. Although they share some basic assumptions (e.g., falsifiability, reproducibility), the various disciplines of science employ vastly different methods to know about reality. Perhaps the methodological differences within the natural sciences are as great as those between the natural and social sciences. Further, the gap between astronomy and biology is at least as wide as that between psychological science and theism. Science is not a monolithic unit of an accepted method, but rather it is a collection of various scientific traditions (Midgley, 2004, 2011). Among other things, postmodernity has concluded that Descartes' search for a single foundation of context-independent, tradition-free knowledge has been unsuccessful.

Regarding Newton's atomist-reductionist model of reality, postmodernists would have us consider that the assumptions of science are "not based on particular scientific evidence" and are themselves extra-scientific in essence (Midgley, 2011, p. xiv). In other words, atomism, reductionism, mechanical materialism, epistemological foundationalism, and scientism are each philosophical conclusions; they cannot be known through the methods of science (Midgley, 2004, 2011). All of science, including psychological science, is rife with extra-scientific claims about reality.

Insufficient Grounds for Exclusion

Theism relies on tradition-based, context-dependent ways of knowing and makes extra-scientific conclusions about reality. But so does psychological science. This is not an attempt to discredit scientific knowing; rather, it is an attempt to defend psychological science from a dangerous misconception. Psychological scientists are able to do good work because of their philosophical assumptions which are unavoidably context-dependent, tradition-based, and extra-scientific (cf. Hayes, Strosahl, & Wilson, 1999). Furthermore, choosing to reject claims that are not tradition-free, context-independent, and scientific would both exclude theism from psychological science and fundamentally undermine the scientific endeavor. It would cut off the nose to spite the face. Although psychological science and theism utilize different methods to know about reality, it does not necessarily follow that they are completely incompatible or irreconcilable. It also does not follow that theism should be excluded from psychological science because it relies on tradition-based, context-dependent ways of knowing and makes extra-scientific conclusions about reality. That conclusion is a bias of scientism, and it ignores many thoughtful appraisals of the modern scientific endeavor. Taken together, these common objections yield insufficient grounds for the exclusion of theism from psychological science.

THE ARGUMENT FOR INCLUDING THEISM

A divine being may or may not exist. Such a determination is beyond the realm of science; it is extra-scientific. Regardless, theism ought to be considered in behavioral science for various reasons. We suggest three: relevance, ethics, and utility, though more could certainly be offered.

Relevance

Social scientists study human experience which has been profoundly shaped by religious values and beliefs throughout history. If psychological science and the clinical methods that emerge from psychological science are to remain relevant to the questions and struggles of everyday living, then religious faith must be considered. Though religion has become less important to United States residents over the past 15 years, the decline is not as remarkable as the persistently high rates of faith. In 2010, 80% still reported religion to be very important or fairly important to them, down 7% from 1992. Almost two-thirds (61%) belonged to a church or synagogue and 39% had attended services in the past seven days (Gallup, 2011).

Psychologists and those studying psychology tend to be less religious than the general population, which may give them a skewed view of the religiousness of others. Table 1 shows the importance of religion to various groups, with data coming from various studies that the authors have been involved with in recent years. Among a large group of university students (n = 1800), 76.1% reported their religion is very or fairly important to them, a number quite consistent with the Gallup poll results just described. In contrast, only 20.7% of American Psychological Association (APA) leaders (divisional presidents and representatives on APA Council) described their religion to be very or fairly important. Rates among other psychology groups vary, but all are substantially lower than the general public: 35.5% of doctoral students, 40.7% psychology interns, 52.5% of doctoral faculty, 23.1% of doctoral program Directors of Clinical Training (DCT), and 29.0% of internship DCTs reported religion to be very or fairly important to them (Vogel, 2011).

While these numbers reflect disparity between psychologists and the general public, it is important to note that psychologists, and those in training, are not utterly non-religious. For example, one-third of doctoral students in psychology and over half of their faculty reported religion to be personally important. Over 15 years ago Shafrankse (1996) concluded, "it appears that psychologists may be more similar than dissimilar to the general population in their religious views and faith commitments" (p. 160). The same holds true today, suggesting that theistic values are important to consider insofar as they are relevant to how many psychologists and psychologists-in-training understand life and even more pertinent to those outside the field of psychology.

Table 1. *Importance of Religion among Various Groups*

Group	N	Mean	Std Dev
Undergraduate students	1800	4.0	1.1
Doctoral psychology students	110	2.7	1.4
Predoctoral psychology interns	59	3.0	1.3
Doctoral faculty	40	3.3	1.4
Doctoral DCTs	26	2.7	1.3
Internship DCTs	38	2.8	1.1
APA leaders	63	2.3	1.2

Notes: All participants answered the question, "How important is your religion to you?" on a 5-point Likert-type scale ranging from 1, *"Not at all important, I have no religion"* to 5, *"Very important, it is the center of my life."* Data were collected as parts of different studies. The undergraduate student data came from Louwerse, McMinn, McMinn, & Aten (2008). Data regarding APA leaders came from McMinn, Hathaway, Woods, and Snow (2009). All other data are from Vogel (2011). DCT = Director of Clinical Training. The overall difference between groups is statistically significant, $F(6, 2129)=60.44$, $p < .001$. Post hoc comparisons using Scheffe tests reveal differences ($p < .05$) between undergraduate students and all other groups and also between APA leaders and doctoral faculty.

Ethics

The inclusion of theism in psychological science is not only a matter of relevance but also a matter of ethics. Psychologists in the APA are supported (if not mandated) by the *Ethics Code* (APA, 2002) to increase scientific knowledge related to the beliefs, experiences, and values of theistic individuals. This is not a new development, as they have been encouraged to do so for almost two decades (see APA, 1992). Including theistic religion in psychological science satisfies an established ethic to demonstrate respect for worldview considerations that are important to most Americans.

There are also reasons to believe the ethical impetus for considering theistic religion within psychological science is growing. As the sociopolitical milieu of the US continues to change, the value of multicultural diversity becomes ever more important (APA, 2003). This is as much the case for theistic religion as it is for any other dimension of diversity, such as ethnicity, sexual orientation, or gender. The APA has responded at an organizational level to the ethic for multicultural sensitivity by launching The Task Force on Enhancing Diversity in the APA, hiring a Chief Diversity Officer, and promoting psychological science to diverse populations (e.g., Anderson, 2008). Theistic religion, as a relevant dimension of multicultural diversity, is ethically important in the APA (e.g., APA, 2003, 2008) and warrants consideration in psychological science.

As our understanding of religion continues to develop, we become increasingly aware of the interconnections between theism and other dimensions of diversity (cf. Constantine, 1999). To be sure, considering theistic religion is helpful to better understand the racial and cultural identities of most, if not all, Americans (Cross, 1995; Harry, 1992; Leong, Wagner, & Tata, 1995; Smart & Smart, 1992; see Vogel, 2011).

Utility

In years past, it was not uncommon to find psychologists trumpeting the deleterious effects of theistic belief (e.g., Ellis, 1962, 1971, 1980, 1983; Walls, 1980), but scientific results showing various health benefits associated with religious and spiritual beliefs demanded a change (e.g., Koenig, McCullough, & Larson, 2001). The flagship journal of the APA, *American Psychologist*, published a special section on health and religion less than a decade ago (Hill & Pargament, 2003; Miller & Thoresen, 2003; Powell, Shahabi, & Thoresen, 2003; Seeman, Dubin, & Seeman, 2003). Though not every religious variable is positively associated with increased health, the beneficial nature of various religious and spiritual activities and beliefs is quite striking.

McMinn, Snow, and Orton (in press) suggested several ways that religion, including theistic religion, may help promote health. First, religion provides a sense of meaning, which can be especially important during difficult seasons of life (Slattery & Park, 2011). The meaning derived through theistic beliefs may also promote altruistic and pro-social behaviors, which have been shown to help mental health (Post, 2005; Schwartz, Meisenhelder, Ma, & Reed, 2002). Second, theists often belong to faith communities that provide social support. Shared beliefs and rituals provide hope and healing during normal life stressors and transitions (see Pargament, 1997). Third, religious communities offer resources and help amidst times of struggle and trouble. Clergy often provide counsel and support for parishioners, and many clergy are open to collaborating with psychologists to help others in times of need (Edwards, Lim, McMinn, & Dominguez, 1999; McMinn, Aikins, & Lish, 2003).

Clinicians have also become increasingly open to considering religion and spirituality, both as a matter of human diversity and as a protective factor in mental and physical health (Aten & Leach, 2009; Aten, McMinn, & Worthington, 2011; Miller & Delaney, 2005; Pargament, 2007; Richards & Bergin, 2005; Sperry & Shafranske, 2005). Rather than trying to disabuse clients of their faulty religious beliefs, as some clinicians once promoted (e.g., Walls, 1980), today's clinical psychologist is mandated both by ethics and research to be respectful of clients' theistic beliefs.

CONCLUSION

More than a century has passed since James (1902/1961) first encouraged psychologists to explore the religious experience. Some (e.g., Allport, 1961; Koenig, McCullough, & Larson, 2001; Plante, 2009; Shafranske, 1996) have taken this task seriously, whereas others (e.g., Ellis, 1962, 1971, 1980, 1983; Walls, 1980) seem to have been reluctant to include theism in psychology. We believe the philosophical assumptions of modern science have been used to justify the usual arguments for excluding theistic religion from psychology. However, the appraisals of postmodernity (e.g., Feyerabend, 2010; Lakatos, 1981) have challenged many core assumptions of the scientific endeavor and called attention to its context-dependent, tradition-based ways of knowing. This does not invalidate psychological science, which has immensely benefited humanity, but rather defends it from the misconception that it is without assumptions that are shared within its particular community. Furthermore, we contend that the relevance, ethical support from the APA, and utility of theistic religion are among the many reasons to include it in psychological science. We hope the split between science and religion over the 20th century will be corrected by a rapprochement during the 21st century.

REFERENCES

Allport, G. (1961). *The individual and his religion*. New York, NY: Macmillan.
American Psychological Association. (1992). Ethical principles and code of conduct. *American Psychologist, 48*, 1597–1611. http://www.apa.org/pubs/journals/amp/index.aspx
American Psychological Association. (2002). Ethical principles of psychologists and code of conduct. *American Psychologist, 49*, 1060–1073. http://www.apa.org/pubs/journals/amp/index.aspx
American Psychological Association. (2003). Guidelines on multicultural education, training, research, practice, and organizational change for psychologists. *American Psychologist, 58*, 377–402. http://www.apa.org/pubs/journals/amp/index.aspx
American Psychological Association. (2008). Resolution on religious, religion-related and/or religion-derived prejudice. *American Psychologist, 63*, 431–434. http://www.apa.org/pubs/journals/amp/index.aspx
Anderson, N.B. (2008). From the CEO: Enhancing diversity in the scientific pipeline. *Monitor on Psychology, 39*(7). Retrieved from http://www.apa.org/monitor/
Aten, J.D. & Leach, M.M. (Eds.). (2009). *Spirituality and the therapeutic process: A comprehensive resource from intake through termination*. Washington, DC: American Psychological Association.

Aten, J.D., McMinn, M.R., & Worthington, Jr., E.L. (Eds.) (2011). *Spirituality oriented interventions for counseling and psychotherapy*. Washington, DC: American Psychological Association.

Buckley, M.J. (1987). *At the origins of modern atheism*. London, England: Yale University Press.

Constantine, M.G. (Ed.). (1999). Spiritual and religious issues in counseling racial and ethnic minority populations [Special Issue]. *Journal of Multicultural Counseling and Development, 24*, 179–181. http://www.jmcdonline.org/

Cottingham, J. (1988). *The rationalists: A history of Western philosophy: 4*. New York, NY: Oxford University Press.

Cross, W.E. (1995). The psychology of nigrescence: Revising the Cross model. In J.G. Ponterotto, J.M. Casas, L.A. Suzuki, & C.M. Alexander (Eds.), *Handbook of multicultural counseling* (pp. 93–122). Thousand Oaks, CA: Sage.

Dawkins, R. (1996). *The blind watchmaker: Why the evidence of evolution reveals a universe without design* (Rev. ed.). New York, NY: W.W. Norton & Company.

Dawkins, R. (2006). *The God delusion*. New York, NY: Houghton Mifflin.

Dennett, D.C. (1996). *Darwin's dangerous idea: Evolution and the meaning of life*. New York, NY: Simon & Schuster.

Dennett, D.C. (2006). *Breaking the spell: Religion as a natural phenomenon*. New York, NY: Viking Adult.

Descartes, R. (2007). *Discourse on method: Meditations on first philosophy*. (D. Weinberg, Trans.). Thousand Oaks, CA: BN Publishing. (Original work published in 1637)

Edwards, L.C., Lim, R.K.B., McMinn, M.R., & Dominguez, A.W. (1999). Examples of collaboration between psychologists and clergy. *Professional Psychology: Research and Practice, 30*, 547–551. doi:10.1037/0735-7028.30.6.547

Ellis, A. (1962). *Reason and emotion in psychotherapy*. Secaucus, NJ: Lyle Stuart.

Ellis, A. (1971). *The case against religion: A psychotherapist's view*. New York, NY: Institute for Rational Living.

Ellis, A. (1980). Psychotherapy and atheistic values: A response to A.E. Bergin's "Psychotherapy and religious values." *Journal of Consulting and Clinical Psychology, 48*, 635–639. doi:10.1037//0022-006X.48.5.635

Ellis, A. (1983). *The case against religiosity*. New York, NY: Institute for Rational-Emotive Therapy.

Fancher, R. (2000). William James. In the *Encyclopedia of Psychology, Vol. 4*, pp. 382–385. New York, NY/Washington, DC: Oxford/American Psychological Association.

Feingold, M. (2004). *The Newtonian moment: Isaac Newton and the making of modern culture*. New York, NY: Oxford University Press.

Feyerabend, P.K. (2010). *Against method* (4th ed.). New York, NY: Verso Books.

Foucault, M. (1972). *The archaeology of knowledge & the discourse on language*. (A.M. Sheridan Smith, Trans.). New York, NY: Pantheon Books.

Gallup Polls, Inc. (2011). *Religion*. Retrieved from http://www.gallup.com/poll/1690/religion.aspx

Harry, B. (1992). *Cultural diversity, families, and the special education system*. New York, NY: Teachers College Press.

Hayes, S.C., Strosahl, K.D., & Wilson, K.G. (1999). *Acceptance and commitment therapy: An experiential approach to behavior change*. New York, NY: Guilford Press.

Hill, P.C. & Pargament, K.I. (2003). Advances in the conceptualization and measurement of religion and spirituality: Implications for physical and mental health research. *American Psychologist, 58*, 64–74. doi:10.1037/0003-066X.58.1.64

James, W. (1961). *The varieties of religious experience: A study in human nature*. Cambridge, MA: Harvard University Press. (Original work published 1902)

Koenig, H.G., McCullough, M.E., & Larson, D.B. (2001). *Handbook of religion and health*. New York, NY: Oxford University Press.

Kuhn, T.S. (1996). *The structure of scientific revolutions* (3rd ed.). Chicago, IL: University of Chicago Press.

Lakatos, I. (1981). Science and pseudo-science. In S. Brown, J. Fauvel, & R. Finnegan (Eds.), *Conceptions of inquiry* (pp. 99–105). London, England: The Open University Press.

Leong, F.T.L., Wagner, N.S., & Tata, S.P. (1995). Racial and ethnic variations in help-seeking attitudes. In J.G. Ponterotto, J.M. Casas, L.A. Suzuki, & C.M. Alexander (Eds.), *Handbook of multicultural counseling* (pp. 441–456). Thousand Oaks, CA: Sage.

Louwerse, K.A., McMinn, M.R., McMinn, L.G., & Aten, J.D. (August, 2008). *Development of a sin awareness scale.* Poster presented at the annual convention of the American Psychological Association. Boston, MA.

Matson, W. (2000). *A new history of philosophy: Volume two: From Descartes to Searle* (2nd ed.). Orlando, FL: Harcourt College Publishers.

McMinn, M.R., Aikins, D.C., & Lish, R.A. (2003). Basic and advanced competence in collaborating with clergy. *Professional Psychology: Research and Practice, 34,* 197–202. doi:10.1037/0735-7028.34.2.197

McMinn, M.R., Hathaway, W.L., Woods, S.W., & Snow, K.N. (2009). What American Psychological Association leaders have to say about *Psychology of Religion and Spirituality. Psychology of Religion and Spirituality, 1,* 3–13. doi:10.1037/a0014991

McMinn, M.R., Snow, K.N., & Orton, J.J. (in press). Counseling within and across faith traditions. In L. Miller (Ed.), *The Oxford handbook of the psychology of spirituality.* New York, NY: Oxford.

Midgley, M. (2004). *The myths we live by.* New York, NY: Routledge.

Midgley, M. (2011). *Philosophy bundle RC: The myths we live by* (Reprint). New York, NY: Routledge.

Miller, W.R. & Delaney, H.D. (Eds.) (2005). *Judeo-Christian perspectives on psychology: Human nature, motivation, and change.* Washington, DC: American Psychological Association.

Miller, W.R. & Thoresen, C.E. (2003). Spirituality, religion, and health: An emerging research field. *American Psychologist, 58,* 24–35. doi:10.1037/0003-066X.58.1.24

Murphy, N. (1997). *Anglo-American postmodernity: Philosophical perspectives on science, religion, and ethics.* Boulder, CO: Westview Press.

Newbigin, L. (1995). *Proper confidence: Faith, doubt, & certainty in Christian discipleship.* Grand Rapids, MI: William B. Eerdmans Publishing Company.

Newton, I. (1999). *The principia: Mathematical principles of natural philosophy.* (I.B. Cohen & A. Whitman, Trans.). Los Angeles, CA: University of California Press. (Original work published in 1687)

Pargament, K.I. (1997). *The psychology of religion and coping: Theory, research, practice.* New York, NY: Guilford Press.

Pargament, K.I. (2007). *Spiritually integrated psychotherapy: Understanding and addressing the sacred.* New York, NY: Guilford Press.

Plante, T.G. (2009). *Spiritual practices in psychotherapy.* Washington, DC: American Psychological Association.

Polanyi, M. (1974). *Personal knowledge: Towards a post-critical philosophy* (corrected ed.). Chicago, IL: University of Chicago Press.

Powell, L.H., Shahabi, L., & Thoresen, C.E. (2003). Religion and spirituality: Linkages to physical health. *American Psychologist, 58,* 36–52. doi:10.1037/0003-066X.58.1.36

Post, S.G. (2005). Altruism, happiness, and health: It's good to be good. *International Journal of Behavioral Medicine, 12*(2), 66–77. doi:10.1207/s15327558ijbm1202_4

Richards, P.S., & Bergin, A.E. (2005). *A spiritual strategy for counseling and psychotherapy* (2nd ed.). Washington, DC: American Psychological Association.

Schwartz, C., Meisenhelder, J.B., Ma, Y. & Reed, G. (2002). Altruistic social interest behaviors are associated with better mental health. *Psychosomatic Medicine, 65,* 778–785. doi: 10.1097/01PSY.0000079378.39062.D4

Seeman, T.E., Dubin, L.F., & Seeman, M. (2003). Religiosity/spirituality and health: A critical review of the evidence for biological pathways. *American Psychologist, 58*, 53–63. doi:10.1037/0003-066X.58.1.53

Shafranske, E.P. (1996). Religious beliefs, affiliations, and practices of clinical psychologists. In E.P. Shafrankse (Ed.), *Religion and the clinical practice of psychology* (pp. 149–162). Washington, DC: American Psychological Association.

Slattery, J.M. & Park, C.L. (2011). Meaning-making and spiritually oriented interventions. In J. D. Aten, M.R. McMinn, & E.L. Worthington, Jr. (Eds.), *Spirituality oriented interventions for counseling and psychotherapy* (pp. 15–40). Washington, DC: American Psychological Association.

Smart, J.F. & Smart, D.W. (1992). Cultural issues in the rehabilitation of Hispanics. *Journal of Rehabilitation, 58*, 29–37.

Sperry, L. & Shafranske, E.P. (Eds.) (2005). *Spiritually oriented psychotherapy*. Washington, DC: American Psychological Association.

Stark, R. (2003) *For the glory of God: How monotheism led to reformations, science, witch-hunts, and the end of slavery*. Princeton, NJ: Princeton University Press.

Stenger, V.J. (2007). *God: The failed hypothesis. How science shows that God does not exist*. New York, NY: Prometheus Books.

Toulmin, S.E. (1992). *Cosmopolis: The hidden agenda of modernity*. Chicago, IL: University of Chicago Press.

Van Belle, H.A. (2005). *Persisting themata and changing paradigms: Explorations in the history of psychology*. Retrieved from http://www.allofliferedeemed.co.uk/Van%20Belle/1008%282%29.pdf

Vogel, M.J. (2011). Examining religion and spirituality as diversity training: A multidimensional study of doctoral training in the American Psychological Association. Manuscript in preparation.

Walls, G.B. (1980). Values and psychotherapy: A comment on "Psychotherapy and religious values." *Journal of Consulting and Clinical Psychology, 48*, 640–641. doi:10.1037//0022-006X.48.5.640

THEISTIC PSYCHOLOGY: A PATRISTIC PERSPECTIVE

*James M. Nelson and Candice Thomason**

ABSTRACT

For a variety of reasons, modern psychology has had an ambivalent relationship with religious understandings of the human person. However, recent work has highlighted the problems with a strictly secular psychology, and authors have begun to develop alternative views that offer exciting possibilities. One of these religious models is theistic psychology, as developed by authors like Richards, Bergin, Slife, and others. What might a theistic psychology look like? A promising possibility for the development of a theistic psychology may be drawn from the Patristic Christian literature, where authors developed sophisticated theistic psychologies in an attempt to understand the struggles of individuals seeking spiritual growth and inner freedom. These models were incarnational and relational, seeing humans as embodied, relational, and spiritual persons. These theistic ideas allowed writers to create sophisticated theories of development and mental illness that integrated the physical, ethical/psychological, and spiritual. Unfortunately, the medicalization of psychology during the modern period destroyed this integrated understanding of the human person, which has made it difficult to develop a psychology that adequately integrates all the elements of our lives. A return to theistic models can help us understand and treat complex problems like depression that depend upon such an integrated understanding.

Keywords: theistic psychology, history and philosophy of science, relationality, attachment, depression

Modern psychology has had an uneasy relationship with religious thought. Early 20th century psychologists such as Freud and Leuba tended to associate religion with pathology and to disparage religious understandings of experience. Psychologists as a group have been found to be consistently less religious than the general population, and a good case can be made that contemporary psychological method and theory are biased against religious and theistic views of the world (Leuba, 1912, 1925; Nelson, 2009; Pierre, 2001; Slife, 2005; Slife & Reber, 2009; Slife & Whoolery, 2006).

While the personal views or even biases of individual psychologists may occasionally play a role in the resistance to religious thought within the

---

* *Author Note*: James M. Nelson, Department of Psychology, Valparaiso University; Candice Thomason, Department of Psychology, Valparaiso University.

Correspondence concerning this article should be addressed to James M. Nelson, Department of Psychology, Valparaiso University, 1001 Campus Drive South, Valparaiso, IN 46383-6493. Email: Jim.Nelson@valpo.edu field, other factors probably play a much more important role. Modern positivistic psychology has traditionally been built on the premise that scientific understandings of the human person are superior to religious ones, and so a true scientific psychology must exclude God and theological understandings (e.g., Churchland, 1996; Comte, 1998; Wilson, 1978). Building a psychology on a religious premise such as theism might be thought to interfere with the naturalistic basis of science or make objectivity impossible (cf. e.g., Hood, Hill, & Spilka, 2009; Tooby & Cosmides, 1992, 2005). Editorial policies of journals, even journals in the area of psychology of religion, have been constructed according to this premise (e.g., Piedmont, 2009).

However, it is doubtful that attempting to protect psychology from religious thought will have its anticipated benefits. From a philosophy of science perspective, positivistic versions of reductive naturalism are deeply flawed, and naturalism itself is a concept too vague to serve as a basis for a coherent approach to science that can both produce new ideas and test old ones. In addition, any scientific theory or research must start with ontological, ethical, epistemological, and methodological assumptions that strongly affect its point of view (Nelson & Slife, in press; Rea, 2002). Taking a position for a reductive naturalism and against theism is no less loaded in assumptions and potential biases than taking a position for it, so the risk to "objectivity" is no different.

Unexpected costs are also apparent. One of the largest of these has been the difficulty the field has had in producing integrated models of the human person that encompass all aspects of life, including our embodied, moral, psychological, and spiritual natures. It seems inherently irrational that a science built on a philosophy that excludes religious or spiritual explanations would ever be able to articulate an understanding of persons that really encompasses the religious or spiritual (cf. Slife, 2005; Slife & Reber, 2009; Slife & Whoolery, 2006).

Some psychologists have begun to recognize the disappointments and problems inherent in a totally secularized psychology, and they have begun to experiment with other models. One example of this is theistic psychology (e.g., Richards, 2005; Richards & Bergin, 2004; Slife, this issue; Slife, 2005; Slife, Mitchell & Whoolery, 2004), which is the view that a full understanding of the human person requires a model which has a place for God. However, *theism* as a concept is quite broad: It requires a specific articulation to make it useful in psychological research or clinical practice. A promising possibility for a specific articulation of theism is to turn to the early Christian or *Patristic* literature, where authors developed sophisticated theistic psychologies in an attempt to understand the struggles of individuals seeking spiritual growth and inner freedom. These writers developed detailed understandings of psychology that provide intriguing integrations of the embodied, emotional, and spiritual aspects of life. This paper will attempt to articulate and explain a theistic psychology based on these Patristic ideas.

This paper will proceed in several stages. First, the development of Patristic models of psychology and mental illness will be discussed. Second, the general characteristics of incarnational Patristic theism will be described. Third, a specific theistic model from this period developed by the Christian writer Evagrius of Pontus will be outlined. Finally, application of the Evagrian theistic model will be illustrated using the example of depression.

Background to Incarnational Trinitarian Theism: Classical Views of Mental Health and Illness

There are many parallels between the contemporary situation in psychology and the intellectual climate in the classical Western world. During the Greek, Hellenistic, and Roman periods, different schools of thought advanced competing views of the human person, mental health, and illness. Essentially, three different approaches existed: religious explanations, philosophical schools, and medical philosophies.

Ancient religious thought emphasized the necessity of persons to be in a positive relationship with divinity and that this relationship could be related to one's physical or mental health and illness. An example of this view was the cult of Asclepius (Edelstein & Edelstein, 1998), where temples were established so the ill could receive healing dreams from the god. Such a view offered a framework for understanding the relationship between the body and spirituality. However, this type of spiritual view was rejected by the development of rational medicine beginning in the 5th century BC (Longrigg, 1998), so that classical thought was unable to develop a synthetic view of physical or mental illness that encompassed both its spiritual and its physical aspects.

Ancient philosophical thought such as Stoicism (Long, 1986) emphasized the ethical and communal aspect of human life. For instance, Epictetus emphasized the need for self-control over our thoughts, feelings, and actions as an essential part of living a good life (e.g., Epictetus, 2008), and Marcus Aurelius stressed the need to develop moral character, take personal responsibility, and understand others as much as possible (Aurelius, 2008). Stoic thought also articulated a sophisticated psychological analysis of the human person as a way of understanding why moral character is important and what barriers prevent people from developing it. Psychology was thus thought to be a means to advance the end of ethical advancement. Spiritual understandings of the human person were largely absent from their work.

Ancient medical thought saw people as primarily material beings. This approach to the human person culminated in the work of Galen. He was a prolific author who pushed a reductionist agenda, reducing the activity of the soul to the functioning of humors in works like *The Faculties of the Soul Follow the Mixtures of the Body*. Unfortunately, he also offered a fragmented model, discussing moral and then physical issues related to health and illness without offering a framework for how they could interact (e.g., Galen, 1952, 1964).

Classical thought thus failed to provide a synthesis of the religious, ethical, psychological, and physical that could form the basis of an understanding of the human person. Mental health and illness were typically approached from only one perspective. This changed with the advent of Patristic thought.

Patristic Theism: Incarnational and Trinitarian

Patristic thought was deeply *theistic*. Furthermore, it was based on a theism that was *incarnational* and *Trinitarian*. This theistic view led to a particular understanding of human nature (anthropological ontology) and human flourishing (anthropological teleology); people were seen as relational persons with material, ethical, and spiritual elements. Human flourishing was inner freedom gained through relationship to God. They rejected a deistic view of religion where God creates the world and then leaves it to its own devices.

Theistic. Patristic authors saw God as active in the world, for instance as a Creator who made all things good and who made humanity in the image of God. It is a God who offers redemption and inner freedom to all who desire it.

Incarnational. The early Christian councils successfully formulated an understanding of Incarnation: how God could become embodied in Christ. This incarnational theism led to a valuing of the body and an appreciation for its relationship to the spiritual. The positive view of the body was in contrast to some classical philosophies like much of neoplatonic thought (e.g., Plotinus, 1991). The incarnational character of the human person was reflected in Christian worship and devotional activities, and the emphasis on somatic practices was designed to purify the body of inordinate attachments. The whole body was thought to be important, as opposed to the specific focus on the brain found in most of modern psychology.

Trinitarian. Later councils struggled with understanding the relationality of a God who is Father, Son, and Spirit. Eastern Christian writers saw the Trinity as essentially relational, for the nature of each of the persons depends on their relationship to the others (Zizioulas, 1985). Western writers like Augustine expressed this relationality in talking about the Spirit as Love binding together the Father and the Son (Augustine, 1956). As humans were thought to be conceived of in the image of God, human nature was seen as having a relational and active component. The human person was thought to be designed to be in relationship with God and with others. Ethics, how we are to treat others, thus becomes a central human concern, and psychological or other barriers to relationships are a focus of keen interest. The relational character of the human person can be found throughout the Patristic literature such as in the literature on monastic and church community (e.g., Benedict, 2001; Holmes, 2000; Veilleux, 1980, 1981) and the literature on spiritual guidance and direction (cf. e.g., Hausherr, 1990). It is also sometimes appreciated in modern psychology as in cultural views of human nature (e.g., Shweder et al., 2006), although an individualistic view of the human person as a detached monad is much more common among Western psychologists.

The theistic thought of the Patristic writers allowed a view of human nature as an integrated whole, allowing writers to develop sophisticated views of development and mental illness that integrated the physical, ethical, and spiritual. Unlike some modern attempts at integration that simply add a little religious content to a current psychological theory, Patristic psychology attempts to build a complete view of the human person based on the central fact of our relationship to God. An important example can be found in the thought and writings by Evagrius of Pontus (e.g., Evagrius, 1972; Sinkewicz, 2003). A theistic psychology based on these writings would be grounded in a number of important assumptions: (a) God is active in the world and in the lives of humans; (b) humans are to be viewed holistically as creatures who are embodied with ethical, psychological, and spiritual natures; (c) the human person is essentially relational in nature and requires a relationship with God to be healthy; (d) when this central relationship is incomplete or absent, people form other kinds of relationships or attachments in its place that are ultimately destructive; and (e) ethical, spiritual, and religious practices are essential in developing a pattern of healthy attachments and relationships.

EXAMPLE: AN EVAGRIAN PSYCHOLOGY AND APPLICATIONS

Evagrius was a highly educated Patristic scholar who spent part of his career writing about the process of spiritual growth that he observed in the Desert Fathers, a group of Christian spiritual seekers who lived in the desert areas of Egypt (Harmless, 2004). His perspective drew on Patristic Trinitarian theism to construct a psychologically sophisticated model of positive and negative forces for growth.

Evagrian theory: In the view of Evagrius, humans are essentially relational. Unlike the weakly relational view of some versions of social psychology that treats relationships as "add-ons" which can affect the behavior of the individual, Patristic authors believed that the human person is not essentially an individual and does not exist outside of relationships. Evagrius argued that because of our essential relationality, people must have a center that becomes a focus for strong connectedness and identity. In the absence of a mature spiritual identity centered on God, we form alternative centers based on disordered attachments or passions (*pathe*) that are ultimately unsatisfying or problematic (e.g., Sinkewicz, 2003, p. 101). A wide variety of things could become objects of inordinate attachment such as food, material possessions, relationships, emotions, and unrealistic views of ourselves held by self or others. These have the ability to become preoccupations or "deadly thoughts" (*logismoi*) that disrupt our relationships and growth. The only real answer to this problem is to form a relationship to God and others who can become a healthy focus for our relationality, leading us to reject inordinate attachments and develop inner freedom (*apatheia*). The emphasis on acceptance of a *higher power* in 12-step programs is reminiscent of this view (Alcoholics Anonymous World Service, 2004). Patristic authors would thus soundly reject the views of authors like Gergen (1991), who have argued that people in the contemporary world have no need for a central focus or identity.

Evagrius thought that inner freedom from disordered attachments was achieved through a lifestyle and series of practices (*praktike*) that engaged body, mind, and spirit. The body was trained through practices like fasting and manual labor. Mental preoccupations and problematic thoughts were challenged with competing thoughts (*antirrhesis*). The spiritual relationship with God was built using practices like prayer and reciting or singing scripture passages. In addition, practices with ethical import such as acts of almsgiving, hospitality, or charity were thought to build virtues that blocked the formation of inordinate attachments. Embodied, ethical, psychological, and spiritual aspects of the person were all addressed in a coordinated system.

Example: Application of Evagrian Theory to the Problem of Depression

How would the Evagrian model work in practice, for instance in the conceptualization and treatment of a specific problem like extended depression? In the Patristic period, the first step would be to identify the cause of the problem. Patristic authors did believe that some depressions were physical in origin and required special treatment. If the person required physical care, this would be provided by others, sometimes in the setting of a community infirmary (Ferngren, 2009). Assuming the depression was not physical in origin, the question would be what kind of inordinate attachments and mental preoccupations were at the heart of the problem. This assessment would typically be done by a spiritual elder who knew the person well and had responsibility for them. Three main possibilities would be considered:

(a). *Disordered desires*. Sadness and depression could be related to the loss of an object or relationship to which the person had become attached, such as a favorite food or material possession. Learning to develop detachment and self-mastery through ethical/spiritual practices like fasting or almsgiving were thought to help the individual develop perseverance and the ability to take a long view, seeing the lost object in a larger perspective and preventing a recurrence of the problem.

(b). *Weariness (accedie)*. Low mood and energy could be related to an inordinate attachment to change and excitement, fostering a continual dissatisfaction with one's place in life. Attempts to change would satisfy briefly, but unhappiness would quickly return. Because this problem is often at its worst during the middle of the day, it became known as the *noonday demon*. Some writers have considered this problem to be equivalent to depression (e.g., Solomon, 2001), but Evagrius considered it to be a separate type of problem. Constant performance of activities like prayer and manual labor were thought to interfere with the rumination and self-absorption at the heart of this weariness.

(c). *Extended sadness or grief* (*lupe*). While periods of sadness are part of normal human experience, Evagrius pointed out that we can hang onto negative emotions, becoming attached to them and allowing these moods to dominate us, thus leading to a loss of inner freedom. He proposed both cognitive and moral solutions to the problem, such as challenging negative thoughts and the practices of hospitality or gift-giving. These practices allowed people to move beyond self-focused attachments to emotions (cf. Nelson, 2009). Dialectical behavior therapy is reminiscent of this Christian insight that hanging on to feelings and reactions can be problematic and lead to difficulty tolerating distress, as it uses techniques based in Zen Buddhism to show the transience of feelings and how detachment from these feelings can aid in emotional regulation (cf. Linehan, 1993; Linehan, Tutek, Heard, & Armstrong, 1994; Robins, 2002).

In all three cases, a combination of ethical activity, psychological technique, and spiritual practice offered a solution to the problem. This suggests that a theistic psychology needs to include a set of practices that flow from the theistic core of the theory. These practices should obviously include spiritual and religious techniques but must also address basic ethical practices and provide a rationale for the way of life that is implied by this ethic.

Theoretical and Historical Barriers to Patristic Theism

Unfortunately, there are barriers that make it difficult for many people to seriously consider a theistic perspective. Some are reluctant due to their attachment to particular views about the nature of science, which may include some beliefs that are questionable or simply untrue (Nelson & Slife, in press). In this case, a simple openness to learn about modern perspectives on philosophy of science may help remove barriers.

Another barrier to the use of theistic psychologies lies in the modern medical model that dominates Western psychological practice. Models from the early modern period (cf. Augstein, 1996; e.g., Prichard, 1835;) had recognized the moral and spiritual components of emotional problems. Unfortunately, one of the main purposes of the medicalization of psychiatry in the 19th century was to destroy the theistic model by removing moral and spiritual components from our understanding of mental illness (cf. Porter, 2002). Positivist versions of science popularized by Comte and Mill at the time saw religion as involving primitive thinking that needed to be replaced by secular science (Comte, 1998; Mill, 2002; Nelson, 2006,

2009). The removal of consideration of moral issues was portrayed as an advantage to the client that would remove any aspect of blame from their condition. Today, mental health practice is largely a secular enterprise.

However, this medicalization also had unintended consequences. Removal of the spiritual and ethical from models of mental illness destroyed the unified Patristic understanding of the human person, which has made it impossible to develop a psychology that adequately integrates the relational, material, ethical, and spiritual aspects of life. A research program that deliberately excludes the religious and spiritual cannot expect to then find a way to coherently include these things in a view of the human person. This was the situation faced in the classical period prior to the advent of theism. Not surprisingly, as modern researchers rediscovered the positive effects of religion and spirituality and wished to bring this back into treatment, they had no theory or set of practices that would work. In addition, the standard medical model makes it extremely difficult to challenge problematic ethical stances taken by our clients, as it is not considered to be integral to the problem. A theistic psychology places a relationship with an active God at the center of the human person and compels us to consider how our relations with others are intimately connected with this central connection.

Conclusion

Theistic psychology, such as the Patristic model discussed here, offers us exciting possibilities. Rather than leading to a loss of scientific objectivity, it provides new ideas for looking at problems like depression from an integrated perspective of body, mind, and spirit. It also helps us understand why some modern approaches to emotional and addictive problems are effective. Hopefully we can move beyond older barriers so that we can take advantage of the theistic viewpoint.

Patristic authors suggest that a strong theistic psychology, and psychology in general, needs to include attention to a number of issues:

(a). Theistic writers need to be clear about the underlying assumptions of their models and be willing to challenge the philosophical inadequacies of competing views.
(b). Any theistic psychology must be based on a strong relational view of the human person with God as the center or nexus of this relationality.

(c). This relationality implies a holistic model of the human person that includes relationship with body, mind, others, and God. In particular, strong relationality means that ethics, how relations should be conducted, must be a part of any theistic psychology.

(d). As a result of (b) and (c), a theistic understanding of psychopathology should focus on human problems as distorted relationships and attachments. Techniques for growth suggested by the theistic psychology must provide a way of repairing distorted relationships.

A return to a theistic psychology offers a ground for constructing a new synthesis that provides a more adequate understanding of persons and better resources for dealing with mental health issues.

References

Alcoholics Anonymous World Service. (2004). *Alcoholics Anonymous: The story of how thousands of men and women have recovered from alcoholism* (4th ed.), New York, NY: Alcoholics Anonymous World Service.

Augstein, H. (1996). J.C. Prichard's concept of moral insanity: A medical theory of the corruption of human nature. *Medical History, 40*, 311–343.

Augustine, St. (1956). On the holy Trinity. In P. Schaff (Ed.), *The Nicene and Post-Nicene fathers, first series* (Vol. 3 pp. 18–312). Grand Rapids, MI: Eerdmans. (Original work written c. 428)

Aurelius, M. (2008). *Meditations* (Farquharson, A.S.L., Trans.). New York, NY: Oxford World's Classics.

Benedict, St. (2001). *The rule of St. Benedict* (L. Doyle, Trans.). Collegeville, MN: Liturgical Press.

Churchland, P. (1996). *The engine of reason, the seat of the soul: A philosophical journey into the brain.* Cambridge, MA: MIT Press.

Comte, A. (1998). Course on positive philosophy. In G. Lenzer (Ed.), *Auguste Comte and positivism: The essential writings* (pp. 71–306). New Brunswick, NJ: Transaction. (Original work published 1830–1842)

Edelstein, E., & Edelstein, L. (1998). *Asclepius: A collection and interpretation of the testimonies.* Baltimore, MD: Johns Hopkins.

Epictetus. (2008). *Epictetus: Discourses and selected writings* (R. Dobbins, Trans.). London, England: Penguin Classics.

Evagrius, P. (1972). *The Praktikos: Chapters on prayer.* Spencer, MA: Cistercian Press.

Ferngren, G. (2009). *Medicine and health care in early Christianity.* Baltimore, MD: Johns Hopkins.

Galen. (1952). *On the natural faculties* (A.J. Brock, Trans.). Cambridge, MA: Harvard University.

Galen. (1964). *Galen on the passions and errors of the soul* (P.W. Harkins, Trans.). Columbus, OH: Ohio State University.

Gergen, K. (1991). *The saturated self: Dilemmas of identity in contemporary life.* New York, NY: Basic Books.

Harmless, W. (2004). *Desert Christians: An introduction to the literature of early monasticism.* Oxford, England: Oxford University.

Hausherr, I. (1990). *Spiritual direction in the early Christian East* (A.P. Gythiel, Trans.). Kalamazoo, MI: Cistercian Press.

Holmes, A. (2000). *A life pleasing to God: The spirituality of the rules of St. Basil.* Kalamazoo, MI: Cistercian Press.

Hood, R., Jr., Hill, P. & Spilka, B. (2009). *The psychology of religion: An empirical approach* (4th ed.). New York, NY: Guilford.

Leuba, J.H. (1912). *A psychological study of religion: Its origin, function, and future.* New York, NY: Macmillan.

Leuba, J.H. (1925). *The psychology of religious mysticism.* New York, NY: Harcourt, Brace.

Linehan, M.M. (1993). *Cognitive-behavioral treatment of borderline personality disorder.* New York, NY: Guilford.

Linehan, M.M., Tutek, D.A., Heard, H.L., & Armstrong, H.E. (1994). Interpersonal outcome of cognitive behavioral treatment for chronically suicidal borderline patients. *American Journal of Psychiatry, 151,* 1771–1776. http://ajp.psychiatryonline.org/journal .aspx?journalid=13

Long, A.A. (1986). *Hellenistic philosophy: Stoics, Epicureans, Sceptics.* London, England: Duckworth.

Longrigg, J. (1998). *Greek medicine from the heroic to the Hellenistic age.* New York, NY: Routledge.

Mill, J.S. (2002). *A system of logic; Ratiocinative and inductive.* Honolulu, HI: University Press of the Pacific. (Original work published 1872)

Nelson, J. (2006). Missed opportunities in dialogue between psychology and religion. *Journal of Psychology and Theology, 34,* 205–216. http://journals.biola.edu/jpt

Nelson, J. (2009). *Psychology, religion, and spirituality.* New York, NY: Springer.

Nelson, J. & Slife, B.D. (in press). Theoretical and epistemological foundations. In L.B. Miller (Ed.), *Oxford handbook of the psychology of religion & spirituality.* New York, NY: Oxford University.

Piedmont, R.L. (2009). Editorial. *Psychology of Religion and Spirituality, 1,* 1–2. doi:10.1037/ a0015253

Pierre, J.M. (2001). Faith or delusion? At the crossroads of religion and psychosis. *Journal of Psychiatric Practice, 7,* 163–172. doi:10.1097/00131746-200105000-00004

Plotinus. (1991). *The Enneads* (S. MacKenna, Trans.). New York, NY: Penguin Books.

Porter, R. (2002). *Madness: A brief history.* Oxford, England: Oxford University.

Prichard, J.C. (1835). *A treatise on insanity, and other disorders affecting the mind.* London, England: Sherwood, Gilbert, and Piper.

Rea, M. (2002). *World without design: The ontological consequences of naturalism.* Oxford, England: Clarendon Press.

Richards, P.S. (2005). Theistic integrative psychotherapy. In L. Sperry, & E.P. Shafranske (Eds.), *Spiritually oriented psychotherapy* (pp. 259–285). Washington, DC: American Psychological Association.

Richards, P.S., & Bergin, A.E. (2004). A theistic spiritual strategy for psychotherapy. In P.S. Richards, & A.E. Bergin (Eds.), *Casebook for a spiritual strategy in counseling and psychotherapy* (pp. 1–32). Washington, DC: American Psychological Association.

Robins, C.J. (2002). Zen principles and mindfulness practice in dialectical behavior therapy. *Cognitive and Behavioral Practice, 9,* 50–57. doi:10.1016/S1077-7229(02)80040-2

Shweder, R., Goodnow, J., Hatano, G., LeVine, R., Markus, H., & Miller, P. (2006). The cultural psychology of development: One mind, many mentalities. In R. Lerner & W. Darron (Eds.), *Handbook of child psychology* (6th ed.): *Volume 1, Theoretical models of human development* (pp. 716–792). Hoboken, NJ: Wiley.

Sinkewicz, R. (Trans.). (2003). *Evagrius of Pontus: The Greek ascetic corpus.* Oxford, England: Oxford University.

Slife, B.D. (2005). Are the natural science methods of psychology comparable with theism? In A. Dueck, & C. Lee (Eds.), *Why psychology needs theology: A Radical Reformation perspective* (pp. 163–184). Grand Rapids, MI: Eerdmans.

Slife, B.D., Mitchell, L.J., & Whoolery, M. (2004). A theistic approach to therapeutic community: Non-naturalism and the Alldredge Academy. In P.S. Richards, & A. Bergin (Eds.), *Case-book for a spiritual strategy in counseling and psychotherapy* (pp. 35–54). Washington, DC: American Psychological Association.

Slife, B.D., & Reber, J. (2009). Is there a pervasive implicit bias against theism in psychology? *Journal of Theoretical and Philosophical Psychology, 29,* 63–79. http://www.apa.org/pubs/journals/teo/index.aspx

Slife, B.D., & Whoolery, M. (2006). Are psychology's main methods biased against the worldview of many religious people? *Journal of Psychology and Theology, 34,* 217–231. http://journals.biola.edu/jpt

Solomon, A. (2001). *The noonday demon: An atlas of depression.* New York, NY: Touchstone.

Tooby, J., & Cosmides, L. (1992). The psychological foundations of culture. In J.H. Barkow, L. Cosmides, & J. Tooby (Eds.), *The adapted mind: Evolutionary psychology and the generation of culture* (pp. 19–136). New York, NY: Oxford University Press.

Tooby, J., & Cosmides, L. (2005). Conceptual foundations of evolutionary psychology. In D. Buss (Ed.), *Handbook of evolutionary psychology* (pp. 5–67). New York, NY: John Wiley.

Veilleux, A. (Trans.). (1980). *Pachomian koinonia, Volume 1: The life of Saint Pachomius and his disciples.* Kalamazoo, MI: Cistercian Press.

Veilleux, A. (Trans.). (1981). *Pachomian koinonia, Volume 2: Pachomian chronicles and rules.* Kalamazoo, MI: Cistercian Press.

Wilson, E.O. (1978). *On human nature.* Cambridge, MA: Harvard University Press.

Zizioulas, J. (1985). *Being as communion.* Crestwood, NY: St. Vladimir's Seminary Press.

SCIENTIFIC THEISM: WHERE THE FORCE OF LOGIC IS DENIED ITS FORCE

*Fiona J. Hibberd**

ABSTRACT

Scientific theism aims to integrate a concept of deity with the key assumptions of science so as to proffer a single self-consistent conceptual system. If successful, it would mean that (a) it is empirically possible for some kind of supreme Being (or Beings) to caus-ally influence this world, and (b) introducing a concept of deity into explanations of our psycho-social life is not contrary to reason. The logically prior issue is whether some kind of supreme Being (or Beings) could possibly exist. This is primarily a conceptual matter to which there are three current approaches deserving of attention: classical theism; Plant-inga's modal argument for God; and Griffin's process theism. However, each is demon-strably flawed. This means that attempts to fashion a coherent concept of deity continue to elude theists; the tag "scientific theism" is still an oxymoron, and a theistic psychology remains an idle fancy.

Keywords: scientific theism, conceptual analysis, dualism, logic

In addressing theism in psychological science, it is perhaps prudent to begin with some distinctions and clarifications. First, I assume that some aspects of religion do not include theism and so to comment on theism is not to comment on the broader subject of religion, on the importance of sacred texts, or on the fact that religious interpretations continue to affect our practices and values. Second, theism is most commonly under-stood as the doctrine that a supreme Being or Beings exists, one that is transcendent from this world but with immanent aspects. I say *world* but it would be more accurate to use the expression *universe as a whole*. By this I mean everything that exists or occurs, has existed or occurred, and will exist and occur.

Theism, then, encompasses monotheism and polytheism. However, in this paper, I limit my comments to monotheism and use the word *God* to refer to the deity. Such usage is common across multiple religions. Third, I assume that a person's belief in "God" is a real situation, a genuine state

---
* *Author Note*: Fiona J. Hibberd, School of Psychology, University of Sydney.
Correspondence concerning this article should be addressed to Fiona J. Hibberd, School of Psychology, Brennan MacCallum Building (A18), University of Sydney, NSW 2006, Aus-tralia. Email: fiona.hibberd@sydney.edu.au

of affairs. When someone has faith in "God," this too is a real situation. Believing and having faith in "God" are genuine phenomena. So, too, are the effects of praying to "God," whatever they may be. (I have used quotation marks to distance myself from any implications regarding God's existence, but I shall not continue this practice throughout the paper. Nevertheless, the reader should assume that quotation marks are there: In referring to God, at no stage do I intend veridicality of reference.) And I assume that, for many, a person's faith is of central importance to their sense of self.

However, my concern here is neither with such experiences, nor with any psycho-social studies of them, nor with the psychotherapy or counseling of clients with theistic beliefs. I focus instead on whether God's existence *could* be real (i.e., whether it is logically possible for there to be some supreme Being). I know this is a matter of little or no consequence to some. For example, Slife & Reber (2009) maintained that theism's validity is less of a priority than its "...promise for psychology..." (p. 129). But what could its promise for psychology amount to if God's existence is not logically possible? Richards and Bergin (2005) went further: They claimed that

> ...the most valid and useful scientific theories and methods are those that acknowledge and provide insight into the role of divine intelligence in the origins and operations of the universe and the life within it, including human development, personality, and therapeutic change. (pp. 314–315)

But, again, this amounts to an uncritical question-begging. It assumes the very point at issue in the theism-science debate: the reality of some supreme Being. Whether God exists is of importance to the discipline of psychology for at least two reasons. First, if God's existence is not real, those psychologists investigating religion and spirituality are studying a very rich and important phenomenon but one that rests on false belief. I take it that all will be aware of this implication for their research. If the study conducted by Delaney, Miller and Bisonó (2007) is representative of American psychologists generally, the latter are apparently five time more likely to deny theism than the American population at large. Second, if God could not possibly exist, then *scientific theism, theistic realism, naturalistic theism* and any other similar doctrine rest on a premise that is false. This would mean that no theory can coherently make God's existence a feature of any explanation of our psycho-social life. *Believing* in God's existence may have explanatory force, but not God's existence per se. In an article entitled "Religion: Modernizing the case for God" (1980, pp. 61–63), *Time*

Magazine described Alvin Plantinga as "America's leading orthodox Protestant philosopher of God." To borrow from Plantinga (2000): "Everything really depends on the *truth* of Christian [sic] belief..." (viii).

Whether a supreme Being could be real is not an empirical matter; it cannot be answered by any empirical test of the research question "Does God exist?" or by relying on reports of religious experiences. Interpretations of any "evidence" will simply beg the question in favor of, or against, the presence of some deity. This is because the "evidence" does not strictly determine the theory that that evidence appears to support. Given a set of data, a particular theory does not follow logically if it is not implied by the data; there will be other possible theories. This is the *underdetermination thesis*; a theory, hypothesis, or prediction is underdetermined by the evidence (cf. Laudan & Leplin, 1991; McMullin, 1995; Newton-Smith, 1980). It is particularly relevant when we make a sizeable leap up the "theoretical food-chain" to explanatory concepts of an increasingly general nature or to concepts that are epistemically inaccessible. It means that if we are to prefer theory$_1$ over theory$_2$, theory$_1$ must have logical or conceptual virtues that theory$_2$ does not have (Kukla, 2001). Therefore, whether a supreme Being could be real must be addressed by *conceptual* test (i.e., by conceptual analysis).

Conceptual analysis involves assessing conceptual structures (such as theories, models, assumptions, concepts, hypotheses) for clarity, coherence, and consistency. This can reveal unacknowledged assumptions and inferences, inadequate definitions, and invalid arguments, thereby exposing that which is logically impossible. When Locke (1706/1924) likened his work to that of an under-laborer "... clearing the ground a little, and removing some of the rubbish that lies in the way to knowledge" (p. 7), conceptual testing is what he had in mind. Such labour is not only the province of philosophers. It is, in fact, an essential component of science because (a) the conceptual structures under review are addressing real scientific issues, and (b) such testing is a necessary condition of the right question being asked in the right way under the right assumptions (Machado & Silva, 2007). The pitfalls of not "clearing the conceptual ground" are captured by Bunge & Ardila's (1987) observation that "... many experimentalists waste precious resources measuring features that have not been adequately conceptualized, thereby producing heaps of useless data" (p. 126). Obviously, the conceptual test of a research question is no less fallible than any empirical test because we are, unfortunately, just as capable of making logical errors as we are of making methodological and observational ones. But given that it can often be shown simply from conceptual analysis that a theory is deficient, precisely why the conceptual test is so often ignored in psychology should be a matter of concern.

To be tested conceptually, the research question becomes "Can there be a coherent concept of deity?" or "Is God's existence logically possible?" If the results suggest that God is logically possible, then God's existence is empirically possible, some version of scientific theism is plausible, as is a theistic psychology. Conversely, if conceptual tests suggest the logical impossibility of God's existence, then it is empirically impossible, no version of scientific theism is plausible, and neither is a theistic psychology; theism would present no challenge to the scientific worldview.

Arguments for God's existence are at least one thousand years old (Oppy, 2011), and many today continue to defend a version of classical theism. Central to classical theism is the conception of a *transcendent* deity. I shall first explain why this entails a notion of God that is not logically possible. The failure of classical theism has led to the prominence, in some contemporary academic circles, of two alternative accounts: Plantinga's ontological argument for God and Griffin's development of process theism. Unsurprisingly, these two accounts receive no mention in the popularist publications of atheists Richard Dawkins, Sam Harris, and Christopher Hitchens. I examine both accounts, albeit in a condensed but, I hope, lucid form. I focus only on their ontological arguments, though each attempts to align a concept of deity with a variety of key philosophical topics, including philosophy of mind and revisions of the standard scientific worldview.

THE NOTION OF *TRANSCENDENCE* IN CLASSICAL THEISM

The notion of transcendence is central to classical or traditional theism. A transcendent deity is one which is "... separate from and over or above the world" (Macquarrie, 1984, p. 31). God is ontologically distinct from this spatio-temporal world. "In classical theism, God acts on the world but the world does not act on God. He affects the world, but is not affected by it" (Macquarrie, p. 40). Although most theists take God to *also* be an active presence in this world (God's immanence), in classical and popular understandings of theism, emphasis is given to the deity's transcendence.

Typically, the deity is characterized not only by a separateness from this world but also by intentional states and associated attributes, such as the ability to create, to inspire, to enlighten, to know, to make decisions, to communicate, and to have the capacity for love and forgiveness (i.e., the deity is personalized). It is taken to be bodiless, omnipresent, omniscient, wholly good and eternal (i.e., the deity has divine qualities). Much has been written about the precise nature of these qualities (e.g., Swinburne, 1996). But the central point is that God's qualities embody a perfection that is contrary to the conditions of anything existing or occurring *in this world*. God is a divine, supernatural, transcendent being whilst also active in this world.

This understanding of God as transcendent is so pervasive that it can be found in the theistic accounts of those who do not identify as classical theists. For example, in *A Spiritual Strategy for Counseling and Psychotherapy*, the psychologists Richards and Bergin (2005) aligned their version of scientific theism with non-classical accounts of God, including the two accounts discussed later in this paper. Yet on many occasions they made reference to a transcendent deity and they made clear their philosophical distance from pantheism, a position which denies that God is ontologically distinct from, and transcendent to, all else that exists. Whilst they may take God to be immanent, they also claimed that "... God exists, is the creator of the universe and life, and communicates with human beings through spiritual means" (Richards & Bergin, p. 314). Here they implied that God is separate from this world because to create anything requires the creator to be distinct or separate from that which she or he creates.

The notion of a transcendent deity is augmented by the supposed existence of God's divine qualities which distinguish God from all living beings. The point is that aspects of God's existence are purportedly of a type different from existence in this world. God's existence is not simply instantiated by a vast range of spatio-temporal occurrences; it is something more than, or besides, that. This is the primary conceptual difficulty for classical theism, and, as we shall see, not only for classical theism. The idea that there is a different mode of existence or being from this world implies a form of dualism and, down through the ages, most philosophers have agreed that dualism is implausible (Passmore, 1970): Why Richards and Bergin ignored this difficulty, I do not know. But they are not alone: The conviction that God in some sense transcends this world is ubiquitous amongst theists. For that reason, the argument against dualism bears repeating.

The Argument against Dualism

Is it logically possible for there to be something divine or supernatural, something other-worldly, something consistent with the classical theist's understanding of God as transcendent? If you think it is possible, you are implicitly invoking two realms or two different ways of being. One is divine, supernatural, and transcendent; the other is the common way of being that characterizes this world. God's mode of existence is different from the mode of this world. "So what?" you might reply, "surely, different kinds of things have different ways of being?" The answer is "no" because existence is not a kind of occurrence, or a type of thing, or a quality, or an attribute. This is reflected in our ordinary language. We do not say, for example, "Some patients exist and some do not," though we do say "Some patients are highly anxious and some are not." So, whilst an anxious state, as a type of occurrence, can be predicated of some, existence cannot. Existence is not a characteristic or quality that anyone has. Existence is not a genuine predicate, and so there are not types, levels, modes, classes, or orders of existence. There are many different kinds of things, many different processes, many different attributes, but there is only a single way of existing or occurring. There can be no qualification with respect to existence. This means that whatever characteristics this single or common way of being has, they are universal. They are the pervasive conditions or features of *all* that occurs. Uncovering these features is the concern of metaphysicians, and in philosophy these pervasive features are called *categories* and the adjective is *categorial*; the word "category" is *not* a synonym for kind, class, sort, or type.

So, if God is conceived as other-worldly, as in supernatural, divine, or transcendent, the implication is that God's existence is of a quite different type to existence in this world. There is a form of dualism. The onus is now on classical theism to explain how God influences this world or components of it (i.e., how there can be a relation between these two modes or realms of existence). That is, classical theism must account for God's effects on *this* world. The problem is that no account of this relation or connection can be given; the apparent relation cannot be accounted for without collapsing the two worlds or modes of existence into one. This is because both relata must be located in a single or common space-time region for the connection to occur. However, a common space-time region is contrary to the notion of God as transcendent, as other-worldly. Passmore (1970) refers to this argument as "the Humpty Dumpty argument" because:

> ... once we break up any system in a certain kind of way, it becomes quite impossible to put the pieces together again in a single situation: and yet, unless they can be so put together, the whole point of the breaking-up is lost. (p. 40)

Assume, for example, that God reveals some truth to you. (In this example, you and God are the two relata.) If God is transcendent, in the sense of other-worldly, the relation of revealing or communicating that God enters into (or stands in) must be in this other-worldly realm. But then if you receive the revelation, you must be other-worldly too. Yet you are not; you are a part of this world. Likewise, if the relation between you and God occurs in this world, then so must both of you. So, if revelation or communication with God is possible, there are not two different realms or worlds. Both you and God must be a part of the same world, namely, this actual world. Setting up a third realm not only invalidates the original two world thesis, it fails to address the logical point: that any relation, in connecting its relata, requires a common realm. It is not logically possible for there to be a connection between two or more relata if they have no common space-time region. And so, a transcendent or other-worldly God is not logically possible. This is why some philosophers and scientists have, over the decades, sought to avoid the classical understanding of theism. A transcendental theistic ontology fails the conceptual test. If there is to be a supreme Being of some kind, it must come under the same set of metaphysical categories that characterize this world.

PLANTINGA'S ONTOLOGICAL ARGUMENT FOR GOD

Many in theology draw on Plantinga's (1974) ontological argument for God, perhaps judging that its reliance on relatively recent developments in modal logic will mean an argument that avoids the difficulties above. Modal statements about possibility (what might be the case) and necessity (what must be the case) are said to refer to a system of logically possible worlds or alternate universes. Logically possible worlds are comprised of non-actual worlds and the actual world. In modal logic, the word *logical* is usually dropped. For example, a statement such as "8 + 3 = 11" is necessarily true; that is, true in all possible worlds, whereas the statement "Julia Gillard is the 27th Prime Minister of Australia" is not necessarily true; there may be possible worlds where Julia Gillard is not Prime Minister or where she is not even a politician. An alternate universe does not imply the dualism discussed above; it does not imply a different set of metaphysical categories from this world. There are hypothesized relationships between possible worlds, such as logical consistency and accessibility, but an alternative universe is one whose history and qualities typically differ from those of our world, rather like works of fiction.

Although the notion of possible worlds is an apparently valuable conceptual tool in some contexts, Girle (2003) judged it unhelpful in answering metaphysical questions. Nevertheless, some contemporary philosophers have few qualms about developing what were initially accounts of our everyday modal locutions (e.g., "Julia Gillard *might be* a teacher") into a metaphysical account of possible worlds. And Plantinga had few qualms about making this the bedrock of his ontological argument for God's existence. (See Oppy, 2011, for an outline of Platinga's argument.) His particular modal system involved an identity across possible worlds including this actual world; he did not restrict which attributes, qualities, properties or objects are necessary or impossible from world to world. For example: if Sigmund Freud was actually phallocentric, not only does Freud have the characteristic of being phallocentric in the actual world, but also, if he exists in certain other possible worlds, Freud has, in every world in which he exists, the characteristic of being phallocentric in that world. This is the highly controversial (though ambiguously named) trans-world identity thesis; there is no possible world that differs in some respect from the actual world.

With that proviso in place, Plantinga then led off with the notion of *maximal excellence* (omniscience, omnipotence, and moral perfection) and predicated *maximal greatness* of an entity that has maximal excellence in *every* possible world. From the premise that "there is a possible world in which there is an entity which possesses maximal greatness," the conclusion "there is an entity which possesses maximal greatness" was drawn. The inference is valid, but only if Plantinga is granted a set of apposite assumptions, including the acceptability of modal logic in dealing with ontological matters and trans-world identity. However, his overall argument is not only controversial but also implausible. It effectively treats *possibly necessary* as equivalent to *necessary*. Moreover, if you begin with the counter-claim that that there is no maximally great being in some possible world and then follow Plantinga's pattern of inference, you can validly conclude that maximal greatness is not exemplified in any world, that this, too, is necessary in every world and is, therefore, necessarily true. Obviously we cannot accept both arguments without contradiction and there is no other reason to accept the premise that maximal greatness is possibly exemplified (for elaborations on this and for other difficulties, see Divers, 2007; Mackie, 1982; Oppy, 2007, 2011; Sobel, 2004). As Plantinga (1974) conceded, his argument "... is not a successful piece of natural theology" (p. 219). And Mackie (1982) concluded that:

The view which is now being popularly disseminated, that recent advances in modal logic permit the construction of arguments which should disturb atheistic or agnostic philosophers, and give some long-awaited comfort to theistic ones, is simply false and quite without foundation (p. 62).

So we are still to find a plausible concept of deity that can be integrated with science.

GRIFFIN'S PROCESS THEISM

One very substantial attempt at integration lies in the naturalistic theism developed by Griffin (2000, 2001). Griffin's thesis was that (a) it is a mistake to assume that God must be transcendent, in the sense of supernaturalist or separate from this world, (b) it is also a mistake to assume that science must rest on atheism, a reductionist materialism, and sensationism (the assumption that we perceive only things that excite our physical sense organs), and (c) *process theism* can reconcile theism and science through a naturalistic, realistic framework that encompasses a *panentheistic* account of God. If Fetzer (2011) is right, Griffin's naturalistic theism is argued for through a straw man conception of science and an overly simplified model of evolution, notwithstanding his intention to adopt "... a more open form of naturalism..." (Griffin, 2000, p. 53). And Pailin's (2002) review of Griffin's *Religion and Scientific Naturalism: Overcoming the Conflicts* offers a list of provisional objections to Griffin's thesis concluding that it "... rests on claims that are not as obviously valid as he [Griffin] deems them to be" (p. 989; an exceptionally lucid and comprehensive overview of process theism is provided by Viney, 2008).

Panentheism means everything (pan) is in (en) God (theos), and the version of theism defended by Griffin is that the universe is part of God, though God is more than the universe in that some of God's attributes are quite unique to God. Griffin draws heavily from Whitehead's expansion of process philosophy into process theology and from Hartshorne's development of the latter. Whitehead's philosophy involves a number of complex and unusual concepts, some prima facie quite implausible. With respect to theism though, it is Whitehead's judgment that the order in this world, the emergence of new forms, our constant experience of possibilities from which we must choose, all signal the existence of "... an all-pervasive actuality worthy of the name God" (Griffin, 2000, p. 89). Whitehead believed that our understanding of reality and that of our own immediate experience is best explained if we include a concept of God in our scientific accounts. This resembles an abductive (or retroductive) inference, more commonly referred to as "an inference to the best explanation." This form of reasoning is central in the development of explanatory theories. Abduction "...consists in studying facts and devising a theory to explain them" (Peirce, 1934, p. 90). So, although a notion of deity is controversial, Whitehead's means of arriving at the notion, via an abductive inference, is standard in theory construction. And crucially, given the problem of dualism (as discussed above), Whitehead insisted that God's influence is constrained by the world's metaphysical nature as well as by the metaphysics of God's nature; that, unlike classical theism, God is not other-worldly. God does not stand outside the principles of metaphysics in order to interrupt them. Instead, God is the "chief exemplification" of such principles (Griffin, 2001, pp. 139–140).

What, then, is process theism's concept of God? Griffin's (2001) preference is for Hartshorne's and Cobb's account rather than Whitehead's. This Griffin (2001) argued, is because Whitehead's notion of God as a single actual entity is not consistent with his dictum that God cannot be otherworldly. God is conceptualized as a social being: "...an everlasting personally ordered society of divine occasions of experience" (p. 157). God's divine influence does not involve interrupting the causal interactions of this world. Importantly, then, process theism recognizes that causation is a metaphysical category and so a condition or feature of anything occurring at all. Causation is involved in the becoming of any actual entity, and this is a temporal process which issues in novelty. This becoming is, according to Whitehead et al., creativity, and so creativity is the primary metaphysical category. Everything that exists has creative power although God is the supreme creator:

> ...God has God's own creative power, distinct from that of the universe of finite actualities. Hence, each finite actual entity has its own creativity with which to exercise some degree of self-determination, so that it transcends the divine influence upon it. (Griffin, 2001, p. 142; I shall not address the thorny issue of whether self-determinism is compatible with causation.)

So, God's creativity does not involve creation *ex nihilio* (out of nothing). God has not created creativity and at no stage could God have ever unilaterally determined what is and what is not. In fact, contrary to classical theism, entities create in God a knowledge of their activity. That is to say, they change God by their activity which God, as omniscient, experiences. This is God's contingent nature. The world's events are contingent in that they could be other than they are and, therefore, God's knowledge of them is contingent: What God knows could always have been different.

So, in what sense is God *more* than the universe? In what sense is God divine and not just a "... puny godling..." (Macquarrie, 1984, p. 180)? Griffin's answer brings us to a concept central to process theism: a dipolar deity. God has attributes that are contrary to one another. Along with God's contingent or consequent nature, there is also God's abstract essence or primordial nature. God as changing is "... temporal, contingent, relative, dependent, changeable, and passible," but God as unchanging has also the attributes of "... timelessness, necessity, absoluteness, independence, and impassibility..." (Griffin, 2001, p. 161). This is God's divine, primordial character which, although it co-exists with the concrete states of God, "... is strictly immutable" (Griffin, p. 158). According to Griffin (2001), omniscience is one attribute of God's abstract essence: God maintains "perfect preservation of the past," with no lapse of memory, no loss of immediacy, regarding past and present actual occasions, as well as envisioning all possibilities eternally.

It is this account of God's primordial character that presents a major obstacle for panentheism. We are told that God, though contingent must exist necessarily, God though changing must be unchanging, though temporal must be non-temporal, and so on (Griffin, 2001, pp. 161–162). To illustrate this, I adapt the example provided by Griffin (p. 162). God's love for you is a concrete state of God but it includes God's necessary existence which is a feature of God's abstract essence. This seems to suggest that God's love for you is a sufficient condition of God's existence; that is, given God's love for you, necessarily God exists. Hence Hartshorne's (1970) claim that these contrasts are "... the ultimate or metaphysical contrarieties [and that]... the two poles of each contrast stand or fall together..." (p. 99). However, this kind of connection obtains everywhere. If you feed your cat, necessarily your cat exists; if I bush-walk in the Blue Mountains, necessarily the Blue Mountains exist, and so on. There is nothing divine or dipolar or primordial about it; it is just a piece of elementary logic. In Griffin's example, there is still no sense in which God is *more than* the universe. Perhaps, then, something else is intended? It should not be that aspects of God's existence are of a different *type* because this would suggest that God is an exception to the categories of metaphysics. And that is precisely the (classical theists') problem that Griffin et al. are concerned to avoid.

Yet avoid it, they do not. God is an exception to the metaphysical "rules" in two respects. First, whilst everything that exists or occurs in this world is causally dependent upon some set of antecedent conditions; that is, to be, or to become, is to be brought about, this does not apply to God's abstract essence. In Hartshorne's (1970) words:

> A theistic philosophy... cannot admit symmetry in this relation of existential dependence, since God is not thought to depend upon any particular creatures for his very existence. Relations to God are intrinsic to a creature, constitutive of its very existence; but relations to the creatures are extrinsic to the mere existence of God (though not to his total actuality, including his contingent qualities). (p. 226)

Setting aside the controversial issue of internal or constitutive relations (see Hibberd, 2005), the point here is that the conditions of God's existence *are not the conditions of existence for anything else*. Your existence is contingent: It is causally dependent upon the occurrence of many, many complex causal interactions. But although God is affected by contingencies, God's *existence* is not contingent: God is not causally dependent upon antecedent events "for his very existence." And so, God stands outside the principles of metaphysics; dualism has not been avoided in process theism, and we are no better off than we were under classical theism.

A second objection pertains to God's supposed temporality and timelessness (in the sense of *everlasting*). Griffin (2000) was surely right in noting that the fundamental nature of temporality is often overlooked. Toomela and Valsiner (2010) have observed that "... one fundamentally important category missing in mainstream psychology is time and all time-related aspects of mind" (p. xi). For example, sensing, perceiving, believing, knowing, etc., involve relations that have a temporal dimension to them. However, the difficulty for process theism is that temporality and its contrary timelessness are improperly conceptualized as attributes. As discussed earlier, an attribute is a kind of feature or characteristic predicated of a subject. Time, however, is categorical—to be, is to be located temporally (and spatially, of course); everything that occurs, occurs sometime and somewhere, a point recognized by Whitehead (1929) and reinforced by Griffin (2000; for example, if I run slowly, this presupposes temporality. Temporality is neither an attribute of myself nor of my running.). The consequence of their mistake is that the deity cannot be dipolar with respect to time because time, as a metaphysical category has no real opposite; it is universal.

In short, although Hartshorne's development of a dipolar deity is critical to panentheism's concept of God, it is nevertheless ill-conceived. It places God's primordial nature *outside* the categorial, metaphysical framework, outside this world's causal nexus. When all existents in this world are subject to the cycle of coming into being and subsequently ceasing to be, God's primordial nature is not. God is not the chief exemplification of all metaphysical principles if God's primordial nature is non-contingent and timeless.

Conclusion

Belief in God is epistemically substandard, not because of any absence of evidence but because there is evidence of absence. This evidence is conceptual. The ontological arguments for God's existence show that a coherent and plausible concept of deity remains unfeasible; it remains contrary to reason. Classical theism ignores the logical impossibility of a transcendental, other-worldly Being. Plantinga's attempt to account for God through modal logic begs the question in God's favor and insists on the equivalence between "possibly necessary" and "necessary". And although Griffin's appropriation of Whitehead's and Hartshorne's process theism is the most commendable recent account of theism, its attempt to identify the way in which God is more than the universe, without being other than or beyond the universe, does not succeed. Their notion of a dipolar deity is one that, in certain respects, transcends the conditions of existence. It is no less a conceptual roadblock for process theism than for classical theism.

In short, there is still no good reason to accept scientific theism, or any other similar doctrine, into psychology. The conceptual evidence points to the logical impossibility of God's existence, ergo the empirical impossibility too. This means that no theory can coherently employ a concept of God in order to explain any aspect of our psycho-social life. Notwithstanding the implicit exhortations of some to deny the force of logic, that logic continues to support the view that theism holds no promise for psychology.

References

Bunge, M., & Ardila, R. (1987). *Philosophy of psychology*. New York, NY: Springer-Verlag.
Delaney, H.D., Miller, W.R., & Bisonó, A.M. (2007). Religiosity and spirituality among psychologists: A survey of clinician members of the American Psychological Association. *Professional Psychology: Research and Practice, 38*(5), 538–546. doi:10.1037/0735-7028.38.5.538
Divers, J. (2007). The modal metaphysics of Alvin Plantinga. In D.-P. Baker (Ed.), *Alvin Plantinga* (pp. 71–92). New York, NY: Cambridge University Press.
Fetzer, J.H. (2011). Evolution and atheism: Has Griffin reconciled science and religion? *Synthese, 178*, 381–396. doi:10.1007/s11229-009-9546-4
Girle, R. (2003). *Possible worlds*. Chesham, England: Acumen.
Griffin, D.R. (2000). *Religion and scientific naturalism*. Albany, NY: SUNY Press.
Griffin, D.R. (2001). *Reenchantment without supernaturalism. A process philosophy of religion*. Ithaca, NY: Cornell University Press.
Hartshorne, C. (1970). *Creative synthesis and philosophic method*. London, England: SCM Press.

Hibberd, F.J. (2005). *Unfolding social constructionism*. New York, NY: Springer.

Kukla, A. (2001). *Methods of theoretical psychology*. Cambridge, MA: MIT Press.

Laudan, L., & Leplin, J. (1991). Empirical equivalence and underdetermination. *The Journal of Philosophy, LXXXVIII*(9), 449–472. doi:10.2307/2026601

Locke, J. (1706/1924). *An essay concerning human understanding* (5th ed.). Oxford, England: Oxford University Press.

Machado, A., & Silva, F.J. (2007). Toward a richer view of the scientific method: The role of conceptual analysis. *American Psychologist, 62*(7), 671–681. doi:10.1037/0003-066X.62.7.671

Mackie, J.L. (1982). *The miracle of theism. Arguments for and against the existence of God*. Oxford, England: Clarendon Press.

Macquarrie, J. (1984). *In search of deity: An essay in dialectical theism*. London, England: SCM Press.

McMullin, E. (1995). Underdetermination. *The Journal of Medicine and Philosophy, 20*, 233–252. http://jmp.oxfordjournals.org/

Newton-Smith, W. (1980). The underdetermination of theory by data. In R. Hilpinen (Ed.), *Rationality in science* (pp. 91–110). Dordrecht, Holland: D. Reidel.

Oppy, G. (2007). Natural theology. In D.-P. Baker (Ed.), *Alvin Plantinga* (pp. 15–47). New York, NY: Cambridge University Press.

Oppy, G. (2011). Ontological arguments. Retrieved from http://stanford.library.usyd.edu.au/entries/ontological-arguments/#OntArg21sCen

Pailin, D.A. (2002). Review. Religion and scientific naturalism: Overcoming the conflicts. *Zygon, 37*(4), 985–990. http://www.zygonjournal.org/

Passmore, J. (1970). *Philosophical reasoning* (2nd ed.). London, England: G. Duckworth & Co.

Peirce, C.S. (1934). *Collected papers of Charles Sanders Peirce* (*Vol. V*). Cambridge, MA: Harvard University press.

Plantinga, A. (1974). *The nature of necessity*. Oxford, England: Oxford University Press.

Plantinga, A. (2000). *Warranted Christian belief*. New York, NY: Oxford University Press.

Religion: Modernizing the case for God: Philosophers refurbish the tools of reason to sharpen arguments for theism. (1980). *Time, 115*(14), 61–63. http://www.time.com

Richards, P.S., & Bergin, A.E. (2005). *A spiritual strategy for counseling and psychotherapy* (2nd ed.). Washington, DC: American Psychological Association.

Slife, B.D., & Reber, J.S. (2009). The prejudice against prejudice: A reply to the comments. *Journal of Theoretical and Philosophical Psychology, 29*(2), 128–136. doi:10.1037/a0017509

Sobel, J.H. (2004). *Logic and theism. Arguments for and against beliefs in God*. Cambridge, England: Cambridge University Press.

Swinburne, R. (1996). *Is there a God?* New York, NY: Oxford University Press.

Toomela, A., & Valsiner, J. (2010). *Methodological thinking in psychology: 60 years gone astray?* Charlotte, NC: Information Age Publishing.

Viney, D. (2008). Process theism. Retrieved from http://stanford.library.usyd.edu.au/entries/process-theism/

Whitehead, A.N. (1929). *Process and reality: An essay in cosmology. Gifford lectures delivered in the University of Edinburgh during the session 1927–28*. Cambridge, England: Cambridge University Press.

THEISTIC PRACTICE AND COMMUNITY INTERVENTION

Kari A. O'Grady*

ABSTRACT

This article asserts that psychotherapists and counselors are most effective in their work with clients when their practice approach aligns with their worldviews. Assessment and intervention strategies for theistic counselors and psychotherapists are proposed. An example of a theistic community intervention conducted following the 2010 earthquake in Haiti is presented. Research conducted in tandem with this intervention found that survivors tended to grow spiritually and psychologically following the earthquake when they experienced the following: (a) perceived daily experiences with God or a higher force, (b) a belief that God or a higher force is aware of them, (c) a sense of community and purpose within the community, and (d) the view that God has and will intervene on their behalf.

Keywords: trauma, theism, community, practice, intervention

The role of theism in psychology and psychotherapy has varied substantially over time and across scholars. Some scholars, including those who might identify themselves as theists, prefer to address psycho-spiritual variables non-theistically as they feel that theism in psychology taints true scientific investigation. Other scholars identify as non-theistic and yet are interested in studying psycho-spiritual variables, so they do so from a non-theistic stance. These two groups tend to feel satisfied with the status quo in which theism is withheld from psychological investigation. Theist scholars tend to be unsatisfied with current conditions in the field.

Many researchers have acknowledged theism by addressing theistic factors as viable areas of investigation within the psychological sciences. Based upon these findings, other scholars have created theistic interventions that are intended to assess and treat psycho-spiritual concerns (Aten, O'Grady, Worthington, 2011; Richards & Bergin, 2005). The movement of theism back into psychology and psychotherapy required a great deal of courage, tenacity, and finesse by our forebears in the field

* Author Note: Kari A. O'Grady, Pastoral Counseling Department, Loyola University Maryland.

Correspondence concerning this article should be addressed to Kari A. O'Grady, Department of Pastoral Counseling, Loyola University Maryland, 8890 McGaw Road, Columbia, MD 21045. Email: mailto:kaogrady@loyola.edu (i.e., William James, Allen Bergin, Gordon Allport, etc.). They opened a door that had been firmly closed by scholars who were fighting to gain a serious foothold for psychology within the scientific community. Although there is ample room to criticize the developmental journey of the field relative to theism, another perspective is that the field is engaged in a natural, necessary, and evolutionary trajectory towards an inclusive, ethical, and sophisticated conceptualization of psychological science and practice.

THEISTIC PSYCHOTHERAPY

Despite some intellectual advancement, some would argue that in many ways, the field is still in its infancy and that we are only able to speculate about the implications of a truly inclusive conceptualization of science in which theism is accepted on an assumptive level. Currently, most theistic scholars still study spirituality as an object of study rather than an acceptable framework for study (O'Grady & Richards, 2011). Also, the few clinicians who are trained in spiritual interventions are trained to understand spiritual issues from a non-theistic mindset and intervene likewise. For example, a clinician trained to assess and address God image issues with a client might be considered to be a theistic psychotherapist. However, this label may be misapplied if the clinician was trained to assess God image as an illusory compensatory feature of the psyche rather than to assess the client's God image based upon his or her actual relationship with God or a higher force (O'Grady & Richards, 2007). The latter form of assessment is based upon a theistic assumption and will likely lead to more cohesive and responsible treatment planning. The former represents a conceptualization of a spiritual variable from a non-theistic lens. Treatment planning created by a theist for a theist but assessed and implemented through a non-theistic approach is likely to be to some degree disingenuous and inconsistent in its delivery. Some may even argue that a clinician cannot be seriously considered a theistic psychotherapist when theism is removed from any level of the practice protocol (Slife, Stevenson, & Wendt, 2010).

A THEISTIC APPROACH TO PRACTICE

A theistic approach to psychological practice would necessarily include a theistic view of the clinician, the client/population, assessment and intervention. The remainder of this article will touch on a few of the implications of theism for these aspects of psychotherapy and community intervention.

A Theistic View of the Clinician

A truly inclusive view of psychotherapy would assume that various worldviews can reasonably underpin and motivate clinicians' approaches to therapy and community intervention. Non-theistic clinicians would likely espouse a worldview that deliberately kept God or a higher force out their views of the world, and thus their approach to clinical work would be void of theistic understanding or expression. Theistic clinicians, on the other hand, would likely espouse a worldview that included a belief in a higher force or God, and thus they would be open to theistic influences and understandings. Additionally, many people espouse a theistic worldview but wish to compartmentalize their beliefs from their clinical work, and they would not, therefore, identify as theistic clinicians.

People's worldviews are likely influenced by their professional training but primarily precede and supersede their training experiences. Their professional training does, however, strongly influence the degree to which they feel safe enough to acknowledge to themselves and/or others the nature of their worldviews (Schulte, Skinner, & Claiborn, 2002). Whether or not someone personally espouses a theistic or non-theistic worldview can best be identified in one's private reflections throughout the day. Questions one might ask oneself to better determine one's worldview could include such questions as:

a) Do I pray to higher forces or God in my private life?
b) Do I attribute some events to divine influences?
c) Do I review my behavior relative to my relationship with God or higher forces?
d) Do I make some choices based on a belief in or relationship with higher forces or God?
e) Do I talk to family or close friends about theological issues from a view that supposes a higher force?

Once psychotherapists and counselors have identified a theistic worldview, they create congruence by aligning their practice with their views. Congruent theistic psychotherapists would most likely approach the counseling context from a different angle than those who do not identify as theistic. Approximately 96% of Western clinicians do espouse a theistic worldview

(Princeton Religion Research Center 2000), so there is critical mass for the justification, development, and expansion of theistically based, empirically tested approaches to psychotherapy and community intervention.

Research has demonstrated that many counselors and psychotherapists who identify as theistic do indeed approach their clinical practice differently than their non-theistic counterparts. For instance, O'Grady and Richards (2010) found that of 333 theistic helping professionals surveyed, 86.6% of the respondents indicated they believe that God may inspire helping professionals in their work with clients and patients, and 74.7% of the respondents indicated that they have personally felt God's inspiration in their professional practice. Respondents in this study indicated that their ability to work with clients and to endure the challenges of clinical work and research endeavors was enhanced through an ongoing relationship with God (O'Grady & Richards, 2011). As such, most theistic psychotherapists likely believe that one important way for clinicians to provide good care for their clients is to nurture their own spiritual lives. Just as clinicians generally agree that obtaining adequate sleep, developing outside hobbies or interests, and engaging in healthy relationships are crucial for job performance in the clinic, theistic clinicians generally concur that nurturing their spiritual lives is a critical component for enhancing performance (Wicks, 2008). In fact, if such self-care were ignored, some psychotherapists might feel hypocritical and unprepared to engage in therapy with their clients. Likewise, studies have shown that counselors' spirituality can serve as a buffer against secondary traumatization in clinicians working with war veterans and other trauma populations (O'Grady, 2011; Trippany, White Kress, & Wilcoxon, 2004; Voss Horrell, Holohan, Didion, & Vance, 2011).

Perhaps most importantly, a theistic view of the practitioner promotes congruence between the internal processing of the therapist and his interaction with clients. Many mainstream theories of psychology address the importance of congruence between beliefs and behaviors for healthy human functioning and for ethical and effective clinical practice (e.g. Lazarus, 1971; Rogers, 1951, Yalom, 1970). Theistic psychotherapists and counselors who treat themselves as spiritual beings are more likely to view their clients as spiritual beings than those who detach their spirituality from their clinical work (Miller & Delaney, 2002).

A Theistic View of the Client

According to the belief systems of many of the major world religions, a theistic perspective of psychology includes the assumptions that (a) God or a higher force has vested interest in human affairs and, at times, inter-action with human activity; (b) humans have a soul or spirit that interacts with other aspects of self, others, and other aspects of reality; (c) humans are inherently social beings; (d) humans have the ability to elect altruistic options over personal gratification; and (e) experiences do not need to be observable to be real (see O'Grady, 2011; Richards & Bergin, 2005). Theistic psychology in practice would manifest as assessments and interventions that emerged from these assumptions, because the clinician would view the client form within these understandings.

For example, because theism espouses the view that God interacts with humans, the therapist might ask the following questions: *How would you describe your past/present relationship with God or a higher force? In what ways, if any, do you experience the God of your understanding in your everyday life?* Further, from a theistic perspective, humans are relational in nature so a therapist might explore clients' relationships, sense of uni-versality, and/or feelings of community or the lack thereof in their lives, and how these relationships impact or emerge from their spirituality. The main point here is that a theistic view of the client frames the client's nature holistically; thus, theories of human functioning such as personal-ity, development, family systems, cognition, and psychopathology would would be constructed non-reductionistically and consistently with the-istic views (Miller & Delaney, 2002). In other words, just as a pet owner would not consider taking her pet goldfish for a walk, giving it a bath, and tossing it a bone because such treatment would defy her beliefs about the nature of a goldfish, theistic psychotherapists would not conduct assess-ments, plan treatments, or intervene with clients in a strictly secular way as it would defy theistic therapists' beliefs about the nature of humans. Neither would they intervene in such way that their clients were made to feel like a "fish out of water," because the very features that define humans were ignored. Piedmont (2005) expressed this well: "When we examine the numinous, we are taking an intimate look at our humanity and what it is that makes our species unique" (p. 269). The assessments and inter-ventions would differ when working with theistic versus non-theistic cli-ents, but the likely viewpoint of the therapist regarding the client's human nature would not alter.

Theistic Assessment

As mentioned earlier, theistic psychological assessment is multidimen-sional in its scope: broad enough to include all aspects of the client, including spiritual features. A number of researchers in the field of the psychology of religion and spirituality have created assessment protocols that tap into theistic aspects of client experiences (see Aten, O'Grady, Worthington, 2011; Richards, Bartz & O'Grady, 2009; Richards & Bergin, 2005). Although there have been a number of assessments that measure people's spiritual and/or religious lives, many of these instruments approach the topic of spiritual and religious assessment non-theistically. One way such protocols can be recognized is by their lack of attention to relational dynamics of spirituality, in particular relationship with a higher force.

For instance, many measures of religious commitment investigate people's religious practice, but they neglect to assess how people's experience with God influences their practice (Hill & Hood, 1999). We do obtain important information when we explore whether or not someone attends church, reads sacred texts, or makes financial contributions to their religious organization; however, if we stop there, we may be overlooking important diagnostic information. How much more fruitful might be an assessment that asked why clients tithe, or what they experience from attending church services, or how their understanding of their sacred texts informs their relationship with the God of their understanding? Such questions would appreciably inform the direction of therapy and the utility of spiritual interventions.

Theistic Intervention

A theistic view of psychology and psychotherapy promotes treatment planning derived from theistically oriented assessment. Theistic interventions include the possibility that both the client and the clinician may experience spiritual transcendence in the therapy session as well as outside of the therapy office. From a theistic perspective, psychotherapists and counselors make efforts to cultivate a therapeutic environment that welcomes spiritual influences (West, 2000). This includes the therapist remaining open to such influences, developing sensitivity to intuitive impressions, and allowing for silence and reflection during the session (O'Grady & Barz, in press; O'Grady & Richards, 2010; Richards & O'Grady, 2007). Communicating empathy, respect, and connectedness with the client also encourages spiritual space in psychotherapy. Interventions might be as simple as asking such questions as *What did you experience in the silence?* Another technique might include asking the client to place a hand over his or her heart and asking, *How are you feeling in your heart in this moment?* Questions of this nature can help foster sensitivity to internal and spiritual processing (O'Grady & Bartz, 2011). As clients become more familiar with calming down and tuning into their internal functioning, they are often able to connect more frequently with their spirituality in the moment (Walsh, 1999).

Clients' prayer life can play an important role in their healing and growth. A theistic psychotherapist explores this aspect of clients' lives with the assumption that clients are experiencing an actual relationship with an existent being and not simply a compensatory or illusory figure (O'Grady & Richards, 2007). This relationship, like other relationships in clients' lives, may be functional and supportive sometimes but harmful or unfulfilling at other times. A non-theistic approach to prayer life assessment and intervention would probably be to ignore it altogether. Psychologists interested in studying spiritual variables or addressing spiritual issues in psychotherapy, may, from a non-theistic viewpoint, treat prayer life as a means to understanding the *real* relationships in the client's life but not worthy of consideration in and of itself. However, a theistic psychotherapist would address prayer life and do so assuming that involvement with a higher force has its own inherent benefits for mental health and emotional well-being and that disruption in prayer life processes may lead to psychological angst (Pargament, Murray-Swank, Magyar, & Ano, 2005). Understanding clients' prayer life can *also* provide important insights into other aspects and relationships of their lives.

For theistically oriented clients, it can be helpful to ask them from time to time if they notice any changes occurring in their relationship with God or a higher force. Research indicates that an individual's relationship with God or a higher force has implications for recovery in trauma situations (Koenig, 2006; Richards, Smith, Berrett, O'Grady, & Bartz, 2009). One question theistic psychotherapists might consider asking their clients who report a traumatic experience is *How has your relationship with God changed since the traumatic event?*

The next section of this article will address implications for theistic community intervention in trauma situations. Community trauma intervention conducted following the 2010 earthquake in Haiti will be presented as the backdrop for this discussion.

THEISTIC PRACTICE IN THE COMMUNITY

The devastating earthquake in Haiti on January 12, 2010 killed over 230,000 people and injured many more. One year later, 1.2 million people were still living in tents. The author and a small team of researchers/counselors conducted research and provided individual and community trauma intervention 6 months following the disaster (O'Grady, Rollison, Hanna, Schreiber-Pan, & Ruiz, 2011). The premise behind waiting 6 months to intervene was due to the investigators' interest in studying how people's relationship with God impacts posttraumatic growth and spiritual transformation following a disaster event. Post-traumatic growth cannot be easily assessed immediately following a trauma event, but is usually best investigated at least 6 months following the event when processes such as meaning making are more fully activated (Tedeschi & Calhoun, 2004). Additionally, they wished to aid in trauma recovery rather than conduct crisis intervention.

Theistic Investigation

While in Haiti, the team conducted both a qualitative and quantitative study. Because the lead investigator is a theistic psychologist, she selected research questions and survey instruments with theistic content. For example, the investigators were interested in exploring posttraumatic growth and spiritual transformation from a relational perspective. The majority of Haitians are theistic (CIA: The World Factbook, 2010), so they determined that investigating an individual's relationship with "God" was appropriate for this population and consistent with the theistic views of the researchers. The research questions were designed to discover how the nature and degree of individuals' relationships with God affected whether or not they experienced growth and/or spiritual transformation following a large scale trauma (O'Grady, et al., 2011). Along with a measure that assessed individuals' relationships with transcendence more generally, they also chose a scale that measured individuals' relationships with "God" specifically (Hall & Edwards, 1996; Underwood & Teresi, 2002). They wanted to determine the impacts of these measures on spiritual and psychological transformation. Studies have demonstrated that spiritual transformation and posttraumatic growth were distinct constructs, with some correlation with one another (Underwood & Teresi, 2002). The researchers/counselors also included questions that queried whether or not participants had encountered religious and spiritual experiences during the earthquake. The qualitative study included semi-structured interview questions regarding experiences with God and meaning-making during and following the earthquake. The type of questions the researchers/counselors asked in their study also guided the way they conducted their interventions.

Theistic Community Intervention

The team worked with local clergy and religious organizations (LDS Charities and Catholic Charities) to learn about the needs of the people prior to intervening. The clergy members stated that a number of members of their congregation had been relocated into tent communities after the loss of their homes. Although the congregants were surrounded by others in the tent community, the immediate and unexpected rearrangement of their social environment created feelings of seclusion. The relocation and losses created both a sense of despair and isolation as well as struggles to make meaning of the event.

Assessment. The members of this community shared stories of profound loss, with nearly all people reporting that they had lost a loved one in the earthquake. Many had also lost their occupations and schools, experienced health declines, and all in the community had been uprooted from their neighborhoods. They expressed deep concern about their futures. The individuals and families also shared stories of faith and their beliefs about God's role during and following the earthquake. Formal and informal assessments of these individuals indicated that daily experiencing God's interaction in their lives, believing that God was aware of them at this time in their lives, and believing that God had a purpose for their lives prompted spiritual transformation and psychological growth and hope for their future and the future of Haiti. The majority (81%) of the people in the community stated that they felt God's guidance or inspiration during the earthquake, with many attributing their survival to this guidance. On the other hand, feeling unneeded and a lack of community instigated symptoms of depression and despair (O'Grady et al., 2011).

Collaboration. Following the meetings with leaders and clergy, and after assessing the members of the community, the team met again with clergy, local leaders, and a volunteer medical doctor to formulate basic treatment planning that would be primarily implemented by the local helpers in the community, including the clergy members after the departure of the research/counseling team. The members of the research/counseling team interacted with the clergy members as "fellow believers" in a higher force. This approach garnered respect and appreciation from the locals towards the team, fostering a sense of fellowship and collaboration. Meeting with the clergy and local leaders allowed for humble, culturally sensitive, and collaborative planning of intervention strategies and the formulation of an expanded treatment team.

Strategy. The strategies were derived from the theistically grounded assessments and constructed based upon theistic assumptions. The

treatment team preceded with the development of a community intervention based upon the assumptions that: (a) God had, could, and likely
would interact on the behalf of those in the community, (b) humans are
inherently social beings, (c) humans have the ability to elect altruistic
behaviors, and often experience a sense of purpose and meaning when
serving others; and (d) experiences do not need to be observable to be
real. Due to the assumption that people are social beings, and because
of their population's expressed feelings of isolation, the treatment team
decided that creating a sense of community was essential. Additionally,
the treatment team determined to activate the community-wide belief
system which assumed that people can find strength, comfort, hope, and
guidance from experiencing each other and the divine. Finally, the treatment team invoked help from God on their behalf and on the behalf of
those they were attempting to help.

   Intervention. The treatment team facilitated a community town meeting, conducted predominately by a respected local leader. The leader
encouraged members of the tent community to share their concerns
and their needs in a public, group gathering. Their concerns and needs
were consistent with the concerns and needs assessed individually by the
counseling/research team previously. The tent community members then
brainstormed about how to strengthen and support one another during
this difficult time. They elected to meet together one day a week for a
prayer meeting and on another day for community "games day." They also
decided to meet together in the evenings to sing songs and hymns and to
meet together in one week with a list of needs and a list of gifts or talents
they possessed. The lists were to be shared with the intention of aligning
needs and gifts. Additionally, they opted to regularly review as families
the changes they experienced in their relationship with God from week
to week. A 6 month follow-up of the tent community indicated that the
community had consistently implemented their plans and that the overall
affect, psychological functioning, and sense of spiritual well-being within
the tent community had improved.

Implications of Theism

This community intervention could have been implemented non-theistically and likely produced positive results. There was not a control group
used for evaluating the outcomes, so the advantages of approaching the
local leaders, clergy, and community members theistically compared to
non-theistically is unknown. There is research, however, that does indicate

that spiritually oriented clients are more willing to openly share and feel an alliance with spiritually oriented therapists and helpers (Richards & Bergin, 2005). Furthermore, given that spirituality is an aspect of culture, a theistic approach with this population demonstrated respect for the local values and customs which has been shown to create sensitive and effective movement within individuals and communities (Leach & Aten, 2010). Finally, from a theistic perspective, invoking divine help on the behalf of another and oneself may enhance and/or alter outcomes (O'Grady & Richards, 2010, 2011; Plante & Sherman, 2001). From a theistic perspective, it is probable that some of the transformation experienced within the tent community is the result of collaborative efforts of the individuals involved and also partly due to divine intervention in response to concerted prayer.

CONCLUSION

A truly theistic approach to psychological practice and community intervention begins with the view that theism is a viable worldview for study and application in clinical work. From this perspective, theistic assumptions that stem from a theistic worldview are explicated to create assessment protocols that inform theistic intervention strategies. The argument for an approach to practice that includes theistic foundations has been presented by numerous outstanding scholars in the field and tested through rigorous research (Nelson & Slife, 2006; Richards & Bergin, 2005; Richards, Hardman, & Berrett, 2007). There seems to be sufficient advancement to transition into an expansive, more inclusive view of psychological science and practice.

Some reputable scholars maintain that theistic assumptions would thwart scientific progress in the field, while others contest that modernistic, non-theistic assumptions interfere with thorough investigation. Regardless of one's position, a common set of best practice guidelines directs practitioners to be congruent in their work with clients. Congruence for non-theistic counselors and psychotherapists implies that they work with clients non-theistically; congruence for theistic psychotherapists and counselors implies that psychotherapists and counselors who espouse a theistic worldview engage in clinical work grounded in the view that a higher force does exist and influences the world and those living in it. A higher standard of congruence would further assume that theistic counselors and psychotherapists may be better equipped to address the concerns of theistic clients than their non-theistic counterparts. *Clinician, know thyself.*

References

Aten, J.D., O'Grady, K.A., & Worthington, E.L. (2011). The psychology of religion and spirituality for clinicians. In J.D. Aten, K.A. O'Grady, & E.L. Worthington (Eds). *The psychology of religion and spirituality for clinicians: Using research in your practice* (pp. 1–12). New York, NY: Routledge.

CIA. The World Factbook. (2010 Oct. 06). Haiti: People: Religions. Retrieved from https://www.cia.gov/library/publications/the-world-factbook/geos/ha.html

Hall, T.W., & Edwards, K.J. (1996). The initial development and factor analysis of the Spiritual Assessment Inventory. *Journal of Psychology and Theology, 24*, 233–246. http://journals.biola.edu/jpt

Hill, P.C., & Hood, R.W. (Eds.). (1999). *Measures of religiosity*. Birmingham, AL: Religious Education Press.

Koenig, H.G. (2006). *In the wake of disaster: Religious responses to terrorism & catastrophe*. West Conshohocken, PA: Templeton Foundation Press.

Lazarus, A.A. (1971). *Behavior therapy and beyond*. New York, NY: McGraw-Hill.

Leach, M.M., & Aten, J.D. (Eds.). (2010). *Culture and the therapeutic process: A guide for mental health professionals*. New York, NY: Routledge.

Miller, W.R., & Delaney, H.D. (2002). Psychology as the science of human nature: Reflections and research directions. In W.R. Miller and H.D. Delaney (Eds.), *Judeo-Christian perspectives on psychology: Human nature, motivation, and change* (pp. 291–308). Washington, DC: American Psychological Association.

Nelson, J.M., & Slife, B.D. (2006). Introduction to the special issue. *Journal of Psychology and Theology. 34*(3), 217–223. http://journals.biola.edu/jpt

O'Grady , K.A. (2011). The role of inspiration in organizational life. *Journal of Management, Spirituality, & Religion, 8*(3), 257–272. doi:10.1080/14766086.2011.599148

O'Grady, K.A., & Bartz, J.D. (2011). Addressing spiritually transcendent experiences in psychotherapy. In J.D. Aten, K.A. O'Grady, & E.L. Worthington (Eds). *The psychology of religion and spirituality for clinicians: Using research in your practice* (pp. 161–188). New York, NY: Routledge.

O'Grady, K.A., & Richards, P.S. (2007). God image and theistic psychotherapy. *Journal of Spirituality and Mental Health, 9*, 183–209. doi:10.1300/J515v09n03_09

O'Grady, K.A., & Richards, P.S. (2010). The role of inspiration in the helping professions. *Psychology of Religion and Spirituality, 2*, 57–66. doi:10.1037/a0018551

O'Grady, K.A., & Richards, P.S. (2011). The role of inspiration in scientific scholarship and discovery: Views of theistic scientists. *EXPLORE: The Journal of Science & Healing (7)* 6, 354–362. doi:10.1016/j.explore.2011.08.004.

O'Grady, K.A., Rollison, D.G., Hanna, T.S., Schreiber-Pan, H., & Ruiz, M.A. (2011). HAITI and faith in times of trauma: Exploring posttraumatic growth and spiritual transformation following the 2010 earthquake. Paper presented for APA Division 36 Mid-Winter Conference: Columbia, MD.

Pargament, K.I., Murray-Swank, N.A., Magyar, G.M., & Ano, G. (2005). Spiritual struggles: A phenomenon of interest to psychology and religion. In W.R. Miller and H.D. Delaney (Eds.), *Judeo-Christian perspectives on psychology: Human nature, motivation, and change* (pp. 245–568). Washington, DC: American Psychological Association.2

Plante, T.G., & Sherman, A.C. (2001). *Faith and health: Psychological perspectives*. New York, NY: Guilford Press.

Piedmont, R.L. (2005). The role of personality in understanding religious and spiritual constructs. In R.F. Paloutzian and C.L. Park (Eds.), *Handbook of the psychology of religion and spirituality* (pp. 253–373). New York, NY: Guilford Press.

Princeton Religious Research Center. (2000). Americans remain very religious, but not necessarily in conventional ways. *Emerging Trends, 22*, 2–3.

Richards, P.S., Bartz, J.D., & O'Grady, K.A. (2009). Assessing religion and spirituality in counseling: Some reflections and recommendations. *Counseling and Values, 54,* 65–79. http://www.aservic.org/counseling-and-values/

Richards, P.S., & Bergin, A.E. (2005). *A spiritual strategy for counseling and psychotherapy* (2nd ed). Washington, DC: American Psychological Association.

Richards, P.S., Hardman, R.K., & Berrett, M.E. (2007). *Spiritual approaches in the treatment of women with eating disorders.* Washington, DC: American Psychological Association.

Richards, P.S., & O'Grady, K.A. (2007). Theistic psychotherapy and the God image. *Journal of Spirituality in Mental Health, 9,* 183–209. doi:10.1300/J515v09n03-09

Richards, P.S., Smith, M.H., Berrett, M.E., O'Grady, K.A., & Bartz, J.D. (2009). A theistic spiritual treatment for women with eating disorders. *Journal of Clinical Psychology, 65,* 172–184. doi:10.1002/jclp.20564

Rogers, C. (1951). *Client-centered therapy: Its current practice, implications, and theory.* London, England: Constable.

Slife, B.D., Stevenson, T.D., & Wendt, D.C. (2010). Including God in psychotherapy: Strong versus weak theism. *Journal of Psychology and Theology, 38,* 163–174. http://journals.biola.edu/jpt

Schulte, D.L., Skinner, T.A., & Claiborn, C.D. (2002). Religious and spiritual issues in counseling psychology training. *Counseling Psychologist, 30,* 118–134. doi:10.1177/0011000002301009

Tedeschi, R.G., & Calhoun, L.G. (2004). Posttraumatic growth: Conceptual foundations and empirical evidence. *Psychological Inquiry, 15*(1), 1–18. doi:10.1207/s15327965pli1501_01

Trippany, R.L., White Kress, V.E., & Wilcoxon, S.A. (2004). Preventing vicarious trauma: What counselors should know when working with trauma survivors. *Journal of Counseling and Development, 82,* 31–36. http://www.counseling.org/Publications/Journals.aspx

Underwood, L.G., & Teresi, J.A. (2002). The Daily Spiritual Experience Scale: Development, theoretical description, reliability, exploratory factor analysis, and preliminary construct validity using health-related data. *Annals of Behavioral Medicine, 24,* 22–34. doi:10.1207/S15324796ABM2401_04

Voss Horrell, S.C., Holohan, D.R., Didion, L.M., & Vance, G. (2011). Treating traumatized OEF/OIF veterans: How does trauma treatment affect the clinician? *Professional Psychology: Research and Practice, 42*(1), 79–86. doi:10.1037/a0022297

Walsh, F. (Ed.) (1999). *Spiritual resources in family therapy.* New York, NY: Guilford Press.

West, W. (2000). *Psychotherapy and spirituality: Crossing the line between therapy and religion.* Thousand Oaks, CA: Sage.

Wicks, R.J. (2008). *The resilient clinician.* New York, NY: Oxford University Press.

Yalom, I.D. (1970). *The theory and practice of group psychotherapy.* New York, NY: Basic Books.

PSYCHOLOGY, THEISM, AND METHODOLOGICAL NATURALISM

Robert A. Larmer*

ABSTRACT

In this essay I argue that attempts to insist that methodological naturalism be regarded as the condition sine qua non of scientific inquiry are mistaken. Scientific inquiry should not be constrained by a methodology which legislates in advance of considering the evidence, that only naturalistic explanations of phenomena be considered acceptable. If there is empirical evidence which suggests the operation of immaterial entities such as the human soul or God, psychologists should be free to consider such evidence, without thereby being deemed unscientific.

Keywords: methodological naturalism, demarcation problem, theism, god of the gaps

The goal of this special issue of *Research in the Social Scientific Study of Religion* is to explore the question of the relation of theism to the science of psychology. To what degree, if any, is it legitimate to appeal to spiritual entities such as God or the human soul in the theory and practice of psychology? Numerous scholars, including a great many theologians, are inclined to reject out of hand any appeal to such entities in explaining events that take place in the world. Bultmann, (1961) a New Testament scholar famous for his insistence that Christianity must be demythologized, expressed this point of view very clearly when he remarked that "it is impossible to use electric light and the wireless and to avail ourselves of modern medical and surgical discoveries, and at the same time to believe in ... [a] world of spirits and miracles" (p. 5). Less dramatically, but equally insistent, the influential contemporary theologian Haught (2004) asserted that "by its very nature, science is obliged to leave out any appeal to the supernatural, and so its explanations will always sound naturalistic and purely physical" (p. 231).

* *Author Note*: Robert A. Larmer, Department of Philosophy, University of New Brunswick.

Correspondence concerning this article should be addressed to Robert A. Larmer, Department of Philosophy, University of New Brunswick, Carleton Hall, 211, Fredericton, New Brunswick, Canada, E3B 5A3. Email: rlarmer@unb.ca

But are matters quite as simple as this? If spiritual entities such as God and human souls exist, then it seems plausible to think they may influence, at least to some degree, what happens in the material world. If one thinks that such entities exist, or that they might exist, then it is important to ensure that one's conception and practice of scientific inquiry does not preclude the possibility of recognizing their causal influence on the world.

This does not mean that for ordinary inquiries, such as why litmus paper turns red when exposed to acid or water changes state when the temperature drops below 32°F, we should look for anything other than physical causes. Theists acknowledge the operation of secondary created physical causes as explaining a great deal of what happens in the world. It is important, therefore, not to overemphasize the degree to which world-view commitments such as naturalism and theism are likely to affect scientific practice. As Lennox (2007) observed, such

> commitments, ... are not likely to figure very largely, if at all, when we are studying *how things work*, but they may well play a much more dominant role when we are studying *how things came to exist in the first place*, or when we are studying things that bear on our understanding of ourselves as human beings. (p. 37)

Where world-view commitments are liable to play a role, however, it is important that we recognize their existence and their influence on how scientific practice is framed. Otherwise, we run the risk of baptizing as metaphysically neutral practices which clearly are not. One does not want to appeal to spiritual causes in cases where they are not operative, but neither does one want to embrace methodologies which will not permit recognizing them in cases where they are operative.

Reasonable though it seems to suggest that scientific inquiry should be conceived and practiced so as to be open to recognizing whatever causes operate, be they material or spiritual, one generally meets stiff opposition to any such suggestion. Science, we are told by both naturalists and many theists, is incapable of ever recognizing the operation of non-material causes. Asked why this is so, the answer given is that it is defined by its commitment to methodological naturalism, that is to say science, qua science, can never legitimately postulate the existence of a non-physical cause.

METHODOLOGICAL NATURALISM AND THE DEMARCATION PROBLEM

Commitment to methodological naturalism as the conditio sine qua non of what it is for an inquiry to be *scientific*, rather than *unscientific*, seems to arise from a desire to resolve what is known in philosophy of science as the demarcation problem. Historically, there have been numerous attempts to specify criteria that allow drawing a hard and fast distinction between what can be considered science and non-science. The motives underlying such attempts have varied. Early demarcationalists were motivated by the assumption that science achieves certainty, whereas other modes of inquiry such as philosophy are only capable of producing opinion. Later demarcationalists, aware that scientific knowledge is subject to uncertainty, have typically attempted to demarcate the line between science and non-science not on epistemic grounds but rather on methodological grounds, claiming that science can be distinguished from non-science on the basis of the methods it employs.

Before directly considering the question of whether adopting methodological naturalism is essential to scientific investigation of phenomena, three general points deserve to be made. First, it deserves emphasis that demarcation criteria are frequently employed as a discrediting device. Given the prestige that science enjoys, it is rhetorically effective if one can cast one's own position as scientific and one's opponent's position as unscientific. Thus Laudan (1996) noted that

> demarcation criteria are typically used as *machines de guerre* in...polemical battle[s] between rival camps...[and] many of those most closely associated with the demarcation issue have...hidden (and sometimes not so hidden) agendas of various sorts. (p. 344)

Rather than critically engage with those with whom one disagrees, it is easier to dismiss their arguments as unscientific and unworthy of being taken seriously.

Second, labels such as scientific or unscientific should not be taken as automatically conferring epistemic warrant or authority. It is fallacious to think that classifying an argument or hypothesis as unscientific, rather than scientific, somehow refutes it. As Stephen Dilley (2010) remarked,

> mere terminological labels do not change epistemic properties. Just as theists cannot lower the epistemic plausibility of [naturalist] hypotheses merely by deeming them "arrogant bluster" so naturalists cannot lower the epistemic plausibility of God hypotheses by labeling them "unscientific." As an epistemic matter, each rival hypothesis must be evaluated on its evidential and conceptual merits. (p. 136)

Refusing to consider empirical evidence that bears on the existence of God or human souls on the grounds that such concepts are unscientific may be rhetorically effective at certain levels of popular discussion, but it is scarcely rationally persuasive. Even if one were to concede the claim of methodological naturalists that all scientific explanations of phenomena must be naturalistic, such a concession is irrelevant to the question of whether a non-naturalistic, that is to say non-scientific, explanation of certain phenomena is superior to a naturalist explanation of the phenomena. Simply labeling the concept of a human soul that is distinct from the body and capable of surviving the death of the body *unscientific* does nothing to resolve the question of whether the phenomena associated with, for example, near death experiences is best explained on the hypothesis that such souls exist. Similarly, insisting that the concept of miracle is unscientific is scarcely a substitute for examining whether events plausibly regarded as miracles actually occur.

Third, philosophers of science are largely agreed that attempts to specify a set of necessary and sufficient conditions that demarcate science from non-science have both failed and are ill-motivated. Having surveyed the failure of demarcation strategies across centuries, philosopher of science Laudan (1996) asserted that "if we...stand...on the side of reason, we ought to drop terms like 'pseudo-science' and 'unscientific' from our vocabulary; they are just hollow phrases which do only emotive work for us" (p. 349). This failure should come as no surprise. The word science comes from the Latin term scientia, which means to know or understand. Knowing and understanding require a disciplined, honest, reasoned approach to whatever it is one studies. What is required, however, in terms of methods for such an approach may vary from discipline to discipline. If one wants to insist on distinguishing science from non-science it should be on the basis of whether a disciplined, honest, reasoned approach was taken, rather than whether a particular methodology that may be appropriate to one discipline or area of study, but not to another, was employed.

This is not to deny that at a practical level we can distinguish between disciplines such as, for example, chemistry and history, or music and physics. It is to claim that what counts as scientific inquiry can be found in all those disciplines, even though their methodologies and aims may differ considerably. The search for absolutely sharp and perfect boundaries between disciplines regarded as sciences and disciplines regarded as humanities, though philosophically tempting, seems ill-founded. Historians may well find themselves making use of chemistry in attempting to date an artifact, and musicians may find themselves studying the physics of music.

Considerations such as these should make one very suspicious of currently fashionable attempts to insist that scientific inquiry requires espousing methodological naturalism. In what follows, I shall briefly consider the various justifications that are routinely given for adopting methodological naturalism. All these attempted justifications, I shall argue, fail to demonstrate that science should be defined in terms of the practice of methodological naturalism.

Attempted Justifications of Methodological Naturalism

Methodological naturalism as metaphysically justified

One might attempt to justify adopting methodological naturalism in the practice of science on metaphysical grounds. Surely, if one is a metaphysical naturalist it makes sense to adopt methodological naturalism as a prerequisite of scientific inquiry. Surely, if like Lewontin (1997), one is a metaphysical naturalist, then one is

> forced by... [an] a priori adherence to material causes to create an apparatus of investigation and a set of concepts that produce material explanations, no matter how counterintuitive, no matter how mystifying to the uninitiated. Moreover, that materialism is an absolute, for... [one] cannot allow a Divine Foot in the door. (p. 31)

The problem metaphysical naturalists have in taking such a stance is that they typically argue that the findings of science support naturalism over and against theism. This is to argue in a circle however, since to adopt methodological naturalism is to guarantee that all phenomena will be viewed as having a naturalistic explanation, no matter how implausible. As Dilley (2010) noted,

> under [methodological naturalism] scientific counter evidence against [metaphysical naturalism] is barred. Since [methodological naturalism] requires that all scientific evidence be given a natural explanation, evidence can never disconfirm [metaphysical naturalism], *no matter what the evidence on hand actually is.* This is not to say that scientific evidence fails to disconfirm [metaphysical naturalism] as a matter of fact, but that it cannot as a matter of principle. Empirical evidence cannot so much as murmur against [metaphysical naturalism], and no rival hypotheses, however, modest, can cast a shadow on its scientific stature. (p. 129)

What this means is that if metaphysical naturalists want to suggest that the findings of science support metaphysical naturalism rather than theism then they cannot, without begging the question, insist that methodological naturalism is a prerequisite of scientific inquiry. It will hardly do to define science in such a way that it cannot provide evidence against metaphysical naturalism and then argue that it supports metaphysical naturalism.

Methodological naturalism as theologically justified
Somewhat ironically, metaphysical naturalists espousing methodological naturalism find themselves keeping company with a number of theologians. Theologians such as Wiles and Kaufman find it inconceivable
that any modern person could think of the world except in terms of an
unbroken web of natural causes. Thus Wiles (1986) insisted that talk of
God's mighty deeds in history must be understood non-literally, that is to
say poetically or symbolically. Such language, in Wiles' view, refers not to
God acting directly in the natural order to produce an event that would
not otherwise occur but rather to the meaning given to certain events
by those experiencing them or hearing of them. Similarly, Gordon Kaufman (1968) found it inconceivable that any modern person could think
of the world except in terms of an unbroken web of natural causes and
their effects.

One suspects that in many cases this insistence that God never intervenes in the world is based on the assumption that it is somehow unscientific to think that the physical universe could be open to other than
physical causes. Insofar as this insistence is genuinely theological, it seems
to appeal to the questionable intuition that it would be unworthy of God
to interact with creation; that for God to in any way intervene in the working of creation is to be guilty of arbitrariness and caprice. Thus David
Jenkins (1987) went so far as to assert that

> a God ... [who inserts] additional causal events from time to time into ...
> [the] universe to produce particular events or trends ... would be a meddling
> demigod, a moral monster and a contradiction of himself. (pp. 63–64)

Underlying assertions such as Jenkins' is the implicit claim that the perfection of God implies that His creation of the universe be along the lines of
a maintenance free machine, and that apart from originating and upholding the existence of the physical universe, God must leave the natural
order absolutely alone. But why think this? Why insist that if God creates it must be along the lines of a maintenance free machine? Why not
think of creation along the lines of a musical instrument, which is created
precisely to be intervened upon? More fundamentally, if, as most theists
believe, creation is conceived as including free agents made in the image
of God, whom God desires to be in loving relationship with, there seems
good reason to think that God might, on occasion, intervene in the natural order in response to their choices and prayers. A parent's intention
to help a son or daughter become a good person may be unchangeable,
but the means by which such help is given is adapted in response to the

child's choices. As Tennant (1925) observed, it is essential that, in seeking to eliminate from our conception of God the anthropic quality of caprice and changefulness, we not fall into the trap of thereby ascribing to Him the equally anthropic qualities of indifference and impassive obstinacy.

Methodological naturalism as inductively justified

An alternative to stipulating that methodological naturalism be accepted on metaphysical or theological grounds is to claim that its acceptance is justified on inductive grounds. Thus McDonald and Tro (2009) claimed that its historical success justifies adopting methodological naturalism, writing that "by induction we rationalize the continued reliance on methodological naturalism as a guide for scientific inquiry" (p. 204).

There are at least two serious objections to this suggestion. First, it does not accurately portray the motivations underlying the adoption of methodological naturalism or how it is actually practiced. Typically, its adherents advocate its adoption on the basis that it is an essential conceptual stipulation of doing science. Thus, in his widely cited *But Is It Science*, Ruse (1996) asserted that "any reliance on a supernatural force, a Creator intervening in a natural world by supernatural processes, is *necessarily* not science" (p. 300, emphasis added). Far from being based on an inductive generalization open to disproof, methodological naturalism appears based on an a priori rejection of the legitimacy of ever postulating a spiritual agent as the cause of a physical event.

Second, the suggestion that acceptance of methodological naturalism is justified on inductive grounds assumes that the progress of science has invariably provided natural explanations of events viewed as caused by spiritual agents. The widespread acceptance of this claim obscures the fact that it is tends to be asserted, rather than argued for. This is unfortunate. One may accept that in certain areas of inquiry, for example the causes of disease, the search for natural causes has been fruitful, yet question the claim that the progress of science invariably makes accounting for certain classes of phenomena in terms of natural causes easier. In the context of our present discussion, the progress of science has not made naturalistic explanations of consciousness or events traditionally viewed as miracles easier but rather harder.

With regard to consciousness, although we have learned a great deal about the brain and no one would deny that its workings are intimately connected with consciousness, our increased knowledge provides no naturalistic account, as naturalist philosopher of mind Kim (1998) noted, of "how ... a series of physical events, little particles jostling against one another, electric current rushing to and fro, and so on, [could] blossom into a conscious experience" (p. 8). Kim, having asserted at the beginning of his *Philosophy of Mind*, that "at bottom, [the mind-body problem] is the problem of accounting for the place of mind in a word that is essentially physical" (p. 9) found himself at the end of his book caught in what he termed a profound dilemma. He wrote,

> If we are prepared to embrace reductionism, we can explain mental causation. However, in the process of reducing mentality to physical/ biological properties, we may well lose the intrinsic, subjective character of our mentality—arguably the very thing that makes the mental mental. In what sense, then, have we saved "mental" causation? But if we reject reductionism, we are not able to see how mental causation should be possible. But saving mentality while losing causality doesn't seem to amount to saving anything worth saving. For what good is the mind if it has no causal powers: Either way, we are in danger of losing mentality. That is the dilemma. (p. 237)

Kim, insisting on naturalism, found himself either having to deny that we are in fact conscious, or alternatively that, although we are conscious, our conscious states have no causal effect on the world, that is to say, what I intend to write in this article is in no way a cause of what actually gets written. That naturalism leads to such a dilemma does not inspire confidence that in either its metaphysical or methodological forms it should be insisted upon in the study of the mind.

Similarly, with regard to what have traditionally been understood as miracles, the advance of science has diminished, rather than enhanced, the prospect of explaining such events naturalistically. For example, advances in our knowledge of chemistry and physiology have not made it less, but rather more, difficult to provide an explanation of how water could turn into wine, or a dead person come back to life, at the spoken word of Jesus. Indeed, it is precisely the difficulty of providing a natural explanation of such events that leads many critics to deny that they occurred. It is hardly a recommendation for methodological naturalism if its effect is to dismiss such events as unhistorical solely on the basis that they defy naturalistic explanation.

Further, claims of miracles and answered prayer are ongoing. There seems no reason why such contemporary claims cannot be scientifically investigated. In many instances, reports of miraculous healing can be investigated in terms of before and after medical records and what we know regarding various diseases and physical ailments. Claims regarding the efficacy of prayer can be, indeed are, investigated by studies designed to test such claims (Harris et al., 1999). If such studies were to establish that there exists a genuine correlation between prayer and positive medical outcomes but that no plausible natural explanation seems possible, should their results be dismissed as unscientific because no explanation in terms of natural causes is liable to be forthcoming? Should an explanation in terms of spiritual agency be automatically dismissed as unscientific on the grounds that scientific investigation can only reveal the operation of natural causes? If one thinks that a goal of science is to uncover the causes of events in the world, then methodological naturalism seems a threat to this goal since it a priori rules out recognizing supernatural causes of events even if such causes exist and operate. As Ratzsch (2000) noted, "if part of reality lies beyond the natural realm, then science cannot get at the truth without abandoning the naturalism it presently follows as a methodological rule of thumb" (p. 105).

The God of the Gaps Objection

An objection that is liable to be raised is that rejecting methodological naturalism leads to what is known as the god of the gaps fallacy. The phrase *god of the gaps* is widely and disparaging used, so much so "that merely labeling an explanation as 'God-of-the-gaps' is often taken to constitute an unanswerable refutation of it" (Ratzsch, 2001, p. 276). The thought seems to be that to take gaps in naturalistic explanations as evidence for immaterial agency is to commit the fallacy of argumentum ad ignorantium, that is to say, an argument from ignorance.

Walton (1996) wrote that the fallacy of argumentum ad ignorantiam is standardly described as an argument that takes either of the following forms:

1. There is no proof (or you have not proved) that *p* is false.
   Therefore *p* is true.

or,

2. There is no proof (or you have not proved) that *p* is true.
   Therefore *p* is false (pp.25–26).

It is clearly fallacious to argue that a statement must be false solely on the basis that it has not been proven true, or that a statement must be true solely on the basis that it has not been proven false. In day to day life, however, it is difficult to find arguments based simply on ignorance. Typically, people do not argue in such a manner. Many arguments which might at first glance appear to commit the fallacy of simply appealing to ignorance reveal themselves on further inspection to implicitly utilize a claim, that if a proposition P were true (or not true) then we should reasonably expect to find evidence for it being true (or not true). When we do not find such evidence we can take this as a kind of evidence that P is false (or true). In such cases, it is a mistake to insist that the argument for concluding that P is false is based simply on ignorance, and is therefore an instance of argumentum ad ignorantiam. Thus psychologists recognize the reasonableness of "lack-of-knowledge" inferences made by experimental subjects, scientists employ the concept of "negative evidence" and historians make use of ex silentio arguments, without falling victim to fallacious reasoning (Walton, 1996, pp. 64–65).

Consider an example. Suppose I am told that there are alligators in the sewers of large city. I and others conduct a thorough and exhaustive search over many months and days, but we never find any trace of alligators. Would I commit the fallacy of argumentum ad ignorantium if I were to conclude that on the basis of a lack of evidence of their presence there are no alligators in the sewers? It seems not, since I have enough positive knowledge of alligators to reasonably expect that if indeed they were in the sewers, there would be positive evidence of their presence. The fact that, after a thorough and exhaustive search, no such evidence is found justifies me in concluding that they are not there.

What this suggests is that someone who takes gaps in naturalistic accounts of certain phenomena as evidence of immaterial agency cannot be automatically dismissed as guilty of fallacious reasoning. What is really at issue is the legitimacy of the claim that, in certain instances, enough can be known about the operation of natural causes to make it reasonable to conclude that at least some gaps in purely naturalistic explanations are evidence of immaterial agency. To revert to our previous examples, might it be argued that we know enough of how the brain functions to legitimately claim that at least some near death experiences are liable to remain impervious to naturalistic explanation (Nichols, 2010), and that if certain events traditionally viewed as miracles actually occurred that they are not susceptible to natural explanation (Larmer, 2011). Put differently, the real issue, which unfortunately gets obscured when the god of the gaps charge is raised, is whether naturalistic explanations are always adequate. As Collins (2000) noted, "by what right may we assume a priori that all 'gaps' are *lacunae ignorantiae causâ* and that none are *naturae causâ*?" (p. 171). If immaterial agents do intervene in the course of nature, then there will exist naturae causâ gaps that are not the result of our ignorance of how natural processes work but rather the result of the fact that a purely natural explanation does not exist. The problem with adopting methodological naturalism as a prerequisite of scientific inquiry is that it guarantees that if gaps of this type exist they can never be recognized as such. Thus Delfino (2007) wrote that,

> when methodological naturalism is understood as a necessary condition of science it is incompatible with realism and its principles of discovery, evidence, and self-correction. We do not know what we are going to discover in advance, but methodological naturalism does not allow for the possibility of discovering the supernatural. We do not know where the evidence we will gather will lead us, but no matter what that evidence is methodological naturalism will not allow us to follow it to a supernatural cause. (Section 3, paragraph 2)

Methodological Pluralism

Those who adopt methodological naturalism typically insist that it is metaphysically neutral, assuming without argument that the methodology one employs can be neatly separated from one's beliefs about the nature or possible nature of reality. Not only is this assumption far from self-evidently true, it seems simply false. If, by way of analogy, I believe that there exist, or may possibly exist, mental states which play a causal role in determining bodily behavior, it makes no sense to adopt methodological behaviorism, since its adoption guarantees the development of psychological theories in which mental states either do not exist or play no causal role in bodily behavior. Only if I am already convinced that mental states do not exist or play no causal role does it make any kind of sense to insist on methodological behaviorism as a prerequisite of developing psychological theories. To insist on its employment in the absence of any justification for disbelieving in the existence of mental states or their causal powers is to beg the question of whether it should be adopted.

Methodological naturalism seems a sensible approach to scientific theorizing if one believes that immaterial agents do not exist, or that if they do they never intervene in the operation of the physical universe. If, however, one believes that a non-natural agent, say God, exists and might possibly intervene in the operation of the physical universe, it will seem wrong-headed to adopt a methodology which forbids positing any such intervention. Insisting that methodological naturalism be adopted implicitly commits one either to the claim that immaterial agents do not exist or to the claim that if they do, they never intervene on the natural order. This, however, begs the important question of whether such claims are justified.

It is important that this point regarding the relation of one's methodology to one's prior beliefs not be allowed to overshadow the role that evidence should play in our theorizing. Regardless of one's particular beliefs, one should maintain certain fundamental evidential allegiances, whether in metaphysics, religion, science, or other human endeavors. The problem with insisting that all scientific inquiry requires adopting methodological naturalism is that it skews from the outset what will count as evidence and what form genuine explanations can take.

I have suggested that methodological naturalism is not a conditio sine qua non of scientific inquiry and that viewing it as such places an intellectual straitjacket on what form explanations may take. As Burtt (1932) has observed,

> there is no escape from metaphysics, that is, from the final implications of any proposition or set of propositions.... If you cannot avoid metaphysics, what kind of metaphysics are you likely to cherish when you sturdily suppose yourself to be free from the abomination? Of course it goes without saying that in this case your metaphysics will be held uncritically because it is unconscious; moreover it will be passed on to others far more readily than your other notions inasmuch as it will be propagated by insinuation rather than by direct argument.... The thinker who decries metaphysics will actually hold metaphysical notions...if he be a man engaged in any important inquiry, he must have a method, and he will be under a strong and constant temptation to make a metaphysics out of his method, that is, to suppose the universe ultimately of such a sort that his method must be appropriate and successful. (pp. 224–226)

It is thus clear that, despite the protestations of the majority of its advocates, methodological naturalism is not metaphysically neutral.

If, as I have argued, methodological naturalism is rejected as essential to the practice of genuinely scientific inquiry, then how should such inquiry proceed? Delfino (2007) advocated replacing methodological naturalism with what he termed methodological neutralism. He suggested that

> scientists should simply search for causes without setting any *a priori* conditions on what ontological status those causes must have. By not setting any *a priori* conditions with respect to ontological status the principle of discovery is not jeopardized in any possible way. By not setting any *a priori* conditions with respect to ontological status we can follow the evidence wherever it might take us. Finally, by not setting any *a priori* conditions with respect to ontological status we can make any corrections necessitated by new evidence. Since the principle of methodological neutralism is more

in harmony with…[these] three principles…it should be preferred over methodological naturalism within a realist conception of science. (Section 3, paragraph 5)

I am sympathetic to Delfino's suggestion. He is surely correct that methodology should not be allowed to trump following the evidence where it leads. I think, however, that he underestimates the practical difficulty of evaluating empirical evidence from a neutral viewpoint. Evidence is always assessed within the context of numerous background beliefs. Consequently, we do not tend to have neutral viewpoints. Rather, we seek to interpret and fit evidence into a prior framework of belief. This is not to say that evidence cannot serve to overthrow or modify such frameworks, but it is naive to think that our prior beliefs have no influence on how evidence is evaluated or even what counts as evidence.

This is in no way to deny that there are principles by which competing world-views or metaphysical systems can be assessed (Larmer, 1988). What it does mean is that evaluating whether a body of data fits better within one large, sophisticated framework of beliefs, say naturalism, than another large sophisticated framework, say theism, is a complex and far from instantaneous process. It seems legitimate therefore to speak, at least at a practical level, of methodological pluralism. In areas where world views such as naturalism and theism clash or might seem to clash, it is reasonable to allow their proponents to explore competing points of view, rather than insisting that all theorizing must be done within the constraints of methodological naturalism. To do so seems a necessary condition of fostering a healthy intellectual environment. Thus, for example, taking seriously the hypothesis that further scientific investigation will emphasise the inadequacy of purely natural causes to explain the full range of phenomena described in near death experiences hardly implies that research cannot continue regarding the possibility of demonstrating that a plausible naturalistic account of such experiences can be given. Far from being a science stopper or encouraging intellectual laziness, such competition holds competing hypotheses to a much higher standard than they would otherwise have to meet.

Conclusion

I conclude that methodological naturalism is not a prerequisite of genuine scientific inquiry and places unjustified constraints of what explanations of phenomena should be considered. Once this is recognized, it becomes possible to contemplate the possibility that certain phenomena are best explained by reference to the agency of God or an immaterial soul. Doing so will help avoid mistakes such as the French astronomer Laplace made when he rejected reports of stones falling from the sky (meteorites) on the basis that his astronomical theory had no place for such phenomena and that reports of these occurrences came from laypersons with no training in celestial mechanics (Jaki, 1989). Science's task is to follow the evidence where it leads and to be open to the possibility that we may be surprised by what is found, not to insist that it either be ignored or forced into the Procrustean bed of a favored theory.

References

Bultmann, R. (1961). New Testament and mythology. In H. Bartsch (Ed., R. Fuller, Trans). *Kerygma and myth* (pp. 1– 44). New York, NY: Harper & Rowe.

Burtt, E.A. (1932) *The metaphysics of modern physical science* (revised 2nd ed). New York, NY: Harcourt, Brace and Company.

Collins, J. (2000) *The God of miracles*. Wheaton, IL: Crossway Books.

Delfino, R.A. (2007). Replacing methodological naturalism. *The Global Spiral*. Retrieved from http://www.metanexus.net/Magazine/Default.aspx

Dilley, S.C. (2010). Philosophical naturalism and methodological naturalism. *Philosophia Christi, 12*(1), 118–141. http://www.epsociety.org/philchristi/

Harris, W.S., Gowda, M., Kolb, J., Strychacz, C.P., Vacek, J.L., Jones, P.G., . . . McCallister, B.D. (1999). A randomized, controlled trial of the effects of remote, intercessory prayer on outcomes in patients admitted to the coronary care unit. *Archives of Internal Medicine, 159*, 2273–2278. doi:10.1001/archinte.159.19.2273

Haught, J. (2004). Darwin, design, and divine providence. In W. Dembsi & M. Ruse (Eds.) *Debating design* (pp. 229–245). Cambridge, England: Cambridge University Press.

Jaki, S. (1989). *Miracles and physics*. Front Royal, VA: Christendom Press.

Jenkins, D. (1987). *God, miracle, and the Church of England*. London, England: SCM Press.

Kaufman, G. (1968). On the Meaning of "Act of God." *Harvard Theological Review, 61*, 175–201. doi:10.1017/S0017816000027991

Kim, J. (1998). *Philosophy of mind*. Boulder, CO: Westview Press.

Larmer, R.A. (1988). *Water into wine? An investigation of the concept of miracle*. Montreal, Canada: McGill-Queen's University Press.

Larmer, R.A. (2011). The meanings of miracle. In Graham H. Twelftree (Ed.) *The Cambridge companion to miracles* (pp. 36–54). Cambridge, England: Cambridge University Press.

Laudan, L. (1996). The demise of the demarcation problem. In M. Ruse (Ed.) *But is it science?* (pp. 337–350). Amherst, NY: Prometheus Press.

Lennox, J. (2007). *God's undertaker: Has science buried God?* Oxford, England: Lion Press.

Lewontin, R. (1997). Billions and billions of demons. *The New York Review of Books, 44*(1), 28–32. http://www.nybooks.com/

McDonald, P., &Tro, N.J. (2009). In defense of methodological naturalism. *Christian Scholar's Review, 38*(2), 201–229. http://www.csreview.org/

Nichols, T. (2010). *Death and afterlife: A theological introduction*. Grand Rapids, MI: Brazos Press.

Ratzsch, D. (2000). *Science and its limits: The natural sciences in Christian perspective.* Downers Grove, IL: Inter-Varsity Press.

Ratzsch, D. (2001). *Nature, design, and science.* Albany, NY: SUNY Press.

Ruse, M. (1996). Witness testimony sheet. In M. Ruse (Ed.) *But is it science?* (pp. 287–306). Amherst, NY: Prometheus Press.

Tennant, F.R. (1925). *Miracle and its philosophical presuppositions.* Cambridge, England: Cambridge University Press.

Walton, D. (1996) *Arguments from ignorance.* University Park, PA: Pennsylvania University Press.

Wiles, M. (1986). *God's action in the world.* London, England: SCM Press.

THE CONCEPTS OF THE INDWELLING SPIRIT AND THE SELF-CRITIC IN THEISTIC THEORY AND RESEARCH

*Richard H. York**

ABSTRACT

This article claims that theists and nontheists interpret data differently based on their different worldviews. Theists interpret some research data as evidence of God's presence because their faith in God allows them to perceive it. Nontheists do not perceive God's presence because their worldview rejects any notion of God in psychological research or theory. However, the data for both theists and nontheists are the results of naturally occurring phenomena. From a theistic perspective, this article argues that God is present and works through the natural phenomena God created; the criterion to determine God's presence is the life-giving nature of any phenomenon. This article presents the concept of the Indwelling Spirit (the IS) or Inner Wisdom as an example of God's presence because this affective-cognitive phenomenon is life-giving to people. The IS is inherent and contains our conscience. It also describes the Self-Critic (the SC), the self-critical inner dialogue, as destructive and demonic. The SC is constructed of internalized images derived from the destructive elements of early relationships with parents and abusive people. These images form a discrete neuropsychological program in the self-image and determine negative feelings about oneself and corresponding behavior. This article proposes research tools to study the IS and SC concepts.

Keywords: theistic psychology, spirituality, self-critic, relationality, theology, psychology

DIFFERENT WORLD VIEWS OF THEISTS AND NONTHEISTS

The central theme of this article involves an insight about people's differing perceptions of the world that are as old as the Buddha. Saddhatissma (1976) tells the story of the Buddha intervening in arguments between some of his students who were debating various philosophical and theological issues until they were fist fighting. The Buddha decided to intervene by telling the parable about a king who put men born blind at various parts of an elephant and asked them to describe it. Each man argued so vehemently for his own description of an elephant that they too began to fight. The king was immensely delighted by the spectacle. "Such,

* *Author Note*: Richard H. York; Psychologist in Private Practice.
Correspondence regarding this article should be addressed to Richard H. York, 248 County Street, New Bedford, MA 02740. Email: richardyork@earthlink.net.

explained the Buddha, is the case of people who have seen one aspect of reality and then dogmatically suppose that they have seen the whole of reality" (Saddhatissma, p. 74).

Most recently, differing worldviews in psychology were discussed in articles about theistic psychology by Helminiak (2010), Nelson and Slife (2006), Slife (2005, 2006a, 2006b), Slife and Reber (2009a, 2009b), Slife and Whoolery (2006), and York (2009). While reading Helminiak's *Zygon* article (March 2010), it occurred to me that differing worldviews were at the center of the debate about theistic psychology. Helminiak argued that theistic psychologists use the assumption that God intervenes in human experience to explain aspects of psychology and psychotherapy to the detriment of psychology as an empirical science; they introduce metaphysics into psychology and use the discredited God of the Gaps theory to explain psychological phenomena. He referred to Occam's razor as the means to reject any notion of God's interventions in psychotherapy or human experience. He asked: Why use God to explain a phenomenon if there are simpler alternative naturalistic explanations? Helminiak separated theology and psychology by defining spirituality without any reference to the presence of God in order to maintain psychology as an empirical science; he wanted psychological theory and psychotherapy to be evidence based without any reference to theological or metaphysical beliefs. Helminiak (2009) defined spirituality as "first and foremost a matter of deliberate pursuit of inner personal harmony, integration, growth, unfolding–in Abraham Maslow's word, self-actualization" (p. 2). It is puzzling that his definition of spirituality is individualistic and does not include relationships or the destructive aspect of human nature which cause problems in relationships with self and others.

That article led me to realize that my discussion of theistic psychology (York, 2009) was unclear about how God intervenes in human experience through the phenomenon of the Indwelling Spirit (the IS). It appeared that I said some examples of the activity of the IS are the evidence of God's presence (or intervention) but others are inherent cognitive processes (see examples below).

I assume that the IS and SC thoughts or voices are cognitive/affective voices (I will use the term *voices* rather than *thoughts* throughout this paper for this reason because these cognitions cannot be separated from emotions). Hersch (2008) argued against separating facts from value and thoughts from emotions in human experience from a phenomenological perspective. He wrote: "abstract splits between such terms as 'reason and emotion,' 'cognition and affect' and other, I believe misguided, dichotomies as those of 'mind versus objectivity' and 'subjectivity versus objectivity' have proven troublesome to both philosophy and science for many years" (p. 201).

The Indwelling Spirit

The definition of the IS in York (2009) is based on Roberto Assagioli's (1965) concept of the Higher Self: "It is the inherent presence of the Triune God who teaches, guides, affirms, heals, and forgives sins, and also contains our conscience.... People describe the experience of their Indwelling Spirit with these faculties" (p. 113). As I read Helminiak's *Zygon* article, I asked myself: How is it possible to resolve the controversy between theists and nontheists? The thought soon popped into my mind: People with a theistic worldview would see God's action in certain phenomena whereas those with a rationalist worldview would not because they reject the notion that psychological phenomena have anything to do with acts of God. This insight led me to conclude that the difference between theists and nontheists is their interpretation of data based on their different worldviews. These insights led me to recognize that the above definition was unclear about God's intervention in human experience through the IS or what kind of affective/cognitive phenomenon it is.

Here are some examples to help make a new definition for the IS concept. The insight that popped into my mind is a good example of how the IS works. It is an example of the teaching or knowledge building or inspiration activity of the IS. It can be interpreted either as God's intervention working through an affective/cognitive process or simply the result of an inherent, internal, intuitive affective/cognitive process of the mind. The worldview of the person would determine which interpretation is made. In other words, as a person of faith, I interpret these insights as the result of God's inner presence working through the IS to teach us new knowledge. Nontheists would reject the notion that God is present at all in scientific theory and research. However, these differences of interpretation have nothing to do with the moral character of the interpreters, (i.e., theists are not the saints and nontheists the sinners). No one should interpret the differing worldviews as involving moral issues in any way.

Another example is from a time when I contemplated why Jews had to endure the suffering of the Holocaust. It did not make sense to me that their suffering was punishment of the sins they committed. The suffering of so many far outweighed the gravity of any sin any of them committed. Then it dawned on me: God was present with them and bore their pain along with them because they were victims of horrific evil. That insight profoundly affected me because I was the victim of rape and covert incest as a child, and it helped me to let go of the pain from those experiences. It also means that God shares the pain of victims of any form of evil. This is an example of both the healing and teaching functions of the IS.

The most common example of the IS activity from clients is the reason they decide to come into therapy. Many clients have told me they initially resisted coming to therapy because they believed they could solve their problems on their own. They reported having a conversation with themselves where one inner voice said: "Oh, I can solve this problem on my own." And another voice said: "You need help with this." Finally, when they recognized they could not do it by themselves, they decided to follow the inner voice that encouraged them to seek help. They finally surrendered to the wise voice that said they could not solve the problem by themselves. This wise voice is an example of the guiding activity of the IS and most often addresses the person as *you* rather than *I*. It is a voice that is commonplace in most people's experience.

In addicts, their addiction often eclipses the activity of the IS. Active addicts say something like: "I know I shouldn't go to the bar, the casino, get drugs, to the porn store, etc., but I need to." The "I know I shouldn't" is their response to the wise voice of the IS telling them that they do not have to continue to use drugs, alcohol, sex, or gamble, etc., but the addict studiously avoids listening to this voice and acts out. If we would be honest with ourselves, we have said similar things to ourselves, often. The paradigm thought is: "I know I shouldn't <u>fill in the blank</u>, but I'm going to anyway."

There are other examples of the IS that may not be interpreted as signs of God's intervention. These are examples of the intuitive cognitive function of the IS. When I was a supervisor of a laboratory, my assistant was a Ph.D. candidate in electronics at MIT. When the instruments failed, as they often did, I was able to find the problem before he did which dismayed him to no end. When he did the trouble shooting, he used a logical set of steps, but I found the problem quicker because the solution answer occurred to me, out of the blue, without using trouble shooting steps. My thought process was not logical because I knew enough about the instruments to let my mind become intuitive. This intuitive or inspirational faculty is also an example of how the IS works all the time. Another example occurred when I was trying to get my television to work. I followed the instruction manual but could not get it to work so I left it. Later on in the day, a thought came to me to click on a function on the menu. It worked. Again, my mind used the information I observed to intuitively come to the solution.

The above examples helped me redefine the IS. I assume that the voices in all these examples were produced by the same affective/cognitive process. Hence it would be intellectually dishonest to exclude the problem solving insights. The first example described a teaching voice and the second, third, and fourth examples described healing and guiding voices. All these voices created insights that affected relationships with others, self, and God. However, the trouble shooting and television examples were insights that solved problems which did not involve human or divine relationships, only electronic instruments.

I now define the IS as the voices produced by inherent affective/cognitive mental processes that Christ in the Holy Spirit of God created in all people to teach, affirm, heal, care for, and forgive people their wrong doings and to produce the person's conscience which the people can choose to use to be more caring, compassionate, nonviolent, and other-centered in all their relationships. Because my faith identifies God's presence, this definition is based on my Christian faith. However, theists from other theological traditions could see this phenomenon as the activity of their God.

The voices of the IS appear to come from a caring "executive secretary" who constantly offers suggestions. The voices remind you about your schedule or suggest what you could do next or suggest different solutions to problems and ways to do things. They occur regularly in our inner dialogue and are often the best alternatives. The conscience voices are like an inner dialogue between the angel and the devil on our shoulders as pictured in cartoons. These conscience voices are assumed to be inherent, not learned. All these voices are data for research because they are empirical aspects of human experience.

However, the same mental process sometimes produces voices that suggest solutions to problems and others that affect human or divine relationships. This raises the question: What is the source of these voices? Are they from God or are they only the result of a mental process? The answer is: Both. By definition the affective/cognitive mental processes produce all the voices; some voices may come solely from these processes and some may be direct interventions from God. It is impossible to tell the source of each voice. God uses these processes as a conduit: God created these processes and remains present in them. Hence I contend that it is immaterial what or who is the source of these voices. Theists and nontheists would probably agree that the voices legitimate data but would differ about the source of the voice. The faith of the theist would interpret the source of the voice as evidence of God's presence whereas nontheists would say the voices were products of a natural mental process. The different interpretations would be the result of their different worldviews. The criterion which theists would use to determine God's presence is whether the voice is life-giving. Being life-giving means that the voices encourage self-affirmation, caring of others, compassion, nonviolence, and other-centeredness in relationships with others, self, God, or the problems people face: These voices are the essence of relationality.

My theology assumes that God maintains a caring presence in all that God created. This presence is a paradox: God is present but does not intervene or control creation regularly but maintains enough control over the natural order to make adjustments when necessary. This type of control is like the designer of a car who later adjusts the car design when it no longer works as it did. The natural laws of creation are an embodiment of caring. The natural order is caring because a caring loving God created it: it is not impersonal like a chemical reaction or genetics of natural selection. However God does not constantly control or intervene in the natural laws: The natural order is caring by definition. God maintains a presence in our mental processes or the rotation of the planets around the sun in order to have ultimate control. This assumption is different from the Deists who believe God created the universe then left it to work according to the laws God created. This assumption does introduce metaphysics into psychological theory. But since the voices of the IS are products of a mental process, it is possible to collect data to do empirical research.

The question is: So what? This theistic interpretation does not add any new knowledge to psychology in and of itself; it is simply a different interpretation which cannot be proved or disproved. No one can prove or disprove that the existence of God because God is not observable. God's presence can only be determined by faith. However, paradoxically God is real. I believe or assume that God has created a world where God is hidden, illusive, and unseen except by faith; God does not want us to be forced to believe. God wants only those who are willing to listen to the call and to ask for help to become more loving in their relationships. The Bible and particularly the parables of Jesus about blindness and deafness demonstrate God's hiddenness. The presence of God through the IS can reassure clients that they are not alone in their struggles. And theists have the option to design a myriad of research projects that determine the impact of the faith of psychologists and clients on relationships.

Meditation and the Indwelling Spirit

Rohr, Wilber, Benson, Siegal, and the whole mindfulness movement have suggested that meditation is a spiritual practice which can produce knowledge and healing with research data to support these claims. Rohr (2011) has written many books and created the Center for Action and Contemplation. His books and Center help people transform their consciousness through meditation practices and community building to become more caring in their various relationships. Wilber (2007) wrote about an *integral science* and established the Integral Institute and a branch called the Integral Spiritual Center. His writings and the Centers assist people to integrate scientific knowledge and spirituality through study and meditation. Benson has written a number of books about the relaxation response and established the Mind/Body Medical Institute. In his recent book (Benson & Proctor, 2010), he reported research that proves meditation can change gene activity in diseases such as hypertension and Parkinson's disease. Siegal has developed a perspective which integrates medical and neurological science into psychotherapy. His recent book (2010) described his approach to psychotherapy using meditation with profoundly healing results.

Initially it was unclear to me how meditation worked to produce knowledge or healing. Then I remembered that some of my IS experiences did just that. It is possible that regular meditation quiets the mind enough to stop the obsessive, self-critical mental chatter. The mind then becomes open to the inherent inner wisdom and healing capacity of the body. However the question still remains: Where does the knowledge and healing come from? Does it come only from within or does it come from within and without?

Another example of my IS voice occurred to me during a meditation. For a period of time, my meditations were becoming boring and no extraordinary experiences were happening. One day during a meditation, this voice came to me saying: We live in the midst of God; we don't have to search for God. I had been searching for what was already present. God is present in every minute of the day as well as in meditation. But in meditation, we experience the silent presence of the activity of God who connects us with all creation.

The Self-Critic

The self-critic (SC) is a more familiar phenomenon. The SC is the common cognitive/affective phenomenon which causes people to be critical of themselves with voices such as *I'm dumb, I'm ugly, You're incompetent, You're no good*. These voices are sometimes *I* thoughts and other times are *You* thoughts. The You voices are usually internalized messages which parents or abusive people have actually said to the person. The I voices are internalized messages that the person has adopted from the critical person. However, some people create their own self-critical voices in response to their experience such as feeling dumb because they have difficulty reading. It is assumed that most people have some form of the SC at some time in their lives, but it can be eliminated if people work at it. People experience these voices as tormenting, critical, or self-hating.

The SC is the result of the negative or destructive aspects of internalized images from early childhood and later. We all construct our self-image by internalizing the relationship between ourselves and our parents and other significant people in our early lives, particularly those who abuse us. These early internalized relationships form both the life-giving and destructive aspects of self-esteem. Children are like sponges; they absorb the emotional interaction between themselves and others as a composite image of early experiences. This composite image forms a neuropsychological program in the neurons of the brain. This program is a video of their early experience. It determines most of people's feelings, self-messages, and behavior. The life-giving aspects of the internalized relationships help people become functional and caring in their relationships. The destructive aspects of these internalized images coalesce into a neuropsychological program to form the self-critic. From childhood on, people become attached to this program; they believe it is them. They give this self-image ultimate authority over them and their behavior. Children tend to relate to their parents and other significant people as if they were gods. For this reason, the self-critical program forms what Jordan (1986) calls false gods or idols. In other words, the attachment to the idols makes people guilty of idolatry or following false gods. This attachment is destructive because it programs people to compulsively repeat the messages of their internalized images in their behavior. But it is more accurate to say people are imprisoned by these idols because they cannot get away from them; they make people miserable at best and often suicidal. The idols usually cause people to be as critical of others as they are of themselves.

The figure below is a diagram of the internalized images which constitute the relational self or the self-image from York (2009, p. 41). The idols which produce the destructive self-beliefs and corresponding behavior are represented in the top of the diagram. Most people have both life-giving and idolatrous behavior. However, this diagram does not illustrate that our relational self does not exist in our bodies alone; it exists between us and others as Siegal (2010) contended. Our relational self has an open door policy; it connects us with others who have had similar experiences that are either life-giving or destructive. That is part of the reason people repeat destructive relationships.

The Self-Critic and Sin and Evil

Now let me introduce the other forbidden topic in psychology avoided by most psychologists, even theistic psychologists: sin and evil. In York (2009), I referred to a number of significant exceptions. Menninger (1973) asked: Whatever became of sin? He criticized the psychological establishment of being willing to talk about destructive behavior but refusing to address the moral implications of various behaviors. Sanford (1981) addressed evil in the collective consciousness from a Jungian perspective. He lamented

THE RELATIONAL SELF

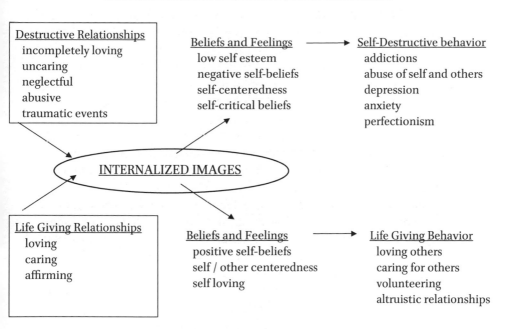

Figure 1. *The Relational Self.*[1]

---

[1] From *A Christian Spirituality and Psychotherapy: A Gay Psychologist's Practice of Clinical Theology* (p. 41) by Richard H. York, 2009, Eugene, OR: Wipf & Stock Publications. Copyright 2009 by Wipf & Stock Publications. Reprinted with permission.

the lack of attention to evil which could lead to our peril as a culture and the need for a psychology of evil.

Stendahl (1976), then a professor at the Harvard Divinity School, was invited to deliver an address at the annual APA Convention on September 3, 1961 about the guilty conscience of the West. He based his thesis on St. Paul's statement in Romans 7:16: "I cannot understand my own actions. I do not do what I want to do but what I hate." He contended that Paul was not talking about his guilty conscience; he was giving his definition of sin. He even made it clear that Paul did not have a guilty conscience because he had accepted the forgiveness of Jesus for his sins of persecuting the church. He contended that the guilty conscience came later from St. Augustine and others who were preoccupied with shame of sin, particularly sexual sins. This passage appeared to describe sin as a compulsive behavior or an addiction: It became the source of my definition of sin.

May (1988) and McCormick (1989) developed this theme of sin and addiction. They both used the Romans 7:16 passage for their theses. May, a psychiatrist, identified a long list of behaviors he considered addictions because they were not life-giving and prevented human freedom. They looked like the old list of venial and moral sins. "*No* addiction is good; *no* attachment is beneficial. To be sure, some are more destructive than others;.... we must also recognize what they have in common: they impede human freedom and diminish the human spirit" (p. 39). McCormick, a religious priest, identified sins which are not from idols. These are social sins like commercialism, militarism, and sexism. He described the connection of these social sins and criminal behavior.

I define sin as (a) the compulsive attachment to idolatrous images and (b) any behavior that is uncaring, harmful, destructive, demeaning, injurious, or abusive to self, others, the earth, and the social order (York, p. 88). The SC neuropsychological program is the source of much sin because it creates compulsive attachments and behavior. People compulsively repeat these attachments and behaviors in their everyday experience in an attempt to gain the love and self-affirmation they were denied in the original relationship. In order to become a healthy adult, people need to let go of their attachment to these childhood idols and choose a life-giving way of relating: in other words, choosing the good and rejecting the evil. This development sometimes requires psychotherapy, but some have matured through "accepting hardships as a pathway to peace" (as noted in Niebuhr's long version of the Serenity Prayer; see Hudson, 2004, p. 12) with the help of others.

The SC neuropsychological program is not evil; no part of any human being is inherently evil. This program is the conduit that evil uses to destroy people. It is destructive because this program takes on a life of its own and focuses people on the destructive elements of the idols. It seduces people to compulsively seek destructive ways to gain the love and well being they never had or lost in the earlier relationships. The evil power works through the destructive aspects of the idols to keep people attached even when the person knows they are being irrational. The evil fans the flames of fear that they will lose themselves or the love of the idol (Bartz, 2009). They fear the abandonment of the idol more than the freedom from abuse which would allow them to be more loving. I had a client who put a loaded gun into his mouth rather than set limits with his uncaring, abusive mother because his father idol was telling him to care for his mother. The clearest examples of this insidiousness are the stories people tell of their alcoholism, drug addiction, sex addiction, or food addiction. It is this insidious, seductive quality of the SC voices that is evil. In this sense, the SC is not only the accumulation of experience, it is a conduit of evil. It is similar to Freud's thanatos principle. Sin is the result of our collusion with attachments and behavior originating from idolatrous images. Evil seduces us through our idols to keep us self-destructive. Our attachment to these self-critical idols makes us guilty of idolatry.

It is relatively easy to differentiate the experience of the SC and IS. The SC is experienced as the opposite of the IS. People feel put down or tormented or terrorized by their SC voices, whereas the IS voices are experienced as affirming, caring, compassionate, and forgiving. However, sometimes the voices point out what people do wrong, but they are not experienced as a demeaning, although they may feel guilty. I believe that the IS was created as an antidote to the SC, but the SC often eclipses the IS. O'Grady & Bartz (in press) have examples of the distinctions in these voices.

The Relationship between Psychology and Theology

One aspect of the theistic/nontheistic controversy is the relationship between psychology and theology. Helminiak has written many articles since 1995 against theistic psychology, even though he believes that God is present in human life, and he is not an atheist. Some psychologists want to keep theological and metaphysical concepts out of psychology, and others want to include theological concepts in the theories and research of psychology.

Yet some of these psychologists forget that Christian theology and psychology share some very significant commonalities. Both disciplines want to heal people so they can be released from a destructive, sinful way of life in order to have healthy, life-giving relationships. Even Freud said the goals of psychoanalysis are love and work: These goals at the least imply a morality. The whole purpose of psychotherapy is to provide a safe environment where people can share the secrets of their lives in order to heal from traumas and to stop being destructive to themselves and others. Almost every page of the New Testament tells a story of Jesus healing people of either physical or mental illnesses. Christian theology describes metanoia as the conversion of people from a sinful to a spiritual way of life, even though they continue to sin. This metanoia is facilitated by the clergy and members of the church. Hence the nexus between psychology and theology cannot be ignored if we are to be intellectually honest.

This nexus of Christian theology and psychology has important implications for both theology and psychology. All theologies throughout the centuries have included either an explicit or an implicit psychology. Current theologians could profit from including current psychology in their formulations as moral theologians and medical ethicists do already. Psychologists could benefit by using a common language with theology. These disciplines cannot ignore their inherent interrelatedness. At the very least, the concepts of both disciplines need to be common when they are dealing with their common issues.

Helminiak (2010) unwittingly created an unnecessary and potentially destructive dualism between psychology and theology. He divorced any connection between a psychology of spirituality and theology. Yet in another article (2011), he recognized the interrelatedness of faith and reason. They "live off each other" and "Both faith and reason are attempts to understand, to know, to appreciate properly" (2011, p. 3). He acknowledged that theology is a way of knowing. However, his divorce of theology from psychology fractures the relationship between faith and reason. His psychology of spirituality puts the reason of science in psychology and relegates faith in God to theology, as if faith has no effect on how people relate. If a religious faith has no effect on behavior, then the faith of people from any religion is nonsense. All religions are intended to transform people from something. Hence psychologists cannot refuse to study the connection between people's faith in God and their behavior, and they need to acknowledge how God is present for these subjects.

Post-modern thought attempts to eradicate such dualisms. These dualisms lead to compartmentalization of the human psyche like Descartes' infamous maxim: "I think; therefore, I am." The thrust of contemporary philosophy is integration and interrelatedness without destroying any of the disciplines (Rohr, 2011, Siegal, 2010; Wilber, 2007). Marriage is the best analogy of the relationship between psychology and theology; two people become one, but they do not eliminate their individuality. They have a healthy pattern of coming together and moving apart throughout their relationship as Dym and Glenn (1993) described. The following symbol (Figure 2) for marriage illustrates one aspect of the nexus between psychology and theology. However, it implies a static relationship between these disciplines instead of the fluidity of Dym's description of couple relationships.

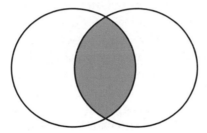

Figure 2. *Symbol for marriage.*

A Theistic Psychologist's View of Psychology as a Science

The limits to objectivity have a long history dating from Kant to Heidegger to Einstein and Oliver. Kant claimed that we human beings cannot know things as they are; we can only know things as they appear to us. The thing itself is beyond our knowing. Hence all perceptions and interpretations of data have some degree of subjectivity. He also introduced the "relational character of nature" (Oliver, 1981, p. 32). Others like Einstein and Oliver (1981) expanded on the inherent relational nature of the universe in opposition to the subject/object epistemology of Descartes and empirical science. I claim that empirical science has done a great disservice to us all. It has posed that we, the observer, are separated from the observed instead of connected to all we see. This subject/object fracture creates a psychological disassociation and loneliness which has to be overcome in order to live fully.

Many theistic psychologists and others have offered a relational, ontological, and experiential model for research to replace the existing subject/object epistemology of current psychology. The main issues are abstractionism and the difficulty of being objective. Slife (2005) made a convincing case for replacing the ontology of abstractionism with relationality. He contended that psychological theory is created by using abstractions from research data which then are applied in psychotherapy practice. Psychologists learn these theories and apply them in psychotherapy. Research methods remove behavior from the context of the relationships that generated it. In other words, research on effective psychotherapy is used to create evidence-based treatments for various disorders such as depression. This endeavor makes depression similar to medical problems like high blood pressure. But depression is a much more complex phenomenon than blood pressure; it involves physiology, neurobiology, and the person's relational history. People with the same criteria for depression are grossly different from one another. Our current diagnostic criteria for depression do not identify a uniform cohort of subjects because people have such different etiologies for depression. It would be essential to identify the idols created by internalized images in order to be sure that the subjects in the research are similar. "Indeed, practices do not *exist*, in an important ontological sense, except in relation to the concrete and particular situations and cultures that give rise to them, implying what we might call a *relational ontology*" (Slife, 2005, p. 158). Richardson (2009) also raised the issue of abstractionism in his discussion of methodological and metaphysical naturalism. In York (2009), I recommended a relational ontology to replace the subject/object epistemology of empirical science in psychology because people are essentially relational. I defined the self as a relational self as described above. Hersch (2008) described a similar relational ontology and the problem of abstractionism in research methods from a phenomenologist's perspective. He contended that relational research is essential, and objective science is illegitimate science. His concept of relative objectivity is similar to my concept of subjective/objectivity (York, 2009). These perspectives could lead to a plethora of new research that would reflect the inherent relationality of all human beings.

D.A. Helminiak (personal communication, August 13, 2009) contends that advances in scientific method for psychology will be generated by the physical sciences. I tend to disagree. The germ for new scientific methods already exists in the social sciences. This germ is the fact that social scientists have to deal with a living system. My high school science teacher showed us his understanding of how science generates knowledge, a picture of a baby smashing a watch to see how it works. They are still doing that as exemplified by the cyclotron between Switzerland and France where physicists are smashing matter in order to learn about the origins of the universe. I doubt that living subjects would agree to be smashed into their component parts to discover how they work, not to mention the fact that most people know that the whole is not the sum of its parts: A system functions differently than the functions of its parts. If social scientists would stop feeling inferior to the physical sciences and start collaborating with mathematicians and other innovative thinkers, a living systems methodology could be created for use by all sciences.

Conclusion

The major theme of this paper is that theistic and nontheists psychologists would interpret the voices of the IS differently based on their different worldviews. Theists would interpret these voices as coming from God, and nontheists would say they are the result of mental processes. I may have given the impression that this theme was the only insight coming from my IS. In actuality, this whole paper is the result of a dialogue between my IS and what I wrote. From my ontological perspective, the "executive secretary" voices of my IS helped me revise my writing to make it more clear; my first draft was unintelligible, even to me. My faith tells me that God is always present with me and with everyone; God may directly intervene through these thoughts, or they may be generated by the natural cognitive/affective mental processes: It does not matter because it is impossible to be certain what the source is. God works through the created order directly and indirectly. I experienced the dialogue about my writing as affirming, teaching, guiding, and life-giving. These characteristics tell me that God is present because these are the criteria that indicate God's presence. Regardless of the source, the cognitive/affective mental processes produce the voices, and these voices are psychological data. My faith interprets them as God's presence because my world view assumes that God is present. Other theistic psychologists would probably agree and nontheistic psychologists would not because their worldview does not include a notion of God's presence. However, most psychologists would probably agree that the voices are legitimate psychological data. It is only faith, not psychological science, which identifies the source of the voices. Other theistic psychologists would be wise to acknowledge whether they are talking about inspiration or about psychological processes.

However, faith is not a benign placebo effect. True faith transforms the believer (Miller & C'de Baca, 2001). This transformation leads to less destructive and more life-giving behavior in relationships. These behaviors can be the subject of myriads of research projects. These projects would include how the faith psychologists affect their work as well as how the faith of subjects affects their relationships.

The other concept is the SC. The self-critic is comprised of voices that are shaming, self-critical, tormenting, and insidious. It has the opposite experience of the IS. These voices are the product of a neuropsychological program created by the destructive aspects of the internalized images of childhood relationships with parents and anyone who was abusive. Children gave these early relationships godlike power. The destructive aspects of these relationships coalesce into the neuropsychological program to form destructive images called idols or false gods. These false gods run people's lives until they are willing to let go of them. People compulsively repeat the destructive relationships in an attempt to get the love they did not get from the original relationships. People are guilty of idolatry because they gave these early relationships ultimate power. It is possible to say that people worship them. As the IS is the conduit for God, the SC is the conduit for demonic forces because these idols are destructive. Addicts are the ones who know the insidiousness of their SC idols.

I have suggested many research projects about the IS, SC, and the behavior produced by true faith. It is essential that the IS and SC are studied together because the voices can easily be confused by subjects. These studies would be invaluable to psychologists, spiritual directors, and many other healers. My dream is to establish an Institute of Psychology, Medicine, Neuroscience, and Theology. People from these many disciplines would do research and treatment together using an integrative, multi-disciplinary approach. The Institute would employ mediation, multi-discipline research, and sharing as means to gain new knowledge. If my colleagues agree, it is time to stop writing ideological and theoretical papers about theistic and nontheistic psychology and start doing research similar to those proposed below in Appendix A.

References

Assagioli, R. (1965). *Psychosynthesis*. New York, NY: Hobbs, Dorman Co.

Bartz, J.D. (2009). Theistic existential psychotherapy. *Psychology of Religion and Spirituality*, *1*(2), 29–80. doi:10.1037/a0014895.

Benson, H. & Proctor, W. (2010). *Relaxation revolution: Enhancing your personal health through the science and genetics of mind body healing*. New York, NY: Scribner.

Dym, B. & Glenn, M.L. (1993). *Couples*. New York, NY: HarperCollins Publishers.

Helminiak, D.A. (March 31, 2009). *The nature of spirituality and its connection with sexuality: An offering for clergy pondering the ethics of homosexuality*. Atlanta Gay Men's Chorus and Saint Mark Methodist Church Invitational Clergy Discussion. Atlanta, GA.

Helminiak, D.A. (2010). Theistic psychology and psychotherapy: A theological and scientific critique. *Zygon, 45*, (1), 47–74. doi:10.1111/j.1467–9744.2010.01058.x.

Helminiak, D.A. (2011). Science and religion, reason and faith, sex and spirituality. *Quarterly Voice of DignityUSA, 10*(2), 1–7. http://www.dignityusa.org/qv.

Hersch, E.L. (2008). A phenomenologist's view of the omnipresence of the evaluative in human experience: Knowledge as a founded mode and the primacy of care. In L. Charland & P. Zachar, (Eds). *Fact and value in emotion* (pp. 193–209). Amsterdam, Holland: John Benjamin Publishing Company.

Hudson, T. (2004). *The serenity prayer*. Grand Rapids, MI: Kregel.

Jordan, M.R. (1986). *Taking on the gods: The task of the pastoral counselor*. Nashville, TN: Abingdon Press.

May, G.G. (1988). *Addiction & grace*. New York, NY: HarperColllins Publishers.

McCormick, P. (1989). *Sin as addiction*. New York, NY: Paulist Press.

Menninger, K. (1973). *Whatever became of sin?* New York, NY: Hawthorn Books.

Miller, W.R. & C'de Baca, J. (2001) *Quantum change: When epiphanies and sudden insights transform ordinary lives*. New York, NY: Guilford Press

Nelson, J.M. & Slife, B.D. (Eds.). (2006). *Philosophical issues in psychology and religion*. Special Issue of *Journal of Psychology and Theology, 34*(3), 191–192. http://journals.biola.edu/jpt.

O'Grady, K.A. & Bartz, J.D. (in press). Addressing spiritually transcendent experiences in psychotherapy. In J.D. Aten, K.A. O'Grady, & E.L. Worthington (Eds.) *The psychology of religion and spirituality for clinicians: Using research in your practice*. New York, NY: Routledge.

Oliver, H.H. (1981). *A relational metaphysic*. New York, NY: Springer.

Richardson, F.C. (2009). Biases against theism in psychology? A comment. *Journal of Theoretical and Philosophical Psychology, 29*, (2). doi:10.1037/a0017689.

Rohr, R. (2011). *Richard Rohr: from Wikipedia, the free encyclopedia*. Retrieved from http://en.wikipedia.org/wiki/Richard_Rohr.

Saddhatissa, H. (1976). *The life of Buddha*. New York, NY: Harper & Row.

Sanford, J.A. (1981). *Evil: The shadow side of reality*. New York, NY: Crossroad Publishing Company.

Siegal, D.J. (2010). *The mindful therapist: A clinician's guide to mindsight and neural integration*. New York, NY: W.W. Norton & Company.

Slife, B.D. (2005). Taking practice seriously: Toward a relational ontology. *Journal of Theoretical and Philosophical Psychology, 24*, (2), pp. 157–78. doi:10.1037/h0091239.

Slife, B.D. (2006a). *Dare we develop a theistic science? The myth of neutrality in psychology's methods*. Paper presented at the 4th Annual Mid-Year Research Conference on Religion and Spirituality, Loyola College, Columbia, MD.

Slife, B.D. (2006b). *Psychology's hidden paradigm and prejudice: Naturalism*. Paper presented at the American University in Cairo, Egypt.

Slife, B.D., & Reber, J.S. (2009a). Is there a pervasive implicit bias against theism in psychology? *Journal of Theoretical and Philosophical Psychology. 29*, 63–79. doi:10.1037/a0016985.

Slife, B.D., & Reber, J.S. (2009b). The prejudice against prejudice: A reply to the comments. *Journal of Theoretical and Philosophical Psychology, 29*, 128–136. doi:10.1037/a0017509

Slife, B.D., & Whoolery, M. (2006). Are psychology's main methods biased against the worldview of many religious people? *Journal of Psychology and Theology, 34* (3), 217–231. http://journals.biola.edu/jpt.

Stendahl, K. (1976). *Paul among Jews and gentiles*. Philadelphia, PA: Fortress Press.

Wilber, K. (2007). *The integral vision: A very short introduction to the revolutionary integral approach to life, God, the universe, and everything*. Boston, MA: Shambhala Publications.

York, R.H. (2009). *A Christian spirituality and psychotherapy: A gay psychologist's practice of clinical theology*. Eugene, OR: Wipf & Stock Publications.

APPENDIX A: RESEARCH PROJECTS TO STUDY THE IS AND THE SC

These concepts need to be studied together because subjects might confuse the SC with the IS voices. Some items to study the SC would be placed between the poles of a 7 point Likert scale; for example: *I'm a failure* to *I'm successful*. The items would determine the thoughts subjects have about their appearance, intelligence, their abilities, lovability, degree of responsibility, or caring for others. They would be asked how they feel (happy, sad, put down, angry) when they hear themselves say the above and who said these things to them in the past, such as no one, mother, father, friend, other person. The demographic items would ask whether they experienced physical, verbal, emotional, and/or sexual abuse.

The first study to measure the IS would include qualitative items which will provide data to construct a scale. These items would be fill-in the blanks such as: What would you say to yourself? For example, I should <u>be perfect</u>. or I should be ___ or I ought to ___ or I must ___. These first items will be used to differentiate the SC voices from the hidden IS ones. Other items will identify the IS voices hidden in the paradigm sentence: I know I shouldn't ___ but I ___. Or I know I should <u>go help my mother</u> but I <u>want to have some fun</u>. An example of an IS guidance item would be: I know (circle the phrase you use) I shouldn't, I was told, or I can't ____ but I ____. An example of an IS conscience item would be: When I did something wrong, (a) I felt guilty and a bad person, (b) felt guilty but not a bad person, or (c) felt guilty and my thoughts helped me learn from my mistake and give an example. Give me examples of when you felt: (a) Guided to ___ by your thoughts, (b) Inspired to ___ by your thoughts, (c) When your thoughts told you that you were wrong to ___.

The following are suggested questions for research projects.

- How do people experience their IS and SC?
- What is the neurobiology of the IS and SC voices?
- What are the factors created by factor analysis of the IS and SC data?
- Do people experience all the types of IS voices described in the definition of the IS?
- Do the IS voices appear to have an otherness quality or simply another mental act?
- What are the life-giving and destructive internalized images which comprise a person's self-image?

- What idols do people live by and what factors do idols create in factor analysis?
- Do idols produce some or all destructive/sinful behavior?
- How can psychotherapy help people become less self-destructive?
- Does the faith of subjects or their beliefs make any difference in their relationships?
- Does the faith of the therapist affect the success of psychotherapy for the clients?
- Can research differentiate between the legalistic and the compassionate people of faith?
- How do Christians and non-Christians who are spiritual or non-spiritual compare in their compassion, nonviolence, rejection of egocentrism, and other-centeredness in their relationships?

These research projects and many others would add important information to the psychology of religion and spirituality.

AN ATHEIST'S GUIDE TO THE DIVINE: THROWING OUT THE BATHWATER BUT KEEPING THE BABY

M. Chet Mirman*

ABSTRACT

It is suggested that the enduring universality and intuitively compelling quality of belief in God is reflective not of its veracity but of the fact that it is simply human nature to believe. The present paper argues that the preoccupation with external spiritual entities, along with the universal propensity to take these reified projections literally, has diverted us from the more constructive task of fostering personal, spiritual transformation via a focus on the religiogenic object representations that underlie these projections. An object relations approach is used to redefine spirituality in a way that shifts the focus from external referents to internal psychic realities. Briefly discussed is a model of ego development that frames transcendence as an ego experience rather than a metaphysical statement, faith as an attitude rather than a belief, and the experience of God as an entirely internal process. Also addressed are the implications of recent work pointing to the existence of two processing systems, one of which enables us to function in the material world, the other in the world of relationships, including a relationship with one's religiogenic internal object representation (i.e., the God image).

Keywords: God, spiritual, religiogenic object representations, atheist, faith as an attitude

WHY WE BELIEVE

There are a number of compelling reasons to believe in the existence of God. Four reasons are discussed below.

Belief in God is One of the More Universal and Enduring Beliefs in Human History

Belief in God has been, and continues to be, so widespread that one might be inclined to say that this alone makes the case. How could so many billions of people be wrong? But might the universality of belief in God be a reflection not of the veracity of the belief but of the fact that it is simply

* *Author Note*: M. Chet Mirman, Illinois School of Professional Psychology, Argosy University\Schaumburg.

Correspondence regarding this article should be addressed to M. Chet Mirman, Illinois School of Professional Psychology, Argosy University\Schaumburg, 999 N. Plaza Drive, Suite 111, Schaumburg, IL 60173–5403. Email: mmirman@argosy.edu.

human nature to believe? Throughout history human beings have had many beliefs that were widely held for long periods of time, like the belief that the earth is flat, that the earth is the center of the universe, and that erratic or crazy behavior is the result of evil spirits or demonic possession. These are all beliefs that, in the absence of information to the contrary, might seem intuitively obvious. The earth does appear flat, the sun does appear to revolve around the earth, and aberrant behavior really does appear to be best explained as possession by a foreign agent like a spirit or demon. As our scientific understanding of the world has progressed, these and many other commonly-held beliefs have fallen by the wayside as they have been replaced by other scientifically-based beliefs. The fact that a belief is popular is not in-and-of-itself a sufficient argument for its veracity. As shall be seen below, belief in God and other *spiritual* phenomena (e.g., creation, souls, the afterlife, etc.) may simply be a human propensity that people retain throughout their life unless they are overridden by the development of other beliefs that conflict with them.

The Complexity and Beauty of the World

How else can we explain how our incomprehensibly complex world came to be, how it functions so beautifully, and how it seems to suit human needs so well other than as the result of its having been designed or created? The world is indeed astonishing in its complexity, as well as in its uncanny suitability for our physical needs (this is more noticeable when compared to other environments like the moon or the bottom of the ocean). The idea that this world was created for us seems like the intuitively obvious explanation.

But an understanding of evolutionary theory points to a different explanation. While the world does indeed seem *as if* it were made for us, it is important to keep in mind that this is the world that we (at least our ancestors) evolved into. The fact that the level of oxygen in the air happens to be pretty close to what human beings ideally need for survival is a result of the fact that our bodies evolved to fit that reality and not the other way around. Similarly, the abundance of appealing sources of nutrition all around us is not a result of the world being created to fit our needs; it too is a result of our ancestors evolving to fit the world they lived in. Those ancestors of ours who did not find the plants and animals around them gustatorily appealing probably did not get enough nutrition to survive. As a result, they were replaced in the battle for gene dominance by those ancestors of ours who did.

The argument that the world is simply too complex and functions too beautifully as an integrated, dynamic system for it to have come to exist as a result of random chance ignores two important facts. First of all, natural selection is not a random process. It is a process that systematically favors certain genes over other ones based on the genes' differential ability to perpetuate themselves. What makes this so difficult for most of us to understand is the scale of the events involved in evolution. The changes involve so many organisms and occur over such tremendously large periods of time that we simply cannot fully grasp the magnitude of these numbers in anything but very abstract ways. The numbers are just too far away from the numbers of our everyday life.

Secondly, to say that the world is too complex to have come to be without a designer or creator simply shifts the problem by replacing many smaller problems with one much larger one. This argument, referred to by philosophers as the *argument from design*, is analogous to taking out a consolidation loan in order to solve one's financial woes. Consider a man who has ten $100 debts. He does not like having so many different debts so he goes to the bank to take out a $1000 consolidation loan in order to pay off the ten $100 debts that he has. Assuming a common interest rate, all he has succeeded in doing is to replace many small debts with one much larger debt that happens to be the same total debt as the sum of the ten smaller debts he had before. The argument for design, by resorting to God in order to explain the origins of the world, has simply replaced many small origin questions with one much larger one that is comparable in magnitude to the sum of the smaller ones. In other words, where did God come from?

Personal Relationship with God

Many people describe having had a personal experience of God or an ongoing personal relationship with God. It is difficult to convince someone that something they have direct personal experience with is not exactly what they think it is. The present paper is not an attempt to deny the experience of those readers who do believe in God but rather an effort to stimulate curiosity about the possibility of creating a new narrative for the subjective experience of God; in other words, it is not exactly what it may appear to be to the experiencer. It is being proposed that the experience of God be taken seriously because there is psychological truth there that is important to understand, a truth that non-theists generally dismiss, and so they often end up throwing out the baby of spirituality along with the bathwater of bad metaphysics. The God explanation of their experience should be taken seriously, but it should not be taken literally. In the same way that Freud was on to something when he discovered penis envy, people who have a direct experience of God are also on to something.

Freud was an astute observer of the workings of the psyche; however, he was not always correct in his conclusions. It can be argued that penis envy was actually a result of Freud's discovery of the fact that women in the late 1800s were indeed envious of men. In those days women could not vote, and they had little power in the family or workplace; from our 21st century perspective, it now seems like an obvious, almost trite, inference to say that women a century ago would be envious about what the possessors of penises had: namely power, freedom, and options that they themselves did not have. But lacking the advantages of the socio-cultural perspective that modern thinkers have, Freud had to rely on his clinical acumen to read between the lines and hear the underlying, often unconscious, concerns voiced by his female patients. Freud discovered a very real phenomenon, envy of men, and then misunderstood and mislabeled what its essence was.

It is being suggested here that this is analogous to what happens to most people who experience the voice of God. It is a real experience that, like penis envy, is nearly universally misunderstood and mislabeled. What is essentially an entirely internal experience, the activation of a particular subset of one's internal object representations, is being projected out, experienced as an external entity that is labeled *God*. While it is naïve to simply dismiss the experience (a la Dawkins), it can be helpful to re-label it in a way that is consistent with what we know about how the psyche functions so that we can learn how to impact that internal relationship in growth-enhancing ways. The nature of this internal process will be elaborated on below.

Belief in God Feels Intuitively Right

God seems like such an obvious answer to so many questions and appears to make so much more sense than the counterintuitive notion of God as nothing more than the product of complex internal processes. We are natural born creationists who believe in the supernatural, according to Bloom (2005). The problem with natural selection, said Bloom, "is that it makes no intuitive sense" (p. 111). Concepts like evolutionary theory and naturalism can override already held, intuitively compelling, universally believed ideas that just make more common sense, but they develop later.

These basic beliefs are more compelling because they are a direct byproduct of how we think about the world.

Kirkpatrick (2005) has characterized religious beliefs as resulting from the basic architecture of the human mind. A byproduct of evolution, religious beliefs are so powerful and intuitively compelling because they are essentially built into our hardwiring.

Reframing the Debate Over the Existence of God

The question of whether or not God exists (as well as other supernatural phenomena, like spirits, souls, the afterlife, etc.) is a longstanding debate that has been framed by a dichotomy of options with misleading implications. Both theists and atheists tend to approach the problem as if the relevant question is whether or not God exists *independent of our experience of him*. (Note: I am using the masculine pronoun when referring to God simply because of the preponderance of references to God across religions as masculine). If, and only if, God exists independent of our experience of him, then he is thought to be real; if not, then he is not. And if he is not real (i.e., if God has no actual external referent), then it is a childish fantasy/delusion that should simply be dismissed. But this dichotomous set of options is misleading and incomplete. Atheists may be correct in asserting that God, like all other spiritual phenomena, is a human creation and thus does not exist independent of our experience of him. But the notion that God is a human creation, that is, a projection of internal processes within our own psyches onto the world, does not lessen its value. In fact, as is the case with our dreams, it is the very reason why it is so valuable. Such creations are to be taken seriously but not literally. To take the experience of God seriously, however, is not the same thing as accepting that there is an actual external referent in the world that exists independent of the psyche of the experiencer.

The remainder of this paper addresses an alternative to this reification model of the experience of God as well as its implications for how we can best foster spiritual growth and development.

REDEFINING SPIRITUALITY

From External Referents to Inner World of Objects

According to object relations theory, our early life relationships with caretakers are the basis for later relationships via the images that we introject:

that is, the internal representations we form of these caretakers. These introjected images are then projected out onto the people we relate to in the world.

Rizzuto (1979) suggested that these introjections are also the basis for the images of God that we develop later. In other words, our experience of God is a function of the same psychological structures that are the basis for all of our relationships. The images that we have of God are simply a subset of these introjections, what has been referred elsewhere by the present author as *religiogenic object representations* (Mirman, 2007).

The parallel between the idealized characterization of God and the way an infant relates to his/her parents is unmistakable. Accompanying these experiences of the idealized, all-powerful, parental Other is a complementary sense of one's self as helpless, needy, weak and dependent. This idea can be found, for example, in the Book of Luke when Jesus says "Truly, I say to you, whoever does not receive the Kingdom of God like a child shall not enter it" (Luke: 18:17, English Standard Version).

The feelings associated with the experience of being loved by an internal idealized parental figure, and the profound sense of wholeness associated with this experience, are core elements of all spiritual experience. The sense of well-being is liberating. The feeling of safety and security, along with the sense of being loved and the attitude of faith (faith that the individual is, and will be, okay) promote the dissolving of defenses, leading in turn to the lifting of barriers between self and the world and the feeling of a loving connection to the world.

This is a familiar state that human beings long to return to:

> The yearning to return to a younger, non-defensive way of being—to recapture lost innocence, to experience awe, wonder and a sense of the sacred, and to feel the sense of being part of something larger than one's own "skin-encapsulated I" (Watts, 1969)—is universal. (Mirman, 2004, pp. 43–44)

Developmental Model of Spirituality: Three Stages of Ego Development

Much has been written about ego development since the time of Ana Freud and other ego psychologists who wrote in the middle of the 20th century, but the present paper proposes a three-stage model of ego development with the following three stages: Primary, Secondary, and Transcendent. Each stage is also a state of ego functioning that can be carried long into adulthood. These three states are also referred to as Defenseless, Defensive, and Non-Defensive, respectively (Mirman, 2008). Individuals in a *Primary* or *Defenseless* state are helpless, dependent, and vulnerable.

They do not yet experience themselves as separate from the world around them, nor do they have the capacity to understand the passing of time. They are unable to act on their environment and lack the capacity to take responsibility for their actions. They are, in short, defenseless in a world that they do not understand and have no real capacity to control. When their needs are anticipated and responded to by their caretakers, they are able to feel joy and delight, but their complete dependence on others, along with their lack of understanding, makes them highly vulnerable to frustration, pain and fear.

As children begin to develop the capacity to experience themselves as separate beings, are able to operate on the world, and understand the passing of time, they gradually enter the *Secondary Stage* in which they adopt a *Defensive mode* of being. In this stage, children learn to protect themselves from the many sources and types of pain and to accumulate supplies, both material supplies and narcissistic supplies. Here, children develop coping tools, including defense mechanisms and security operations, that help them to protect themselves and to navigate their way around the world of things as well as that of people. As their coping tools become more developed and more relied on, they become more rigid, more guarded, and better defended against pain. They are more preoccupied with protecting their ego and with the accumulation of protective supplies of various types (desirable traits, material possessions, the respect and good will of others, etc.). Despite the development of these coping tools, individuals in a Defensive state feel more vulnerable and more at risk of harm and of loss, and so they cling to their increasingly identified-with defense mechanisms and security operations.

Those individuals who advance to the third stage of ego development, the *Transcendent Stage*, are able to transcend the protective ego operations of the Secondary Stage and function in a relatively *Non-Defensive* manner. This third stage is marked by a greater level of comfort with self and an internal environment of more loving messages from their parental object representations; it is as if they carry with them a portable self-esteem supporting claque that quietly applauds approval and love of their very Being. It should be noted that an important, common variant of this dynamic involves a distinctly different message: "Although you are inherently defective, if you submit to my will, my love will make you whole, and I will take care of you." While these two messages are clearly quite different from each other, their impact is similar in that both lead to relative freedom from the need for these individuals to be on guard to protect their ego and thus engenders a loosening of their grip on their defenses.

The resulting increased availability of inner resources enables these individuals to be more open to their inner experience and to feel more connected to the world around them. This freedom from the need for the protective vigilance of their wary ego opens them to experiences of awe and wonder and enables them to feel gratitude and love, as well as a sense of the sacred or the divine.

Several points are worth briefly noting about this model: First of all, individuals in a Secondary Ego State, afraid of feeling helpless, powerless, and out of control, are essentially defending against regressing back to a Primary Ego State, and so they cling to the coping tools of the Secondary Ego State at the cost of being blocked from moving forward to the Transcendent Ego State. In essence, their fear of being defenseless keeps them defensive and so deprives them of the opportunity to experience the spiritual joys of being non-defensive.

Second, for most people these ego states are in constant flux. Most of us spend most of our lives controlled by the need to anticipate and plan for the future, hoarding narcissistic supplies and guarding against dangers of various types. We think strategically, and we often experience things (including people) as means to other ends. Dominated by chronically activated security operations, we suffer from ego fatigue and yearn to return to a younger, non-defensive way of being: to recapture lost innocence; to experience awe, wonder, and a sense of the sacred; and to feel the sense of being part of something larger than one's own *skin-encapsulated I*. Third, the Transcendent Ego State has a good deal in common with the Primary Ego State. While clearly different levels of organization, they do have in common the relative absence of the defenses and rigidity of the secondary, defensive ego state that keeps the individuals who are in that state feeling separate from the world and overly preoccupied with the mundane (secular?) tasks required to maintain their fragile, elusive security.

The Experience of God as a Relationship

It is being suggested here that the experience of God is a relational one. It is a relationship with an internal representation of *Other* that promotes a sense of well-being that is similar to the feelings associated with being loved by a powerful parent. Of course it is also a relationship that has the power to trigger the angst that accompanies the experience of having fallen out of grace with that parental figure; it feels very much like being in trouble for being bad. Spirituality, then, is best thought of not in terms of what one is able to locate *out there* (e.g., God, spirits, etc.), but rather as a particular kind of internal experience. In short, it involves the transcendence of one's normal (i.e., secondary stage) ego functioning, an experience that produces a sense of other-worldliness. This experience is associated with the felt sense of a loving presence and the sense of one's self as loved and lovable that accompanies it. For Kirkpatrick (2005), when an individual feels a secure attachment to what he/she characterizes as God, this produces a subjective sense of wellbeing that has properties that are described in religious terms. These include feeling loved and thus free to love, feeling awe, wonder, and a sense of the divine, and a sense of being in a state of grace. It is being suggested here that the feelings associated with being loved by an internal idealized other and the profound sense of well-being and wholeness associated with this experience are core elements of all spiritual experience. Feeling accepted and loved is liberating, centering, and exhilarating. Consider the way that experiences of God are typically described. "I submitted to God's will," "I felt bathed in his love," "I knew the glory of God," etc. It is a wonderful feeling that involves pleasing, and getting the approval of, one's loving, internal parent image. Whether or not one believes that there is a God that exists out there, how one experiences that God is largely a function of the nature of the self-representation that has been activated and the representation of Other that is being projected out onto that Being.

Faith Revisited: Faith as an Attitude Rather Than a Belief

Faith is generally thought of in terms of the tenacity of one's belief system, especially one's belief in God. "Do you have faith?" really means: "Do you believe in God?" and "How strong is your conviction about this belief?" Kierkegaard (1844/1981) wrote that God cannot be proven by logic to exist and that faith is not based on evidence. He claimed that faith involves making a commitment despite this and that it is only by making a *leap to faith* that one can find God. (Note: Kierkegaard is often misquoted as having used the term a *leap of faith*). Neo-Atheists like Dawkins and Harris, also buying into this definition of faith, have roundly criticized it as "pernicious ... and evil ... because it requires no justification" (Dawkins, 2006, p. 347), characterizing it as "consoling" but not based on evidence and therefore not true (Harris, 2005, pp. 67–68).

But faith can also be seen as an *attitude* towards the world, an attitude of what the psychoanalyst Erik Erikson would call "basic trust" (Fowler, 1981, p. 48). The essence of the experience is that it involves the *felt sense* of a loving parental presence: that is, a loving internal object representation that does not necessitate the actual presence of something or someone that exists independent of one's self. As is the case with most internal object representations, there is a wide range in the degree to which individuals are conscious of the voice of their object representations, as well as the way they experience the values that are derived from them. As an individual's superego develops, his/her values are increasingly internalized, becoming more ego syntonic and experienced less as the voice of the Other. This felt sense is not necessarily a consciously experienced voice. In fact, the vast majority of the time there is no conscious awareness of this voice; what is noticed is the impact of the message. It could be argued that because the object representation is not consciously experienced as a separate entity that it might be more accurately described as an *as-if* experience; in other words, there is no actual voice heard, but the individual is reacting as if there were. When there is conscious awareness of this voice, a subset of those experiences produces the narrative that the individual is in God's presence. This felt sense of a loving presence is generally found in healthy, psychological functioning, even when there is no God narrative. It is being suggested here that rather than debating whether there actually is an external referent to the subjective sense of God's presence (i.e., that God really exists independent of our experience of him), or the even more common battle over whose God is the better or more genuine God, what should be focused on is how to foster religiogenic object representations that underlie an *attitude of faith*. There may or may not actually be a God (I happen to hold the unprovable belief that there is no such external Being), but either way, the focus should be on the internal experience. In other words, how can we help people to be more loving and to live lives characterized by awe, wonder, and a sense of the sacred, via support for the quest to transform the relationships in their inner world?

Faith is really a developmental process that is analogous to belief in karma. A mature understanding of karma is not the belief that if you behave well, then good things will happen to you. Rather it is the belief that repeated acts of kindness and generosity will benefit you by fundamentally altering your soul (and thus your behavior) in ways that tend to lead to positive systemic changes in the social systems that you are part of (friendships, family, work relationships...). (Note: this should not be confused with the belief that if you help a little old lady cross the street you should immediately run out and buy lottery tickets because something good is about to happen to you.)

As a result of early life experiences in which the world (i.e., one's caretakers) is responsive to individuals' needs, faith that the world will continue to take care of them gradually gives way to faith in their own inner resources as adequate to handle what the world presents. Mature faith is thus not really the sense of confidence that the world (e.g., an external God) will be accommodating to one's needs and wants. It is confidence in one's self, confidence that is derived from supportive internal object representations. In short, it is not confidence that the world will treat you well; it is confidence that you will be okay, even if it does not.

TWO PROCESSING SYSTEMS

The dual nature of the universe has long been described by writers from various cultures and religious disciplines, most notably Descartes' division of the world into mind and body. It is being argued in the present paper, however, that this is not a reflection of there being two distinct worlds but rather of two ways of reacting to and organizing the world, each of which is the product of a different processing system.

Buber (1958) wrote that "the world is twofold for man in accordance with his twofold attitude," (p. 19) an attitude that is reflected in two types of relationships: I-Thou and I-It. In an I-It relationship, the individual treats other people as objects to be used. The individual in an I-It relationship relates to the world in terms of his or her own needs: that is, as objects that can serve that individual's own interests. Of course, I-It relationships are not always undesirable, and in fact, are necessary for taking care of the ordinary, mundane tasks of everyday life. The It world Buber claimed, "stands together in time and space." "Without It a human being cannot live," he wrote, "but whosoever lives only with that is not human" (pp. 43–44).

This is in contrast to I-Thou relationships, which he described as an encounter between two people which is direct, mutual, and holistic. The other person is experienced as a sacred Thou that is an end in-and-of-itself rather than a means to some goal, and so that individual is free of the objectification of the other. Buber wrote that human life consists of an oscillation between I-Thou and I-It, and that I-Thou experiences are, in fact, rare.

Along the same lines, Durkheim (1912/1995) wrote that the essence of religion can be found in its division of the world into two categories: the sacred and the profane. The sacred was said to be the world of the numinous, transcendental, or extraordinary, while the profane referred to the realm of everyday utilitarian activities. Anticipating the insights of modern psychology, he noted that objects are not themselves sacred or profane; rather, whether or not an object or activity is seen as sacred is dependent on the meaning that is bestowed by the people experiencing it.

Psychologists today have reexamined this split and have begun to characterize it as the product of two systems of thought rather than two types of things in the world (Barrett, 2004; Bloom, 2005). Unlike most writers, who believe that religion developed because it served a function (survival, comfort, social, etc.), Bloom has written that religion's emergence was basically an accident. He pointed out that we evolved to have two processing systems. One system is used for dealing with the physical world, while the other for the psychological/social world. Physical things are seen as being controlled by the laws of nature, whereas psychological things (like people) are seen as having minds, intentions, beliefs, goals, and desires that are not governed by the same principles. The adaptive value of a system that helps individuals to navigate their way around the physical world is fairly obvious, but there is also adaptive value in being able to function socially: Those ancestors of ours who could not do this sufficiently well to be accepted by the group were left to their own devices in a dangerous world, reducing the likelihood that they would survive or find a mate, which in turn made them less likely to contribute their genes to the gene pool.

Dealing with the psychological/social world requires a different set of tools than that used in the physical world. These tools are based on the human propensity to infer agency, that is, to have a *theory of mind* about others that allows them to empathize with them. That ability is crucial for the ability to predict how other people will behave and for getting along with them. While both of these are useful today, they had obvious survival value for our prehistoric ancestors as those members of the group that were unable to understand how to function socially with the rest of the group were, for a variety of reasons, less likely to survive and thus contribute their genes to the gene pool. However, as useful as this second system is, according to Bloom, our system of social understanding is overly active and so is activated even at times that offer no adaptive advantage (e.g., getting angry at your Xbox when it defeats you in a game).

Barrett (2004) referred to the mechanisms that underlie this overactive social system as *hyperactive agency detection devices*, and Boyer referred to this propensity as *hypertrophy of social cognition* (Boyer, 2001). According to Barrett, human beings have a built-in bias to perceive agency, even when there is clearly no intention there. For example, human beings have often seen rain as a result of the will of God (or gods), who is providing water for their crops to reward them for good behavior. And who does not get angry at a vending machine that accepts money but fails to deliver the requested soft drink, as if it intended to frustrate or cheat them? Barrett saw belief in God as an "almost inevitable consequence of the kinds of minds we have" (2004, p. 91). Most of what we believe is a result of mental tools that operate outside of our awareness, and even what we believe consciously is driven largely by these unconscious beliefs.

Barrett also talked about human beings as having two types of beliefs: reflective and non-reflective. Reflective beliefs are the result of conscious thought processes and are less compelling than non-reflective beliefs. What we consciously believe is often fueled by our unconscious non-reflective beliefs, and these beliefs then lead to after-the-fact rational explanations for these automatic beliefs. Non-reflective beliefs are automatic, spontaneous, and universal; they require no thought or reflection. They feel natural, and they feel intuitively true. Examples of non-reflective beliefs are dualism, creationism, selfhood, souls, and God.

Do Atheists Exist?

As a consequence of our social/psychological processing system, human beings have a number of propensities in the way they think: First of all, we are natural born dualists. The presence of these two systems gives rise to a duality of experience whereby we experience the world of material things as separate from the world of intentions and desires. As Bloom stated,

> it seems intuitively obvious to us that the physical body and a conscious entity—a mind or soul—are genuinely distinct. We don't feel like we *are* our bodies. Rather, we feel that we *occupy* them, we *possess* them, we *own* them. (2005, p. 109)

Bloom pointed out that while the notion of an immaterial soul that can be separated from the body conflicts with how most scientists look at this, nevertheless, it just feels right. And once the notion of the mind as separate from the body has been established, it is a short cognitive jump to having a mind that can live even after the body is gone, thus heaven and the afterlife.

There are a number of such spiritual beliefs that feel intuitively right. The reason that they feel so right is that they are a byproduct of our biologically-based mental structure and so could be said to be built into our hard-wiring. While these beliefs never completely disappear, they can be inhibited by higher order beliefs. The theory of natural selection, for example, is a complex theory that is clearly counterintuitive; no one is born believing that reduced death rates resulting from random genetic mutations that happen to be adaptive are the basis for the evolution of all life. But once an individual is exposed to and then develops an understanding of natural selection, this theory generally comes to override the more intuitively appealing belief in a creator. So, while some individuals deny that God actually exists, this belief never completely disappears; it simply goes underground as other beliefs supersede it. (Just ask a self-proclaimed atheist to describe to you the God that he/she doesn't believe in!) This is analogous to developing the capacity to inhibit the impulse to murder or steal. Most people live their lives without actually killing or stealing, and they may not even have a strong awareness of such desires, but this does not mean that under the surface these more primitive impulses have been entirely eliminated.

FOSTERING AWE, WONDER, AND A SENSE OF THE DIVINE: FROM EXTERNAL ABSOLUTES TO INTERNAL RESPONSIBILITY

Religion, at its best, is a collective effort to foster experiences of the sacred. Hill et al. (2000) echoed this view when they described religion as the methods involved in the search for the sacred that are supported by a particular group of people. However, this characterization has the drawback of seeming to imply that what is being sought is something outside of the self, the search for a holy grail of sorts. It is suggested here, instead, that an experience of the sacred is an entirely internal process. Sacredness is not a *property* of a person, place, thing or activity: It is a projection of an internal attitude onto that external person, place, thing or activity. In other words, it is the meaning that we give to it. Considerable blood has been spilled over the ages in the quest to save the souls of the world's heathens, infidels, and nonbelievers by helping them to worship the correct god. This is nearly always a byproduct of the mistake of confusing one's inner world with the world around them. It is easier to understand the sacred as something to be found out there rather than as a type of experience to be fostered via a focus on one's own psyche. Watts (1969) wrote that the problem with religion as it is generally practiced is that religion is actually like a thumb pointing the way along a path, but unfortunately, most adherents end up sucking the thumb.

The process of internalization is an important aspect of human psychological development. This can be seen in the development of one's superego, one's experience of the sacred, and in one's relationship with God. The maturation of the superego is essentially the gradual integration of messages that originated outside of the self. Children move from behaving morally in order to get praise and avoid punishment, to following rules simply because rules should be followed, to experiencing things as absolute good or evil, to eventually taking responsibility for the values they hold as their own. This can be illustrated by looking at how an individual feels about stealing. At first, the child refrains from stealing in order to avoid punishment. Over time, this evolves into a rule that must be obeyed ("thou shalt not steal"). This then becomes the belief that stealing is bad or evil; it is an absolute moral truth. This attitude was exemplified by Kant when he described morality as part of a transcendent realm that is outside of the natural order of the world (Kant, 1797/1996). Unlike nature, which he characterized as a determined world of cause and effect, he saw the realm of morals as a matter of free will, with the individual making a choice about whether or not to comply with universal moral law. For Kant, good and bad were absolute truths; our task is to discover those truths and live by the *categorical imperative* of following them simply because they are right and so we *ought to*. This absolutist, transcendentalist way of thinking about stealing evolves to the next level of moral development, in which the people choose not to steal because they know they will feel bad about violating their own moral code. They understand that it may feel wrong, it may even feel like the violation of a universal moral truth, but they understand that it is really their own value, even if everyone around them seems to share the same value. The fact that so many people have very similar moral values is not a coincidence. Human beings have similar brains, and thus have similar attitudinal tendencies; these attitudinal tendencies are typically experienced as absolute good and evil. It can be speculated that the more innately, biologically based a particular value or belief is, the more compelling it is, and so the more likely it is to be experienced as a universal moral absolute.

This developmental tendency for increasing internalization can also be found in the way that human beings experience the sacred. Is an ancient Torah scroll sacred? Would a wine cup that had been used by Jesus be a sacred object? To say that something is sacred is generally thought to be making a statement about that object (or person or activity) that transcends any reference point. It implies that it has the *property* of sacredness and that therefore it is sacred independent of anyone's experience of it. But might there be another way of understanding what it means to say that something is sacred? That is, might someone's characterizing something as sacred actually be a statement about the observer's subjective experience of that object, that is, the meaning that it has for that individual? As an individual matures, the experience of sacredness becomes increasingly internalized as there is a shift from seeing something as having the property of sacredness to seeing it as something that matters to him or her in a sacred way. In other words, the individual is able to take greater responsibility for the meaning that that thing has for him or herself.

While I was an undergraduate at the University of Illinois, I studied karate. Several times a week I would bow as I entered the dojo for two hours of what felt like an other-worldly experience of focus and discipline. The sensei, or teacher, was treated with almost priestly respect. We had rituals as well as requirements and prohibitions (e.g., someone leaving the dojo would not turn their back and just walk out; the proper way to leave was to back out and, of course, bow respectfully). We had essentially created a sacred space to practice this discipline. But was there anything intrinsically sacred about this dojo? Well, not exactly. In fact, it was actually just a smelly, old gymnasium that had been built over 60 years earlier. Still, those of us who were able to react to the dojo as if it really were sacred, that is, as if it had the property of sacredness, had a different kind of experience than those who could not.

Finally, the principle of equating maturity with greater internalization and the assumption of greater personal responsibility for one's own experience can also be seen to apply to experiences of God. The experience of God is, at bottom, a relationship: a relationship with internalized object representations that are derived from the relationships with our early life caretakers. Initially the image of an idealized parental figure is projected out onto the world and produces the compelling sense of there being a supernatural being out there who is real and whose presence has a powerful impact on the world. For many, this relationship with God becomes fixed in time, and God remains a reified, externalization of their internal object representation. While the internal representation is a permanent fixture in the psyche, as individuals continue to take increasing responsibility for their inner world, the relationship they have with this projected parental Other evolves. As the individual matures, and the object representation becomes increasingly integrated and owned as part of his/her own psyche, the individual's experience of God changes. God is experienced less and less as an external entity that has supernatural power in the material world, and increasingly as a voice from within that demands to be paid attention to. Much like Jung's warning about the destructive consequences of ignoring the archetypes of our collective unconscious

(Jung, 1938), it is at our peril that we ignore the voice of this religiogenic object representation.

ARE SPIRITS NECESSARY FOR SPIRITUALITY? REDEFINING SPIRITUALITY

Religion, at its best, is centered around the pursuit of the experience of the sacred. The experience of love, gratitude, awe, and wonder, along with a sense of the magical and the divine, are universal goals for most of the great religious traditions. Supernatural entities like God, souls, and spirits are core elements of most religious narratives, but are they really necessary for the achievement of a rich spiritual life? Spirituality is generally thought of as a transcendent experience that involves attunement to the spirit world. It is suggested here that what is transcended is not the natural world, per se, but rather one's own ego-based concerns that underlie the preoccupation with events in the natural/material world: in short, the mundane problems that are derived from the need for security in our everyday life. The ability to shift one's attention from ordinary ego-based concerns to higher order needs (as described by Maslow, 1970) is a core element of spiritual intelligence.

SO WHAT TO DO?

Religious naturalism is a philosophy that states that there is nothing that operates outside of the laws of nature (in other words, there is no such thing as the supernatural) but that this should in no way lessen our sense of awe in response to the wonders of nature. A leading figure in this movement, Goodenough wrote in *The Sacred Depths of Nature* that a scientific account of nature can "call forth appealing and abiding religious responses" (Goodenough, 1998, p. xvii). But religious naturalists are a small group. It is simply not that easy to look beyond the traditional ways of understanding the nature of the world. It is much easier to see Gods, souls, spirits, demons, the afterlife, and moral absolutes than it is to explore the complex inner world that these sorts of constructs are derived from. When at a movie theater, it is easy to forget that what is being watched on the screen in front of you is really just a projection; the source is the projector in the dark little room behind you.

There is an old joke about a police officer who finds a drunken man crawling around on his hands and knees under a street light one night. When asked what he was doing he tells the officer that he is looking for his keys. After twenty minutes of crawling around together on the sidewalk, the officer finally asks the man if he is sure that this is where he lost his keys. The man replies that he actually thinks he lost them across the street. "Then why are you looking here?" asked the officer. "Because the light is better here," replies the man.

Such has been the search for answers to questions about the nature and workings of the universe, the origins of human beings, and the paths to a more spiritual life. The light has always been better when we have looked to religion, specifically to God, for answers. As our ability to maneuver in the material world has developed, what has been learned has increasingly usurped traditional religion's role as the default answer to such questions. Nevertheless, the vast majority of people, from poor uneducated third world peasants to modern, highly educated westerners, continue to look to God for answers, particularly when asking questions about spiritual life.

But the fact that the light is better there does not in-and-of-itself make it a better place to look for answers. It is being argued here that spiritual growth is an internal process that involves a transformation of one's psyche. So, while there may be less light in the black box of the psyche, we ought to make use of the rapidly growing understanding of just how things operate in that black box as our modus operandi when dealing with questions about spiritual growth rather than the better lit externalized reifications of internal processes. Despite the nearly universal preoccupation with the qualities of the external referent that is God, at bottom, the subjective experience of God is essentially an internal relationship. And consequently what needs to be focused on is the relationship itself, not the qualities of the external referent (since it is really just a projection of internal representations anyway). Ultimately what people really want is to live a life that is characterized by a felt sense of loving, divine presence. We will never get there as long as we continue to confuse our externalized reifications of inner processes, with the inner processes themselves. Imagine instead, a world in which people are focused on maximizing the spiritual quality of their (and others') lives, where the narcissistic need to make others conform to our own beliefs is replaced by respect for the possibility of many paths to more fully human, self-actualized lives, and where you have the paradox of individuals cooperating to support the ultimately solitary quest to live a life that is characterized by love, a sense of awe and wonder, and a felt sense of the sacred.

REFERENCES

Barrett, J.L. (2004). *Why would anyone believe in God?* Walnut Creek, CA: AltaMira Press.

Bloom, P. (2005). Is God an accident? *The Atlantic Monthly, 296*(5), 105–112. http://www.theatlantic.com/

Boyer, P. (2001). *Religion explained: The evolutionary origins of religious thought.* New York, NY: Basic Books.

Buber, M. (1958). *I and thou.* New York, NY: Charles Scribner's Sons.

Dawkins, R. (2006). *The God delusion.* Boston, MA: Houghton Mifflin Co.

Durkheim, E. (1995). *The elementary forms of religious life.* New York, NY: The Free Press/Simon & Schuster. (Original work published 1912)

Fowler, J.W. (1981). *Stages of faith: The psychology of human development and the quest for meaning.* New York, NY: Harper Collins Publishers.

Goodenough, U. (1998). *The sacred depths of nature.* New York, NY: Oxford University Press.

Harris, S. (2005). *The end of faith: Religion, terror, and the future of reason.* New York, NY: W.W. Norton & Company.

Hill, P.C., Pargament, K.I., Hood, R.W., McCullough, M.E., Swyers, J.P., Larson, D.B. & Zinnbauer, B.J. (2000). Conceptualizing religion and spirituality: Points of commonality, points of departure. *Journal for the Theory of Social Behavior, 30*(1), 51–77. doi:10.1111/1468-5914.00119

Jung, C.G. (1938). *Psychology and religion: West and east.* Collected Works, Vol. 11. New Haven, CT: Yale University Press.

Kant, I. (Trans. 1996). *The metaphysics of morals.* Cambridge, England: Cambridge University Press. (Original work published 1797)

Kierkegaard, S. (1981). *The concept of anxiety.* Princeton, NJ: Princeton University Press. (Original work published 1844)

Kirkpatrick, L.A. (2005). *Attachment, evolution, and the psychology of religion.* New York, NY: The Guilford Press.

Maslow, A. (1970). *Religion, values, and peak experiences.* New York, NY: The Viking Press.

Mirman, M.C. (2004). The subjective experience of God. *American Journal of Pastoral Counseling, 7*(2), 41–54. doi:10.1300/J062v07n02_04

Mirman, M.C. (2007, March). *The psychology of religion: Does it explain religion or just explain it away?* Paper presented at Division 36 Mid-Winter Annual Conference, Loyola College, Columbia, MD.

Mirman, M.C. (2008, February). *Are spirits necessary for spirituality?* Paper presented at Division 36 Mid-Winter Annual Conference, Loyola College, Columbia, MD.

Rizzuto, A.-M. (1979). *The birth of the living God.* Chicago, IL: The University of Chicago Press.

Watts, A. (1969). *Psychotherapy east and west.* New York, NY: Ballantine Books.

A TALE OF TWO THEISTIC STUDIES: ILLUSTRATIONS AND EVALUATION OF A POTENTIAL PROGRAM OF THEISTIC PSYCHOLOGICAL RESEARCH

Jeffrey S. Reber, Brent D. Slife, and Samuel D. Downs

ABSTRACT

Two empirical research studies are described that illustrate the potential value of joining conventional social science and theistic religion in a theistic program of psychological research. The first study shows how a theistic program of psychological research tweaks the existing psychological research on the formation of God attachment to include a new assessment, experiences of God. The results of Study 1 indicate that experiences of God are an important predictor of theists' attachment to God, even when controlling for parental attachment. The second study exemplifies how theistic ideas can lead to a new program of psychological research, in this case research on implicit attitudes toward faith and science, and can generate new scientific instruments such as the modified Implicit Association Test used in this study. The results of Study 2 suggest that education and training in psychology may lead theistic psychology students to implicitly endorse a secular stereotype that they consciously reject. Implications of the findings of both studies are discussed and the heuristic value of a theistic program of psychological research is explored.

Keywords: Theistic psychology, God image, faithism, religion, prejudice, research

In this paper, we are interested in describing two examples of a theistic approach to psychology that have produced rigorous empirical and quantitative research. Conventional science and theistic religion have long been considered relatively independent of one another (e.g., Dixon, 2008), but we would like to show how this traditional chasm can be bridged. To be sure, the scientific method has been used to investigate the religious in fields like the psychology of religion. Yet, these investigations still consider science and religion to be ultimately independent because religious ideas are not typically used to frame the hypotheses or explain the data. Here we show in these two examples how conventional social science and theistic religion can truly be joined.

---

* *Author Note*: Jeffrey S. Reber, Department of Psychology, Brigham Young University; Brent D. Slife, Department of Psychology, Brigham Young University; Samuel D. Downs, Department of Psychology, Brigham Young University.

Correspondence regarding this article should be addressed to Jeffrey S. Reber, Department of Psychology, Brigham Young University, 1001 Kimball Tower, P.O. Box 25543, Provo, UT 84602. Email: jeff_reber@byu.edu

Research in the Social Scientific Study of Religion, Volume 23
© *Koninklijke Brill NV, Leiden, 2012*

The first example shows how existing research can be tweaked to produce this joining. One would think that psychological research on people's representations of God had already effected this joining, but to this point, researchers have rarely considered theistic hypotheses or explanations in their research on people's God image (e.g., O'Grady & Richards, 2008). We describe how a theistic program of research suggests empirically testable theistic hypotheses that have been mostly overlooked by conventional psychological researchers, such as the hypothesis that theists' experiences of God contribute to the development of their God image.

The second example shows how theistic ideas can lead not only to a whole new program of research but also to the development of new scientific instruments. Psychologists have long been interested in implicit attitudes and beliefs and their effects on each other and on behavior (Gawronski & Payne, 2010). A theistic approach to psychology suggests a host of as yet uninvestigated studies in this important research area. As one illustration, we describe the preliminary results of an empirical study that examines the impact of education and training in psychology on theists' implicit theistic and naturalistic attitudes and beliefs.

EXAMPLE 1: THE GOD IMAGE

As we have described (Slife, Reber & Lefevor, this issue), a theistic worldview assumes that God is actively and currently involved in psychological phenomena in a difference making way. This assumption opens the theistic psychologist up to aspects of psychological phenomena and ways of studying them that have rarely been considered. One such phenomenon is the development of theists' God image. Conventional God image researchers assume that theists' early childhood experiences with parents and other authority figures are a significant contributor to the development of their representations of God (Reinert & Edwards, 2009). However, they often exclude experiences with one important authority figure for theists, God, even though these experiences might also contribute to the development of theists' God images (e.g., Cassibba, Granqvist, Costantini, & Gatto, 2008). The thoroughgoing theist, on the other hand, is explicitly interested in experiences of God and would form a hypothesis to test whether and to what extent experiences with God predict theists' God images. The test of this hypothesis, as we will illustrate, could closely follow the methodology already used in conventional God image research, with a few modifications.

Methodology

Given attachment theory's emphasis on experiences with parents, the methodology typically used in God image research relies primarily on self-reports of childhood experiences and parental attachment. That is, using either an interview (e.g., the Adult Attachment Interview) or a survey (e.g., Parental Attachment Measure) God image researchers gather data about participants' experiences with their parents. They then examine those experiences in order to assess the extent to which they were positive or negative and indicative of a secure or insecure parental attachment style. They also assess participants' God image, typically using a self-report instrument like the God Attachment Measure to examine whether the participants' God image is more positive or negative, secure or insecure. Then, they correlate the two measures to test the extent to which parental attachment predicts God attachment. If there is a significant positive correlation, the researchers typically conclude that the hypothesis has been supported that experiences with parents, which develop a secure or insecure parental attachment style, contribute to a similar style of attachment to God and a God image that is consistent with the image of one's parents and other authority figures.

In researching this topic, conventional researchers typically have not included the possible role that experiences of God might play in the development of theists' attachment to God. Their reasons for leaving this potentially important variable out of their studies are rarely explained or justified by a methodological rationale. Lawrence (1997), for example, simply asserted without any empirical support or theoretical explanation that "the God representation . . . is not based directly on experiences of God" (p. 214). O'Grady and Richards (2008) have closely reviewed the God image literature looking for something more than Lawrence's just-so assertion. They came to the conclusion that "this neglect seems to come from an underlying atheistic presupposition that because God is not real, a real relationship with him could not possibly be part of the explanation of God image formation" (p. 189). Slife and Reber (2009a) have also critically examined this exclusion of experiences of God and trace the omission of experiences of God to the naturalistic worldview underpinning conventional psychological research.

Given that the exclusion of experiences of God appears to be based primarily on the worldview of the researchers conducting the study and not on the basis of a methodological justification, we decided to include experiences of God in our God image study. In our own consideration of this research variable, we could see no in principle methodological reason for excluding reports of one set of experiences and including the other. Participants' reports of their experiences of God are as describable, measurable, and statistically analyzable as their reports of experiences of parents or any other experience. By including experiences of God as a research variable in our study, we were able to evaluate the extent to which experiences of God correlate with theists' attachment to God just as conventional researchers examine the degree to which experiences of parents correlate with attachment to parents.

The Current Study

In light of the theoretical and methodological parallels and modifications just described, we have conducted a theistic psychological study that investigates the extent to which theistic participants' attachment to God is positively correlated with their personal experiences with God. Specifically, we hypothesized that experiences with God account for a significant percentage of the variance in participants' attachment to God, even when controlling for the variance accounted for by parental attachment. Results confirming this hypothesis would suggest that experiences with God could be a necessary factor in theists' development of their attachment to God, which, together with parental attachment, accounts for a large portion of the variance in the phenomenon.

Participants. Eighty-five undergraduate students who self-identified as theistic were recruited for participation in this study from two private religious institutions, Brigham Young University and Trinity International University. The average age of participants was 20.5 and 66% of the participants were female. Fifty-three percent of the participants (all from BYU) self-identified as Latter-Day Saint (LDS), 8% indicated that they were protestant Christian, 29.4% listed their religion as evangelical Christian, and 9.4% self-identified as "Other."

Instruments. Three instruments were used in this study: the Parental Attachment Measure (PAM), the God Attachment Measure (GAM), and the Experiences with God Measure (EGM).

The PAM is a retrospective self-report measure of parent-child attachment modified from Collins and Read's (1990) Adult Attachment Measure and Hazan and Shaver's (1987) adult attachment descriptions. The PAM and the instruments from which it was developed are designed to assess participants' adult attachment styles, which Bowlby (1973) asserted, "are tolerably accurate reflections of the experiences those individuals have actually had" (p. 235). The PAM consists of 18 Likert-type items evenly divided into three subscales: dependence, anxiety, and closeness. The dependence subscale measures the participants' perceived ability to rely on their parents with higher scores indicating more dependence. The anxiety subscale measures feelings of uncertainty about being loved and/ or abandoned and is reverse scored with higher subscale scores indicating less anxiety about the relationship. The closeness subscale measures the warmth of the relationship with parents with higher scores indicating a closer relationship. The items for each subscale are summed together for a subscale score. The subscales may also be totaled for an overall measure of parental attachment with higher scores indicating more secure attachment. The PAM has a Cronbach's reliability coefficient of .84.

The GAM is a modification of the PAM that is designed to assess participants' attachment to God using the same questions as the PAM with the references to parents replaced with references to God. As with the PAM, the GAM consists of 18 Likert-type items evenly divided among three subscales (dependence, anxiety, and closeness) that are scored and totaled in the same manner as the PAM. The GAM has a Cronbach's reliability coefficient of .82. Both the PAM and GAM have been used in several previously published peer-reviewed research articles.

The EGM was created for the purposes of this research as a self-report measure of participants' experiences with God. A research team consisting of a professor, a graduate student, and three undergraduate students generated the items for the instrument. Each person came up with 10 possible items that were compiled into a larger list. The team met together to remove any redundant or confusing items and reduced the number of items to 18. The wording of each item was adjusted to make sure it was similar to the wording of the items used by parental attachment researchers to examine experiences of parents.

Similar to the PAM and GAM, the items were formatted into a Likert-type scale with "*never*" and "*frequently*" as anchors. The items were then reviewed by a sample of students in the professor's psychology course to ensure clear wording and fit with their experiences of God. Examples of the items included in the final instrument include: "I have experienced God comforting me when I am sad," "God has touched my heart," and "I have experienced God's presence when I worship." Four items concerning negative experiences with God were also included, such as "I have experienced God's anger toward me." These four items were reversed scored and summed with the other 14 items for a total score derived from 18 total questions. Higher scores on the EGM indicate more positive experiences with God. The 2-week test-retest reliability of the EGM is .88.

Procedure. Participants were provided with a hyperlink to the online survey. After giving consent each participant took the survey, which consisted of four parts: a demographics questionnaire, the PAM, the GAM, and the EGM. The survey took approximately 10 minutes to complete. Following their completion of the survey, participants were debriefed and thanked for their participation.

RESULTS

PAM/GAM correlation. Consistent with the findings of previous research, we found a moderate, positive correlation between participants' overall scores on The PAM and their overall scores on the GAM (see Table 1). Correlations for all subscale scores were also significant. These findings support the hypothesis that parental attachment is a moderate predictor of theists' attachment to God and that specific styles of attachment to parents are significantly correlated with the specific forms of attachment to God. Following the common practice for statistically determining the variance contributed by each measure to the correlation between all measures (Baba, Shibata, & Sibuya, 2004), we then conducted a partial correlation analysis. A partial correlation analysis determines the portion of the variance in the PAM-GAM relationship that is accounted for by PAM by statistically removing the variance in the PAM-GAM correlation that is accounted for by the EGM measure.

The results of the partial correlation analysis show that when you control for the variance in the PAM-GAM correlation that is accounted for by EGM, the correlation between PAM and GAM reduces by 26%, and the variance in the PAM-GAM relationship that is accounted for by PAM, when controlling for the effects of EGM, is cut by almost half. This suggests that although parental attachment is a predictor of God attachment and is a necessary condition for understanding God attachment, it is probably insufficient to explain God attachment. It may even be the case that the prediction power of parental attachment is attenuated by experiences with God. Further analyses will help us better interrogate this possibility.

EGM/GAM correlation. Consistent with the theistic hypothesis of this study, results show that there is a strong, positive correlation between respondents' overall EGM scores and their overall GAM scores, and EGM

Table 1. *Bivariate and Partial Correlation Coefficients of Parental Attachment Measure (PAM), God Attachment Measure (GAM), and Experiences with God Measure (EGM), with Variance Estimates.*

Correlated Measures	Bivariate Correlation (r)	r^2	Variable Controlled	Partial Correlation (r)	r^2	Variance Reduced
PAM-GAM	.38**	.14	EWG	.28*	.08	43%
PAMdep-GAMdep	.41**	.17		.28*	.08	53%
PAManx-GAManx	.40**	.16		.34**	.12	25%
PAMcls-GAMcls	.32**	.10		.21	.04	33%
EGM-GAM	.52**	.27	PAM	.47**	.22	19%
EGM-GAMdep	.74**	.55	PAMdep	.70**	.49	11%
EGM-GAManx	−.52**	.27	PAManx	−.49**	.24	11%
EGM-GAMcls	.54**	.29	PAMcls	.49**	.24	17%
PAM-EGM	.27*	.07	GAM	.10	.01	86%
PAMdep-EGM	.32**	.10	GAMdep	.02	.00	100%
PAManx-EGM	−.22*	.05	GAManx	−.02	.00	99%
PAMcls-EGM	.29**	.08	GAMcls	.14	.02	75%

$*p < .05$ $**p < .01$

is also a strong predictor of participants' GAM subscale scores (see Table 1). This supports the idea that experiences with God are strongly associated with theists' attachment to God and their particular form or style of attachment. In order to determine the proportion of variance in the EGM-GAM relationship that can be accounted for by EGM with the effects of PAM on the EGM-GAM correlation statistically removed, we conducted a partial correlation.

Results show that there was only a slight decrease in the variance accounted for in the EGM-GAM relationship by EGM when the effects of PAM are removed, indicating that the EGM is a significant predictor of GAM with or without the variance contributed by PAM to that relationship. These findings suggest that experience with God may be a necessary factor in the development of theists' attachment to God in its own right. That is, its predictive utility with regard to theists' attachment to God appears to be largely undiminished by the inclusion or exclusion of parental attachment. A final analysis will help determine whether this is likely the case.

PAM/EGM correlation. To fully interrogate the relationship among these three measures and to better understand the contribution of EGM to GAM, it is necessary to examine the relationship of the predictor variables, PAM and EGM. If the correlation between these two measures is high and if the variance accounted for in the relationship between the PAM and EGM is not due primarily to each variable's relationship to GAM, then it is possible that the measures are not that different. In other words, it could be, as conventional researchers have suggested, that experiences with God are strongly influenced by or even developed out of parental attachment. To examine this possibility we correlated participants' overall EGM scores and their composite PAM scores, as well as the PAM subscale scores.

The overall correlation between the two measures was small and positive but significant (see Table 1). However, a partial correlation analysis, which controls for the variance in the PAM-EGM relationship that is due to the GAM, shows a significant decrease in the PAM-EGM correlation. Indeed the correlation drops to insignificant levels. This means that only 1% of the variation in the PAM-EGM correlation can be accounted for by PAM or EGM when the variance in the relationship accounted for by GAM is statistically removed. This suggests that theists' experiences with God and parental attachment are not directly associated with each other. Each phenomenon appears to be related to the other only by virtue of their each being related to God attachment.

Discussion

The results of this study suggest at least three potentially valuable contributions to the God image research literature. First, they support the hypothesis that experiences of God are strongly associated with theists' attachment to God; not as a derivative of parental attachment but as a particular and particularly strong predictor of theists' attachment to God. Second, they support the methodological claim that experiences of God are as assessable as experiences of parents and any other experiences. Granted, the EGM is an initial foray into the development of instruments that could measure these experiences and will need further validation in future research studies before it can become a vetted measure. However, this statement could be said of any new psychological measure that is being developed and tested. We hope other researchers will test the EGM and develop additional measures, both quantitative and qualitative, that can more fully interrogate and validate the assessment of this important phenomenon. At the very least it will be important to identify which types of experiences of God are most predictive of particular attachment styles, something that was not studied in this research, but would better parallel the parental attachment instruments that have been developed.

Third, the results of this study add support for a theistic form of attachment theory. That is, the findings seem to indicate that attachment theory could be reasonably and productively adapted to an understanding of theists' relationship to God, a relationship that for theists is just as real and important, if not more so, than their relationship to their parents. Our study does suggest that experiences of God might contribute to God attachment in much the same way that experiences of parents appear to contribute to parental attachment. Why not develop a theistic theory of attachment to frame theistic psychologists' understanding of this phenomenon and to generate additional hypotheses to test various aspects of the theory? Such an approach falls right in line with conventional researchers' conceptualization of a scientific program of psychological research.

EXAMPLE 2: IMPLICIT THEISTIC AND NATURALISTIC ATTITUDES

We have just reviewed a study that illustrates how a theistic worldview opens up new possibilities for studying and theorizing about a topic that has been the focus of a great deal of conventional research. Now, we will review a study that illustrates how a theistic worldview opens up possibilities for developing entirely new programs of research, investigating psychological topics that have been overlooked by conventional researchers and that promote the development of new scientific instruments and theories. One example of a new program of research that we are currently developing investigates the effects of implicit attitudes and beliefs about naturalism, theism, and the relationship between the two.

We have discussed in our theoretical paper in this special issue and elsewhere (Reber, 2006; Slife & Reber, 2009a; Slife, Reber & Faulconer, in press) the widely held secular assumption that science is an objective and unbiased method of investigation, and faith is a subjective perspective that differs among religions and individuals and can lead to biased perceptions and explanations (for examples of this assumption see Helminiak, 2010 and Alcock, 2009). We have also traced this secular assumption to the *myth of neutrality* (Flashing, 2010) that often accompanies the naturalistic worldview, which is "the central dogma of science" (Leahey, 1991, p. 379). Finally, we have challenged the myth of neutrality by showing that naturalism and theism are distinct worldviews built on alternative sets of assumptions that lead to different implications for how psychologists understand people, the world, and God. Put in the simplest terms, the naturalistic worldview assumes that God is not necessary to psychological explanation, and a thoroughgoing theism assumes that God is necessary. Given this fundamental incompatibility, we conclude that naturalism is not neutral with regard to theism.

To support our conclusion, we have described some of the historical effects of psychology's adoption of the naturalistic worldview on theism, including the exclusion of God from psychology texts; method practices that discriminate against including theistic hypotheses, measures, and explanations; and the omission of theism from theistic theories that are adopted into psychology (Slife & Reber, 2009a). We have also shown that when theistic concepts are omitted, they are replaced by naturalistic explanations and conceptions (Slife & Reber, in press). In this sense, naturalism does not just exclude God but fosters a replacement worldview. In considering these and other potential consequences of naturalism for theism, we have also wondered whether psychology's adoption of naturalism might have demonstrable effects on theists' beliefs and attitudes, including the beliefs and attitudes of theistic psychologists (Reber, 2006; Slife & Reber, in press). In developing this study, we specifically wondered whether education and training in psychology might have an effect on theistic students' attitudes and beliefs about theism and naturalism. Following our theoretical work on the relationship of naturalism and theism (Slife & Reber, this issue; 2009a; 2009b) we decided to examine whether theistic students' implicit attitudes and beliefs would become more naturalistic as a consequence of their training and education in scientific psychology. More precisely, we tested the hypothesis that their implicit theistic attitudes and beliefs would become more naturalistic as their education and training in psychology increased, as evidenced by their greater unconscious acceptance of the secular stereotype that science is objective and fair and faith is subjective and biased.

Researchers have long been interested in the relationship between higher education and students' religiosity more generally. Early research in this area strongly suggested that students' religious practices and beliefs declined as their college education increased (e.g., Caplovitz & Sherrow, 1977). By 1983, the finding seemed so compelling and consistent that the sociologist Hunter boldly concluded, "It is a well-established fact that education, even Christian education, secularizes" (p. 132). More recently, researchers have been much more circumspect about drawing these conclusions. Some have even found in studies of more current datasets (e.g., Lee, 2002) and meta-analyses based on research from the last two decades (e.g., Pascarella & Terenzini, 2005) that at least since 1990, there has been a consistent finding that most students' religious convictions actually increased during college.

In fact, sociologists Uecker, Regner, and Vaaler (2007) found that young adults who did not attend college were significantly more likely to attach less importance to religion since adolescence than young adults who are currently enrolled in college or who have earned a college degree. Uecker et al. (2007) did find that some religious practices tend to decline during college, such as church attendance, but "the religious belief systems of most students go largely untouched for the duration of their education" (p. 1683). Based on their review of the literature and their own findings, Uecker et al. concluded that "a college education is not the secularizing force we presumed it to be" (p. 1683). According to researchers Albrecht and Heaton (1998), this conclusion is especially true of young adult Mormon college students (the population of interest in our study), most of whom attend one of BYU's three campuses and whose explicit religious beliefs, attitudes and even practices, like church attendance, appear to increase during college.

It is important to note that virtually all of these findings have to do with conscious and explicit attitudes and beliefs. Recent research on prejudices and stereotypes, however, distinguishes between explicit and implicit attitudes, with the latter being prejudicial or biased even when the former are not (Blair, 2001). Based on this literature and the findings previously described, we hypothesized that the theistic students in our study would begin college with explicit attitudes that are favorable toward theism and that there would be no significant change in explicit attitudes as education level and class change. However, their explicit attitudes do not tell the whole story. As we have asserted in this special issue and elsewhere, it is psychologists' implicit theistic attitudes which are more likely to be influenced by the naturalistic worldview and its secular implications (e.g., Slife & Reber, 2009a, 2009b). Consequently, consistent with the implicit stereotype and prejudice research, we expect our theistic sample to explicitly reject the secular stereotype across all education-levels and class standing while implicitly becoming more accepting of the stereotype as their education and training in psychology increases.

The Study

If, as we have argued (Slife, Reber & Lefevor, this issue), psychology's naturalistic method assumptions are not neutral toward theism, then it is reasonable to assume that these assumptions are a kind of hidden ideology of its own and thus might have demonstrable effects on alternative beliefs and attitudes, such as those of theistic psychology students, particularly their implicit beliefs and attitudes. We focus our hypotheses on implicit theistic attitudes and beliefs because explicit attitudes and beliefs tend to be consciously controlled and may reflect the social and religious norms of the university environment where the students are located. The psychology students who participated in this study are all enrolled at Brigham Young University, a private religious institution of higher education, and are all members of the LDS church, with the vast majority attending at least 4 years of LDS seminary education. Given the natural religious pressures of an institution like BYU and its supporting church, it is highly likely that participants' explicit attitudes with regard to theism and naturalism will reflect public conformity with the religious norms and values of the broader institutional culture.

Implicit attitudes and beliefs, on the other hand, tend to be more unconscious and therefore are less likely to be controlled by the conscious mind and are less likely to reflect public conformity with the norms and values of the broader religious culture. At the same time, because these students are actively religious members of the LDS church and have chosen to attend a university supported by that church, we thought it highly likely that their implicit attitudes about theism at the beginning of their education in psychology would be favorable. In this sense, studying a theistic population would allow us to effectively test whether and to what extent participants' implicit attitudes might change from being initially more favorable toward theism to being more favorable toward naturalism near the end of their educational experience.

IAT

Researchers have long been interested in the role implicit attitudes and beliefs play in human thought, feelings, and actions. However, they have also had to be quite creative in developing instruments that would bypass or get behind the controlled attitudes that people explicitly express. In 1998, Greenwald, McGhee, and Schwartz introduced an instrument that they believed can be used to examine implicit attitudes and beliefs, the Implicit Association Test (IAT). Initially designed to examine implicit stereotypes, biases, and prejudices, the IAT has been used in thousands of studies to examine hundreds of topics across a variety of domains (Project Implicit, 2011). It has also been subjected to numerous tests of reliability and validity and used in several meta-analyses (e.g., Greenwald,

Poehlman, Uhlmann & Banaji, 2009; Nosek, Greenwald & Banaji, 2005). It appears to be a very rigorous method of examining automatic thoughts and feelings and has become the primary instrument psychologists use to study implicit attitudes and beliefs (Nosek, Greenwald & Banaji, 2007).

How does the instrument work? The basic premise of the instrument is that the speed of response with which a word is sorted into its proper category will differ, on the average, in trials where the category label is paired with another category label that is stereotypically associated with it (e.g., insect and bad) as opposed to trials where the category label is paired with another category label that is not stereotypically associated with it (e.g., insect and good). The assumption is that it should take longer to correctly sort words when the category labels are paired in the nonstereotypical way than the stereotypical way, indicating an implicit preference toward the stereotypical category pairing. The IAT used in this study follows this same standard procedure that Greenwald and his colleagues have developed and has been tested and validated numerous times (Greenwald, Nosek & Banaji, 2003). However, in order to examine implicit attitudes favoring theism or naturalism, we modified the IAT category labels and sorting words to test whether theistic psychology students come to implicitly adopt the popular secular stereotype that faith is biased and subjective and science is fair and objective as their education and training in psychology increases. Details of our modification are fully described in the instrument section.

Method

Participants. Two hundred seventy-seven participants were recruited to participate in this study. Undergraduate students were recruited from psychology courses offered at BYU. Graduate students in psychology and psychology department faculty were recruited via an email requesting their participation. Participant ages ranged from 17 to 64 years with an average age of 22.49. Just slightly over half of the participants were female (52%), and 98% indicated that they currently believed in God.

It is important to note that although most students at BYU are theistic and LDS, their education and training is similar to that of students at other comparable institutions. The psychology department curriculum conforms closely to the recommended curriculum for psychology majors published by the American Psychological Association (2007). Graduate students also follow a curriculum that is APA accredited. Faculty have been educated in APA accredited doctoral programs at universities that adhere to the APA guidelines for psychology education, and the texts they use in their courses are widely used across the discipline.

This strongly suggests that the education and training of the sample used in this study is not different from that of other institutions. Teachers are encouraged to integrate faith in their teaching, but there is no consistent way in which this is practiced or monitored. If anything, the integration of faith and teaching should work to support the implicit theistic attitudes of the participants, making them more resilient to change as a result of their exposure to psychology education. It should also be noted that the psychology degrees offered at BYU are scientific degrees (BS, MS, and Ph.D.), indicating that the scientific method is strongly emphasized by the department. For example, all undergraduate majors have to complete a set of four fairly standard courses in psychological statistics, research methods, measurement, and scientific writing that is strongly oriented toward scientific methods.

Procedure. After signing up to participate, participants were sent a link to the study that they could complete online when they had the time and privacy to complete the study in a comfortable and attentive manner. After opening the link and completing the consent form, a new window opened with instructions for completing the modified IAT. The instructions used were essentially the same as the instructions used in Greenwald et al.'s (2003) standard application of the IAT. After reading the instructions, the participants hit the space bar and the study began. Following completion of the IAT, the participants received their difference score and were informed that their score indicated either a strong, moderate, mild, or no preference for science over faith or for faith over science. Following the completion of the IAT, participants closed the window and responded to a demographic questionnaire and a 20-item explicit attitudes about faith questionnaire designed to assess participants' explicit attitudes towards faith and people of faith compared to science. After the participants completed the explicit attitudes questionnaire, a message appeared on the screen that thanked them for their participation and debriefed them. After reading the debriefing the study was complete, and the participants closed the window.

Instruments. There were two instruments used in this study: an explicit attitudes about faith measure and an implicit attitudes about faith measure, which is a modification of the IAT.

Explicit Attitudes about Faith: In order to examine participants' agreement with the stereotype that people of faith are prone to bias and subjectivity, and scientists are objective and fair, we first examined the research literature to see if any other instruments had been developed and used to examine this belief. In our review of the social science literature on this and related topics, we could find no study that used an instrument of any type designed to measure explicit attitudes toward faith and people of faith, and no instrument specifically focused on the stereotype of interest in this study. There were several instruments that measured negative attitudes among the religious directed toward the non-religious or toward different religions but none that looked at stereotypes or negative attitudes directed toward religion or faith in general and certainly none toward theism. Consequently, we designed our own instrument to assess this as yet untested construct. We developed 20 questions that examined attitudes toward faith and in several cases used wording that contrasted attitudes toward faith with attitudes toward science, which was consistent with the format of the IAT used in this study.

The first step in the process of developing the questions was to brainstorm about possible items that examine the stereotype that associates faith with bias and science with fairness. A large list was compiled by each of the participants on the research team, which included two faculty, two graduate students, and five undergraduate students. The research group then narrowed the number of items by removing redundant items and items that might confuse participants or not fit the stereotype. The resulting 20 items were then pretested for test-retest reliability over a two week period (Cronbach's alpha = .88). Given that there were no other measures that explicitly tested the stereotype or attitudes toward faith and people of faith generally, we could not conduct validity tests.

Implicit Attitudes about Faith: The IAT used in this study was an adaptation of the standard IAT format used for implicit prejudice studies. The four category labels that were used in this study were *Science, Faith, fair*, and *biased*. The selection of these category labels reflects the popular secular stereotype that science is an objective and value-free method that is neutral with regard to other worldviews and faith is a subjective perspective that differs among religions and individuals and promotes bias. In this way, our implicit and explicit measures assessed the same secular stereotype using different but comparable methods.

Following the standard procedure for administering the IAT, the IAT used in this study consisted of seven trials. The first two trials were learning trials designed to teach participants which words belong to which categories. The first trial presented "Science" and "Faith" on opposite top corners of the computer screen. A word (e.g., experiment) flashed in the middle of the screen, and the participants assigned it to the proper category (Science) as quickly as possible. All twenty words that belonged to the category of "Science" or "Faith" were randomly ordered and presented to the participants for sorting. The second trial presented the category labels "fair" and "biased" on opposing top corners of the screen. Each of the 20 words that belonged to those two categories was randomly selected and presented to the participants for sorting.

The third and fourth trials presented the category labels paired together in the stereotypical format with "Science" and "fair" listed together on one side of the screen and "Faith" and "biased" paired together on the other side. In the third trial, 20 words were randomly selected from the 40 words from all four categories. In the fourth trial, all 40 words were presented for sorting in random order. The average speed with which participants hit the key associated with the proper location of the category label was recorded across the two trials. In the fifth trial (another learning trial), the categories "Faith" and "Science" were presented, but their location on the top corners of the screen was reversed. All 20 words associated with those category labels appeared in the middle of the screen for sorting in random order. For trials six and seven, the category labels "fair" and "biased" were added to the top corners of the screen in their original locations, so now in the nonstereotypical manner "Science" and "biased" appeared on the same side and "Faith" and "fair" appeared on the other side. In the sixth trial, 20 of the 40 words were randomly selected and presented on the middle of the screen for placement in the proper category. In the seventh trial, all 40 words appeared and were sorted. Average speed of response was recorded across both trials and compared to the average response speed for trials three and four.

A difference score (d) was calculated for each participant. A positive difference score indicated that participants took longer to properly assign words to categories when the words were paired nonstereotypically than when category labels were paired stereotypically, suggesting a more naturalistic attitude. A negative score indicates that the participant took longer to assign words to their proper categories when the words were paired stereotypically than when they were paired nonstereotypically, suggesting a more theistic attitude. A score at or near zero indicated no difference in speed of accurate response and suggested no preference for naturalism or theism.

Results

Explicit attitudes. As a check on our hypothesis that explicit attitudes about faith were unlikely to reveal any change from theistic attitudes toward naturalistic attitudes, we first examined the results of the Explicit

Attitudes about Faith measure. Descriptive statistics revealed that participants' scores on this measure were primarily at the lower end of the points possible for the total. With a range of possible total scores from 20–140, with 20 representing very strong disagreement with the naturalistic stereotype and 140 representing very strong agreement with the naturalistic stereotype and 80 as the midpoint (neither agreeing nor disagreeing with the stereotype), the average total score across all respondents was 58.64 (SD = 11.66) which falls closest to the *disagree* score on the measure. This indicates that on average, participants disagreed with the naturalistic stereotype that science is fair and faith is biased.

Inferential tests (one-way ANOVA) were conducted to see if participants' explicit attitudes about faith differed according to their educational level (e.g., bachelor's degree) and class standing (e.g., freshman). Omnibus tests found no significant differences overall for each variable suggesting, as we predicted, that explicit attitudes about the naturalistic stereotype do not change as education and training in psychology increases (see Table 2).

Table 2. *Descriptive and Inferential Statistics for Education Level and Class by Explicit and Implicit Attitudes about Faith.*

Level of Education	Explicit Attitude		IAT score	
	Mean	*SD*	*Mean*	*SD*
High School Degree (n = 8)	56.63	14.12	−.47	.23
Associate's Degree (n = 28)	55.39	11.58	−.38	.33
Some College (n = 183)	58.86	11.91	−.19	.42
Bachelor's Degree (n = 25)	57.72	10.05	−.15	.54
Graduate School (n = 12)	63.17	8.79	.10*	.26
Master's Degree (n = 8)	59.50	9.12	.21	.54
Doctoral Degree (n = 5)	64.20	15.42	.31	.42
Omnibus ANOVA Test	$F(6, 261) = .94, p = .47$		$F(6, 262) = 4.98, p <.001\ \eta_p^2 = .10$	
Class Standing	Mean	SD	Mean	SD
Freshman (n = 55)	60.69	12.21	−.26	.35
Sophomore (n = 44)	57.95	12.00	−.24	.46
Junior (n = 69)	58.65	12.19	−.22	.44
Senior (n = 57)	56.72	10.69	−.11	.46
Graduate Student (n = 17)	63.29	10.92	.15**	.39
Omnibus ANOVA Test	$F(4, 236) = 1.48, p = .21$		$F(4, 237) = 3.78, p = .005\ \eta_p^2 = .06$	

* Differs significantly from High School Degree (mean difference = .57, p = .001), Associate's Degree (mean difference = .48, p = .001), and Some College (mean difference = .28, p = .035).
** Differs significantly from Freshman (mean difference=.41, p = .006), Sophomore (mean difference = .39, p = .019, and Junior (mean difference = .37, p = .016).
Note: All post-hoc comparisons conducted using Games-Howell test.

Implicit attitudes. In order to test our hypothesis that implicit theistic attitudes change towards naturalistic attitudes as education and training in psychology increase, we compared participants' IAT difference scores across education level and class standing. Descriptive statistics (see Table 2) show that average difference scores on the IAT do differ by both education level and college class and do so in the predicted direction. When we consider this change in light of the absence of change in explicit attitudes, the results indicate that the implicit attitudes not only change in the predicted direction but also in the opposite direction of participants' explicit attitudes. This opposition suggests that this shift is not merely a product of social desirability or demand characteristics, a finding that increases the validity of both measures, but may reflect an unconscious move toward endorsing a secular stereotype that the participants consciously deny.

Inferential statistics (one-way ANOVA) were conducted with difference scores as the dependent variable and both education level and class standing as independent variables to test whether the pattern of differences in average IAT scores is statistically significant. As Table 2 displays, omnibus tests show a significant difference in the pattern of means of difference scores for both education level and class standing, which supports the hypothesis that increased education and training in psychology changes implicit theistic attitudes toward naturalistic attitudes. Post-hoc analyses indicate that although the pattern of change in difference scores consistently moves away from theism toward naturalism, as predicted across education level and class standing, significant differences between means only emerge at the graduate level. This would suggest that graduate education and training in psychology may have the strongest impact on the shift from implicit theistic beliefs to naturalistic beliefs that appears to mark the educational path of psychologists generally.

Discussion

The results of this study are supportive of our hypothesis and suggest the likelihood that an education in psychology, which includes training in natural science methods, may not be neutral with regard to the faith of students in psychology. On the contrary, it would appear that the more the education and the higher the class level of the respondent, the less likely the person is to implicitly believe that faith is fair. Once students are at the post-graduate level, they are likely to implicitly accept the secular stereotype that faith is biased, which would suggest that they have developed an implicit prejudice against a vital part of their own faith. We do not have space to consider all the implications of these findings, but we can say that they do offer support for the theoretical case we have made in this special issue (Slife, Reber & Lefevor) and elsewhere (Slife & Reber, 2009a) that naturalism is not neutral with regard to theism, and there are real consequences of an education in naturalistic methods and explanation for the implicit theism of theistic psychology students.

Of course, as with our image of God study example, this study is only an initial foray into this new area of psychological study, and the research results are preliminary. Consequently, additional research and validation of the new instruments developed for use in this study are required. For example, at this point, we have only collected the cross-sectional data that supports our hypothesis that implicit attitudes about theism and naturalism differ by class standing and education level. At this juncture, we have no reason to believe that cohorts across the educational levels are any different on issues related to faith and science biases that would change these results in a longitudinal study. Still, it will be necessary to collect longitudinal data that pairs within-subject analyses of implicit attitude changes with the between-subject results we already have. If the longitudinal data are consistent with the cross-sectional data, our hypothesis will be significantly reinforced.

As with any new program of research, lingering questions requiring further research remain. For example, researchers will need to examine whether this implicit attitude change is unique to psychology or is common across social science disciplines, the natural sciences, arts and humanities, and perhaps even any university education regardless of the students' major. At the same time, it might be important to examine whether increased education and training in particular subdisciplines of psychology have a different effect on implicit theistic and naturalistic attitudes than education and training in other specializations. Also, our study did include five participants with doctoral degrees, which was the group manifesting the highest implicit endorsement of the secular stereotype. It would be interesting and important to further investigate this population to see if there are differences by specialization among doctoral psychologists as well. It would also be important to examine these implicit attitudes and any potential changes in them among populations that are not theistic or religious.

Each of these studies and others that we do not have space to list would provide a clearer understanding of this implicit attitude change phenomenon and would also provide further tests of the reliability and validity of the new instruments developed. And this is but one possible area of focus in this new program of research. Another area of potential research would be to examine whether the change in implicit theistic attitudes toward naturalistic attitudes and stereotypes is accompanied by changes in behavior. Do theistic psychology students, for example, change the ways they talk about psychological phenomena as their education increases? Will their explanations of happiness or depression, which may have included theistic elements at the beginning of their education, exclude those elements by the time they graduate or enter graduate school? This is but one example of the numerous studies of the behavioral effects of this implicit attitude change that could be conducted.

Conclusion

As we hope to have made clear in our review of these two example studies, theistic programs of research have great heuristic potential, suggesting a whole host of possible hypotheses and research studies as well as prompting the modification and development of new scientific instruments. In our view, this is the epitome of good science: rigorous investigation using a variety of methods and instruments that is theory driven and produces results that inform, reform, and refine theory and increase our understanding of important psychological phenomena. Yet, without considering the possibility that existing method assumptions of psychology might not be neutral with regard to theism, it would likely never occur to conventional psychological researchers to look at these kinds of issues and consider these theistic and faith-related questions.

Given the large number of theists, including theistic psychologists, theistic psychology students, theistic therapy clients, and theistic research participants, it appears to us to be potentially worthwhile and even important to put theistic hypotheses and theories to the test. As we stated in our theoretical paper (Slife, Reber & Lefevor, this issue), we are not requiring the inclusion of theistic programs of research. On the contrary, if theistic programs of research fail to yield results that increase psychologists' understanding of human beings and phenomena, then we should let them fall by the wayside as would any unproductive research program. If however, the selective attention and explanatory focus of the theist adds to, complements, and perhaps even corrects misconceptions about human psychology, as our example studies might do, then we suggest that theistic programs of psychological research be given a chance to compete in the marketplace of scientific investigation.

REFERENCES

Albrecht, S.L., & Heaton, T.B. (1998). Secularization, higher education, and religiosity. In J. Duke (Ed.) *Latter-day Saint social life: Social research on the LDS church and its members* (pp. 293–314). Provo, UT: Religious Studies Center, BYU.

Alcock, J.E. (2009). Prejudice or propaganda? *Journal of Theoretical and Philosophical Psychology, 29*, 80–84. doi:10.1037/a0016968

American Psychological Association. (2007). *APA guidelines for the undergraduate psychology major.* Washington, DC: Author. Retrieved from www.apa.org/ed/resources.html

Baba, K., Shibata, R., & Sibuya, M. (2004). Partial correlation and conditional correlation as measures of conditional independence. *Australian and New Zealand Journal of Statistics, 46*, 657–664. doi:10.1111/j.1467-842X.2004.00360.x

Blair, I.V. (2001). Implicit stereotypes and prejudice. In G.B. Moskowitz (Ed.), *Cognitive social psychology: The Princeton symposium on the legacy and future of social cognition* (pp. 359–374). Mahwah, NJ: Lawrence Erlbaum.

Bowlby, J. (1973). *Attachment and loss: Volume 2. Separation: Anxiety and anger.* New York, NY: Basic Books.

Caplovitz, D., & Sherrow, F. (1977). *The Religious drop-outs: Apostasy among college graduates.* Beverly Hills, CA: Sage Publications.

Cassibba, R., Granqvist, P., Costantini, A., & Gatto, S. (2008). Attachment and God representations among lay Catholics, priests, and religious: A matched comparison study based on the adult attachment interview. *Developmental Psychology, 44*, 1753–1763. doi:10.1037/a0013772

Collins, N.L., & Read, S.J. (1990). Adult attachment, working models, and relationship quality in dating couples. *Journal of Personality and Social Psychology, 58*, 644–663. doi:10.1037/0022-3514.58.4.644

Dixon, T. (2008). *Science and religion: A very short introduction.* New York, NY: Oxford University Press USA.

Flashing, S. (2010). The myth of secular neutrality: Unbiased bioethics. Retrieved from http://www.cbhd.org/content/myth-secular-neutrality-unbiased-bioethics

Gawronski, B., & Payne, B.K. (2010). *Handbook of implicit social cognition: Measurement, theory, and application.* New York, NY: The Guilford Press.

Greenwald, A.G., McGhee, D.E., & Schwartz, J.K.L. (1998). Measuring individual differences in implicit cognition: The Implicit Association Test. *Journal of Personality and Social Psychology, 74*, 1464–1480. doi:10.10.7/0022-3514.74.6.1464

Greenwald, A.G., Nosek, B.A., & Banaji, M.R. (2003). Understanding and using the Implicit Association Test: An improved algorithm. *Journal of Personality and Social Psychology, 85*, 197–216. doi:10.1037/0022-3514.85.2.197

Greenwald, A.G., Poehlman, T.A., Uhlmann, E., & Banaji, M.R. (2009). Understanding and using the Implicit Association Test: III. Meta-analysis of predictive validity. *Journal of Personality and Social Psychology, 97*, 17–41. doi:10.1037/a0015575

Hazan, C., & Shaver, P. (1987). Romantic love conceptualized as an attachment process. *Journal of Personality and Social Psychology, 52*(3), 511–524. doi:10.1037/0022-3514.52.3.511

Helminiak, D.A. (2010). Theistic psychology and psychotherapy: A theological and scientific critique. *Zygon: Journal of Religion and Science, 45*, 47–74. doi:10.1111/j.1467-9744.2010.01058.x

Hunter, J.D. (1983). *American evangelicalism: Conservative religion and the quandary of modernity.* Piscataway, NJ: Rutgers University Press.

Lawrence, R.T. (1997). Measuring the image of God: The God image inventory and the God image scales. *Journal of Psychology and Theology, 25*, 214–236. http://journals.biola.edu/jpt

Leahey, T.H. (1991). *A history of modern psychology.* Englewood Cliffs, NJ: Prentice Hall.

Lee. J. (2002). Religion and college attendance: Change among students. *The Review of Higher Education, 25*, 369–384. doi:10.1353/rhe.2002.0020

Nosek, B.A., Greenwald, A.G., & Banaji, M.R. (2007). The implicit association test at age 7: A methodological and conceptual review In J.A. Bargh (Ed.), *Social psychology and the unconscious: The automaticity of higher mental processes* (pp. 265–292). New York, NY: Psychology Press.

Nosek, B.A., Greenwald, A.G., & Banaji, M.R. (2005). Understanding and using the Implicit Association Test: II. Method variables and construct validity. *Personality and Social Psychology Bulletin, 31*, 166–180. doi:10.1177/0146167204271418

O'Grady, K., & Richards, P.S. (2008). Theistic psychotherapy and the God image. In G. Moriarty & L. Hoffman (Eds.), *God image handbook for spiritual counseling and psychotherapy: Research, theory, and practice* (pp. 183–209). Binghamton, NY: Haworth Pastoral Press.

Pascarella, E.T., & Terenzini, P.T. (2005). *How college affects students: A third decade of research.* San Francisco, CA: Jossey Bass.

Project Implicit. (2011). Bibliography articles—Listed alphabetically by primary researcher. Retrieved from https://implicit.harvard.edu/implicit/demo/background/biblioresearcher.html

Reber, J.S. (2006). Secular psychology: What's the problem? *Journal of Psychology and Theology, 34*, 193–204. http://journals.biola.edu/jpt

Reinert, D.F., & Edwards, C.E. (2009). Attachment theory, childhood mistreatment, and religiosity. *Psychology of Religion and Spirituality, 1*, 25–34. doi:10.1037/a0014894

Slife, B.D., & Reber, J.S. (2009a). Is there a pervasive implicit bias against theism in psychology? *Journal of Theoretical and Philosophical Psychology, 29*, 63–79. doi:10.1037/a0016985

Slife, B.D., & Reber, J.S. (2009b). The prejudice against prejudice: A reply to the comments. *Journal of Theoretical and Philosophical Psychology, 29*, 128–136. doi:10.1037/a00117509

Slife, B.D., & Reber, J.S. (in press). Conceptualizing religious practices in psychological research: Problems and prospects. *Pastoral Psychology.*

Slife, B.D., Reber, J.S., & Faulconer, J.E. (in press). Implicit ontological reasoning: Problems of dualism in psychological science. In R. Proctor & J. Capaldi (Eds.), *Psychology of science: Implicit and explicit reasoning.* New York, NY: Oxford University Press USA.

Uecker, J.E., Regner, M., & Vaaler, M.L. (2007). Losing my religion: Social sources of religious decline in early adulthood. *Social Forces, 85*, 1667–1692. doi:10.1353/sof.2007.0083

WHEN GOD TRULY MATTERS:
A THEISTIC APPROACH TO PSYCHOLOGY

*Brent D. Slife, Jeffrey S. Reber, and G. Tyler Lefevor**

ABSTRACT

Our study of the philosophy of social science has led us to realize that many psychologists, including ourselves, have participated in a kind of popular myth, sometimes known as the *myth of neutrality*. The primary feature of this myth is the supposition that the research findings and conceptual practices of secular psychology are essentially neutral to or compatible with various worldviews, including theism. We first attempt to dispel this myth. Instead of being bias-free or bias-minimized, the research and practice of psychologists presupposes certain assumptions or biases about the world. We explicate some of the more important assumptions of conventional methodology and practice and compare these assumptions to the theistic assumption of a currently and practically relevant God. We find that theistic conceptualizations are considerably different from secular conceptualizations, not only in their hypotheses about psychological events but also in their practical applications to psychological problems. These differences, we believe, suggest the need for a theistic approach to psychology as a complement to our currently secular approach to psychology. We describe how this is possible by pointing to several applied branches of this theistic approach, including other articles of this special *Journal* issue, which relate to programs of research and approaches to practice.

Keywords: religion, philosophy of social science, naturalism, theism, methodology

As psychologists who are interested in science and religion, we have long been intrigued by what the inclusion of God might mean for psychology. In our early careers, we presumed like many other psychologists that psychological research and practice were essentially neutral to or compatible with this inclusion. In other words, we assumed that even though the data and practices of psychology were not originally formulated with God in mind, due to the secular nature of the discipline, the notion of a deity was nevertheless compatible with the information generated. After all, we reasoned, secular psychologists were dealing with the same world

* *Author Note*: Brent D. Slife, Department of Psychology, Brigham Young University; Jeffrey S. Reber, Department of Psychology, Brigham Young University; G. Tyler Lefevor, Department of Psychology, Brigham Young University.

Correspondence regarding this article should be addressed to Brent D. Slife, Department of Psychology, Brigham Young University, 1001 Kimball Tower, P.O. Box 25543, Provo, UT 84602. Email: brent_slife@byu.edu as the theist, so any objective data should apply to all concerned, theist and a-theist alike.

Our subsequent study of the philosophy of social science has since led us to realize that our initial assumptions were wrong. We now believe that we originally participated in a kind of popular myth, sometimes known as the *myth of neutrality* (e.g., Armstrong, 2011; Bernstein, 1983; Flashing, 2010; R. Bishop, 2007; S. Bishop, 1993). The primary feature of this myth is the supposition that the research findings and conceptual practices of secular psychology are essentially neutral to or compatible with various worldviews, including theism. This myth kept us from recognizing that even the research of psychologists presupposes certain assumptions about the world. These assumptions may remain hidden from the researcher, but they are always active in shaping the investigators' interpretations of their findings. Psychological research, in this sense, does not map or describe the world in an unbiased manner; it *interprets* the world in light of the assumptions researchers presuppose. Indeed, we believe there is no methodology that avoids this interpretive element, so the assumptions informing or shaping any set of methods should be explicated and examined in relation to its findings.

In this paper, we first describe how we arrived at these current beliefs, including the reasons that lead us now to question the neutrality and transparency of our methods. We then explicate some of the more important assumptions of conventional methodology and compare these assumptions to the theistic assumption of a currently and practically relevant God. We find that theistic conceptualizations are considerably different from secular conceptualizations, not only in their hypotheses about psychological events but also in their practical applications to psychological problems. These differences, we believe, suggest the need for a theistic approach to psychology as a complement to our currently secular approach to psychology. We conclude by describing several applied branches of a theistic approach, including other articles of this special *Journal* issue that relate to programs of research and approaches to practice (Johnson & Watson, this issue; Nelson & Thomason, this issue; O'Grady, this issue; Reber, Slife, & Downs, this issue).

THE MYTH OF NEUTRALITY

As we are using the phrase here, the myth of neutrality means that methods, whether research or therapeutic, are thought to be neutral to or compatible with worldviews other than those that the methods assume. Our concern here is that psychologists think of this neutrality as if their methods are transparent and unbiased windows to the real objective world. Many psychological researchers recognize that their methods involve unproven assumptions or prejudgments about the world to be investigated. Yet they routinely report their findings as if the myth of neutrality is still in effect. They do not typically report their method assumptions, nor do they critically evaluate them in relation to their findings or to alternative method assumptions. Instead, these methods are typically understood as a neutral or universal logic that attempts to sweep away the subjective elements of human experience, such as biases and assumptions, to reveal the uninterpreted, assumptionless objective world (Schweigert, 2006; Slife, Reber, & Faulconer, in press).

Consider a few prominent research methods texts in this regard. In one such text, Mitchell and Jolley (2007) explained that the purpose of the scientific method is to search for "objective evidence that does not depend on the scientist's theory or personal viewpoint" (p. 4), supposing the scientific method to be the instrument that gathers such untainted evidence. In another widely adopted methods textbook, Schweigert (2006) described the scientific method in terms of systematic observations made in an objective manner: "This approach is adopted so that the results of the research will be meaningful, unambiguous, and uncontaminated by the biases of either the participants or the researcher" (p. 2). We could cite one methods text after another (e.g., Dyer, 2006; Marczyk, DeMatteo, & Festinger, 2005; Ray, 2006), but suffice it to say that they are virtually unanimous in presenting the traditional scientific method as the ultimate means of avoiding bias and discovering the uninterpreted reality of the natural world.

Unfortunately, these texts present naïve views of science and the scientific method, views that must ignore a large philosophy-of-science literature to maintain their naiveté. This literature shows how all methods entail unproven assumptions or prejudgments about the world to be investigated, whether or not the researcher is aware of or even endorses them (Bishop, 2007; Okasha, 2002; Rescher, 1999; Spackman & Williams, 2001; Sugarman & Martin, 2005; Wiggins, 2011; Yanchar, Gantt, & Clay, 2005). Because the formulation of any method occurs before any investigation using the method, this formulation necessarily involves pre-investigatory beliefs or presuppositions about the world in which the method is to be used. What else would guide a method's formulation other than assumptions about how such a method would be successful in investigating a particular as-yet-uninvestigated world? This is not to say that these suppositions are mere guesses. Method formulators have presumably interacted with their world in many important ways that suggest assumptions. Still, these formulators have no evidence about the world that comes from the method yet to be formulated, so all methods have to rely on these unproven suppositions as their conceptual foundations. In other words, all methods are not revealers of an uninterpreted or assumptionless world; all methods, and thus all findings, are informed and shaped by assumptions that interpret this world.

With quantitative methods, for example, the world that matters to science is presumed to be observable, replicable, and quantifiable (e.g., Ray, 2006). In other words, the more important events for science, before investigation has begun, are thought to be observable (public) events rather than unobservable (private) events, replicable events rather than nonreplicable events, and quantifiable events rather than unquantifiable events. To be clear, we do not question whether these particular events should be the more important events for science; our point here is that their importance is decided philosophically (epistemologically), before formal investigation has begun. In this sense, the importance of observable, quantifiable, and replicable events for science comes not from empirical fact but from philosophical fiat. Yet these assumptions have become so commonplace and powerful that many researchers believe that any parts of the world that do not fit them should be either turned into phenomena that suits them (i.e., operationalized) or considered outside the purview of science (e.g., Hibberd, 2009; Marczyk et al., 2005). These notions of fit and purview become a de facto kind of *scientific selective attention* (to certain events over others), as if the suppositions of method can and should define the interests of scientists and dictate the importance of certain phenomena to science.

Researchers typically also engage in another aspect of methodological interpretation: *explanation of results.* Without a keen awareness of method assumptions and their philosophical nature, researchers are likely to extend their implicit method worldview to explain or interpret the data generated. Indeed, why would they presume a particular view of the world when formulating and being trained in the method and then abandon that worldview once the data have been gathered and require analysis and explanation (Richardson, Fowers, & Guignon, 1999; Slife, Reber, & Richardson, 2005)? We will later say more about the role of method assumptions in explanatory practices. For now, the primary issue is how completely understandable it is that method assumptions, which are rarely identified but implicitly purveyed in research methods texts and courses, have become the mindset of researchers and thus the preferred explanatory framework for interpreting the data generated in psychological studies (cf. Slife & Williams, 1995).

Our point here is not that these forms of interpretation, selective attention and explanation, are necessarily bad or problematic. Indeed, these forms of interpretation are probably involved in any method. The point is that they are rarely examined critically (because they are assumed and often taken for granted). Therefore, it seems completely legitimate to question whether a certain set of assumptions—what could be termed a *method worldview*—is the only or best set of assumptions for our methods.

Some researchers might understandably claim that the success of conventional methods is evidence of the effectiveness of the traditional method worldview. We would certainly agree. Yet, it should be recognized that this claim is an opinion, not a scientifically proven fact. Indeed, it is an opinion in which the same assumptions that inform the method are likely to frame the criteria of success for making the claim. In point of fact, no scientific investigation has compared the effectiveness of method worldviews, partly because some method worldview would need to be presumed in doing so. This presumed worldview would itself selectively attend to some things over others and explain the data from the perspective of its own method assumptions without these assumptions being tested. Perhaps more importantly, the effectiveness of one set of methods does not preclude the effectiveness of another set of methods or the complementary effectiveness of both sets of methods. The rise of qualitative methods in psychology is a case in point, especially when these methods are properly recognized to originate from a different method worldview or set of worldviews than traditional quantitative methods (Gelo, Braackman, & Benetka, 2008; McGrath & Johnson, 2003; Slife & Gantt, 1999; Slife & Melling, in press; Wiggins, 2011).

COMPARING WORLDVIEWS

Should other candidates be considered for method worldviews, both for research and for practice? We recognize that many scientists experience what Bernstein (1983) called "Cartesian anxiety" about opening up the canon of science (p. 16). They feel anxious about too many method worldviews complicating and perhaps even subjectifying science (Alcock, 2009). We should acknowledge that we suffer a bit from this anxiety ourselves. Nevertheless, psychologists should also realize that this canon is not sacred, nor is it empirical. It is a particular method worldview or epistemology that was not itself derived scientifically. Without some comparison to other method worldviews, the discipline risks unknowingly deploying an arbitrary or a problematic method worldview. The method worldview of many qualitative methods has undoubtedly been helpful in this regard, but their similarity to conventional quantitative methods has not led generally to a greater understanding of the assumptions underlying these methods (e.g., Packer, 2011; Slife & Williams, 1995).

As we will describe here, a theistic worldview has several qualities to recommend it as a supplementary or complementary method worldview. First, it presents a fairly direct contrast to many secular scientific assumptions, allowing psychologists to become more aware of their current method assumptions. Second, the number of people, both scholar and layperson alike, who subscribe to a theistic worldview is substantial, including the primary consumers of psychological information (Richards & Bergin, 2005). Third, many scholars consider theism to be the main rival to a conventional scientific (naturalistic) worldview in Western culture (e.g., Armstrong, 2011; Griffin, 2000; Smith, 2001). Fourth, theism may be an important intellectual resource for psychologists, especially in view of its long tradition of some of the world's greatest scholars considering important psychological issues (Nelson & Thomason, this issue). Fifth, theism will attend to other aspects and explanations of psychological phenomena that conventional methods may overlook, making it a potentially valuable supplement or complement, much as the qualitative worldview presently functions in the discipline.

Before we can properly address theism's potential relevance and value to the discipline, we first need to understand a bit more about why a theistic worldview has been excluded historically from psychology. Space constraints prevent a fuller and more complex treatment (cf. Griffin, 2000; Maier, 2004; Slife & Reber, 2009a), but it is probably fair to say that most psychologists assume that psychology was founded as a secular discipline. What is probably less well known is that secularism did not originally exclude theistic religions (Pannenberg, 1996; Reber, 2006). In fact, many early American psychologists viewed theism and psychology as mutually supportive (cf. Maier, 2004; Slife & Reber, 2009a). Only with the advent of modern forms of secularism, especially those inhabiting scientific disciplines, did psychology detach itself from faith (Maier, 2004) and move toward what historian of psychology Leahey (1991), calls the "central dogma" of psychological science, *naturalism* (p. 379). Naturalism is the system of assumptions or method worldview that psychologists acquired, perhaps without complete awareness, when they adopted historically the methods of the natural sciences.

Naturalism

Naturalism can be defined in a host of ways (Bishop, 2009; Griffin, 2000; Praetorius, 2003), but for the purposes of this article it has two main related features: its lawfulness and its godlessness. Some philosophers of science distinguish between two types of naturalism: methodological and metaphysical. However, these philosophers differ on how sharp this distinction should be, with Bishop (2009), for example, asserting a fairly sharp distinction and Cowan and Spiegel (2011) preferring a more blurred relationship (Spiegel, personal communication, July 29, 2011; see also Plantinga, 1997). Here, we subscribe to the latter. As our previous section on "The Myth of Neutrality" shows, all methods require pre-investigatory assumptions about the world in which they are to be successful, so naturalistic methods have to make assumptions just like another other methods, including implicit metaphysical assumptions about the type of world in which they will be operating.

The natural world is considered to consist of a network of laws and principles that govern the natural world. From this perspective, God could be the creator of these natural laws (deism), but God cannot remain involved after creation, at least not in any unlawful manner, because this involvement would disrupt the lawfulness or the regularity of these laws, rendering them ineffectual and unpredictable. Hence, most forms of naturalism assume that God does not exist in any way that really matters (i.e., makes a difference) in the world. God may be relevant for some naturalists in the sense of creation (deism) or in the sense of some supernatural world (dualism), or even in the sense of an invisible hand that merely upholds or sustains the laws of nature. God cannot, however, be actively involved (in a difference-making way) in the current natural world of psychological events. Instead, natural laws or principles, especially as postulated in theories, are the preferred understanding of these events.

The influence of naturalism's lawfulness and godlessness is evidenced most obviously in the myriad universal theories of psychology (with these universals attempting to be lawful) as well as in the almost complete absence of any mention of God in the articles and texts of psychology (Slife & Reber, 2009a). If God were considered to be involved in a difference-making way, psychologists would necessarily take these divine activities into account in their research and practices. However, even researchers who investigate God-associated topics, such as how people attain their *image of God*, frequently do not consider experiences with God to be important, even when their participants are theists (cf. O'Grady & Richards, 2008: Slife & Reber, 2009a). As we will see, divine influences are deemed, before investigation, to be unimportant and thus are not conceptualized or investigated. This conception of naturalism, then, is a relatively "soft" or "weak" one because it presents naturalism as merely assuming that God is not required for the research, theory, or practice of psychology. Naturalists in this sense are not necessarily anti-God or anti-theist per se. As mentioned in the introduction, this weak naturalistic position was our own position in our early careers.

Theism

This position is not, however, our current position. To understand our current position we must first define theism, which, like naturalism, can be conceptualized in a number of ways. However, the functional relevance of God (not God's irrelevance or passivity) is the central thrust of any theistic worldview, by definition. As philosopher/theologian Plantinga (2001) described it, "God is already and always intimately acting in nature which depends from moment to moment . . . upon divine activity" (p. 350). Thus, unlike a soft or weak definition of naturalism, where God is not essentially required, a theist would at least argue that God is essentially required for any theistic conceptualization in psychology.

Moreover, a thoroughgoing theist would need to apply this conceptualization to all psychological events. We emphasize "thoroughgoing" here because a popular intellectual position is partial theism, where one postulates a difference-making God for some locations (e.g., the supernatural) and some times (e.g., creation) but not for other locations and other times. This partial theism position, we believe, is itself a viable method worldview. However, it necessarily implies that the other locations (e.g., the natural world) and other times (e.g., post-creation) do not require a functionally relevant, difference-making God, and thus a weak naturalistic worldview is implied at these other locations and times. We refer to our distinction here between thoroughgoing and partial theism as strong and weak theism in other contexts (e.g., Slife, Stevenson, & Wendt, 2010).

The upshot is that a thoroughgoing theism requires that God be at least postulated as a difference-maker in all aspects of psychology. As theoretical psychologist Richardson has noted (F. Richardson, personal communication, May 19, 2010), we do not have to be theists to argue that this is the position of a thoroughgoing theist. In other words, we are making a logical (i.e., from definition) argument here rather than a theological or religious argument. We also recognize that this assumption of God's encompassing involvement could be quite wrong and thus not yield any important contribution to psychology. Yet, a number of psychologists and consumers of psychological information make this assumption privately. Why not evaluate the assumption and give theism a chance in the marketplace of scientific ideas?

We realize in saying "scientific ideas" that it can be jarring to many psychologists to even consider theism as a potentially scientific idea, especially in view of their secular and naturalistic training. Theistic perspectives, especially when used to conceptualize research and practice, have long been implicitly, if not explicitly, illicit in science. Yet, if we are going to challenge the myth of neutrality and compare the method assumptions of different worldviews, we have to operate with a view of science that is broader than any particular epistemology (empiricism) or method worldview (naturalism). The hallmark of science is the investigation of ideas, with investigation and method allowable in a variety of forms, including qualitative and perhaps even theistic forms. To identify science with a particular epistemology and/or method worldview is to decide before investigation what philosophies work best. This position seems singularly unscientific to us.

Our thrust, instead, is: Why not allow several method worldviews some disciplinary space to operate, especially if they are already widely endorsed, to see what fruit they can pragmatically bring to bear? Clearly, psychologists cannot study the world without method assumptions, so some preliminary assumptions are inevitable. Moreover, because they make methods possible, these assumptions are not themselves tested through the methods. The assumption that observable phenomena are important, for example, is not itself tested through methods that require observability. Only alternative method worldviews make the evaluation of method assumptions possible. They contrast with and thus expose these implicit assumptions, allowing them to be compared pragmatically and thus evaluated for their usefulness. Indeed, this approach to methods embraces the scientific humility that Myers (2009) and others consider so vital to sciences of all stripes.

Distinctions Between Naturalism and Theism

Crucial to this evaluation process is a clear sense of the distinctions among method worldviews. Unlike the myth of neutrality where the naturalistic worldview appeared to be compatible with all (or many) alternative world-views, and thus sufficient for psychological investigation alone, we are attempting to show how we believe that naturalism and theism are sub-stantially different from one another. The theistic psychologist assumes that God's activity is at least a necessary factor (with perhaps other neces-sary factors) for a complete study and explanation of psychological phe-nomena, whereas the naturalistic psychologist denies this requirement.

As we will see in the next section, this conceptual difference leads to practical differences not only in topics that are often viewed as involving God, such as prayer and images of God, but also in topics that are often not considered to be connected with God at all, such as neuroscience and child development. This extension to less traditional topics derives from the thoroughgoing variety of theism we are exploring here: God could be involved in events and topics that are not typically understood in this manner. In this sense, the theistic assumption of an active, relevant God is not an add-on God (i.e., merely added on to naturalistic conceptions) but is rather an assumption that could potentially lead to all manner of different psychological conceptualizations. We will discuss examples of these reconceptualizations in the second half of the article.

Reconceptualization can also refer to another important distinction between theism and naturalism that bears some elaboration. It involves the first of the two features of naturalism, the lawfulness feature, because theists and naturalists are both interested in the regularities or repeated patterns of nature. Natural theology, for this reason, has long been a vital portion of many theistic traditions. Yet, the meaning of these patterns is quite different for the theist and naturalist, as Taylor (2007) explained in his book, *A Secular Age*, using Christianity as his example of theism:

> Modern science offers us a view of the universe framed in general laws. The ultimate is an impersonal order of regularities in which all particular things exist, over-arching all space and time. This seems in conflict with Christian faith, which relates us to a personal Creator-God, and which explains our predicament in terms of a developing exchange of divine action and human reaction to his interventions in history... (p. 362)

This quote from Taylor not only indicates the conflict or difference between naturalism and theism, but Taylor also seemed to distinguish two very different meanings of order in the two perspectives: one an impersonal, lawful, and determined order and the other a personal, divine, and obedi-ent order, at least for this particular (Christian) tradition of theism. The point here is that the common term "order" denotes the importance of regularities for both perspectives, hence the possibility of some complementary work between researchers from the two worldviews. Still, it must be noted that the nature, source, and meaning of order is substantially different and could conceivably lead to very different hypotheses and practices, even with the regularities of the world.

Perhaps more intriguingly, many thoroughgoing theists, such as many Abrahamic theists (e.g., Jews, Muslims, Christians), are also vitally interested in the *irregularities* of the world, for lack of a better term. Naturalism presupposes that nothing outside the natural order makes a difference, whereas robust theism is always open to the possibility that God is involved in the world in ways that show up to us as irregular. These irregularities could include the singular, the one-time, or even the unique events of the world: events that are not exactly lawful or exhibit repeated patterns and thus are not replicable in a naturalistic sense. Indeed, it is the irregular that most notably distinguishes the two worldviews, primarily because naturalism selectively attends to the lawful or replicable and relegates the irregular to categories like *error variance*. What if, for the sake of argument, God is also involved in the current world in all sorts of irregular ways, ways that take into account our singular contexts and minister to us in a tailored, perhaps even a one-time manner? If this is possibly true, then the worldviews of naturalism and theism are generally different, both in the meanings of world regularities and in the import of world irregularities.

Consequently, there is the possibility, at least, that these general differences mean that a theistic approach to psychology could have a unique contribution to the discipline. We do not doubt the contribution of the method worldview of naturalism to psychology; we just wonder about the potential supplemental contribution of a different worldview, theism. As Smith (2001) argued, theism and naturalism are the two major worldviews of Western (and much of Eastern) culture. Why not allow them both to have a shot at illuminating and interpreting the psychological world?

PRACTICAL IMPLICATIONS

But this question clearly begs another question: "How?" How would a theistic approach actually work in the research, theory, and practice of psychology? This may seem particularly problematic when one of the main differences between the two method worldviews of naturalism and theism hinges on an unobservable, divine entity. Yet, it may help considerably to recognize that the theist's postulation of a practically relevant God is a theoretical or philosophical premise for conceptualizing psychological events and problems, not an object to be tracked or a variable to be measured. Analogous to the assumption of lawfulness, which helps the naturalist to formulate hypotheses and conduct tests, the assumption of God's activity helps the theist to do the same.

To understand this analogy between the naturalist's laws and the theist's God, it might be helpful to note that naturalism itself (indeed, most any method worldview) assumes unobservable entities (Bridgman, 1993). The notion of a natural law is a case in point. We are aware that such laws are frequently considered the most important concepts of science, yet they hold a peculiar status in this regard because they are not, in principle, observable. Some scientists view them as invisible forces, others see them as empirical generalizations, and still others view them as logical proofs or mathematical descriptions (Dixon, 2008). However they are conceived, they are inferred from observables because they are not in themselves observable. With respect to the law of gravity, for example, we clearly see our footprints in the sand and our pounds on the scale, but these are the postulated manifestations of this law; they are not the law itself. The law itself is an unseen entity that supposedly governs or influences these manifestations, much like God is an unseen entity that supposedly governs or influences world manifestations. In this sense, God may not be observed, but that does not mean that the influence of God cannot be deduced and its manifestations measured, just as with natural laws.

Efforts toward drawing these deductions and measuring these manifestations have been necessarily preliminary, to be sure, but they have clearly borne important fruit. These efforts can reasonably be divided into the familiar categories of research, theory, and practice, which we use here to briefly sketch some psychological applications of theism. In each category, we first provide an example of how a theist might see naturalistic findings or practices as potentially misleading. This does not mean that a naturalistic worldview does not yield important findings or enhance psychology's understanding of the phenomena it studies. It just means that we first want to show aspects of the phenomena and explanations that traditional methods might miss or deemphasize so as to highlight the possibly unique contribution of a theistic psychology. We then point to more positive theistic contributions in each category as evidenced by several articles in this special *Journal* issue that follow fairly directly from our conceptualization, specifically Reber, Slife, and Downs' research on image of God and prejudice, Nelson & Thomason's work on theistic resources for psychological theory, O'Grady's description of some of the more important practical applications of theism, and Johnson & Watson's pluralistic vision for a theistic approach to psychology.

Research

Psychological research may, in some sense, be the most important of these three categories because the scientific method is frequently viewed as a transparent (bias-free or bias-minimized) view of the world. As we mentioned, this was our early view of psychological research methods, and it led us to believe that there were no other necessary or credible scientific ways to investigate the world. Yet, as we have also described, we understand now that psychologists do not have to identify science with a particular epistemology, such as empiricism, or a particular method worldview, such as naturalism. Indeed, we believe, along with a considerable philosophy-of-science literature, that this identification inappropriately commits researchers to particular investigative strategies before they have compared them.

A proper comparison requires, we believe, greater awareness of alternative method worldviews, which is just one of the many virtues that a theistic approach brings to psychological research. In other words, theism provides at least a contrasting perspective to help illuminate other perspectives and raise our collective consciousness about the assumptions underlying conventional methods. As we will see, however, this contrasting worldview does not have to mean a wholly different philosophy of science, and thus set of methods. Theism can move in the direction of another philosophy of science, which we will explore in due course, but we would argue that theism also has important practical implications for conventional forms of inquiry.

Problematic findings. As mentioned, we begin each major category with examples of what naturalistic researchers have potentially missed or overlooked *from a theistic perspective.* We emphasize this last phrase because what is considered to be overlooked is somewhat in the eye of the beholder, but then that is our point: We need to understand that methods are "beholders" or interpretive in nature. A theistic interpretive framework, just as a naturalistic interpretive framework, brings with it a different selective attention and explanatory base. Consequently, it will likely select for different things and explain them differently. Perhaps the most obvious examples of these differences involve psychology-of-religion topics that have often been associated with theistic conceptualizations, such as prayer and worship. From a theistic perspective, naturalism (by its very exclusion of God) cannot represent either theistic phenomena or a theist's experience properly.

Slife and Reber (in press), for example, attempt to show how many studies of theistic prayer miscast the meaning of this prayer and the theist who prays. As philosopher of social science Bishop (2007) argued, one of the major aspects of social science research methods is their instrumentalism, the notion that whatever is investigated is properly construed as an instrument of humankind's benefit. In this instrumental sense, theistic prayer is routinely interpreted in the research literature as ultimately for the benefit of the person who prays. Depending on the theistic tradition, this instrumental interpretation can completely misrepresent the theist's experience and meaning of prayer. Even petitionary prayer, for instance, is frequently understood noninstrumentally within many theistic religions as an acknowledgment of the person's dependence on God (Bowker, 2011/1997; Livingstone, 2011/2000; Wieand, 1953). Yet, research operationalizations often presume instrumentalism because of method assumptions rather than because of the phenomena under study. The upshot is that these assumptions move the study's measures away from the theist's actual experiences (Slife & Reber, in press).

Quantitative and qualitative investigators also participate in another bias from a theistic perspective: the exclusion of God in definitions of religious constructs. Forgiveness research, for example, frequently excludes what many theists would consider essential components of the forgiveness process, such as receiving forgiveness and the capacity to forgive from God (Macaskill, 2005). A theistic program of research, on the other hand, would explicitly consider the possibility of theistic factors in both the definition and study of forgiveness. A quantitative study of forgiveness might compare the outcomes of participants whose forgiveness process includes God with participants whose process does not include God. A qualitative study might explore the ways in which experiencing God's forgiveness might facilitate a participant's capacity to forgive another person. These studies are not possible without a theistic worldview.

O'Grady and Richards (2008) also documented how image-of-God researchers rarely consider the possibility that God could be a factor in a person's development of his or her image of God (see also Slife & Reber, 2009a). Surveys and interviews rigorously assess a participant's experiences with human authority figures, but few of these studies attempt to assess a participant's experiences with God. Indeed, this omission is typically not even discussed; it is just assumed, without any investigation or justification. If asked, these researchers might justify their omission by noting that experiences with God are not observable, but we would remind them that experiences with any authority figures are not publicly observable (Slife & Reber, 2009b). Both require participants to report in a survey or an interview their recollection of what those experiences were. When participants in these studies are asked, "Did you have loving experiences with your parents?" why can't theistic participants be asked similar questions about their experiences with God? This inclusion would uphold both the principles of empirical methods and a theistic worldview.

Theistic empirical studies. In fact, as we report (Reber, Slife, & Downs, this issue), we have conducted a theistically oriented, image-of-God study where survey questions reflected these theistic sensibilities. Our data clearly support the claim that a large portion of the variance in participants' image of God stems from experiences of God. This study was conducted with actively religious participants who may be viewed as biased in reporting these experiences, so it might be important to use this survey with other types of participants (e.g., nonreligious, nontheistic). Even so, the possibility of such bias is an issue with any self-report measure, including those conventionally used in image-of-God studies. Perhaps more importantly, our study did not eliminate questions about the participants' experience with God before the investigation was conducted.

Reber, Slife, & Downs (this issue) also describe another example of a theistic study that shows how theistic sensibilities may lead not only to new hypotheses but also to new methods and measures. Regarding theistic hypotheses, we predicted that teaching naturalistic psychology moves even theistically oriented students away from their theistic beliefs. Our reasoning for this hypothesis was that naturalism is a disguised or hidden ideology and thus not a neutral set of assumptions, especially with regard to theists. In this sense, naturalistic psychology teaches students who were originally biased in favor of theism and theistic explanations to explain themselves and others in naturalistic terms (i.e., without God's practical activity). For example, theistic students, who would have originally explained their own and others' happiness with God as an active influence, would, after an undergraduate education in psychology, tend to explain their own and others' happiness without God as an active influence.

There are many ways, we believe, to investigate this hypothesis, but we anticipated that few participants at our religious institution of higher education (Brigham Young University) would admit or perhaps even recognize this change in biases. In other words, we predicted that these students' conscious and explicit theism would remain intact across their

undergraduate education, especially in view of BYU's inherently religious environment. However, we also predicted that their implicit biases
would shift increasingly toward scientific naturalism across their years of
undergraduate work because implicit biases are less easily monitored. To
measure this implicit shift, we adapted the Implicit Association Test to
gauge these implicit biases, as Reber, Slife, & Downs (this issue) describe.
This new instrument is an example of how a theistic approach fosters
the development of new measures. The results are preliminary and only
cross-sectional data are currently available, but they are clearly in line
with these theistic predictions. Perhaps more importantly, they suggest
the possibility not only that theistic students do shift their biases but also
that supposedly neutral psychological findings and practices can move
students to a different implicit understanding of the world.

So far, we have discussed only topics that are traditionally associated
with theism: image of God and theistic beliefs. However, we would argue
that even traditionally secular psychological topics can be reconceptualized
and rendered theistically. Prosocial behavior, a vital topic in secular social
psychology, could be viewed from a theistic perspective as God prompting
a person to altruistic action. The theist Plantinga (1997), for example, has
long argued that secular science has completely misunderstood the prosocial behavior of theists such as Mother Teresa. The theistic researcher
could consider the possibility of theistic motives, which are no more or
less observable than any other motives studied by prosocial researchers, in either quantitative or qualitative investigations (Reber, 2006).

Theistic philosophy of science. These types of empirical theistic studies
do not preclude, from our perspective, the possibility of theists developing
their own philosophy of science, and thus their own ways of advancing
knowledge. After all, if theism is a wholly different method worldview,
then it has its own implications for how methods should be developed.
This development is obviously a formidable undertaking, so we do not
presume to describe it here, even in outline form. Nevertheless, it should
be noted that theistic epistemologies and methods already exist in many
seminaries and institutions of higher learning (Plantinga, 1993; Stiver,
2003), and several psychological researchers have done some preliminary
thinking about theistic philosophies of science (e.g., Johnson, 2007; Slife
& Whoolery, 2006).

Theory

The second major category of theistic practical implications for psychology involves psychological theories and conceptions. The usual personality

theories have long been viewed as sufficiently comprehensive and diverse, if not too diverse, to accommodate human thought and behavior (Slife, in press). For the thoroughgoing theist, however, few if any of the mainstream theories make the pivotal assumption of a currently and practically relevant God. Indeed, they all assume that cognition, emotion, personality, and behavior can be adequately explained without the God assumption (i.e., they are naturalistic). This is not to preclude the possibility that some theories might be more sympathetic to theism than others. Jung's work, for example, is sometimes cited as including these sympathies (cf. Slife, in press). Nevertheless, the God assumption is typically avoided scrupulously in theorizing. Indeed, as we will see, even when clearly theistic theories are imported from theistic religion, the God assumption is often excised from them.

Problematic theory. Just as some image-of-God researchers have often ruled out or overlooked theistic possibilities, so too some psychological theorists have imported philosophies steeped in theism and then ruled out or overlooked their theistic bases. One of the more striking instances of this involves the importation of Buber's work, most famously by Rogers, but we could discuss the theistic work of any number of other scholars whose philosophies have been imported into psychology, including Macmurray (1961), Kierkegaard (1974), and Levinas (1969). According to Buber (1958), God is the "ground and meaning of our existence" (p. 135), making all "spheres in which the world of relation arises" possible, including "our life with nature... our life with men [and]... our life with spiritual beings" (p. 6). Indeed, God is so inherent in all relations for Buber that even the atheist's I-Thou relations are bound up with God. In his words, "when he too who abhors the name, and believes himself to be godless, gives his whole being to addressing the Thou of his life... he addresses God" (p. 76).

Buber's assertion of God's inseparability from all relationships was corroborated repeatedly by his primary translator and interpreter, Friedman. Friedman regularly quoted Buber's comments to this effect, including in several of his articles Buber's mission statement:

> If I myself should designate something as the 'central portion of my life work,' then it could not be anything individual, but only the one basic insight... that the I-Thou relation to God and the I-Thou relation to one's fellow man are at bottom related to each other. (Friedman, 1970, p. 99; see also Friedman, 1982, p. 232 and Friedman 1985, p. 421)

Yet, in our review of the many psychology articles that address Buber's I-Thou relationship, we found that virtually all of them excluded God from their description and explanation of his work (cf. Slife & Reber, 2009a). The authors of these papers often noted Buber's religious background and the role of his Hasidism in his theory of I-Thou, but they stopped short of describing the connection of Buber's religious influence to his foundational premise that God is the ground for all I-Thou relations. Surely, these authors would find the deletion of a foundational concept from some other theory to be an extremely problematic and unscholarly practice, comparable to leaving the conception of reinforcement out of Skinner's operant conditioning or ignoring the materialism of Marx's sociological theory. However, in the case of Buber's theory, the disciplinary bias against theism is apparently so pervasive and so unconscious that it is not only perfectly acceptable to exclude God from the I-Thou account but also completely unnecessary to explain the reason for this exclusion. The story is frequently the same for many other theistic theorists and philosophers.

Theistic resources for psychologists. Nelson & Thomason's work (this issue) is fortunately a notable exception. They not only include the theistic core of major theistic thinkers, but they also show how these thinkers are genuine resources for psychologists in their theorizing. A theist can, of course, operate from any number of traditions, including Islam and Jew, among others, but much of Nelson's work is set in the Christian tradition, especially the early Church Fathers of the Patristic era. Nelson and Thomason describe how these early scholars solved many theoretical puzzles that befuddle psychological theorists today. Perhaps most notably, several Patristic writers dealt with the issues surrounding a truly holistic or relational understanding of human being in a theistically spiritual manner. From this perspective, part of anyone's mental health and well-being is a healthy and intimate relationship with one's God, an element that is missing in today's psychology, at least formally. Yet, Nelson and Thomason explain not only how a God can be included in psychology but also how a viable holism for mind, body, and spirit is conceivable.

Practice

Psychological practices, such as therapy and parenting, can themselves be viewed as methods of a sort; they involve techniques and strategies for advancing knowledge about the people involved, much as scientific methods advance knowledge about the world. Unlike scientific methods, however, therapeutic methods are more likely to be understood as guided by theories of change and personality. Yet, these theories are themselves underlain with systems of assumptions that we could call worldviews (Rychlak, 1981), and these worldviews partake of the same secularism and naturalism as most other sets of ideas in mainstream psychology (Richardson, 2005; Richards & Bergin, 2005; Slife, in press). Consequently, psychotherapists are likely teaching, often without client or therapist awareness, that God is not a necessary condition in the events, problems, and sufferings of their lives (Slife, Stevenson, & Wendt, 2010). Clients are generally taught to explain themselves and each other as if God did not matter. Again, we admit that this teaching could be correct, but, as we will see, the notion that God does not matter is often merely assumed and taught implicitly in therapy, rather than explicated and examined with sensitivity and awareness.

Problematic practice. As a supplement to the implicit naturalism pervading mainstream therapy practices, several psychotherapists have recently initiated a movement toward the inclusion of theistic therapy practices (e.g., Richards & Bergin, 2004; York, 2009). In general, we applaud this movement and believe that O'Grady (this issue) describes some of the best contributions of this movement in her fine article. Nevertheless, there are many therapy approaches that are sometimes represented as theistic when theism is little more than a minor add-on. This notion of add-on means that the supposed neutrality of naturalistic therapy practices and their compatibility with other approaches, including theism, permits them to be used in conjunction with (i.e., merely added to) theistic conceptions and strategies. For example, one can supposedly add on a theistic prayer to an ongoing behavior therapy and remain completely consistent with the main tenets of behaviorism.

Our contention, however, is that naturalistic and theistic conceptions are logically incompatible. Recall that theism assumes that God is necessary to psychological events, and naturalism, one of the tenets of behaviorism, denies this requirement. In this sense, a theistic add-on (e.g., theistic prayer) is not logically compatible with a fundamentally naturalistic treatment technique or strategy. While God is recognized in the prayer, God is not part of the behaviorist's explanation of the client's problem, nor is God viewed as important to the therapy strategy. This incompatibility does not mean that therapists cannot use both theistic and naturalistic practices in the same therapy session. Indeed, we do not question that both practices might even be used effectively. We only question whether the therapy should be considered theistic or thoroughly theistic when such "theistic" practices are treated as mere add-ons to naturalistic practices, add-ons that assume that God does not make a meaningful difference in the other facets of therapy.

Slife, Stevenson, and Wendt (2010) reviewed several of these attempts to combine naturalism and theism and found them to be problematic from a theistic perspective. They described and exemplified three such types. The first type, *compartmentalized theism*, occurs when the therapist's private theistic beliefs are compartmentalized from his or her professional theories and practices. These therapists may be theists personally, but their professional theories and explanations do not reflect theism as a core philosophy, and, in fact, are often identical to secular and naturalistic approaches. The second type, *peripheral theism*, includes peripheral aspects of theism within the context of therapy, such as prayer and forgiveness. These peripheral aspects can be conceptualized as requiring an active God. However, more often therapists conceptualize these practices naturalistically because the therapists assume the practices work through more conventional psychological mechanisms, and thus treat them as if an active God is not necessary. The final type of theism, partial or *inconsistent theism*, clearly advocates the vital and present activity of God, not just in privacy or in peripheral aspects. Yet, we would consider it a partial theism because there are many other aspects of the therapy's theories, methods, and practices (e.g., mechanistically understood biological interventions) that may not be viewed as requiring an active God.

We readily acknowledge that some psychotherapists may view these combinations of naturalism and theism as potentially beneficial. After all, they might say, not every client will agree with the assumptions and biases of a theistic approach, which is surely an important point. Nevertheless, it is also important to note that this point applies with equal force to naturalistic approaches. Naturalism is itself a set of assumptions and biases, a worldview or an ideology, about which many clients, both theistic and non-theistic, might not agree (Richards & Bergin, 2004). For this reason, we believe it is ethically imperative to identify the conceptual assumptions of all psychotherapies in order to provide clients with the information needed to allow some type of informed consent. A lengthy discourse would rarely be necessary; therapists rarely provide details about their model of change. Still, we suspect that many theistically inclined clients will be interested to know that many conventional therapy theories and their applications are not unbiased with respect to the client's theism, and, in fact, these therapies do not include a currently active God in some portion of their conceptions.

Multiplicity of theistic practices. We praise the work of O'Grady (this issue) for avoiding this nettle of naturalistic/theistic combinations in her fine contribution to this special *Journal* issue. She reviews a host of practical applications that are not only consistently and thoroughly theistic but also rigorously conceptualized and investigated. These include general clinical interventions as well as a more specialized account of individual and community trauma, providing an instructive illustration of an implementation in the recent disaster in Haiti. In all her conceptualizations, she avoids the temptation to syncretize the naturalistic and the theistic, and yet she provides what appear to be viable approaches to these important therapeutic issues.

Johnson and Watson (this issue) take up the issue of theistic practice in another way in their intriguing article. They cast a vision for a theistic approach to psychology that entails meetings and note-trading not only across various forms of theism, including Animism, Polytheism, Monotheism, Trinitarian theism, Pantheism, Panentheism, and Atheism, but also across various forms of transcendence, including Hinduism, Buddhism, Taoism, and New Age representatives. Trading notes across these traditions would not preclude working within them. Christians could work on specifically Christian approaches to psychology, and Muslims would work on Islamic approaches to the discipline, and so on. However, that work would be examined in relation to the work of other traditions as part of a larger whole, much like the interdisciplinary work of many universities. Perhaps even more intriguingly, subsections of these meetings could explore commonalities across associated traditions, such as the Abrahamic religions of Islam, Judaism, and Christianity.

Johnson and Watson's vision of a theistic approach to psychology is obviously anything but monolithic. As dialogue commences among these worldviews, those aspects and explanations of the world that are selected for attention or ignored by any particular tradition or set of traditions would be illuminated by their similarity and contrast with alternative views from other traditions. This dialogue, after all, is the nature of truly engaging the other. The relations of difference within and among theistic and transcendence communities, according to Johnson and Watson, would be an essential part of a theistic approach to psychology. They conclude their article by declaring not only the need for respect in this dialogue but also the need for conviction. Conviction makes the relations of difference among the adherents and outsiders clear, allowing for truly productive dialogue, Johnson and Watson argue. Indeed, outsiders are not even viewed as outsiders without the involvement of adherents.

Interestingly, in psychology the case could be made that theism is the outsider, showing as it does the convictions and adherency, not neutrality, of conventional psychological methods by its contrasting worldview.

Conclusion

At this juncture, we would like to think that we have made a case for a theistic approach to psychology. We have attempted to show that the more conventional researcher does not cover the same ground or even conceptualize the world in the same way as the theist, leading to alternative theories, hypotheses, measurement instruments, and therapy strategies. Indeed, from a theist's perspective, many important conceptions and variables are presently being overlooked, given the selective attention and explanations of any methodology, including the one prevailing in mainstream psychology currently. This prevalence is also an important concern because dominant conventions and philosophies are often so pervasive that they operate in the background, without awareness or examination. Allowing a theistic worldview to have a formal foothold in the discipline would at least permit it to serve as a contrasting worldview and thus a point of reference for mainstream method assumptions. We recognize, of course, that there are those who either are not interested in theism or perhaps have anti-theistic sensibilities. We believe that the theistic researcher or therapist should be appropriately sensitive to these sensibilities. Still, we also believe that a similar sensitivity to theistic sensibilities is needed on the part of the nontheist, especially when theists make up the vast majority of psychology's clientele.

References

Alcock, J.E. (2009). Prejudice or propaganda. *Journal of Theoretical and Philosophical Psychology, 29*, 80–84. doi:10.1037/a0016968

Armstrong, D. (2011). Philosophy of science and the impossibility of epistemological "neutrality" and "objectivity." http://web.archive.org/web/20030604150349/http://ic.net/~erasmus/RAZ520.HTM

Bernstein, R.J. (1983). *Beyond objectivism and relativism: Science, hermeneutics, and praxis.* Philadelphia, PA: University of Pennsylvania Press.

Bishop, R.C. (2007). *The philosophy of the social sciences.* New York, NY: International Continuum Publishing.

Bishop, R.C. (2009). What is this naturalism stuff all about? *Journal of Theoretical and Philosophical Psychology, 29*, 108–113. doi:10.1037/a0016967

Bishop, S. (1993). Science and faith: Boa constrictors and warthogs? *Themelios, 19*, 4–9. http://thegospelcoalition.org/publications/

Bowker, J. (2011/1997). *Concise Oxford dictionary of world religions*. Retrieved from Encyclopedia.com. http://www.encyclopedia.com/topic/Prayer.aspx#2. *Encyclopedia of Religion*.

Bridgman, P. (1993). *The logic of modern physics* (reprint ed.). Salem, NH: Ayer. (Original work published 1927)

Buber, M. (1958). *I and thou* (2nd ed.). New York, NY: Charles Scribner's Sons.

Cowan, S.B., & Spiegel, J.S. (2011). *The love of wisdom: A Christian introduction to philosophy*. Nashville, TN: Academic Press.

Dixon, T. (2008). *Science and religion: A very short introduction*. New York, NY: Oxford University Press.

Dyer, C. (2006). *Research in psychology: A practical guide to methods and statistics*. Malden, MA: Blackwell Publishing.

Flashing, S. (12/29/10). The myth of secular neutrality: Unbiased bioethics. http://www.cbhd.org/content/myth-secular-neutrality-unbiased-bioethics

Friedman, M. (1970). Interrogation of Martin Buber. In S. Rome & B. Rome (Eds.), *Philosophical interrogations* (p. 99). New York, NY: Torch Books.

Friedman, M. (1982). Walter Kaufmann's mismeeting with Martin Buber. *Judaism, 31*, 229–239.

Friedman, M. (1985). Martin Buber's influence on twentieth century religious thought. *Judaism, 34*, 417–432.

Gelo, O., Braakmann, D., & Benetka, G. (2008). Quantitative and qualitative research: Beyond the debate. *Integrative Psychological & Behavioral Science, 42*, 266–290. doi:10.1007/12124-008-9078-3

Griffin, D.R. (2000). *Religion and scientific naturalism: Overcoming the conflicts*. Albany, NY: SUNY Press.

Hibberd, F.J. (2009). Sham reasoning, Humpty Dumpty, and the burden of proof. *Journal of Theoretical and Philosophical Psychology, 29*, 91–96. doi:10.1037/a0017208

Johnson, E. (2007). Towards a philosophy of science for Christian psychology. *Edification: Journal of the Society for Christian Psychology, 1*, 5–20. http://christianpsych.org/wp_scp/publications/edification/

Kierkegaard, S. (1974). *Fear and trembling* (W. Lowrie, Trans.). Princeton, NJ: Princeton University Press.

Leahey, T.H. (1991). *A history of modern psychology*. Englewood Cliffs, NJ: Prentice Hall.

Levinas, E. (1969). *Totality and infinity: An essay on exteriority* (A. Lingis, Trans.). Pittsburgh, PA: Duquesne University Press.

Livingstone, E. (2011/2000). *Concise Oxford dictionary of the Christian church*. Retrieved from Encyclopedia.com. http://www.encyclopedia.com/topic/Prayer.aspx#3. *Encyclopedia of Religion*.

Macaskill, A. (2005). Defining *forgiveness*: Christian clergy and general population perspectives. *Journal of Personality, 73*, 1237–1266. doi:10.1111/j.1467-6494.2005.00348.x

Maier, B.N. (2004). The role of James McCosh in God's exile from psychology. *History of Psychology, 7*, 323–339. doi:10.1037/1093-4510.7.4.323

Marczyk, G., DeMatteo, D., & Festinger, D. (2005). *Essentials of research design and methodology*. Hoboken, NJ: John Wiley & Sons, Inc.

Macmurray, J. (1961). *Persons in relation*. Amherst, NY: Humanity Books.

McGrath, J.E., & Johnson, B.A. (2003). Methodology makes meaning: How both qualitative and quantitative paradigms shape evidence and its interpretation. In P.M. Camic, J.E. Rhodes, & L. Yardley (Eds.), *Qualitative research in psychology* (pp. 31–48). Washington, DC: American Psychological Association.

Mitchell, M.L., & Jolley, J.M. (2007). *Research design explained* (6th ed.). Belmont, CA: Thomson Wadsworth.

Myers, D.G. (2009). *Psychology* (8th ed.). New York, NY: Worth Publishers.

O'Grady, K., & Richards, P.S. (2008). Theistic psychotherapy and the God image. In G. Moriarty & L. Hoffman (Eds.), *God image handbook for spiritual counseling and psychotherapy: Research, theory, and practice* (pp. 183–209). Binghamton, NY: Haworth Pastoral Press.

Okasha, S. (2002). *Philosophy of science: A very short introduction.* New York, NY: Oxford University Press USA.

Packer, M.J. (2011). *The science of qualitative research.* Cambridge, MA: Cambridge University Press.

Pannenberg, W. (1996). How to think about secularism. *First Things, 64,* 27–32. http://www .firstthings.com/index.php

Plantinga, A. (1993a). Divine knowledge. In C.S. Evans & M. Westphal (Eds.), *Christian perspectives on religious knowledge* (pp. 49–65). Grand Rapids, MI: Eerdmans.

Plantinga, A. (1997). Methodological Naturalism? *Origins & Designs, 18.* Retrieved from http://www.arn.org/docs/odesign/od181/methnat181.htm

Plantinga, A. (2001). Methodological naturalism? In R.T. Pennock (Ed.), *Intelligent design creationism and its critics: Philosophical, theological, and scientific perspectives* (pp. 339–362). Cambridge, MA: MIT Press.

Praetorius, N. (2003). Inconsistencies in the assumptions of constructivism and naturalism. *Theory & Psychology, 13,* 511–539. doi:10.1177/09593543030134004

Ray, W.J. (2006). *Methods: Toward a science of behavior and experience* (8th ed.). Bellmont, CA: Thomson Wadsworth.

Reber, J.S. (2006). Secular psychology: What's the problem? *Journal of Psychology and Theology, 34,* 193–204. http://journals.biola.edu/jpt

Rescher, N. (1999). *The limits of science* (revised ed.). Pittsburgh, PA: University of Pittsburgh Press.

Richards, P.S. & Bergin, A.E. (2004). A theistic spiritual strategy for psychotherapy. In P.S. Richards & A.E. Bergin (Eds.) *Casebook for a spiritual strategy in counseling and psychotherapy* (pp. 1–32). Washington, DC: American Psychological Association.

Richards, P.S. & Bergin, A.E. (2005). *A spiritual strategy for counseling and psychotherapy* (2nd ed.). Washington, DC: American Psychological Association.

Richardson, F.C. (2005). Psychotherapy and modern dilemmas. In B.D. Slife, J.S. Reber, & F.C. Richardson (Eds.), *Critical thinking about psychology: Hidden assumptions and plausible alternatives* (pp. 17–38). Washington, DC: American Psychological Association.

Richardson, F.C., Fowers, B.J., & Guignon, C.B. (1999). *Re-envisioning psychology: Moral dimensions of theory and practice.* San Francisco, CA: Jossey-Bass.

Rychlak, J.F. (1981). *Introduction to personality and psychotherapy: A theory construction approach* (2nd ed.). Boston, MA: Houghton Mifflin.

Schweigert, W.A. (2006). *Research methods in psychology: A handbook* (2nd ed.). Long Grove, IL: Waveland Press Inc.

Slife, B.D. (in press). Religious implications of Western personality theories. *Pastoral Psychology.*

Slife, B.D., & Gantt, E. (1999). Methodological pluralism: A framework for psychotherapy research. *Journal of Clinical Psychology, 55,* 1–13.doi:10.1002/(SICI)1097-4679 (199912)55:12<1453:AID-JCLP4>3.0.CO;2-C

Slife, B.D., & Melling, B. (in press). Method decisions: Quantitative and qualitative inquiry in the study of religious phenomena. *Pastoral Psychology.*

Slife, B.D., & Reber, J.S. (2009a). Is there a pervasive implicit bias against theism in psychology? *Journal of Theoretical and Philosophical Psychology. 29,* 63–79. doi:10.1037/ a0016985

Slife, B.D., & Reber, J.S. (2009b). The prejudice against prejudice: A reply to the comments. *Journal of Theoretical and Philosophical Psychology, 29,* 128–136. doi:10.1037/a00117509

Slife, B.D., & Reber, J.S. (in press). Conceptualizing religious practices in psychological research: Problems and prospects. *Pastoral Psychology.*

Slife, B.D., Reber, J. S., & Faulconer, J.E. (in press). Implicit ontological reasoning: Problems of dualism in psychological science. In R. Proctor & J. Capaldi (Eds.), *Psychology of science: Implicit and explicit reasoning.* New York, NY: Oxford University Press.

Slife, B.D., Reber, J., & Richardson, F. (2005). *Critical thinking about psychology: Hidden assumptions and plausible alternatives.* Washington, DC: American Psychological Association Press.

Slife, B.D., Stevenson, T., & Wendt, D. (2010). Including God in psychotherapy: Weak vs. strong theism. *Journal of Psychology and Theology, 38*, 163–174. http://journals.biola .edu/jpt

Slife, B.D., & Whoolery, M. (2006). Are psychology's main methods biased against the worldview of many religious people? *Journal of Psychology and Theology, 34*, 217–231. http://journals.biola.edu/jpt

Slife, B.D., & Williams, R.N. (1995). *What's behind the research? Discovering hidden assumptions in the behavioral sciences.* Thousand Oaks, CA: Sage.

Smith, H. (2001). *Why religion matters: The fate of the human spirit in an age of disbelief.* San Francisco, CA: Harper.

Spackman, M.P., & Williams, R.N. (2001). The affiliation of methodology with ontology in a scientific psychology. *The Journal of Mind and Behavior, 22*, 389–406. http://www .umaine.edu/jmb/

Stiver, D. (2003). Theological method. In K. Vanhoozer (Ed.), *Postmodern theology* (pp. 170–185). New York, NY: Cambridge University Press.

Sugarman, J., & Martin, J. (2005). Toward an alternative psychology. In B.D. Slife, J.S. Reber, & F.C. Richardson (Eds.), *Critical thinking about psychology: Hidden assumptions and plausible alternatives* (pp. 251–266). Washington, DC: American Psychological Association.

Taylor, C. (2007). *A secular age.* Cambridge, MA: The Belknap Press of Harvard University Press.

Wieand, A.C. (1953). *The gospel of prayer: Its practice and psychology as revealed in the life and teachings of Jesus.* Grand Rapids, MI: WM. B. Eerdmans Publishing Company.

Wiggins, B.J. (2011). Confronting the dilemma of mixed methods. *Journal of Theoretical and Philosophical Psychology, 31*, 44–60. doi:10.1037/a0022612

Yanchar, S.C., Gantt, E.E., & Clay, S.L. (2005). On the nature of a critical methodology. *Theory & Psychology, 15*, 27–50. doi:10.1177/0959354305049743

York, R.H. (2009). *A Christian spirituality and psychotherapy.* Eugene, OR: Resource Publications.

PSYCHOLOGY AND REVELATION

Robert C. Bishop*

ABSTRACT

Does Christian theism have any positive resources to offer psychology? Revelation offers
one fruitful possibility by encouraging us to think seriously about the nature of human
beings. Although there are many kinds of revelation (e.g., in the physical and personal
realms), I focus on the most worrisome case, that of special divine revelation, and draw out
some implications for human inquiry that are often missing from psychological research.

Keywords: Christian theism, methodological naturalism, psychology, revelation, self-
interpreting beings

> [A]ll knowledge is a species of Revelation.
>
> Coleridge (1956, p. 388)

> [M]odernity promised us a culture of unintimidated,
> curious, rational, self-reliant individuals, and it pro-
> duced...a herd society, a race of anxious, timid,
> conformist "sheep," and a culture of utter banality.
>
> Pippen (1990, p. 22)

Instead of exploring the propriety or impropriety of admitting theistic perspectives and commitments into the domain of psychological
inquiry, I want to explore a different avenue. Namely, are there theological resources in the form of revelation that might prove helpful for psychology? So as to avoid too much abstraction, I will focus specifically on
Christianity rather than theism in general. I will begin by exploring the
general concept of revelation, then move to what revelation might offer in
particular. The flow of my exploration will move from the context of natural science inquiry, where issues are often more straightforward, to that

* *Author Note*: Robert C. Bishop, Department of Physics, Wheaton College.

I want to thank Stanton Jones, Frank Richardson, and Brent Slife as well as two referees
for useful conversations and comments that improved this essay.

Correspondence regarding this article should be addressed to Robert C. Bishop, Department of Physics, Wheaton College, 501 College Avenue,Wheaton, IL 60187. Email: Robert
.Bishop@wheaton.edu

of psychological and social inquiry, where there are some unique issues requiring careful attention. I seek to illustrate that a plausible Christian approach to psychological inquiry can draw on revelation for beneficial insights that secular approaches might miss (although in some instances, secular approaches may surreptitiously be drawing on revelation unawares).

My general approach follows that of the early Christian theologians who, in the context of a culture saturated in Greek philosophical thought that maintained the universe was eternal, struggled to understand what the New Testament implied about an origin for creation. Irenaeus, Basil, and Augustine, drawing on revelation, developed new arguments, articulations and insights for ex nihilo creation rather than simply asserting the idea on authority or missing it altogether (Gunton, 1998).

I will not offer a justification for revelation but rather will assume a provisional default status for its plausibility and existence and see what comes from it. For a philosophical defense of such a *default and challenge* form of justification, see Williams (2001).

THE CONCEPT OF REVELATION

Let me start with a very broad definition of revelation that will then be refined and fleshed out over the course of the next several pages: *knowledge received as a gift standing in need of understanding* (Gunton, 1995). The giver could be some feature of nature, a human being, or God. The very idea of revelation raises a serious question with familiar Enlightenment contours: Does revelation undercut human capacities for discovering truth, rendering us passive recipients of truth rather than active inquirers? In other words, we appear to be forced into choosing between revelation or the autonomy and integrity of human reason:

> Because it is believed that revelation takes away our autonomy and leaves us in thrall to the authority of others ... it becomes necessary to replace it with pure untrammelled reason. On the other hand, if reason is autonomous and self-sufficient, we do not need revelation. We only need to find things out for ourselves. (Gunton, 1995, p. 21)

Historically, such a dilemma led to the typical Enlightenment rejection of revelation in favor of reason. I want to suggest this is a false dilemma because revelation actually turns out to be crucial to our rationally engaging the world.

Revelation in the Physical Domain

Rational inquiry into the physical world initially appears the least plausible as a domain where revelation takes place, but this impression is misleading. Even such an Enlightenment Father as Kant recognized that reason "must approach nature in order to be taught by it," though not as a passive student who merely soaks up what her teacher has to say (Kant, 1933, B xiii, p. 20). Revelation as gift involves the idea of being taught, and even Kant recognized that learning from nature was central.

The best accounts of the history and philosophy of science typically emphasize the provisional nature of scientific truths: We could learn something tomorrow forcing us to either reinterpret some current scientific truth or perhaps replace it wholesale. In that light, natural science inquiry is an activity that mediates provisional truths about the physical world. This is to say that natural science inquiry reveals or discloses truth about the physical world as scientists engage that world. Moreover, natural scientists do not have unmediated access to facts or truths about the physical domain. These facts and truths involve the mediation of the instruments they use and the theoretical structures they deploy but also the background knowledge and presuppositions scientists carry with them (Hacking, 1983; Kuhn, 1996; Gauch, 2002; Tauber, 2009). What these facts and truths mean is mediated by the experimental and theoretical practices of the various scientific communities struggling to understand these various domains of reality as well as their crafting good interpretations of those domains. The physical world reveals itself to natural scientists as they engage it through their research frameworks and background assumptions. These frameworks and background assumptions can either enable scientists to form more accurate or more distortive interpretations of nature (Gunton, 2006; Kuhn, 1996; Polanyi, 1974). Ultimately, physical truths are mediated through the interpretations of research communities as they explore together and sift each other's work.

The idea that experimental and theoretical practices are ultimately aimed at producing interpretations of the natural world is not new but traces back to the foundations of the new experimental philosophy of the 17th century as expounded, for example, by Boyle (Sargent, 1995; Wojcik, 1997). Interpretations are less accurate or more accurate, less distortive or more distortive, of the objects of study. For Boyle and other scientific revolutionaries from the 17th century, experimental and theoretical methods were means of putting human investigators into the best position to engage and interpret creation's disclosures mediated by evidence with as much clarity as possible. For the founders of the Scientific Revolution, this clarity included seeing all of nature as God's creation and understanding God's regular ways of working in creation through the laws and processes of nature. Boyle exemplified how the scientific revolutionaries viewed the exploration of nature as revelation:

> The book of nature is a fine and large piece of tapestry rolled up, which we are not able to see all at once, but must be content to wait for the discovery of its beauty, and symmetry, little by little, as it gradually comes to be more and more unfolded, or displayed. (Boyle, 1965, p. 796)

Not only does the book metaphor suggest that interpretation is central, it is humans engaged in inquiry who through discovery unfold the book of nature. Perhaps the most striking contemporary example is how the quantum realm is disclosed under experimentation. If physicists configure an experiment to reveal the wave-like character of quantum systems, then wave-like behavior is what they see. In contrast, if they configure an experiment to reveal the particle-like character of quantum systems, then particle-like behavior is what is disclosed to them.

Far from being a distanced, mechanical process, ideally natural science investigation discloses physical reality to natural scientists through the mediation of creative interrelationships among their instrument manipulations, bodies which engage those instruments, senses mediated by their bodies, thinking and theorizing, affective and evaluative stances, background knowledge, and presuppositions that come from the affordances and constraints of histories in families, communities, schools, and research environments (e.g., Osbeck, Nersessian, Malone, & Newstetter, 2011).

Revelation, as I have been describing it so far, appears central to natural science inquiry and knowledge and is often reflected in the language of scientific discourse. Consider the following from Adami (2006, p. 61): "More phylogenetic analysis revealed that precisely two amino acid substitutions resulted in the glucocorticoid receptor phenotype-aldosterone insensitivity and cortisol (and DOC) sensitivity." The revelation to which Adami referred comes about through careful genetic sleuthing, based on some plausible assumptions, into the possible history of the formation of a particular hormone-receptor system. Plenty of hard work, creative experimentation, and interpretation were involved so revelation in the physical realm largely involves active engagement (though there may also be plenty of instances where knowledge is received more passively). These are the hallmarks of revelation in the physical domain.

Revelation in the Personal Domain

In comparison, the idea of revelation seems much more plausible in the personal domain than in the physical. Suppose someone you thought was your friend starts shunning you after she has experienced some success that supposedly is independent of anything you did for her. Through this painful experience, her feelings and lack of concern for you are revealed by her actions, and new insight into her is disclosed to you. We are dependent on the words and actions of others to mediate the disclosure to us of who they really are: how they feel about various things, what they think about issues, how they conceive of themselves and their communities, and so forth. We cannot genuinely know another person unless she opens herself to us.

Knowledge in the personal domain is mediated through the words and actions of others as well as through our bodily senses. Moreover, this knowledge is mediated through our ways of understanding persons in general as we are constantly interpreting other people through our background knowledge and prior understandings (see below). Similarly, knowledge revealed through psychological and social inquiry is mediated through various kinds of laboratory experiments, survey instruments, and other forms of observation and engagement all also involving interpretation.

In particular, knowledge of persons is *embodied knowledge* because bodies partly constitute the kinds of persons we are, and because it is only through our embodiment that we reveal ourselves to others. Moreover, knowledge of persons is *relational knowledge* because we only have knowledge of other persons as we are in some form of relationship with them. Indeed, much of what we know about ourselves comes through our relationship with others, whether these be family, friends, or rivals. Likewise, whatever knowledge is gained through psychological inquiry is both embodied and relational because that knowledge depends upon embodied beings participating in laboratory or survey studies, where they must perform tasks bodily as well as depending on relationships among subjects, technicians, and observers.

Revelation and Knowledge

All knowledge, then, whether of the physical or personal realms, comes by revelation mediated through our relations with the other (either impersonal or personal other). Furthermore, we come to understand the world, both natural and social, through our being part of it (Polanyi, 1974; Taylor, 1992). This brings us to a crucial question: Is revelation in the physical and personal domains significantly different from God's self-revelation mediated through Trinitarian action, community, tradition, and Scripture?

Christianity historically has distinguished God's revelation into general and special revelation. General revelation is taken to be a very general and limited form of disclosure or unfolding of knowledge about God through creation. Special revelation is the specific, detailed disclosure or unfolding of knowledge in Scripture of God's redemptive plans and purposes culminating in the person and work of Jesus. There is a third distinction: *creation revelation*, detailed knowledge of creation disclosed through engaging creation (Bavinck, 2003, pp. 341–342; Goheen, 1996). This latter form of revelation is basically what I was describing in the previous two subsections.

As Gunton (1995, p. 31), on whose work I will be drawing, pointed out, "If Jesus Christ is in any sense the revelation of God, then the Bible, as the sole source of our knowledge of him, is unavoidably at the heart of any doctrine of revelation." So does the Christian conception of special revelation have important contrasts with revelation in the physical and personal realms? The problematic takes the form of the problem of authority: The authority of the Bible as often conceived by Christians appears to cut deeply against modern notions of human autonomy. We should especially be on guard against the tendency to be overconfident in our interpretation of special revelation. Overconfidence generally leads to devaluing others and deficient intellectual conclusions among other bad consequences. Christianity sometimes has fallen to temptation to replace the authority of God's revelation with overconfidence in the Church's institutional authority. When assessing revelation and its authority, we should not make the mistake of confusing that authority with this overconfidence, a distinction that from the Enlightenment forward has been difficult to make but is important to maintain.

There are several things to say in response to this undeniable tension. First, all knowledge of the physical and personal realms is revealed knowledge mediated through various means as indicated above. Here, there is a significant parallel between these forms of revelation and special revelation: The knowledge of special revelation is also mediated to us through practices such as worship, prayer, and interpretation; through attempting to live in light of that revelation; through Christian communities coming to an understanding of the Bible; through the formation and interpretation of creeds, and so forth.

Second, for revelation in the physical and personal realms, humans, whether scientists or not, rely on the provisional authority we must give the other in the form of the natural world, other persons, or other societies. Indeed, data cannot have any evidentiary status in the absence of such provisional authority (Kant's injunction that we "must approach nature in order to be taught by it"). Such authority is not located in individuals nor in institutions but in the reality of being. For example, the physical world and other persons place some demand on us to conform our thinking, feelings, and ways of apprehending to the way the physical world actually is or the genuine nature of other persons. The Enlightenment, then, was not really a movement seeking to get rid of all authority. Rather, it was a movement seeking after what it considered proper authority (e.g., human reason) in contrast to improper authority (e.g., the institutional Church). So there is an often unappreciated role for provisional authority of the other in these cases of revelation that parallels the role of provisional authority in the biblical case.

Third, a general Christian theology of revelation, essentially what I am articulating in the first portion of this essay, necessarily draws on several Christian doctrines. For instance, the doctrine of creation (Bishop, 2011) implies creation is intelligible, the kind of thing that can be known (i.e., creation was made to be revelational). This is consistent with revelation in the physical and personal realms. The doctrine gives a theological reason to expect these realms to be knowable (though not exhaustively). Moreover, a Christian theology or doctrine of anthropology takes humans to be rational beings fashioned in the divine image. The kinds of intellectual capacities we have along with our particular embodiment are means through which knowledge of the created order is gained (i.e., creation reveals itself through our engagement with it). Taking the doctrines of creation and anthropology together, our knowledge and understanding of the physical and personal realms is not a distanced, objectified knowledge because it is mediated through our being part of and dwelling in the world we come to know.

On the Christian view, one additionally needs a pneumatology, a theology or doctrine of the Holy Spirit, to understand revelation. The Spirit enables human beings to both indwell the world and exercise our capacities so that knowledge and understanding of both the physical and the personal are possible to their fullest extent given our limitations. Furthermore, it is God's Spirit who enables us to recognize and grasp truth by coming under the provisional authority of truth when conforming our thinking to it in whatever realm it is found. That knowledge and truth in these realms is not final but subject to ongoing interpretation and elaboration is also a gift, as the Spirit enables us to pursue ongoing engagement with

knowledge and truth. Again there is a parallel between how these doctrines underwrite human knowing in the physical and personal realms
and their role in human knowing in special revelation. If the Christian
doctrines of creation, anthropology, and pneumatology are on the mark,
there are no mediation-free ways to understand Scripture just as there are
no mediation-free ways to understand nature.

As a final point, "Revelation speaks to and constitutes human reason,
but in such a way as to liberate the energies that are inherent in created
rationality" (Gunton, 1993, p. 212). One of the ways revelation in the physical and personal realms does this is by enabling human engagement with
and discovery of the nature of created reality (e.g., we study phenomena,
uncover facts and relationships, find food for thought, etc.). Special revelation is no different in this regard except that it enables forms of human
thought and action not available when relying on revelation in the physical and personal realms alone. This essay is an exploration of how special
revelation also speaks to and shapes human reason when we are open to
listening to, struggling with, interpreting, and learning from it. This kind
of open-ended dialogue with special revelation also parallels our open-
ended dialogue with revelation in the physical and personal realms.

What Has Special Revelation Done for You Lately?

While these parallels between the cases of revelation in the physical
and personal realms and the case of special revelation may go some way
towards relaxing our modern tensions, there is also the issue of whether
or not special revelation has been helpful to human inquiry in general and
in the sciences in particular. While there is much that can be said on this
topic, I will confine myself to one unique contribution of biblical revelation to modern science: *ontological homogeneity*.

All intellectual roots of modern Western culture (ancient Egypt, Mes-
opotamia, Greece, Rome, and Medieval Islam) uniformly accepted the
celestial realm as being of a different order of being (divine, infinite, perfect) from the terrestrial (mundane, finite, imperfect, changeable). The
divine is not investigated in any of these cultures in the same manner as
the mundane. In contrast, early Christian thinkers struggled with biblical
revelation and their own Greek philosophical context, eventually coming
to a recognition that the only distinction in being was that of Creator
and created: The being of everything created—terrestrial and celestial—is
homogenous.

The ontological homogeneity of celestial and terrestrial realms advocated
by Basil of Caesarea and John Philoponus, resurrected by Duns Scotus and,

later, Galileo proved decisive for seeing nature more accurately as it really is. Taking biblical revelation seriously in the face of the strength of neo-Platonic and Aristotelian hierarchies was an ongoing struggle within Christianity (Gunton, 1998), but once the likes of Galileo, Kepler, Boyle, Descartes, and Newton grasped hold of ontological homogeneity, the exploration of nature was never the same. The doctrine provided the seeds motivating Galileo, Kepler, and the other scientific revolutionaries to see celestial and terrestrial regions as of the same order of being: finite, composed of the same material, operating by the same principles. Newton's grand synthesis was the culminating flowering of these seeds. Particularly relevant for psychology, ontological homogeneity provided the theological basis for seeing continuities between humans and the rest of creation long before Darwin's theorizing gave this impulse concrete expression. That many lost sight of such revealed continuities over the centuries does not show that the seeds of continuity were not always there, but those seeds began to come into sharp focus in the systematic study of nature in the 19th century.

In summary, the natural and human sciences owe a debt to this uniquely Christian insight from special revelation. As such, all modern scientific investigation draws on a distinctly Christian resource rooted in the conviction that God in Jesus Christ created all things. In this sense, the idea that God can somehow be excised out of or cordoned off from psychology, or scientific inquiry more broadly, boarders on incoherence.

Others have explored the debts modern science owes to distinctly Christian thought (e.g., Foster, 1934; Nebelsick, 1992). Harrison (2009) has traced how the Christian doctrine of fallen human nature played an important role in motivating and shaping the development of scientific methods of investigating nature in the 16th and 17th centuries that were open to public scrutiny. Jaki (1987) explored the uniqueness of the Hebrew conception of linear time versus the cyclical views of other ancient cultures and how the linear view contributed to the advent of modern science (though Jaki sometimes oversells the role of biblical thought in the formation of modern science). An example of theological resources from revelation contributing directly and substantially in natural science inquiry is found in Faraday (Cantor, 1991). That Christianity has historically been an enemy of science is one of the well-worn myths of our times (e.g., Numbers, 2010).

Special Revelation and Methodological Naturalism

One worry many have about breaking down any walls sealing religious perspectives out of scientific inquiry is that the very ideals and practices of natural science may have to be radically reshaped. I do not think this worry has any justification in Christian thought. This is not to say that there are no arguments that scientific methods must be substantially modified to accommodate a uniquely Christian approach to scientific inquiry. It is only to say that both the history of Christian theology and of science seriously undercut such arguments.

A fundamental implication of a Christian theology of nature, based on special revelation, is that creation has a *contingent rationality*. There are two senses of contingent here: (a) creation is contingent in that it depends upon God for its very existence, and (b) creation is contingent in that God could have made a wide variety of creations but chose one in particular. The contingency of creation implies that we have to investigate it to discover what kind of nature creation has. The rationality of creation refers to the order given to creation, an order or nature that is intelligible (hence on the Christian view, creation's nature is revelatory).

Here is one of the theological roots for *methodological naturalism*. As conceived and practiced by the founders of the Scientific Revolution, methodological naturalism is a commitment to use particular methods of inquiry for the limited purposes of discovering the nature or order of creation and its workings. For instance, the theoretical and experimental methods of physics focus on understanding matter, energy, and their interactions with no further commitment to any picture of reality where *only* matter, energy, and their interactions exist. Natural science methods, then, seek to reveal physical facts and regularities without prejudging whether physical facts and regularities exhaust reality. So even though we could give a physical explanation of how a cue ball's striking an eight ball sent the latter into the corner pocket, our explanation carries no implication that God is absent or inactive in this situation.

Methodological naturalism is justified theologically in the following way. If all things were created through and for Christ and for their own sake as the doctrine of creation maintains (Bishop, 2011; Colossians 1:15–16; Gunton, 1998; John 1:1–3), then truly knowing and understanding created things requires that we take them on their own terms. In the natural sciences, methodological naturalism, as expressed by Philoponus, Jean Buridan, Galileo, Boyle, and Newton, among others, is the injunction to take created things on their own terms so that their natures can be understood as accurately as possible. This means that we do not treat created things as divine or as fronts for the real activity of God or, what amounts to the same thing, as shadows behind which *genuine reality* is working. Instead, we treat electrons, volcanoes, planets, stars, and animals as having genuine natures and relationships, as responding to and contributing to order, and seek to put ourselves in the best methodological and epistemological position to explore all that they have to teach us about themselves.

So far as I know, the injunction to take *all things* on their own terms is a unique contribution of Christian theology to Western thought, based on special revelation, mediated by the doctrine of creation and its implication of ontological homogeneity. There may be other religious or metaphysical views in other places and times that emphasize taking all things on their own terms, but they made no contribution to the development of Western science. Although it takes centuries for this injunction to thoroughly permeate thought about nature, it is one of the keys to the founding of modern science. In natural science inquiry, we are so used to thinking about studying things on their own terms that the theological roots of this commonplace insight are largely forgotten.

Special Revelation and Psychological Inquiry

With this background in place, I want to draw out some implications and suggestions for what a theologically serious psychology could be like.

Taking Things on Their Own Terms: Self-Interpreting Beings

Although methodological naturalism works nicely in the natural sciences, in the social and behavioral sciences, it is problematic (Bishop, 2009; Richardson, 2009). However, the underlying theological idea that created things have genuine natures and should be understood on their own terms has much to offer psychology. For example, when we take human beings on their own terms, we see that we are self-interpreting beings (Bishop, 2007; Richardson, Fowers, & Guignon, 1999; Taylor, 1985a, 1985b, 1992). We are always engaged in ongoing evaluation and interpretation of who we are and who we want to be, of the kind of society and world in which we live, of what is most dear and of concern to us, and so forth. The self-interpreting nature of human beings is deeply involved in everything we do; hence, any inquiry failing to take this feature of humanity into account likely yields only limited or distorted views of human action.

The insight that humans are self-interpreting beings has had a rocky history in human inquiry. For instance, Mill (1843) dropped this insight out of his approach to human inquiry relying exclusively on natural science methods. In contrast, Dilthey (1958) preserved this insight in his arguments that understanding in the human realm does not come from reliance on natural science inquiry alone. And the struggle to maintain this insight has continued into contemporary psychology. It is typical for advocates of this insight to shun natural science methodologies such as correlation studies wholesale, just as it is typical for advocates of the latter methodologies to shun all forms of interpretive approaches to inquiry.

Although I think this revelation-derived idea that proper inquiry takes things on their own terms counsels us to always be aware of the self-interpreting nature of human beings in our research, there is no need to create a false choice between correlational and other natural science methodologies, on the one hand, and interpretive approaches, on the other. The former approaches may be uniquely useful in discerning important patterns in human action and experience that might not otherwise be discernable by other means. Likewise, making use of such methods in no way implies that the only form of understanding available to the psychologist is that of quantitative relationships among decontextualized variables. The crucial point is that all methods and evidence involve interpretation and should be handled with care.

Often this forced choice is the product of an unexamined adherence to an objectifying approach to human inquiry: Studying things by abstracting away from so-called subject-related qualities such as the meanings of and relationships among things showing up within our ordinary values, aims, and concerns (Bishop, 2007, pp. 113–122). Taking an objectifying stance means regarding the natural and social realms as being independent of the meanings these realms have for human subjects. Instead, these realms are reduced to a network of objects and efficient causes.

Several important points should be noted about objectification as an exclusive approach to human inquiry. First, this stance is only made possible by a number of cultural affordances that have everything to do with shifts in human ways of conceiving and interpreting the world (e.g., Taylor, 2007; Turner, 1985). All forms of inquiry require background assumptions and interpretations. Even the notions of objectivity and objectification have changed over time (Daston & Galison, 2010). Second, objectification involves excising the values and meanings making up the everyday life-world of human experience. We only engage in this kind of abstraction against substantial background commitments and values and for particular purposes. Third, objectification in human inquiry has proven problematic to say the least (e.g., Bernstein, 1976, 1983; Bishop, 2007; Richardson, Fowers & Guignon, 1999; Slife & Williams, 1995; Taylor 1985a, 1985b). A key reason for objectification's failure when applied to the human realm is that it represents as much a moral as an epistemological ideal. This moral ideal can be seen, for example, in the Enlightenment drive towards emancipation through insisting that moral good comes from objectifying and investigating hypotheses about the social realm that lead to liberating people from antiquated superstitions and false authorities. Such moral implications derive from a viewpoint already animated by a moral vision of the good life for human beings.

Objectification may be a thoroughly appropriate stance to take towards understanding the properties of electrons, molecules, and stars. However, when applied to human activities and our ways of coping with our world, objectification distorts the human phenomena under study by treating self-interpreting beings as being no different in kind from electrons, molecules, and stars (quite the value judgment!). One may be able to investigate and describe the physical properties of stars without implicitly or explicitly judging whether it would be better if the star formed in a different way or place. But when investigating and describing human activity, such judgments about what is good are essentially unavoidable (Bishop, 2007).

For instance, Bernstein (1976) showed how objectification in human inquiry, though purportedly fostering "value-neutral, objective claims subject only to the criteria of public testing," turn out to harbor "disguised ideology." These "proposed theories secrete values and reflect controversial ideological claims about what is right, good, and just" (1976, p. 31), reflecting a "total intellectual orientation" (1976, p. 51) anchored in a complete package of tendentious high Enlightenment ideals such as individualism, instrumentalism, and emancipation. As an example, several thinkers have analyzed different versions of liberal individualism, a disguised ideology that pervasively shapes much human inquiry (e.g., Bishop, 2007; Richardson, Fowers & Guignon, 1999; Taylor 1985a, 1985b). This is a particular ethical vision or understanding of the nature of human action and the good life stressing *negative liberty*—what we are free from rather than what we are free for—and defends individual autonomy (the very value that so many feel is threatened by revelation). This one-sided emphasis obscures our cultural embeddedness and downplays the value of lasting social ties. It advocates thoroughgoing neutrality towards and distancing from all values as a way of promoting particular basic and laudable ends such as liberty, tolerance, individuality, dignity, and human rights (more values, ironically). Simultaneously, liberal individualism's insistent characterization of human action and motivation as exclusively self-interested and utilitarian undermines our capacity to respect and cherish others. Thus, liberal individualism tends to erode our devotion to the admirable modern ideals of freedom and justice, the very ideals that it seeks to promote.

Liberal individualism, with its emphasis on human autonomy and liberty likely accounts for the fact that we moderns miss the role authority plays in our learning about and coming to understand the physical and personal realms. Since the Enlightenment, Western society has been so focused on promoting individual autonomy over all forms of authority that we fail to see the extent to which as knowing subjects we have to place ourselves under the provisional authority of electrons, volcanoes, stars, other people, etc., to learn what they have to teach us. Western society's one-sided emphasis on individualism and autonomy is a prime source of our modern discomfort with and rejection of the provisional authority of traditions and institutions, whether those be religious, political or otherwise, and most pointedly our dismissive rejection of special revelation. Special revelation is neither irrational nor defies reason; however, special revelation's claim that some things can only be known *through a source other than human reason* could not be tolerated by the Enlightenment's celebration of human reason and individual autonomy.

Remarkably, such disguised ideology is part and parcel of the seemingly innocent commitment to studying human actions and involvements through exclusive use of natural science methods (Bernstein, 1976; Bishop, 2007; Taylor, 1985a, 1985b). Such disguised ideology is on full display when psychologists require religious commitments and practices be formulated in clear, objective, publicly (i.e., scientifically) testable propositions. A defense of these natural science methods based on science or on standard models of rationality cannot be offered because both of these already presuppose the objectification that is in question.

When we take fully on board the insight that humans are self-interpreting beings, it becomes clear that these natural science approaches to human inquiry as well as the cultural ideals animating them are also interpretations of the social realm. For instance, dozens of recent correlational studies have found a positive, moderate, statistically significant relationship between (a) scores on a variety of measures of common religious commitment and practices, and (b) scores on a number of different scales assessing mental and physical health or well-being (McCullough, Pargament, & Thoresen 2001; Pargament, 2001). Whatever such findings disclose about human life is not a matter of simply discovering correlations and producing statistical analyses. Such findings, as well as the methods used to uncover them, involve interpretation.

First, these are hardly value-neutral findings. The religious commitment and practice measures adopted by the investigator reflect his or her judgment as to what are normal or worthwhile religious activities. Moreover, the scales of health and well-being employed reflect the investigator's opinion concerning what are desirable outcomes in living.

Second, it would be a mistake to construe these findings as demonstrating a clear instrumental relationship between religion and well-being. Rather, these commitments and activities, as well as the conditions of well-being or peace of mind, are different facets or ingredients of a particular way of life. They seem to go together to a modest extent as aspects of a particular way of being human at one point in time. We have to decide what we think about that way of being as a whole because there is no way to objectively evaluate it in terms of its effects.

Whether we like it or not, such findings and any interpretation we place on them are deeply value-laden. We can all imagine someone who values physical and social success or domination above everything else in life. To such a person, religious attitudes such as acceptance or peace of mind would seem trivial or escapist, much mental turmoil might be interpreted as excitement or a sign of vitality, and high blood pressure deemed a badge of honor! In fact, many of us think such spiritual values as finding genuine meaning in suffering and adopting a forgiving attitude toward others have much to recommend them. Yet no one can attain a view from nowhere to demonstrate this outlook as a good or worthy one. Conclusions about what is worthwhile or significant have no real meaning outside of being worked out by members of a community in their struggle to discern things in a deeper or wiser way, a struggle full of surprises and at least some degree of learning through suffering.

This kind of research into religion and well-being is in every way a living part of the human struggle for clarity, decency, and wisdom. The research was motivated and generated by that struggle in the first place, and what sense or meaning we make of it will depend upon our vantage point and concerns at a given point in this struggle. For self-interpreting beings, this process of sense-making is a two-way street. Psychologists interpret and explain human activity, but often their understanding (and, indeed, the very terms of their understanding) of this activity change or develop in the process (similar to how partners in a conversation influence one another's outlook and values in unpredictable ways). The same two-way process takes place between reported results and the way they are assimilated and interpreted by citizens, students, and other psychologists. The meaning of these findings and the very realities of human activity or social life may alter as a result of how these findings are received and interpreted. For example, secular readers of these studies on religion and well-being may be prompted to reevaluate their opinion of religion as something usually backward or even harmful to human welfare. Meanwhile, readers more sympathetic to religious values may be prompted to question whether the emphasis on health and well-being in this research and current religious culture perhaps points to a penchant they may have for looking at religion only in terms of its personal benefits or payoffs. Or perhaps religious adherents may find these results challenge them to question whether their own emphasis on personal well-being has blinded them somewhat to suffering and injustice in the world to which they probably should attend more pointedly, even at the cost of some of their comfort and security. In such ways, the meanings we live by and our psychological accounts of them will mutually influence one another and change over time.

Certainly, taking fully on board the insight that humans are self-interpreting beings places severe limitations on the traditional pretensions of mainstream psychology to objective, final truths about the human realm. At the same time, it also reconnects us morally and existentially with our world: the human realm we are trying to understand.

Taking Things on Their Own Terms: Relationality

The injunction to take things on their own terms has a further implication for human inquiry. If we are to genuinely take things on their own terms, we must also consider the context in which they are situated. Put another way, we must consider the *relatedness* of the thing in question to other things because that relatedness patly constitutes what the thing of interest to us is (Gunton, 1993; Slife, 2004). This also is not a new insight. In the 17th century, Boyle, for instance, insisted that "A body is not to be considered barely in itself, but as it is placed in, and is a portion of the universe" (Boyle 1965, p. 303). A contemporary example of this from the natural sciences would be genes. The functionality of a particular gene is largely constituted by that gene's relationship to all the other genetic material in the genome. A geneticist cannot understand what a particular gene is by only studying it in isolation from the rest of the genome.

In the study of human beings as self-interpreting, our relationality is inescapable. Ontologically, self-interpreting beings are always in relationship with and significantly shaped by others. We are related to other humans through family, friendship, and rivalry; to communities and societies in which we live as well as read about or see on television; to masses of ideas forming a kind of intellectual sea all around us; and to the values and ideals that permeate our lives even if we are largely unaware of them, as well as being in relationship to the physical realm. At some level, self-interpreting beings are always engaged in the ongoing process of understanding, responding to, working out, adopting, modifying, or rejecting the myriad things with which we are related, by which we are shaped, and through which we are enabled to act in the world.

Put this way, the relationality of persons is somewhat obvious if too often taken for granted or ignored. However, in human inquiry we face an important question: Which forms of relatedness lead to inauthentic autonomy, domination, and distortion, and which forms enable true autonomy (Gunton, 1993)? For instance, much (if not most) human inquiry treats people as if they are individual atoms, each bearing properties, and are related to each other by forms of efficient causal and instrumental influence, what Slife (2004) called *weak relationality* and Taylor called *weak world-shaping relations* (Bishop, 2007, pp. 23–25). Any other forms of relationship among people actually violate the kind of neutrality towards values and the individualistic autonomy endorsed by liberal individualism. So human relationships are conceptualized as strictly efficient-causal and instrumental. However, that has the consequence of pressing the particularity of persons into a generic individualism. Our uniqueness tends to be minimized, and our differences become significant sources of social and political threat rather than a positive social and political good. In this way, Western societies tend to channel human autonomy towards sameness and conformity (Gunton, 1993).

Our modern world is awash in conformity, if not downright tyranny, in numerous forms of fundamentalism (religious, atheist, and political), totalitarianism, drives towards herd mentality and consumerism, public opinion, markets and marketing, fads of fashions and gadgets, the worship of ideological purity, the compulsion in many quarters to force all human intellectual activity into an idealized model of natural science, just to name a few. And there is evidence in the world of social and psychological theory of forms of homogeneity threatening to undermine human freedom and integrity. One only has to look at 19th and 20th century theories still haunting us today: scientism, behaviorism, Freudianism, sociobiology, doctrines of determinism and reductionism, among others. Ironically, human freedom and creativity was needed to formulate such theories which, in turn, entirely explain human freedom and creativity away, radically depersonalizing all humans in the process. The weak forms of human relatedness promoted in human inquiry, and much social and political policy, actually undercut rather than enable genuine autonomy and individuality.

This tendency towards homogenization of individuals shows up squarely in natural science approaches to the study of the human realm. Efficient-causal and instrumental relationships are quantifiable, and the reduction of human individuality to a narrow range promotes the identification of behavioral patterns that might be studied in systematic fashion. Genuine uniqueness of every person threatens this behavioral reduction, while the rich relationality of genuine human life tends to resist quantification. Natural science inquiry tends to picture everything as mechanically inter-related via efficient cause-effect chains (Bishop, 2007). This mechanical picture is a particularly damaging form of homogenization that appears schizophrenic:

> It is one of the many contradictions of modernity that side by side have developed a view of the person as essentially indistinguishable from, identical in being with, the non-personal universe, and a view of the person as so discontinuous with the matter of the world as to be an alien within it. Naturalistic views of the human deriving from a view that everything, whatever it is, should be subject to the same kind of scientific theorizing, have encouraged an equally unbalanced stressing of subjectivity, consciousness, rationality, and all those things which make us appear utterly different from the material world. (Gunton, 1993, p. 174)

Moreover, liberal individualism not only fails to preserve and encourage genuine autonomy and authentic individuality, it also promotes a distorting picture of persons as punctual selves who manipulate or use everything outside of the self (the body, other people, the material world) as raw materials for securing and promoting their individual well being (Gunton 1993; Taylor, 1995). There are no alternatives for action or relationship with others in the physical or personal realms when the only two means of relationality are efficient causation and instrumentalism. Our being as persons is pictured as wholly drawn from within ourselves and our ability to manipulate the others surrounding us, rather than pictured as deeply influenced by mutually constitutive relationships with others, where the kind of person you distinctively are is shaped by the relationships you have to other persons and things.

Special revelation from the Christian tradition has something to say here, through the doctrine of the Trinity, a theologically mediated revelation of the divine, as a rich pattern for our relationality. The three persons of the Trinity are what they are and who they are in their particularity in virtue of their relationship with each other. That is to say that Father, Son, and Spirit co-constitute each other; they are bound up together with making each other what they are. This is not a static form of being and relationship; instead, there is a dynamic interrelatedness in the Trinity where Father, Son, and Spirit always mutually constitute each other while enabling each other to be particularly who they are and engage creation and salvation in particular ways suited to who they are as persons (Gunton, 1993). Here we have a picture of diversity and particularity in unity, not a homogenizing of the persons of the Trinity so that they become identical. Rather, Father, Son, and Spirit are being in community.

Likewise, creation, both the physical and personal realms, is what it is in virtue of its relationship to the Trinity through God's creating, upholding, redeeming, enabling, and perfecting activity (Gunton, 1998). The physical and personal realms are not what they are in virtue of some bundle of internal properties they have; rather, they are what they distinctly are in virtue of their relationship to God as well as each other. Just as the Father, Son, and Spirit mutually contribute to and make possible each other's identity and particularity, so the physical and personal realms mutually contribute to and make possible each other's identity and uniqueness. There is diversity and particularity that is enabled by virtue of everything being related to everything else, yet there is a unified order to the created realm.

In particular, humans are what we distinctly are in our being and personality in virtue of our relationship to God, creation, and each other. Our involvements with others are necessary shapers of who we are as particular persons, as in Slife's *strong relationality* and Taylor's *strong world-shaping relations* (Bishop, 2007, pp. 23–25). The personal realm is characterized by a dynamic relationality as persons have ongoing mutually constituting influence on each other. This is part of the "dynamic order" of creation

> that is summoned into being and directed towards its perfection by the free creativity of Father, Son and Holy Spirit. That orientation of being is, of course, distorted and delayed by sin and evil, and returns to its directedness only through the incarnation and the redeeming agency of the Spirit. But evil distorts the dynamic of being, does not take it away. (Gunton, 1993, p. 166)

Our being as persons is shaped through a web of relations that is dynamic in that while we are being shaped by these relationships, we also are continually interpreting and reinterpreting those relations and ourselves in light of those relations. We each bring our particular slant to this web of relations: The web both enables us to be the particular individual persons we are while at the same time we engage that web out of our particularity.

Instead of a problematic drive toward homogeneity, the picture is one of diversity and particularity in a unifying relational social order. We are *being in community*.

One form this takes for us is a dialogical or conversational dynamic (Bakhtin, 1981; Dunn, 1996; Guignon, 1991; Richardson, Rogers, & McCarroll, 1998; Scheff, 2004; Taylor, 1991). There are a number of internal dimensions to these dynamics. For instance, my past experiences, traditions, and involvements shape my current self-understanding. As well, my present understanding of myself sheds light and new understanding on my past experiences, traditions, and involvements. In turn I have a further illuminated grasp on who I am. Similarly, my current picture of my future (my goals, my dreams, the kind of person I imagine I want to become, etc.) shapes my current self-interpretation leading to a further refined understanding of my past. Furthermore, my present view of myself also colors my picture of the future which then further clarifies and illumines my current self-understanding.

This dialogical dynamic is not just internal. It is made possible by the dialogical nature of the relationships I have with the traditions of family and community, my family ties, friends, colleagues and rivals, books I read, music I hear, movies and television shows I watch, the unforeseen surprises and disappointments of my life and so forth. Part of how I currently envision myself is due to my relationships with spiritual and intellectual mentors who have shaped me not only through their care for and interest in me but also through my desire to learn from and become more like them. One form this dynamic can take is my imagining what I might currently be like if I could have appropriated more from my mentors earlier in my life. How much further down my desired path would I be? Or, under reflection, I may come to realize that I am much further in my development as a person, scholar, friend, and minister than I realized because of how my mentors have shaped me. The bottom line is that I could not possibly be the person I now am, or the person I am striving to become, without the significant involvements of others in my life.

This inherent relationality of self-interpreting beings is in strong tension with the objectifying tendencies of mainstream psychological inquiry which seeks to decontextualize the self as its means for understanding (cf. Bishop, 2007; Richardson, Fowers & Guignon, 1999; Slife & Williams, 1995; Webb, 1993). This decontextualized or atomistic view of the personal realm pictures that realm as a set of objectified social structures and systems mediating the interactions of an amalgamation of separate individuals and their qualities (e.g., Bishop, 2005). To the degree that psychological theory and practice miss out the relationality of persons is the degree to which it distorts its research subjects, promotes inauthentic autonomy, and participates in the homogenizing tendencies of contemporary Western societies.

Taking Things on Their Own Terms: Psychology of Religion Research

If the world is a creation, as special revelation indicates, then the physical and personal realms have their own particular being: relational being as we have seen. The world is what it is created to be and is becoming what it is created to become. There is no necessary expectation that the activity of the Trinity in creation should show up as evidence detectable in test tubes and telescopes. Rather, the world shows itself to be the creation of God by its created nature, a nature that is distinct from the divine nature of the Trinity. The modern tendencies towards displacing divine nature into the created order either as a search for evidence for God or as a means of replacing God with creation lay at the root of some of the most disquieting tendencies of modern Western culture (Gunton, 1993, 1998). Taking this created, relational being on its own terms in the personal realm has implications for psychological inquiry. I will use one study in the psychology of religion that is illustrative of much work in this area.

Cassibba, Granqvist, Costantini, and Gatto (2008) studied religious attachment drawing on attachment theory. Attachment theory, as Cassibba et al. described it, is a mechanical approach to understanding human action, positing a "genetically based attachment behavioral system" that selects "attachment figures" which are "represented" in the system. Behaviors are then explained accordingly. For example, on this view young children tend to select the caregiver who "spent the most time caring for the child" as their "principal attachment figure... The caregiver's sensitivity to the child's signals is in turn believed to determine the nature of the child's cognitive-affective representations... of self and others" (Cassibba et al., 2008, p. 1753). The references to "representations," "signals" and determination all indicate a mechanical, efficient-causal framework for their analysis.

Within this framework, the authors often referred to *God representations* rather than understandings or interpretations of God. The former is a kind of scientized, propositionalized construal of the latter, transmuting their subjects' understandings and commitments regarding God into what appears to be a scientifically assessable state analyzable in an efficient cause-effect framework. However, note that this transmutation and research framework are themselves interpretations of social realities. So the very way that Cassibba et al. framed their hypotheses and research approach started with not taking religious people's understandings and commitments on their own terms (the same could be said of the secular attachment representations invoked for comparison with religious attachments) but offered an alternative interpretation of their research subjects from the get go. Moreover, Cassibba et al. conceptualized a person's relationship with God as largely instrumental with God being "a safe haven when distressed," "a secure base for exploration," "an important source of felt security," a means "to regulate distress," and a "compensation" for insensitive parents (Cassibba et al., 2008, p. 1754). In other words, research subjects were pictured in this study as only being subject to weak world-shaping relations with respect to God and others, which clearly transmutes Christian understandings of a relationship with God into something different than it is for Christians.

One of their research questions was whether "intense religious devotion" (e.g., being a Catholic priest) "might be set in motion by a history of insecure attachment in the secular attachment domain, where the individual's perceived relationship with God comes to serve a surrogate attachment function that assists in regulating distress," or whether this "religiosity . . . stems from a history of secure attachment in which the individual's perceived relationship with God signals an extension of his or her prior secure relationships" (2008, p. 1755). This question encodes natural science-like hypotheses formulated in efficient-causal and instrumental terms limiting the possible interpretations for a person becoming a Catholic priest or nun to two possible efficient causes. No consideration was given to traditional Christian ideas such as a woman receiving a calling on her life to serve Christ through convent life, or a man discovering that his spiritual gifts are for pastoral ministry. The possibility that God is actually at work in such people's lives was completely discounted by Cassibba et al.'s interpretations, so the research subjects' own self-interpretations and understandings were ignored in favor of supposedly objectified measures in a validated attachment scale (though any such scale can only reflect what its deviser considers to be a good, meaningful life).

On all counts, Cassibba et al.'s study missed the mark of taking things on their own terms as self-interpreting beings. Of course, priests and nuns could be confused or deluded in their self-understandings, so their interpretations need to be probed. But the same goes for Cassibba et al.'s interpretations which involved a framework that homogenizes research subjects for the sake of identifying quantifiable research outcomes at the expense of pursuing understanding of actual lived experience. For instance, the feelings of security and peace many priests and nuns report may be a byproduct of fulfilling their calling in Christ and serving through their giftedness rather than a representation of God being an instrumental means to gaining security.

Although much could be said about Cassibba et al.'s results, I will focus on only one illustrative example: "The fact that most of the priests and religious who were included in this study appear to be continuously secure" (2008, p. 1760). Leaving aside how the study's notion of security is colored by the cultural ideal of liberal individualism and treated as an unquestioned good, Cassibba et al. presented this finding as initially counter intuitive since

> the priests and religious of this study have withdrawn to a secluded life in the convent or Church, where they abstain from reproduction and from becoming primary caregivers to children... and their secure working models thus fail to transmit to the next generation. (2008, p. 1760)

Cassibba et al. only imagined that a person's influence is passed on to future generations through their parental care-giving instead of other kinds of involvements (e.g., priest or nun as a role model that may inspire children and youths).

Given the kinds of rich lives priests and nuns forego, Cassibba et al. explained their security as follows: (a) In every known human culture in history, many well-adjusted individuals have embraced life philosophies where deities hold a central place.

> It is notable, however, that when securely attached individuals do so, some anthropomorphic features in general and benevolent features (e.g., loving, caring) in particular seem to be attributed to the transcendent, which makes the transcendent reminiscent of the secure individual's primary attachment figure. (2008, p. 1760)

One wonders what instruments were used to determine the secure attachment of the ancient Israelite prophets, 3rd century Desert Fathers, or Mohamad, say, to establish the validity of such a generalization. Here, Cassibba et al. merely projected their contemporary picture of Western security attachment into the past and into other cultures organized quite differently from ours. Also, (b) The priests and nuns formed

> close relationships with *imagined figures* such as the Virgin Mary (the perfect mother) and Christ (the perfect bridegroom)... the adult human mind has an enormous degree of flexibility and capacity for imagination (e.g., the attribution of a mind to *nonobservable entities*). (2008, p. 1760, emphasis added)

leading even the most well-adjusted individuals away from "the normative scenario" (i.e., spousal relationships) to cloistered or celibate life (2008, p. 1760). On Cassibba et al.'s interpretation, God, Jesus, and the Virgin Mary cannot be anything other than imaginary, "empirically unsubstantiated, invisible" agents (2008, p. 1753).

Attachment theory is an attempt to come to grips with meaningful human ties. When operationalized in terms of efficient causation and instrumental agency, it loses its grip on the meaningfulness of our human relationships and commitments. Perhaps researchers have some sense for the meaningfulness of human life, but the drive to produce validated natural-science-like research squeezes this meaningfulness out. It is clear that the "relational influences" in Cassibba et al.'s research subjects are efficient cause-effect relations among cognitive representations, rather than the real flesh and blood relationships of human beings with each other and certainly not the relationship these subjects have with the Triune God through Christ. The strong relational reality of the personal realm, as well as the reality of God, were weakened if not suppressed from the beginning by the way the study was framed. Cassibba et al.'s disguised cultural ideals deprived their research subjects of genuine individuality and shunted them into a distorting homogeneity conforming to those ideals. For example, the idea that God might create different individuals with particular callings and particular gifts to serve particular purposes never entered into Cassibba et al.'s intrepretations. Their liberal individualist expectations and commitment to a natural science approach ruled out any such particularity from the start. Instead, the individuality of human beings was submerged into the same efficient cause-effect order as that of the physical realm. Furthermore, the idea that people might actually choose through an autonomy that is both shaped and empowered by their relationships with others to serve God in particular ways was ruled out from the beginning by these same cultural ideals and a strictly natural science interpretation.

As an alterative, instead of picturing these priests and nuns as liberal individualist, instrumental actors, what if we draw on revelation and the self-interpreting, relational nature of people, picturing them as being in community along the Trinitarian lines sketched earlier? Persons in this image are fundamentally relational and that relationality is centered on love in the form of gift and reception rather than on self-interest and utility. Sacrifice, so hard to understand in modern times through terms of self-interest and utility, stands at the very center of this image:

God the father *"gives up"* his only Son, allows him to be delivered into the hands of sinful men. Jesus *lays down* his life, and, particularly but not only in the theology of the Letter to the Hebrews, *offers* his humanity, made perfect through suffering to the Father. So it is with the Spirit. As the *gift* of the Father he is the ... first fruits ... of the perfecting action of God in Christ ... It is the Father's *giving* of the Son, the Son's *giving* of himself to the Father and the Spirit's enabling of the creation's *giving* in response that is at the centre. (Gunton, 1993, p. 225, emphasis added)

There is a rhythm or dynamic of giving and receiving within the Trinity and in the Trinity's actions. Similarly, as created in this image (Gunton, 1992, 1998), priests and nuns give up particular kinds of familial relationships while receiving other kinds of communal relationships. They offer their humanity so that others may receive service and ministry. They are enabled to give themselves in these ways by the Spirit and through the relational nature they have as being in community. As self-interpreting beings following their particular calling as they understand it, they see themselves as giving their all not for what they may gain (security) but out of love for God and other persons. Christianity's understanding of love includes a transcendence of the self in a willingness to forbear and forgive the faults of others, sacrifice for their good, and consider the needs and interests of others before considering our own. This is a significantly different way of life than altruism, a modern category that distorts love and gift into something more instrumental and mechanical. Satisfactions flowing as a byproduct of this way of life no doubt will be the kinds of peace and security registering on Cassibba et al.'s surveys and interviews, but it is just that: a byproduct of fulfilling a greater calling. These priests and nuns perhaps see more clearly than most of us that gift and reception are constitutive of human life, not self-fulfilment:

[A] Christian view of life will here come into sharpest conflict with modernity and ... its "myth of fulfillment." The doctrine that the calling of the person is to fulfill himself or herself is both individualist and a characteristic fruit of the transcendental pretense that would make the world circle around the sun that is the individual. The false transcendentality that is the ideological basis of modernism mistakes the character of human relationality. Because in modernity individual self-fulfilment has displaced God from the centre of the world, it makes itself the centre of things, and so uses both person and world as means to its ends. (Gunton, 1993, pp. 226–227)

If seeking truth means being serious about taking things on their own terms, then psychological studies should come to grips with the dynamically relational, self-interpreting nature of human beings (and should come to grips that such studies are interpretive practices; see Taylor, 1985b). Otherwise, psychologists run the danger of churning out studies that ultimately bear little resemblance to human realities and that shed little genuine insight into human action. With an appropriate theological grounding, we can do much better than this. Yet, we should not underestimate how difficult it is to give full weight to relationality and self-interpreting beings and resist falling into objectification.

Taking Things on Their Own Terms: Taking Stock

I began by exploring the concept of revelation in the physical and personal realms and their parallels with that most troubling concept to moderns, special revelation. Methods used in natural science inquiry have their theologically mediated roots in special revelation in the idea of taking things in nature on their own terms so as to understand what they genuinely are as accurately as possible. If this is true, when psychological inquiry draws only on the natural sciences, because the latter have such a track record of success, without first thinking through what it means to take the objects of inquiry of psychology on their own terms, it is very likely that such research will end up distorting its understanding of human beings. Indeed, human inquiry generally suffers from a diminished or defective conception of relationality, a weak form shaped largely in term of efficient causation and instrumental action (Bishop, 2007; Slife, 2004). A Christian viewpoint helps us both diagnose this deficient view of human relationality and see our way to a richer, more genuine conception of that relationality. Revelation does speak to human reason "in such a way as to liberate the energies that are inherent in created rationality" (Gunton, 1993, p. 212) so that inquiry can be richly furthered.

To some degree, then, psychology already draws on revelation for its approaches to understanding human beings, whether it currently acknowledges this debt or not. In several senses, that I have tried to illustrate, there is no clean separation between psychology and Christianity as is so often taken for granted by both sides in the theism-psychology debates. Psychology may often draw very poorly on these roots and suffer as a consequence. Perhaps it is time to transform the propriety question (Is it appropriate to allow God into psychology?) into the question of how robustly should psychology engage with Christian insights and understandings. Insights resulting from the mediation of revelation within the Western tradition are already involved in our social relationships and psychological inquiry and can help us avoid both objectification and relativism by taking our subjects of study on their own terms. One might urge that we can take this latter insight on board but drop traditional religious understandings. However, there may be much to be gained from the human struggle such understandings mediate to us about our humanity, keeping us focused on what makes us genuinely human.

REFERENCES

Adami, C. (2006). Evolution: Reducible complexity. *Science, 312*(5770), 61–63. doi:10.1126/science.1126559

Bakhtin, M. (1981). *The dialogical imagination: Four essays by M.M. Bakhtin*, (M. Holquist, Ed). Austin, TX: University of Texas Press.

Bavinck, H. (2003). *Reformed dogmatics, Volume I: Prolegomena* (J. Bolt, Ed., J. Vriend, Trans). Grand Rapids, MI: Baker Academic.

Bernstein, R. (1976). *The restructuring of social and political theory*. Philadelphia, PA: University of Pennsylvania Press.

Bernstein, R. (1983). *Beyond objectivism and relativism: Science, hermeneutics and praxis*. Philadelphia, PA: University of Pennsylvania Press.

Bishop, R.C. (2005). Cognitive psychology: hidden assumptions. In B. Slife, J. Reber, & F.C. Richardson (Eds.) *Critical thinking about psychology: Hidden assumptions and plausible alternatives* (pp. 151–170). Washington, DC: American Psychological Association.

Bishop, R.C. (2007). *The philosophy of the social sciences*. London, England: Continuum.

Bishop, R.C. (2009). What is this naturalism stuff all about? *Journal of Theoretical and Philosophical Psychology, 29*, 108–113. doi:10.1037/a0016967

Bishop, R.C. (2011). Recovering the doctrine of creation: A theological view of science. *Scholarly Papers*. http://biologos.org/projects/scholar-essays

Boyle, R. (1965). *The works of the honorable Robert Boyle* (T. Birch, Ed.). Hildersheim, Germany: Georg Olms. (Original work published 1772)

Cantor, G. (1991). *Michael Faraday: Sandemanian and scientist. A study of science and religion in the nineteenth century*. London, England: Macmillan.

Cassibba, R., Granqvist, P., Costantini, A., & Gatto, S. (2008). Attachment and God representations among lay Catholics, priests, and religious: A matched comparison study based on the adult attachment interview. *Developmental Psychology, 44*, 1753–1763. doi:10.1037/a0013772

Coleridge, S.T. (1956). *Collected letters of Samuel Taylor Coleridge, Volume II, 1801–1806* (E.L. Grigg, Ed.). Oxford, England: Clarendon Press.

Daston, L., & Galison, P. (2010). *Objectivity*. Brooklyn, NY: Zone Books.

Dilthey, W. (1958). *Gesammelte schriften, Volume V*. Stuttgart, Germany: B.G. Teubner.

Dunne, J. (1996). Beyond sovereignty and deconstruction: The storied self. *Philosophy and Social Criticism, 21*, 137–157. http://psc.sagepub.com/

Foster, M. (1934). The Christian doctrine of creation and the rise of modern natural science. *Mind, 43*, 446–468. doi:10.1093/mind/XLIII.172.446

Gauch, H. (2002). *Scientific method in practice*. Cambridge, England: Cambridge University Press.

Goheen, M. (1996). Scriptural revelation, creational revelation, and natural science: The Issue. In J.M. Van der Meer (Ed.) *Facets of faith and science, Volume 4: Interpreting God's action in the world* (pp. 341–343). Lanham, MD: University Press of America.

Guignon, C. (1991). Pragmatism or hermeneutics? Epistemology after foundationalism. In J. Bohman, D. Hiley, & R. Schusterman (Eds.) *The interpretive turn* (pp. 81–101). Ithaca, NY: Cornell University Press.

Gunton, C.E. (1992). *Christ and creation*. Eugene, OR: Wipf & Stock.

Gunton, C.E. (1993). *The one, the three, and the many: God, creation, and the culture of modernity. The 1992 Bampton lectures*. Cambridge, England: Cambridge University Press.

Gunton, C.E. (1995). *A brief theology of revelation*. London, England: T & T Clark.

Gunton, C.E. (1998). *The triune creation: A historical and systematic study*. Grand Rapids, MI: Eerdmans.

Gunton, C.E. (2006). *Enlightenment and alienation: An essay towards a trinitarian theology*. Eugene, OR: Wipf & Stock.

Hacking, I. (1983). *Representing and intervening*. Cambridge, England: Cambridge University Press.

Harrison, P. (2009). *The fall of man and the foundations of science*. Cambridge, England: Cambridge University Press.

Jaki, S. (1987). *Science and creation*. Edinburgh, Scotland: Scottish Academic Press.

Kant, I. (1933). *Critique of pure reason* (N.K. Smith, Trans.). London, England: Macmillan.

Kuhn, T. (1996). *The structure of scientific revolutions* (3rd ed). Chicago, IL: University of Chicago Press.

McCullough, M.E., Pargament, K.I., & Thoresen, C.E. (2001). *Forgiveness: Theory, research, and practice*. New York, NY: Guilford.

Mill, J.S. (1843). *System of logic, ratiocinative and inductive*. London, England: John W. Parker.

Nebelsick, H. (1992). *The renaissance, the reformation, and the rise of modern science*. Edinburgh, Scotland: T&T Clark.

Numbers, R. (2010). *Galileo goes to jail and other myths about science and religion*. Cambridge, MA: Harvard University Press.

Osbeck, L.M., Nersessian, N.J., Malone, K.R., & Newstetter, W.C. (2011). *Science as psychology*. Cambridge, England: Cambridge University Press.

Pargament, K.I. (2001). *The psychology of religion and coping: Theory, research, practice*. New York, NY: Guilford.

Pippen, R.B. (1990). *Modernism as a philosophical problem*. Oxford, England: Blackwell.

Polanyi, M. (1974). *Personal knowledge: Towards a post-critical philosophy* (2nd ed.). Chicago, IL: University of Chicago Press.

Richardson, F.C. (2009). Biases against theism in psychology? *Journal of Theoretical and Philosophical Psychology, 29*, 122–127. doi:10.1037/a0017689

Richardson, F.C., Fowers, B., & Guignon, C. (1999). *Re-envisioning psychology: Moral dimensions of theory and practice*. San Francisco, CA: Jossey-Bass.

Richardson, F.C., Rogers, A., & McCarroll, J. (1998). Toward a dialogical self. *American Behavioral Scientist, 41*, 496–515. doi:10.1177/0002764298041004004

Sargent, M.-A. (1995). *The diffident naturalist: Robert Boyle and the philosophy of experiment*. Chicago, IL: University of Chicago Press.

Scheff, T. (2004). Is hatred formed by hidden shame and rage? *Humanity & Society, 28*, 25–39. http://uhaweb.hartford.edu/doane/humanityandsociety1.htm

Slife, B. (2004). Taking practice seriously: Toward a relational ontology. *Journal of Theoretical and Philosophical Psychology, 24*, 157–178. doi:10.1037/h0091239

Slife, B., & Williams, R. (1995). *What's behind the research? Discovering hidden assumptions in the behavioral sciences*. Thousand Oaks, CA: SAGE.

Tauber, A.I. (2009). *Science and the question for meaning*. Waco, TX: Baylor University Press.

Taylor, C. (1985a). *Philosophical papers, Volume 1: Human agency and language*. Cambridge, England: Cambridge University Press.

Taylor, C. (1985b). *Philosophical papers, Volume 2: Philosophy and the human sciences*. Cambridge, England: Cambridge University Press.

Taylor, C. (1991). The dialogical self. In J. Bohman, D. Hiley, & R. Schusterman (Eds.) *The interpretive turn* (pp. 304–314). Ithaca, NY: Cornell University Press.

Taylor, C. (1992). *Sources of the self: The making of the modern identity*. Cambridge: MA Harvard University Press.

Taylor, C. (1995). *Philosophical arguments*. Cambridge, MA: Harvard University Press.

Taylor, C. (2007). *A secular age*. Cambridge, MA: Belknap Press.

Turner, J. (1985). *Without God, without creed: The origins of unbelief in America*. Baltimore, MD: The Johns Hopkins University Press.

Webb, E. (1993). *The self between: From Freud to the new social psychology of France*. Seattle, WA: University of Washington Press.

Williams, M. (2001). *Problems of knowledge: A critical introduction to epistemology*. New York, NY: Oxford University Press.

Wojcik, J.W. (1997). *Robert Boyle and the limits of reason*. Cambridge, England: Cambridge University Press.

WORLDVIEW COMMUNITIES AND THE SCIENCE OF PSYCHOLOGY

Eric L. Johnson and P.J. Watson*

ABSTRACT

Since its founding, modern psychology has been based on the worldview of naturalism, and its rules of discourse conform to naturalism. However, there are other intellectually respectable worldviews that humans hold. A human science that seeks to be comprehensive in its description of human beings ought to permit other kinds of worldview discourse and require researchers to be more explicit about their own worldviews and the worldviews of their research subjects. An example of a research agenda in which worldviews are explicitly factored into the research is summarized.

Keywords: worldview, naturalism, theism, theistic psychology

In the West, psychology is commonly assumed to be identical with *modern* psychology, the version of psychology that originated in the late 1800's. This confusion is understandable. Within decades of its founding, modern psychology formed a discrete, professional discipline, bounded by the application of natural sciences methods to the study of human beings, resulting in a rich, scientific literature containing innumerable novel contributions to our understanding of human beings, and it was quickly embraced by the West's major educational institutions. In light of these developments, it is not surprising that modern psychology became the exclusive framework for understanding individual humans in the 20th century. What is not as widely appreciated is that these significant disciplinary developments were entirely confounded with the acceptance of the worldview of naturalism. The authors of this article believe that it is possible to decouple the naturalistic worldview from the powerful psychological research agenda of the past 100 years with which it has been wed, so that other worldviews can also empower and contribute to that agenda.

* *Author Note*: Eric L. Johnson, School of Theology, Southern Baptist Theological Seminary; P.J. Watson, Department of Psychology, University of Tennessee at Chattanooga.

Correspondence concerning this article should be addressed to Eric L. Johnson, Southern Baptist Theological Seminary, Box 2381, 2825 Lexington Rd., Louisville, KY, 40280. E-mail: ejohnson@sbts.edu

The members of an intellectual community share certain basic beliefs about reality, called a *worldview*. A worldview is the subset of one's entire system of beliefs that ground and legitimize the rest of one's beliefs: They form the presuppositions for all other suppositions. Many terms have been used for this meta-concept: Husserl and others used *life-world*; Heidegger referred to *preunderstanding*, and coined the phrase *Being-in-the-World*; Wittgenstein discussed *forms of life* and *language games*; Lyotard preferred *metanarrative*; Foucault wrote of *epistemes* and *systems of institutions and disciplinary practices*; P.J. Watson originated *ideological surround*; Kuhn used the terms *paradigms* and *disciplinary matrices* and Lakatos *research programs* to refer to analogues in science; and there are others (Naugle, 2002). These are not synonyms, and they each have their strengths. Nevertheless, worldview is the most commonly used term for this concept-family, so it will be our term of choice in this article.

The challenge in this conceptual area is that a person's basic assumptions are rarely carefully articulated. Rather, they tend to guide one's thinking and living implicitly. As a result, most adherents are not very aware of their worldview beliefs.

The need for greater worldview awareness would seem to be important for all disciplines, but it is especially important for the human sciences. This is because human beings are in large part constituted by their beliefs. Therefore, the basic beliefs a community has about human beings will shape the psychological form of its members. Complicating matters further, in the human sciences, human beings are simultaneously the subjects and the objects of the investigations. As a result, worldview influences operate on both observer and observed.

Naturalism is the worldview that assumes that only natural entities exist and that beliefs are justified only by the methods of empirical science (Danto, 1967; Post, 1995). As a result, naturalism is especially oriented to the empirical, the objective, the measurable, and quite often the material. Those holding a worldview consider its basic assumptions to be true, and therefore the contrary worldview beliefs of others to be false. However, the success of natural science methods and the belief that they lead to the greatest possible objectivity that humans can attain seem to have created a sort of *halo effect* that has led naturalist human scientists to be especially susceptible to dogmatism regarding the objectivity, validity, and freedom from bias of their worldview assumptions.

The problem here is that it is not possible to prove, either logically or empirically, one's worldview beliefs (see Slife, Reber, & Lefevor, this issue). They are simply assumed, perhaps for good reasons, but they cannot be proven true to the satisfaction of those who do not already subscribe to them. It is a curious fact of human life that a necessary circularity attends some of our most cherished and important beliefs, including beliefs in the general validity of one's perceptions, clear and simple memories, reasoning, the testimony of others, the existence of other persons, indeed the existence of whatever one is presently experiencing (a problem nicely dramatized in the movie *The Matrix*; see Audi, 1998; Plantinga, 1993). Many worldview beliefs are similar. The fact is there are many worldview beliefs that appear to be logically and empirically compatible with the universe within which we live.

Since its founding, modern psychology has assumed a naturalistic worldview and has excluded reliance on other worldview beliefs in its discourse. Early on, as modern psychology sought to differentiate from its intellectual rivals, its worldview beliefs had to be more explicit. James (1890/2007), for example, declared in his classic *The Principles of Psychology*, that "psychology is a natural science" (Vol. 1, p. 183). However, over the ensuing decades, its worldview sank into the rarely acknowledged realm of assumptions, so that today, outside of articles in the philosophy of psychology, naturalistic worldview beliefs are rarely discussed in contemporary psychology; they have become the air that we breathe. Consider, for example, that there is no entry for naturalism (or anything comparable) in the *Encyclopedia of Psychology* (Kazdin, 2000), perhaps our generation's definitive overview of contemporary psychology.

QUESTIONING THE REQUIREMENT OF NATURALISM FOR CONTEMPORARY PSYCHOLOGY

The value of natural science methods and an empirical orientation for psychology is indisputable. There are many reasons, however, to question the hegemony of the worldview of naturalism in contemporary psychology. To begin with, not all thoughtful humans believe that that worldview is even valid. Some philosophers, for example, have argued that naturalism is inherently self-contradictory (Craig & Moreland, 2000; Goetz & Taliaferro, 2008). Moreover, philosophers of science in the latter half of the 20th century have criticized the naïve positivism that gave rise to modern psychology's commitment to naturalism, for example, a rejection of metaphysics (Seager, 2000). Some believe that naturalism involves assumptions which give psychologists a truncated view of human beings, for example, that discounts personal agency or freedom (Martin, Sugarman,

& Thompson, 2003). Similarly, for most of the 20th century, a strict adherence to natural science assumptions led modern psychology to avoid investigating topics such as virtues, moral awareness, and transcendence (apart from their being treated as mere social beliefs), which positive psychology researchers have now demonstrated can be investigated empirically. One wonders how many other valid psychological phenomena may have been neglected because of the biases of naturalism.

Conversely, allowing other worldviews into contemporary psychology could lead to additional psychological discoveries. Dialogue with those with whom we disagree is one of the best ways to advance one's understanding, to become more aware of one's own assumptions, and to correct one's errors and distortions. Bakhtin called this the other's "surplus of vision" (Morson & Emerson, 1990, pp. 53–54): Others can see things about oneself that one cannot. Minorities (like theists) are especially helpful, because they may more easily recognize the bias of majorities. Sciences necessarily begin with generalizations and universal claims. However, as they mature, they pursue greater accuracy, detail, and comprehensiveness. In recent decades, cross-cultural psychology enriched contemporary psychology by opening it up to non-Western psychological phenomena. Likewise, allowing diverse worldviews in contemporary psychological discourse would likely lead to a more complex and sophisticated understanding of human beings (Slife, Reber, & Lefevor, this issue).

To be blunt, requiring public adherence to naturalism and the enforcement of naturalistic discourse rules is also questionable from an ethical standpoint. It is a curious thing that most people studied in modern psychology have not held to naturalism, yet its exclusive worldview requirements produced a naturalistic psychology of those human beings. To whom does the discipline belong? It could even be argued that naturalistic exclusivism constitutes a form of censorship that often accompanies the influence of any unquestioned regime of power.

To those concerned that opening contemporary psychology up to other worldviews would destroy its unity, it must be pointed out that naturalism is not as unifying as might be believed. This is partly because there are significantly different kinds of naturalism: ontological or strong, supervenient or non-reductive, and methodological, as well as humanist and postmodernist versions (Jobling, 2001; Post, 1995), and such variation is represented in modern psychology. Just consider the differences in the methods and content of evolutionary psychology, radical behaviorism, object relations theory, cognitive psychology, feminist psychology, positive psychology, and social constructivism.

The Psychologies of Other Worldview Communities

If we allow ourselves to think outside the ethnocentrism of modern psychology and its assumptions, there is plenty of evidence of the existence of other psychologies cross-culturally and in the history of humankind, most of them based on alternative worldviews. In the West, relatively well-developed psychologies can be found in ancient Greece, ancient Rome, Judaism, Christianity, and Islam; and in the East in Hinduism, Buddhism, and Taoism, and each of these consists of additional subgroups. Many of these psychologies have been discussed by contemporary historians of psychology and other scholars (Brett, 1951; Charry, 1998; Foucault, 2005; Hergenhahn, 2008; Nussbaum, 1994; Robinson, 1995; Viney, King, & Woody, 2008; Watson & Evans, 1991). These psychologies can of course be distinguished in terms of their level of intellectual sophistication, investigative methods, number of documents, institutional development, number of findings, forms of people-helping, and basic assumptions or worldview, among other things; by most of these standards, modern psychology has been unquestionably the most productive, uncovering innumerable previously unrecognized psychological features of human beings. Nonetheless, this fact does not warrant the wholesale exclusion of the psychologies of all other worldview communities from the discipline of psychology for the simple reason that the intellectual accomplishments of one group do not guarantee the invalidity of the work of other groups.

The Necessarily Pluralistic Nature of the Science of Psychology

What worldviews and their communities are distinctive enough to warrant inclusion in a worldview classification scheme relevant for psychology? Such organizational questions have to be addressed in most sciences, including linguistics (distinguishing dialects and languages), biology (e.g., families), and geography and anthropology (people groups). The formation of a definitive list for psychology would have to be a communal affair, involving the input of all worldview communities. Perhaps the greatest problem facing such a project is that such classifications could be based either on substantive psychological distinctives (e.g., the Buddhist concept of *no-self*) or on a priori sociocultural distinctives, out of respect for different communities (e.g., Islamic and Jewish psychology). It would seem that legitimate reasons can be given for both approaches.

In the meantime, the following is a plausible beginning, based on both conceptual and communal criteria: *naturalism*: ontological, supervenient, humanist, postmodernist, Marxist, and classical Buddhist; and *supernaturalism*: idealistic monist (Hindu, Taoist, and New Age), panentheist, monotheist (Judaism, Islam), Trinitarian theist (Christianity), deist, polytheist (found in ancient cultures, and some contemporary religions, including Shinto and some traditions of Hinduism and Buddhism), and animist (Markham & Ruparell, 2001; Meister, 2011; Smith, 2009; Young, 2009). We should add that thorough consistency and coherence in worldview beliefs is an ideal (at least conceptually). Most people, however, are more or less syncretists; that is, they incorporate beliefs from more than one worldview. Regardless of the validity of the previous organizational scheme, taking worldview seriously in contemporary psychology would require work (writing texts/teaching/counseling) that is mindful of this diverse and pluralistic context.

Given the enormous complexity of human beings, it seems very likely that some psychological topics will be more and some less affected by worldview considerations, depending on whether or not the psychological feature is particularly *worldview-dependent*. Greater worldview dependence seems to be a function of the feature's susceptibility to sociocultural influence, multi-level complexity (for example, its nature as biopsychosocial as well as ethicospiritual), existential or experiential quality, and the extent to which it is constituted by values. Lesser worldview dependence is indicated by the feature being characterized by greater mechanistic and organismic qualities.

As a result, there will likely be greater overall agreement among worldview communities regarding psychological features that are largely a function of mechanistic or organismic dynamics, such as neural networks, stimulus-response units, cognitive structures and processes, drive motivation, and basic social processes (like social influence). By contrast, there will likely be less agreement among worldview communities regarding uniquely human motivation, personality structures and processes, psychopathology, definitions of human maturity and flourishing, psychotherapy models, complex social processes (attribution, definitions of love), and ethical and spiritual dynamics. Where worldview communities share assumptions, they can and should work together on psychological topics. Consequently, some hierarchy of worldview consonance might guide collaborative psychological work, with most worldview communities collaborating commonly to a greater extent in neuropsychology but forming more sub-community collaborations in areas of psychology that are more worldview-dependent, where naturalists (ontological and supervenient), theists (Jewish, Christian, Muslim), and monists (Hindu, Taoist, New Age), for example, might be expected to work more closely together, within their respective worldview families.

Even in the latter areas, however, we would expect benefits from dialogue and studying the psychological work of other worldview communities. In fact, some subgroups may find it easier to collaborate with members of other worldview communities on certain topics, rather than with certain members of their own worldview community. For example, humanist and postmodernist naturalists and theists might collaborate on research on human freedom.

In addition, depending on the richness of their community's intellectual resources, individual worldview communities ought to do psychological work according to their particular perspective. For example, Jewish psychologists might work on a distinctly Jewish psychology (e.g., see Spero, 1992), and Buddhists on a distinctly Buddhist psychology (e.g., see Kwee, Gergen, & Koshikawa, 2006), and so forth. Nonetheless, as in cross-cultural psychology, such worldview-specific work would be included within a comprehensive science of human beings. The rest of the article will illustrate worldview-sensitive empirical research by reviewing a particular theistic psychology research program.

An Example of a Theistic Psychology Research Program

Development of a theistic psychology requires accomplishment of three research objectives. First, theistic psychologists will need to empirically articulate and describe the real life implications of their worldview. A theistic tradition will express itself in the psychology of its followers. A full understanding of that psychology will require psychometrically sound measurement devices and sophisticated qualitative and critical studies that have *tradition validity* in allowing religious believers to express the lived experience of their faith. Second, theistic psychologies will need to interact effectively with the psychologies of nonreligious worldviews. Research based upon nonreligious perspectives will yield invaluable insights into religion. Sometimes, however, nontheistic psychologies may operate from ideological presumptions that can misrepresent the full psychological implications of theistic commitments. Theistic psychologists will also have ideological blind spots of their own that can sometimes make it difficult for them to discern the legitimate insights of the nontheistic psychologies. Theistic psychologists, therefore, will need methods that allow them to formally determine whether findings based upon nontheistic frameworks are insightful or misleading. Impartiality is an important scientific ideal (Lacey, 1999); truly impartial nontheistic researchers will presumably want to be open to such data as well. Third and finally, theistic psychologists from one tradition can and should interact with theistic psychologists from another in clarifying religious commitments more broadly.

Investigating the Psychology of a Theistic Worldview Tradition

Psychological adjustment within theistic systems can be very different from adjustment as depicted by nontheistic psychologies. One famous description of this contrast occurred in the work of Rieff. In his last published book, for instance, Rieff (2007) contrasted the *creedal personality* of Western theistic traditions with a *therapeutic personality* that increasingly dominates contemporary society. The experience of *unpleasure* or guilt after pleasure is for nontheistic social scientists like Freud and Weber a sign of neurosis or social pathology. Personal efforts to relate such guilt to God's grace then become symptoms of an immature submissiveness associated with transferences from early experiences with authority figures. Within a secular worldview, the therapeutic task is to eliminate the guilt and resolve the transferences.

For those with theistic commitments, however, beliefs in sin and in God's grace underlie humane forms of social life that require resistances to and rejections of tendencies that threaten the common good. As Reiff explained, "sin enlarges the truths of resistances and supplies a certain unity to the style of our rejections" (p. 200). The turn to God's grace then expresses "the commanding presence of authority" within the creedal personality: "In our opposition to him, in his opposition to us, that figure enforces those disciplines of obedience, through guilt in relationship to himself, by which societies are constituted" (Reiff, p. 53).

Rieff's analysis illustrates the claim that religious and nontheistic worldviews have different psychologies. To fully understand the psychological consequences of religion, theistic psychologies must empirically investigate their worldview in projects that clarify what adjustment means within a faith tradition. Indeed, one series of studies developed preliminary measures of beliefs about sin and grace in order to examine the dynamics of psychological functioning that are relevant to many theistic traditions. Sin-related beliefs predicted adjustment, and a covariance with beliefs about grace was important in explaining such effects

(Watson, Morris, & Hood, 1988a, b). Later development of more psycho-metrically sophisticated instruments further confirmed the positive poten-tials of both types of beliefs in, for example, greater self-esteem and lower levels of pathological narcissism, depression, and anxiety (Watson, Mor-ris, Loy, Hamrick, & Grizzle, 2007; Sisemore et al., 2010). Especially note-worthy was the additional finding that Christians in counseling displayed lower beliefs in grace than those who were not in counseling (Sisemore et al.). Within a theistic worldview, the therapeutic task would not be to eliminate the guilt and resolve the transferences. Instead, the task would be to clarify beliefs in sin, beliefs in grace, and the religiously meaningful connections between the two. The result of such theistic therapy presum-ably would be the better adjustment of a creedal personality that could more forthrightly face personal shortcomings (i.e., sins) with a confidence that the love of God would support progress in becoming the person one ought to become (i.e., sanctification).

While the availability of more sophisticated sin and grace measures makes it possible to test hypotheses about the dynamics of the creedal personality (Watson, Chen, & Sisemore, 2010), this research is more impor-tant here for its broader implications. First, such studies suggest that full insight into the creedal personality will require the development of spe-cifically theistic psychologies. The ideological assumptions of nontheistic psychologies will presumably lack the conceptual resources that could offer a full analysis of personality as socially constructed within a religious tradition. Second, this focus on sin and grace was meant to be illustrative. Understanding the theistic personality will, of course, require empirical investigations into a broad array of additional constructs. Finally, argu-ments in favor of a theistic psychology should not be limited to any par-ticular religious tradition. These studies into sin and grace explored the worldviews of Christian participants, but Muslim scholars, to cite only one possible example, will need to build up an Islamic psychology through empirical investigations of their own tradition. This need has been exem-plified in recent attempts to develop scales for measuring the psychologi-cal experience of Ramadan (Khan & Watson, 2010; Khan, Watson, Chen, Iftikhar, & Jabeen, in press).

Research Strategies for Interacting with Nontheistic Psychologies

Recent research has demonstrated that ideological contrasts between the-istic and nontheistic psychologies can and should be the explicit focus of empirical investigations that clarify both (Watson, 2011). Religious and psychological commentators, for example, have both argued that the orthodox Christian emphasis on sin is wholly incompatible with the self-actualization promoted by humanistic psychology (e.g., Ellis, 1980; Vitz, 1995). *Empirical translation schemes* make it possible to test such assumptions. In this procedure, Christians responded to a humanistic self-actualization scale along with potential translations of each item into Christian discourse (Watson, Milliron, Morris, & Hood, 1995). Positive correlations between an original statement and a corresponding translation revealed some compatibility between the two forms of adjustment and also made it possible to construct a valid Christian measure that was empirically analogous to the humanistic measure.

Such data did not mean, however, that the two worldviews are easily compatible. In another study using a *correlational marker procedure*, Christians responded to a self-actualization scale that consisted of items taken directly from the writings of humanistic theorists (Watson, Morris, & Hood, 1989). Christians also responded to an intrinsic religious motivation scale that served as a marker of their religious commitments. Positive correlations of this marker with a self-actualization item revealed *pro-religious* expressions of self-actualization whereas negative correlations identified *anti-religious* items. Most noteworthy was the discovery that pro-religious and anti-religious items correlated negatively with each other when psychometric standards of internal reliability require that such relationships be strongly positive. This humanistic measure, therefore, was neither wholly compatible nor wholly incompatible with Christian forms of psychological maturation. Christian and humanistic understandings of psychological maturation instead seemed to be incommensurate.

Further evidence of complexities appeared in a study using *statistical controls for ideological language* (Watson, Morris, & Hood, 1987). In this investigation, Christians responded to an array of scales measuring healthy self-functioning and religious commitment. Relationships between these two sets of constructs were largely nonsignificant, although a few negative correlations did appear. Research participants also responded to an anti-religious self-actualization scale and an anti-humanistic measure of Christian beliefs in sin and guilt. Statistical procedures then controlled for the anti-religious and anti-humanistic language of these measures, with the result that correlations between Christian commitments and healthy self-functioning became overwhelmingly positive. Once again, the results suggested that Christian and psychological understandings of adjustment operated within incommensurate ideological systems. Statistical controls for those ideological factors proved to be useful in clarifying the adjustment of Christian self-functioning.

Other procedures exist for evaluating ideological factors in the analysis of theistic and nontheistic psychologies (see Watson, Hood, & Morris, 1988; Watson, 2010). A more general point deserves emphasis, however. Theistic psychologies are organized according to different worldview assumptions than nontheistic psychologies. This is another reason why it is important to conduct research programs that examine psychological functioning that takes into account the underlying worldview system itself.

Interacting with Diverse Theistic Psychologies

Again, development of theistic psychologies also makes it possible to bring diverse religious perspectives into research dialogues that can clarify theistic commitments more generally. In one recent study, for example, Muslims in Australia and Malaysia responded to a new Islamic Religious Reflection Scale (Dover, Minor, & Dowson, 2007). Confirmatory factor analysis identified four dimensions within this measure that could be combined into a single higher order Muslim Religious Reflection factor. The content and factor structure of this instrument supported the claim that Muslim commitments can encourage a religious complexity rather than rigidity in Islamic thinking.

A subsequent American study translated items from this instrument into Christian language in an attempt to promote dialogue across religious traditions (Watson, Chen, & Hood, 2011). An exploratory factor analysis revealed that this Christian Religious Reflection Scale contained separate Faith and Intellect Oriented Religious Reflection factors that appeared to have polarized psychological implications. The two factors, for example, correlated negatively with each other. Faith Oriented Reflection also correlated positively with an intrinsic religious orientation and negatively with openness to experience, whereas Intellect Oriented Reflection displayed the opposite pattern. Additional procedures controlled for ideological factors associated with the measurement of religious fundamentalism and demonstrated that foundational Christian commitments to the Bible could be consistent with both Intellect and Faith Oriented forms of reflection.

Is Islamic Religious Reflection polarized as well? An Iranian study recently attempted to answer that question by administering the Islamic Religious Reflection Scale to samples that included students from an Islamic seminary in Qom studying to become mullahs (Ghorbani, Watson, Chen, & Dover, in press). Confirmatory factor analysis demonstrated that the two factors did indeed appear in Iran. Especially noteworthy was the further observation that Faith and Intellect Oriented forms of Islamic

Religious Reflection correlated positively rather than negatively with each other. Both also predicted greater cognitive complexity in contrast to the negative relationship that had been observed for Faith Oriented Reflection in the United States.

Such studies illustrate the potentials inherent in the empirical development of multiple theistic psychologies and for developing dialogue within and between theistic traditions. Religious reflection can operate differently in different cultural contexts. Additional research will need to explain why such contrasts occur. Perhaps, in a theocratic society like Iran, religious forms of reflection will be consistent with dominant ideological perspectives that nurture their development. Christian forms of reflection, at least in a society like the United States, may instead struggle to develop within the ideological conflicts of *culture wars* that operate within the more secularized West. A less sympathetic cultural surround may mean that the psychological expression of Christian Religious Reflection will necessarily occur in less straightforward ways. Research may eventually support other explanations. The more important and general point, however, is that by comparing different theistic psychologies such theoretically important issues become clearer. Nontheistic researchers would presumably appreciate the need for such research as well.

Towards a More Just and Comprehensive Worldview-Conscious Psychology

We imagine a future for contemporary psychology that entails an increasing awareness regarding the hegemony, biases, and limitations of naturalism on the field, resulting in a more just, humane, and comprehensive science of psychology, one that takes into explicit account the worldviews of all researchers and those humans they are investigating. Such a development would usher in a new era of dialogue that is more open to the surplus of vision of those holding other worldviews and could lead to another enormous leap in psychological knowledge (perhaps analogous to the application of natural science methods to the study of human beings, instigated by modern psychology). However, true dialogue is characterized by mutual respect as well as personal conviction. According to Bakhtin (Morson & Emerson, 1990), genuine dialogue is fostered by those who believe they have something worthwhile to learn from their dialogue partner and also that they have something worthwhile to say. What do you think?

REFERENCES

Audi, R. (1998). *Epistemology: A contemporary introduction ot the theory of knowledge.* New York, NY: Routledge.

Brett, G.S. (1951). *Brett's history of psychology* (R.S. Peters, Ed.). London, England: George Allen & Unwin. (Original work published 1912–1921)

Charry, E.T. (1998). *By the renewing of the mind: The pastoral function of Christian doctrine.* New York, NY: Oxford University Press.

Craig, W.L., & Moreland, J.P. (2000). *Naturalism: A critical analysis.* New York, NY: Routledge.

Danto, A.C. (1967). Naturalism. In P. Edwards (Ed.), *The encyclopedia of philosophy* (Vol. 5, pp. 448–450). New York, NY: Macmillan and The Free Press.

Ellis, A., (1980), Psychotherapy and atheistic values: A response to A.E. Bergin's "Psychotherapy and religious values." *Journal of Consulting and Clinical Psychology, 48,* 635–339. doi:10.1037//0022-006X.48.5.635

Dover, H., Miner, M., & Dowson, M. (2007). The nature and structure of Muslim religious reflection. *Journal of Muslim Mental Health, 2,* 189–210. doi:10.1080/15564900701614858

Foucault, M. (2005). *The hermeneutics of the subject* (G. Burchell, Trans.). New York, NY: Palgrave Macmillan.

Ghorbani, N., Watson, P.J., Chen, Z., & Dover, H. (in press). Varieties of openness in Tehran and Qom: Psychological and religious parallels of faith and intellect oriented Islamic religious reflection. *Mental Health, Religion, & Culture.*

Goetz, S., & Taliaferro, C. (2008). *Naturalism.* Grand Rapids, MI: Eerdmans.

Hergenhahn, B.R. (2008). *An introduction to the history of psychology* (6th ed.). Florence, KY: Wadsworth.

James, W. (2007). *The principles of psychology. Volume 1.* New York, NY: Cosimo Classics. (Original work published 1890)

Jobling, J. (2001). Secular humanism. In I.S. Markham & T. Ruparell (Eds.), *Encountering religion: An introduction to the religions of the world.* New York, NY: Blackwell.

Kazdin, A.E. (Ed.). (2000). *Encyclopedia of psychology.* Washington, DC: American Psychological Association and New York, NY: Oxford University Press.

Khan, Z.H., & Watson, P.J. (2010). Ramadan experience and behavior: Relationships with religious orientation among Pakistani Muslims. *Archive for the Psychology of Religion, 32,* 149–167. http://www.brill.nl/archive-psychology-religion

Khan, Z.H., Watson, P.J., Chen, Z., Iftikhar, A., & Jabeen, R. (In press). Pakistani religious coping and the experience and behavior of Ramadan. *Mental Health, Religion, & Culture.* doi:10.1080/13674676.2011.582862

Kwee, M.G.T., Gergen, K.J., & Koshikawa, F. (Eds.), *Horizons in Buddhist psychology.* Chagrin Falls, OH: Taos Institute Publications.

Lacey, H. (1999). *Is science value free?* London, England: Routledge.

Markham, I.S., & Ruparell, T. (2001). *Encountering religion: An introduction to the religions of the world.* New York, NY: Blackwell.

Martin, J., Sugarman, J., & Thompson, J. (2003). *Psychology and the question of agency.* Albany, NY: SUNY Press.

Meister, C. (Ed.). (2011). *The Oxford handbook of religious diversity.* New York, NY: Oxford University Press.

Morson, G.S., & Emerson, C. (1990). *Michail Bakhtin: Creation of a prosaics.* Stanford, CA: University of Stanford Press.

Naugle, D.K. (2002). *Worldview: The history of a concept.* Grand Rapids, MI: William B. Eerdmans.

Nussbaum, M.C. (1994). *The therapy of desire: Theory and practice in hellenistic ethics.* Princeton, NJ: Princeton University Press.

Plantinga, A. (1993). *Warrant and proper function.* New York, NY: Oxford University Press.

Post, J.F. (1995). Naturalism. In R. Audi (Ed.), *The Cambridge dictionary of philosophy* (pp. 517–518). New York, NY: Cambridge University Press.

Reiff, P. (2007). *Charisma.* New York, NY: Vintage Books.

Robinson, D.N. (1995). *An intellectual history of psychology.* Madison, WI: University of Wisconsin Press.

Seager, W. (2000). Metaphysics, Role in science. In W.H. Newton-Smith (Ed.), *A companion to the philosophy of science* (pp. 283–292). New York, NY: Blackwell.

Sisemore, T.A., Arbuckle, M., Killian, M., Mortellaro, E., Swanson, M., Fisher, R., & McGinnis, J. (2010). Grace and Christian psychology—Part 1: Initial measurement, relationships, and implications for practice. *Edification: The Transdisciplinary Journal of Christian Psychology, 4*(2), 57–63. http://christianpsych.org/wp_scp/publications/edification/

Slife, B.D., Reber, J.S., & Lefevor, T. (2012). When God truly matters: A theistic approach to psychology. *Research in the Social Scientific Study of Religion, 23,* (this issue).

Smith, H. (2009). *The world's religions.* New York, NY: HarperOne.

Spero, M.H. (1992). *Religious objects as psychological structures: A critical integration of object relations theory, psychotherapy, and Judaism.* Chicago, IL: University of Chicago Press.

Viney, W., King, D.B., & Woody, W.D. (2008). *A history of psychology: Ideas and context* (1st ed.). Englewood Cliffs, NJ: Prentice Hall.

Vitz, P.C. (1995). *Psychology as religion: The cult of self-worship* (2nd ed.). Grand Rapids, MI: William B. Eerdmans.

Watson, P.J. (2010). Christian rationality and the postmodern context: The example of Rational-Emotive Therapy within a Christian ideological surround. *Edification: The Transdisciplinary Journal of Christian Psychology, 4*(1), 64–74. http://christianpsych.org/wp_scp/publications/edification/

Watson, P.J. (2011). Whose psychology? Which rationality? Christian psychology within an ideological surround after postmodernism. *Journal of Psychology and Christianity, 30,* 306–315. http://caps.net/membership/publications/jpc

Watson, P.J., Chen, Z., & Sisemore, T.A. (2010). Grace and Christian psychology—Part 2: Psychometric refinements and relationships with self-compassion, depression, beliefs about sin, and religious orientation. *Edification: The Transdisciplinary Journal of Christian Psychology, 4*(2), 64–72. http://christianpsych.org/wp_scp/publications/edification/

Watson, P.J., Chen, Z., & Hood, R.W., Jr. (2011). Biblical foundationalism and religious reflection: Polarization of faith and intellect oriented epistemologies within a Christian ideological surround. *Journal of Psychology and Theology, 39,* 111–121. http://journals.biola.edu/jpt

Watson, P.J., Hood, R.W., Jr., & Morris, R.J. (1988). Existential confrontation and religiosity. *Counseling and Values, 33,* 47–54. doi:10.1002/j.2161-007X.1988.tb00739.x

Watson, P.J., Milliron, J.T., Morris, R.J., & Hood, R.W. Jr. (1995). Religion and the self as text: Toward a Christian translation of self-actualization. *Journal of Psychology and Theology, 23,* 180–189. http://journals.biola.edu/jpt

Watson, P.J., Morris, R.J., & Hood, R.W., Jr. (1987). Antireligious humanistic values, guilt, and self esteem. *Journal for the Scientific Study of Religion, 26,* 535–546. doi:10.2307/1387103

Watson, P.J., Morris, R.J., & Hood, R.W., Jr. (1988a). Sin and self-functioning, Part 1: Grace, guilt, and self-consciousness. *Journal of Psychology and Theology, 16,* 254–269. http://journals.biola.edu/jpt

Watson, P.J., Morris, R J., & Hood, R.W., Jr. (1988b). Sin and self-functioning, Part 2: Grace, guilt, and psychological adjustment. *Journal of Psychology and Theology, 16,* 270–281. http://journals.biola.edu/jpt

Watson, P.J., Morris, R.J., & Hood, R.W., Jr. (1989). Sin and self-functioning, Part 5: Antireligious humanistic values, individualism, and the community. *Journal of Psychology and Theology, 17,* 157–172. http://journals.biola.edu/jpt

Watson, P.J., Morris, R.J., Loy, T., Hamrick, M.B., & Grizzle, S. (2007). Beliefs about sin: Adaptive implications in relationships with religious orientation, self-esteem, and measures of the narcissistic, depressed and anxious self. *Edification: Journal of the Society for Christian Psychology, 1,* 57–67. http://christianpsych.org/wp_scp/publications/edification/

Watson, R.I., Sr., & Evans, R.B. (1991). *The great psychologists: A history of psychological thought* (5th ed.). New York, NY: HarperCollins.

Young, W.A. (2009). *The world's religions: Worldviews and contemporary issues* (3rd ed.). Englewood Cliffs, NJ: Prentice Hall.

THEISM AND NON-THEISM IN PSYCHOLOGICAL SCIENCE: TOWARDS SCHOLARLY DIALOGUE

Kari A. O'Grady and Richard H. York

We hope that you enjoyed the articles included in the discussion of theism and non-theism in psychological science. We now address the areas of reflection we posed in the opening article of the special issue section. In this article, we consider personal worldviews, the role of *groupthink* in the formulation and maintenance of theistic and non-theistic positions, and the need for innovative approaches for encouraging future dialogues on the topics posed by the authors in this issue.

REFLECTING ON PERSONAL WORLDVIEWS

The term *worldview* originates from the German word, *Weltanschauung* and has been described as:

> A commitment, a fundamental orientation of the heart, that can be expressed as a story or in a set of presuppositions (assumptions which may be true, partially true, or entirely false) which we hold (consciously or subconsciously, consistently or inconsistently) about the basic construction of reality, and that provides the foundation on which we live and move and have our being. (Sire, 2009, p. 20)

Personal worldviews are most easily recognized in the private ponderings and questions that occupy our thoughts. Personal worldviews can be altered by external influences and pressures but are considered by most to be a fundamental aspect of selfhood (Smart, 2000). Given the differences in personal worldview, it is not surprising that a special issue on theism in psychology would produce a kaleidoscope of perspectives on the topic.

A few of the contributors to this issue are concerned about divergent worldviews in psychological science as they fear the discrepancies may undermine the legitimacy of the field, our ability to conduct rigorous research, and our capacity to formulate consistent, best practice standards. Indeed, most would agree that an "anything goes" approach to psychological science and practice would not only cause research regression but also reduce the level of care we are able to provide to others.

Research in the Social Scientific Study of Religion, Volume 23
© *Koninklijke Brill NV, Leiden, 2012*

On the other hand, a few of the authors in this issue consider the acceptance of some worldviews and the rejection of others by powerful players in the field to be a form of prejudice and/or dictatorship. Currently, the most widely accepted worldviews in psychological science are those void of theistic assumptions, so those with theistic worldviews often feel marginalized and denigrated. Most would concur that a totalitarian approach to the development of any form of thought, including scientific thought, is less than desirable.

How, then, do we encourage a rigorous, serious study of human beings without a consensus about the fundamental way we approach and understand the world and those that live in it? Is it the impossibility of this task that makes the consideration of it so vital to the progress of psychological science? Could it be that reconciliation of worldviews would inevitably prove to be the decline of the field?

Avoiding Group Think

Social psychologists have suggested that homogenous societies are prone to groupthink. Groupthink is likely to occur when a group: (a) collectively evaluates and rationalizes the decisions it makes, (b) promotes uniformity of ideas, (c) assumes a censorship role towards outside views, and (d) exclusively selects information that supports their perspectives. Some of the deleterious effects of group think are (a) decrease in creativity, (b) lack of inventiveness, and (c) reduced ability to engage in rational decision making. An effective means for combating group think is to invite contradictory perspectives into the discussion, thus setting up a monitoring system for the group's ideas (Janis, 1982).

We do not typically frame the face-off between theism and non-theism in psychological science as being prone to groupthink. However, when we become overly defensive in our positions, and our views about theism in psychological science become too polarized, we may need to evaluate the influence of groupthink in the development and maintenance of our views. If we are not invulnerable to the effects of groupthink, we may wish to brainstorm about strategies for inviting contradictory frameworks of thought as we formulate and disseminate our views.

Supporting Between Group Dialogue

From this vantage point, it might be prudent to seek out those with divergent worldviews to help us scrutinize our previously under-challenged

	Theism in Psychological Science	No Theism in Psychological Science
Theistic Personal Worldview	Group A	Group B
Non-Theistic Personal Worldview	Group C	Group D

Figure 1. *Personal Worldviews and Positions of Theism in Psychological Science.*

assumptions and approaches to psychological science. Scholars and clinicians interested in the psychology of spirituality and religion should be encouraged to actively seek out colleagues in the field who have the same interests of study but espouse opposite worldviews and/or differing viewpoints about approaching psychological science theistically. Figure 1 illustrates configurations of various groups of people relative to their personal worldviews and their views about approaching psychological science theistically.

Currently, there is little cross-talk in the field between most of these groups, and there are even fewer *invited* discussions between the groups. In modernity, the most vocal configuration has been those in Group D. These folks tended to have the most prominent influence on the development of the field, and they encountered little scrutiny in the assumptions that they employed to establish the field. Several members of this group have a vested and active interest in keeping theism out of psychological science. Group B represents people who identify as theist but prefer to adhere to the rules established by Group D. Individuals from this group will, at times, engage in a fight to keep theism out of psychological science despite their personal worldviews. Group A consists of those who have theistic personal worldviews and argue that theism should be considered as a framework for psychological science. They are unsatisfied with the standards set forth by Group D, and they often engage in battle with this group. Group C is comprised of individuals, such as Teo (2009), who are non-theistic in their personal worldviews but see the value of considering theism in psychological science. They are unlikely to engage in battle, and when called to arms, they are usually somewhat tentative in their positions.

The proposal is that we seek out those from differing categories of groups (e.g. those who identify with Group B collaborate or consult with those in Group C) to help elevate our work and to raise the standard of scholarship and practice in the field. By avoiding group think, we open the door for revolutionary ideas and improved decision making in our science and practice. This may require a re-consideration of the role of the "other."

ENCOURAGING FUTURE DIALOGUES

The call to dialogue between those with differing viewpoints stretches well beyond an appeal to return to our respective corner of the ring, and it requires more than just tolerance of the other. Tolerance requires civility, whereas dialogue promotes personally transformative valuing of the other (Islam, 2007). Gadamer (1982) took this idea a step further by suggesting that in order to engage in genuinely open dialogue, we must make efforts to understand and empathize with what it is like to *be* the other. It is difficult to stand in the ring with someone we understand in this way. Perhaps the process of understanding and valuing the views of the other groups (see Figure 1) will elevate the study of the psychology of spirituality and religion to a level in which we are less inclined to defend our views and more eager to invite the "other" to critique our work. Islam (2007) elucidated this idea by stating, "Might [intellectual] dialogue not be better served if we considered all humans as part of a single speech community, with various dialects of the same language, whose speakers can thereby exert meaningful influence upon one another?" (p. 705).

We may never gain consensus as a scientific community about the fundamental way we approach and understand the world and those that live in it, but we might agree that uniformity of thought in this way is not conducive to good scholarship and practice. The guiding framework for rigorous research and the development of best practice protocols could be established through a system of checks and balances proffered by intentional intergroup dialogue. Perhaps we could agree to set a standard for the study of the psychology of religion in which between group dialogue is fostered through such criteria as: (a) peer reviews of journal manuscripts conducted between groups, (b) professional conference symposia or panels intentionally comprised of those from diverse groups, (c) theories explicitly developed out of respectful discussion between groups, and (d) practice protocols established in consultation with those from divergent groups.

This special issue has presented an arena of viewpoints on the topic of theism in psychological science and practice from some of the top scholars in the field. The contributors come from a variety of religious, geographical, and educational backgrounds and represent diverse world-view perspectives. The richness of diversity has contributed to a stimulating discussion on the topic. Additionally, we, as the special issue editors, have posed some provocative considerations for future dialogue. We hope that scholars across disciplines will consider collaborative discussions about theism in psychological science with those who represent divergent positions. We are optimistic that this kind of respectful and humble dialogue will refine and advance our study of the human condition and will model ethical and sophisticated scholarship and practice for the field.

REFERENCES

Gadamer, H-G. (1982). *Hegel's dialectic: Five hermeneutical studies.* New Haven, CT: Yale University Press.

Islam, G. (2007). Virtue ethics, multiculturalism, and the paradox of cultural dialogue. *American Psychologist, 62*(7), 704–705. doi:10.1037/0003-066X.62.7.704

Janis, I. (1982). *Groupthink: Psychological studies of policy decisions and fiascoes.* Boston, MA: Houghton Mifflin.

Sire, J.W. (2009). *The universe next door: A basic worldview catalog* (5th edition). Downer's Grove, IL: Intervarsity Press.

Smart, N. (2000). *Worldviews: Crosscultural explorations of human beliefs.* Upper Saddle River, NJ: Prentice Hall.

Teo, T. (2009). Editorial. *Journal of Theoretical and Philosophical Psychology, 29*(2), 61–62. http://www.apa.org/pubs/journals/teo/index.aspx

AUTHORS' BIOGRAPHIES

Dr. Robert C. Bishop is the John and Madeleine McIntyre Endowed Professor of Philosophy and History of Science and Associate Professor of Physics. His research involves history and philosophy of science, philosophy of physics, philosophy of social science, and philosophy of mind and psychology. He is particularly interested in chaos and complex systems and their philosophical implications. Dr. Bishop's most recent book is *The Philosophy of the Social Sciences* (Continuum International Publishing Group, June 2007).

Dr. Mark J. Cartledge is the Director of the Centre for Pentecostal and Charismatic Studies at the University of Birmingham, UK. He is involved in a number of academic societies and networks, including the European Research Network on Global Pentecostalism (GloPent), and he edits the network's journal, *PentecoStudies: An Interdisciplinary Journal for Research on the Pentecostal and Charismatic Movements* (Equinox). His most recent book is entitled: *Testimony in the Spirit: Rescripting Ordinary Pentecostal Theology* (Ashgate, 2010).

Samuel D. Downs is in his last year as a doctoral candidate for applied social psychology at Brigham Young University. His research focuses on interpersonal perceptions and includes his work in psychology of religion about theists' perceptions of God. For his dissertation, he addresses the contextual forces impacting attributions of actors and observers to choice, situation, and disposition using Milgram's obedience paradigm. He is also interested in the philosophical foundations of psychological science.

Tyler A. Gerdin is pursuing a doctoral degree in clinical psychology from George Fox University. His developing professional interests are the integration of Christianity and psychology, psychodynamic therapies, and geriatric development and assessment.

Dr. Fiona J. Hibberd is Senior Lecturer in the School of Psychology at the University of Sydney where she teaches the history and philosophy of psychology, conceptual issues in research methods, and psychoanalysis. She publishes papers on the philosophical underpinnings of psychology, has been visiting researcher at the University of Durham (UK), the City University of New York and the Vrije Universiteit (Amsterdam), and is the author of *Unfolding Social Constructionism* (2005).

DR. ERIC L. JOHNSON is Lawrence and Charlotte Hoover Professor of Pastoral Care at Southern Baptist Theological Seminary. A contributing editor for the *Journal of Psychology and Theology*, the *Journal of Spiritual Formation & Soul Care*, and *Edification*, he has edited the book *Psychology and Christianity: Five Views* and written *Foundations for Soul Care: A Christian Psychology Proposal*. He is also the director of the Society for Christian Psychology.

DR. ROBERT A. LARMER is currently Chair of the Philosophy Department at the University of New Brunswick, Fredericton campus. He has served as President and Vice-President of the Canadian Society of Christian Philosophers, as well as on the executive of the Canadian Philosophical Association and the Evangelical Philosophical Society. His research interests are primarily concerned with the interface between science and theology, although he has also published in the areas of philosophy of mind and applied ethics. His hobbies include chess, fishing, and gardening.

G. TYLER LEFEVOR, B.S. earned his bachelor's degree in psychology from Brigham Young University. He is currently working towards his Ph.D. in counseling psychology at the University of Miami. His research interests include the philosophical underpinnings of psychology, the intersection between psychology and religion, and the moral dimensions of psychology.

DR. GINA MAGYAR-RUSSELL is Assistant Professor of Pastoral Counseling at Loyola University Maryland and Adjunct Assistant Professor of Psychiatry and Behavioral Sciences at The Johns Hopkins School of Medicine (JHSOM) in Baltimore, MD. She is a licensed psychologist who specializes in psychological and spiritual adjustment following adverse health events. She has co-authored several papers on religion/spirituality and health, as well as depression and anxiety, in a variety of medical patient populations.

DR. MARK R. MCMINN has a Ph.D. in clinical psychology from Vanderbilt University. He is Professor of Psychology at George Fox University and a former president of the American Psychological Association's Division 36, Society for the Psychology of Religion and Spirituality.

M. CHET MIRMAN, PH.D. is a practicing clinical psychologist and an Associate Professor of Psychology at the Illinois School of Professional Psychology at Argosy University-Schaumburg. His recent papers and presentations include: the psychology of religion; desire, object relations and psychopathology; ego development and spiritual transformation; the psychology of morality; and religious naturalism. He received his Ph.D. in clinical psychology from Michigan State University in 1984.

JUDITH A. MUSKETT graduated from Nottingham University in 1980 with a degree in English Studies and received her M.A. in Public and Social Administration from Brunel University in 1986. She was research assistant at the Culham College Institute for Church-Related Education, and professional assistant at the London Diocesan Board for Schools, before serving for nearly 20 years as an Assistant Registrar at the University of Oxford. She is now completing her Ph.D. in Theology at York St. John University. Her research field is the Friends' associations of Anglican cathedrals, and she has recently published articles in peer-reviewed journals on the establishment of the Friends in the 1920s and 1930s and on their royal patronage, past and present.

DR. JAMES M. NELSON holds a M.Div. from Fuller Theological Seminary and a Ph.D. in clinical psychology from Washington State University. He has been a faculty member at Valparaiso University since 1987, and he is a member of both Division 24 (Theoretical/Philosophical Psychology) and Division 36 (Psychology of Religion and Spirituality) of the American Psychological Association. He recently completed a year as a visiting scholar in the Department of Theology at the University of Notre Dame.

DR. KARI A. O'GRADY earned a Ph.D. in counseling psychology from Brigham Young University. She is an assistant professor in the pastoral counseling department at Loyola University Maryland. She currently serves as the early career professional's chair for Division 36 (Society for the Psychology of Religion and Spirituality) of the American Psychological Association.

DR. RALPH L. PIEDMONT is professor of pastoral counseling at Loyola University Maryland. He is the founding editor of *Psychology of Religion and Spirituality*, the official journal of Division 36 (Society for the Psychology of Religion and Spirituality) of the American Psychological Association. He is also the co-editor of *Research in the Social Scientific Study of Religion*.

DR. JEFFREY S. REBER is associate professor of psychology at Brigham Young University. His research interests include critical thinking about psychology, the relationship between religion and psychology, the meaning and possibility of altruism, and relational social psychology.

DR. BRENT D. SLIFE is currently Professor of Psychology at Brigham Young University. Honored recently with an APA Presidential Citation for his contribution to psychology, Dr. Slife has served as the President of the Society of Theoretical and Philosophical Psychology and on the editorial boards of seven journals. He has authored over 180 articles and seven books, including *Critical Thinking about Psychology* (2005), *Taking Sides* (2011), *Critical Issues in Psychotherapy* (2001), and *What's Behind the Research?* (1995).

CANDACE THOMASON is a graduate student at Valparaiso University studying in the joint degree program in Law and Psychology.

MICHAEL J. VOGEL is pursuing a doctoral degree in clinical psychology from George Fox University. His professional interests are ever expanding and currently include the integration of Christianity and psychology, psychodynamic psychotherapy, and religious and spiritual dimensions of diversity.

DR. P.J. WATSON is U.C. Foundation Professor of Psychology at the University of Tennessee at Chattanooga. His research interests focus on the psychology of religion with recent coauthored projects examining samples in Iran, Pakistan, China, and Tibet in addition to those from the United States. He currently is an editor of *Edification: The Transdisciplinary Journal of Christian Psychology*.

TERESA A. WILKINS is a clinician and a doctoral candidate in pastoral counseling at Loyola University Maryland. She has served as the editorial assistant for *Research in the Social Scientific Study of Religion* and as an assistant for the Mid-Year Conference on Religion and Spirituality, a joint partnership of Division 36 of the American Psychological Association and the Pastoral Counseling Department of Loyola University Maryland.

DR. RICHARD H. YORK is a psychologist in private practice. He recently discovered that he is a reconciler. His personal and professional life has been a struggle to reconcile the conflicts between science, theology, and spirituality. These conflicts needed to be reconciled in order to become a healthy gay man and to work as a science teacher and laboratory technician. He studied for the Episcopal priesthood and later got his Ph.D. in pastoral psychology. This struggle eventually produced a book about theistic psychology: *A Christian Spirituality and Psychotherapy: A Gay Psychologist's Practice of Clinical Theology*.

MANUSCRIPT REVIEWERS

In addition to the preceding authors, many scholars and scientists have made significant contributions to the publication of this volume. They have anonymously screened the initial versions of these and other submitted manuscripts for methodological rigor and scientific significance. They also have provided the authors with invaluable suggestions for improving their papers prior to the authors making their final revisions. The editors and the authors appreciate their expert services. Not only have they improved the quality of the research reported here, they also have contributed to the quality of the field of the social scientific study of religion.

SUBJECT INDEX

NAMES INDEX